Chevrolet Colorado & GMC Canyon Automotive Repair Manual

by Jay Storer
and John H Haynes
Member of the Guild of Motoring Writers

Models covered:

Chevrolet Colorado and GMC Canyon - 2004 through 2008
Two- and four-wheel drive versions with inline four-cylinder
and five-cylinder engines

(24027 - 1M2)

ABCDE
FGHIJ
KLMNO
PQR

Haynes Publishing Group
Sparkford Nr Yeovil
Somerset BA22 7JJ England

Haynes North America, Inc
861 Lawrence Drive
Newbury Park
California 91320 USA

Acknowledgements

Wiring diagrams provided exclusively for Haynes North America, Inc by Solution Builders.

© **Haynes North America, Inc. 2007, 2009**
With permission from J.H. Haynes & Co. Ltd.

A book in the Haynes Automotive Repair Manual Series

Printed in the U.S.A.

ISBN-13: 978-1-56392-753-9
ISBN-10: 1-56392-753-5

Library of Congress Control Number 2009921401

While every attempt is made to ensure that the information in this man-ual is correct, no liability can be accepted by the authors or publishers for loss, damage or injury caused by any errors in, or omissions from, the information given.

Contents

Haynes mechanic and photographer with a Chevrolet Colorado

About this manual

Its purpose

The purpose of this manual is to help you get the best value from your vehicle. It can do so in several ways. It can help you decide what work must be done, even if you choose to have it done by a dealer service department or a repair shop; it provides information and procedures for routine maintenance and servicing; and it offers diagnostic and repair procedures to follow when trouble occurs.

We hope you use the manual to tackle the work yourself. For many simpler jobs, doing it yourself may be quicker than arranging an appointment to get the vehicle into a shop and making the trips to leave it and pick it up. More importantly, a lot of money can be saved by avoiding the expense the shop must pass on to you to cover its labor and overhead

costs. An added benefit is the sense of satisfaction and accomplishment that you feel after doing the job yourself.

Using the manual

The manual is divided into Chapters. Each Chapter is divided into numbered Sections, which are headed in bold type between horizontal lines. Each Section consists of consecutively numbered paragraphs.

At the beginning of each numbered Section you will be referred to any illustrations which apply to the procedures in that Section. The reference numbers used in illustration captions pinpoint the pertinent Section and the Step within that Section. That is, illustration 3.2 means the illustration refers to Section 3 and Step (or paragraph) 2 within that Section.

Procedures, once described in the text, are not normally repeated. When it's necessary to refer to another Chapter, the reference will be given as Chapter and Section number. Cross references given without use of the word "Chapter" apply to Sections and/or paragraphs in the same Chapter. For example, "see Section 8" means in the same Chapter.

References to the left or right side of the vehicle assume you are sitting in the driver's seat, facing forward.

Even though we have prepared this manual with extreme care, neither the publisher nor the author can accept responsibility for any errors in, or omissions from, the information given.

NOTE

A **Note** provides information necessary to properly complete a procedure or information which will make the procedure easier to understand.

CAUTION

A **Caution** provides a special procedure or special steps which must be taken while completing the procedure where the Caution is found. Not heeding a Caution can result in damage to the assembly being worked on.

WARNING

A **Warning** provides a special procedure or special steps which must be taken while completing the procedure where the Warning is found. Not heeding a Warning can result in personal injury.

Introduction to the Chevrolet Colorado and GMC Canyon

Introduced in 2004, the Chevrolet Colorado and the GMC Canyon are the newest generation of GM intermediate or "mid-size" trucks, replacing the Chevy S-10 and GMC Sonoma models. These vehicles are available in a number of configurations that include a standard cab, an extended cab and a four-door crewcab model, all available in 2WD or 4WD versions. The vehicles covered by this manual are equipped with an inline four-cylinder engine or an inline five-cylinder engine, coupled with a five-speed manual transmission or four-speed automatic, both with overdrive.

The chassis layout is conventional with a front-mounted engine transmitting power to the rear wheels via the transmission. On 4WD models, in addition to power being delivered to the rear axle and wheels, a transfer case transmits power to the front differential then to the wheels through independent driveaxles.

2WD models feature independent front suspension with coil spring/shock absorber units. An independent front suspension with

torsion bars is used on 4WD models. At the rear, all models have a solid rear axle supported by two parallel leaf springs and shock absorbers.

The power-assisted steering is rack-and-pinion. The steering unit is mounted to the frame aft of the front wheels. All models have a power assisted disc-type front and drum-type rear brake system with an Anti-lock Brake System (ABS) as standard equipment.

Vehicle identification numbers

Vehicle identification numbers

Modifications are a continuing and unpublicized process in vehicle manufacturing. Since spare parts manuals and lists are compiled on a numerical basis, the individual vehicle numbers are essential to correctly identify the component required.

Vehicle Identification Number (VIN)

The Vehicle Identification Number (VIN), which appears on the Vehicle Certificate of Title and Registration, is also embossed on a gray plate located on the left (driver's side) corner of the dashboard, near the windshield (see illustration). The VIN tells you when and where a vehicle was manufactured, its country of origin, make, type, passenger safety system, line, series, body style, engine and assembly plant.

VIN engine and model year codes

Two particularly important pieces of information found in the VIN are the engine code and the model year code. Counting from the left, the engine code letter designation is the 8th character and the model year code is the 10th character.

On models through 2006 the engine codes are:

8 ..... 2.8L inline four-cylinder MFI (LK5)
6 ..... 3.5L inline five-cylinder MFI (L52)

On 2007 and later models, the engine codes are:

9 .....2.9L inline four-cylinder (LLV)
E .....3.7L inline five-cylinder (LLR)

On the models covered by this manual the model year codes are:

4 2004
5 2005
6 2006
7 2007
8 2008

Vehicle Safety Certification label

The Vehicle Safety Certification label is attached to the rear edge of the driver's door (see illustration). The label contains the name of the manufacturer, the month and year of production, the Gross Vehicle Weight Rating (GVWR), the Gross Axle Weight Rating (GAWR) and the certification statement. On most models, the label also includes the OEM tire sizes and pressures.

Service Parts Identification label

Located on the inside of the glove compartment door, this label contains information about the options on your vehicle and the paint and trim codes (see illustration). This information is important when ordering parts or when bodywork and repainting is done.

Engine Identification Number (EIN)

The Engine Identification Number (EIN) is stamped into the lower left side of the block, near the oil pan. Additionally, an engine I.D. label is affixed to the rear of the valve cover.

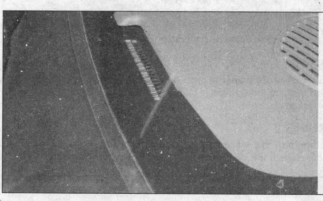

The VIN plate is visible from the outside of the vehicle, through the driver's side of the windshield

The Vehicle Safety Certification label is affixed to the driver's side door end or post

The Service Parts Identification label contains information on options and trim/paint codes

Transmission Identification Number (TIN)

The Transmission Identification Number (TIN) for automatic transmission models is stamped or etched into the bottom of the transmission case, to the rear of the fluid pan **(see illustration)**. On five-speed manual transmission models, the number is on a metal tag attached near the transmission mount.

Transfer case identification label

The transfer case identification information is on a tag affixed to the rear side of the case **(see illustration)**.

Typical automatic transmission identification number location

Location of the transfer case identification tag

Recall information

Vehicle recalls are carried out by the manufacturer in the rare event of a possible safety-related defect. The vehicle's registered owner is contacted at the address on file at the Department of Motor Vehicles and given the details of the recall. Remedial work is carried out free of charge at a dealer service department.

If you are the new owner of a used vehicle which was subject to a recall and you want to be sure that the work has been carried out, it's best to contact a dealer service department and ask about your individual vehicle - you'll need to furnish them your Vehicle Identification Number (VIN).

The table below is based on information provided by the National Highway Traffic Safety Administration (NHTSA), the body which oversees vehicle recalls in the United States. The recall database is updated constantly. For the latest information on vehicle recalls, check the NHTSA website at www.nhtsa.gov, or call the NHTSA hotline at 1-888-327-4236.

Recall date	Recall campaign number	Model(s) affected	Concern
12/5/05	05V552000	2006 and 2007 Chevy Colorado/GMC Canyon	Vehicles were shipped with tire and loading information labels listing an inaccurate vehicle capacity weight.
4/26/06	06V139000	2004 through 2006 Chevy Colorado/GMC Canyon	Faulty brake light switch. Brake lights may fail to come on when brakes are applied, or may stay on all the time.
8/9/06	06V307000	2006 and 2007 Chevy Colorado/GMC Canyon	Certain vehicles fail to comply with the requirements of Federal Motor Vehicle Safety Standard No. 110, "Tire selection and rims." These vehicles have an incomplete tire rim designation on the certification/tire label located on the driver's door edge. In addition, the label may also be missing the tire load rating on the label. Although this information is not required by the standard, if a tire of a lesser load rating is installed, the tire may not be able to sustain the loads encountered during use. If a customer replaces a wheel and only relies on the rim size designation that is indicated on the label, a wheel that is of a different rim contour designation may be installed. It may be difficult or impossible to mount the tire on a wheel with the wrong contour. If the tire is mounted on the wheel with the wrong contour, the wheel and tire may not perform as intended, which could increase the risk of a crash.

Buying parts

Replacement parts are available from many sources, which generally fall into one of two categories - authorized dealer parts departments and independent retail auto parts stores. Our advice concerning these parts is as follows:

Retail auto parts stores: Good auto parts stores will stock frequently needed components which wear out relatively fast, such as clutch components, exhaust systems, brake parts, tune-up parts, etc. These stores often supply new or reconditioned parts on an exchange basis, which can save a considerable amount of money. Discount auto parts stores are often very good places to buy materials and parts needed for general vehicle maintenance such as oil, grease, filters, spark plugs, belts, touch-up paint, bulbs, etc. They also usually sell tools and general accessories, have convenient hours, charge lower prices and can often be found not far from home.

Authorized dealer parts department: This is the best source for parts which are unique to the vehicle and not generally available elsewhere (such as major engine parts, transmission parts, trim pieces, etc.).

Warranty information: If the vehicle is still covered under warranty, be sure that any replacement parts purchased - regardless of the source - do not invalidate the warranty!

To be sure of obtaining the correct parts, have engine and chassis numbers available and, if possible, take the old parts along for positive identification.

Maintenance techniques, tools and working facilities

Maintenance techniques

There are a number of techniques involved in maintenance and repair that will be referred to throughout this manual. Application of these techniques will enable the home mechanic to be more efficient, better organized and capable of performing the various tasks properly, which will ensure that the repair job is thorough and complete.

Fasteners

Fasteners are nuts, bolts, studs and screws used to hold two or more parts together. There are a few things to keep in mind when working with fasteners. Almost all of them use a locking device of some type, either a lockwasher, locknut, locking tab or thread adhesive. All threaded fasteners should be clean and straight, with undamaged threads and undamaged corners on the hex head where the wrench fits. Develop the habit of replacing all damaged nuts and bolts with new ones. Special locknuts with nylon or fiber inserts can only be used once. If they are removed, they lose their locking ability and must be replaced with new ones.

Rusted nuts and bolts should be treated with a penetrating fluid to ease removal and prevent breakage. Some mechanics use turpentine in a spout-type oil can, which works quite well. After applying the rust penetrant, let it work for a few minutes before trying to loosen the nut or bolt. Badly rusted fasteners may have to be chiseled or sawed off or removed with a special nut breaker, available at tool stores.

If a bolt or stud breaks off in an assembly, it can be drilled and removed with a special tool commonly available for this purpose. Most automotive machine shops can perform this task, as well as other repair procedures, such as the repair of threaded holes that have been stripped out.

Flat washers and lockwashers, when removed from an assembly, should always be replaced exactly as removed. Replace any damaged washers with new ones. Never use a lockwasher on any soft metal surface (such as aluminum), thin sheet metal or plastic.

Fastener sizes

For a number of reasons, automobile manufacturers are making wider and wider use of metric fasteners. Therefore, it is important to be able to tell the difference between standard (sometimes called U.S. or SAE) and metric hardware, since they cannot be interchanged.

All bolts, whether standard or metric, are sized according to diameter, thread pitch and length. For example, a standard 1/2 - 13 x 1 bolt is 1/2 inch in diameter, has 13 threads per inch and is 1 inch long. An M12 - 1.75 x 25 metric bolt is 12 mm in diameter, has a thread pitch of 1.75 mm (the distance between threads) and is 25 mm long. The two bolts are nearly identical, and easily confused, but they are not interchangeable.

In addition to the differences in diameter, thread pitch and length, metric and standard bolts can also be distinguished by examining the bolt heads. To begin with, the distance across the flats on a standard bolt head is measured in inches, while the same dimension on a metric bolt is sized in millimeters (the same is true for nuts). As a result, a standard wrench should not be used on a metric bolt and a metric wrench should not be used on a standard bolt. Also, most standard bolts have slashes radiating out from the center of the head to denote the grade or strength of the bolt, which is an indication of the amount of torque that can be applied to it. The greater the number of slashes, the greater the strength of the bolt. Grades 0 through 5 are commonly used on automobiles. Metric bolts have a property class (grade) number, rather than a slash, molded into their heads to indicate bolt strength. In this case, the higher the number, the stronger the bolt. Property class numbers 8.8, 9.8 and 10.9 are commonly used on automobiles.

Strength markings can also be used to distinguish standard hex nuts from metric hex nuts. Many standard nuts have dots stamped into one side, while metric nuts are marked with a number. The greater the number of dots, or the higher the number, the greater the strength of the nut.

Metric studs are also marked on their ends according to property class (grade). Larger studs are numbered (the same as metric bolts), while smaller studs carry a geometric code to denote grade.

It should be noted that many fasteners, especially Grades 0 through 2, have no distinguishing marks on them. When such is the case, the only way to determine whether it is standard or metric is to measure the thread pitch or compare it to a known fastener of the same size.

Standard fasteners are often referred to as SAE, as opposed to metric. However, it should be noted that SAE technically refers to a non-metric fine thread fastener only. Coarse thread non-metric fasteners are referred to as USS sizes.

Since fasteners of the same size (both standard and metric) may have different strength ratings, be sure to reinstall any bolts, studs or nuts removed from your vehicle in their original locations. Also, when replacing a fastener with a new one, make sure that the new one has a strength rating equal to or greater than the original.

Tightening sequences and procedures

Most threaded fasteners should be tightened to a specific torque value (torque is the twisting force applied to a threaded component such as a nut or bolt). Overtightening the fastener can weaken it and cause it to break, while undertightening can cause it to eventually come loose. Bolts, screws and studs, depending on the material they are made of and their thread diameters, have specific torque values, many of which are noted in the Specifications at the beginning of each Chapter. Be sure to follow the torque recommendations closely. For fasteners not assigned a

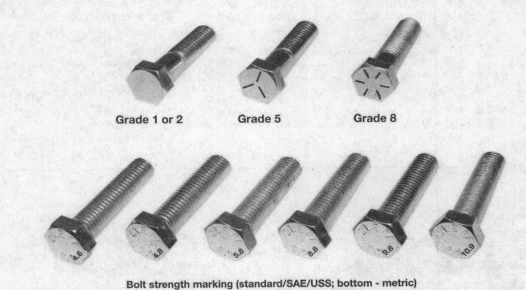

Grade 1 or 2   Grade 5   Grade 8

Bolt strength marking (standard/SAE/USS; bottom - metric)

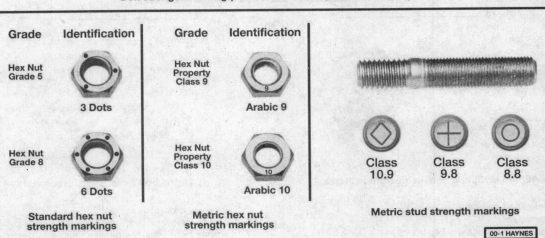

Grade	Identification
Hex Nut Grade 5	3 Dots
Hex Nut Grade 8	6 Dots

Standard hex nut strength markings

Grade	Identification
Hex Nut Property Class 9	Arabic 9
Hex Nut Property Class 10	Arabic 10

Metric hex nut strength markings

Class 10.9   Class 9.8   Class 8.8

Metric stud strength markings

specific torque, a general torque value chart is presented here as a guide. These torque values are for dry (unlubricated) fasteners threaded into steel or cast iron (not aluminum). As was previously mentioned, the size and grade of a fastener determine the amount of torque that can safely be applied to it. The figures listed here are approximate for Grade 2 and Grade 3 fasteners. Higher grades can tolerate higher torque values.

Fasteners laid out in a pattern, such as cylinder head bolts, oil pan bolts, differential cover bolts, etc., must be loosened or tightened in sequence to avoid warping the component. This sequence will normally be shown in the appropriate Chapter. If a specific pattern is not given, the following procedures can be used to prevent warping.

Initially, the bolts or nuts should be assembled finger-tight only. Next, they should be tightened one full turn each, in a crisscross or diagonal pattern. After each one has been tightened one full turn, return to the first one and tighten them all one-half turn, following the same pattern. Finally, tighten each of them one-quarter turn at a time until each fastener has been tightened to the proper torque. To loosen and remove the fasteners, the procedure would be reversed.

Component disassembly

Component disassembly should be done with care and purpose to help ensure that

Metric thread sizes	Ft-lbs	Nm
M-6	6 to 9	9 to 12
M-8	14 to 21	19 to 28
M-10	28 to 40	38 to 54
M-12	50 to 71	68 to 96
M-14	80 to 140	109 to 154
Pipe thread sizes		
1/8	5 to 8	7 to 10
1/4	12 to 18	17 to 24
3/8	22 to 33	30 to 44
1/2	25 to 35	34 to 47
U.S. thread sizes		
1/4 - 20	6 to 9	9 to 12
5/16 - 18	12 to 18	17 to 24
5/16 - 24	14 to 20	19 to 27
3/8 - 16	22 to 32	30 to 43
3/8 - 24	27 to 38	37 to 51
7/16 - 14	40 to 55	55 to 74
7/16 - 20	40 to 60	55 to 81
1/2 - 13	55 to 80	75 to 108

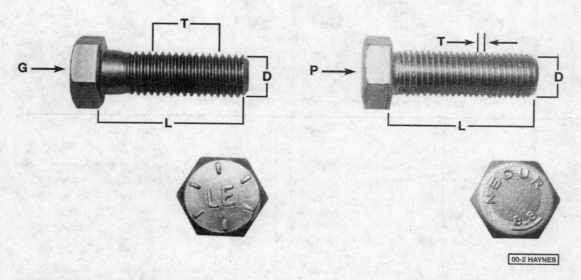

Standard (SAE and USS) bolt dimensions/grade marks

G   Grade marks (bolt strength)
L   Length (in inches)
T   Thread pitch (number of threads per inch)
D   Nominal diameter (in inches)

Metric bolt dimensions/grade marks

P   Property class (bolt strength)
L   Length (in millimeters)
T   Thread pitch (distance between threads in millimeters)
D   Diameter

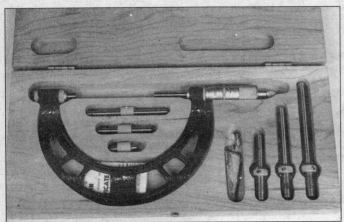

Micrometer set

Dial indicator set

the parts go back together properly. Always keep track of the sequence in which parts are removed. Make note of special characteristics or marks on parts that can be installed more than one way, such as a grooved thrust washer on a shaft. It is a good idea to lay the disassembled parts out on a clean surface in the order that they were removed. It may also be helpful to make sketches or take instant photos of components before removal.

When removing fasteners from a component, keep track of their locations. Sometimes threading a bolt back in a part, or putting the washers and nut back on a stud, can prevent mix-ups later. If nuts and bolts cannot be returned to their original locations, they should be kept in a compartmented box or a series of small boxes. A cupcake or muffin tin is ideal for this purpose, since each cavity can hold the bolts and nuts from a particular area (i.e. oil pan bolts, valve cover bolts, engine mount bolts, etc.). A pan of this type is especially helpful when working on assemblies with very small parts, such as the carburetor, alternator, valve train or interior dash and trim pieces. The cavities can be marked with paint or tape to identify the contents.

Whenever wiring looms, harnesses or connectors are separated, it is a good idea to identify the two halves with numbered pieces of masking tape so they can be easily reconnected.

Gasket sealing surfaces

Throughout any vehicle, gaskets are used to seal the mating surfaces between two parts and keep lubricants, fluids, vacuum or pressure contained in an assembly.

Many times these gaskets are coated with a liquid or paste-type gasket sealing compound before assembly. Age, heat and pressure can sometimes cause the two parts to stick together so tightly that they are very difficult to separate. Often, the assembly can be loosened by striking it with a soft-face hammer near the mating surfaces. A regular hammer can be used if a block of wood is placed between the hammer and the part. Do

not hammer on cast parts or parts that could be easily damaged. With any particularly stubborn part, always recheck to make sure that every fastener has been removed.

Avoid using a screwdriver or bar to pry apart an assembly, as they can easily mar the gasket sealing surfaces of the parts, which must remain smooth. If prying is absolutely necessary, use an old broom handle, but keep in mind that extra clean up will be necessary if the wood splinters.

After the parts are separated, the old gasket must be carefully scraped off and the gasket surfaces cleaned. Stubborn gasket material can be soaked with rust penetrant or treated with a special chemical to soften it so it can be easily scraped off. **Caution:** *Never use gasket removal solutions or caustic chemicals on plastic or other composite components.* A scraper can be fashioned from a piece of copper tubing by flattening and sharpening one end. Copper is recommended because it is usually softer than the surfaces to be scraped, which reduces the chance of gouging the part. Some gaskets can be removed with a wire brush, but regardless of the method used, the mating surfaces must be left clean and smooth. If for some reason the gasket surface is gouged, then a gasket sealer thick enough to fill scratches will have to be used during reassembly of the components. For most applications, a non-drying (or semi-drying) gasket sealer should be used.

Hose removal tips

Warning: *If the vehicle is equipped with air conditioning, do not disconnect any of the A/C hoses without first having the system depressurized by a dealer service department or a service station.*

Hose removal precautions closely parallel gasket removal precautions. Avoid scratching or gouging the surface that the hose mates against or the connection may leak. This is especially true for radiator hoses. Because of various chemical reactions, the rubber in hoses can bond itself to the metal spigot that the hose fits over. To remove

a hose, first loosen the hose clamps that secure it to the spigot. Then, with slip-joint pliers, grab the hose at the clamp and rotate it around the spigot. Work it back and forth until it is completely free, then pull it off. Silicone or other lubricants will ease removal if they can be applied between the hose and the outside of the spigot. Apply the same lubricant to the inside of the hose and the outside of the spigot to simplify installation.

As a last resort (and if the hose is to be replaced with a new one anyway), the rubber can be slit with a knife and the hose peeled from the spigot. If this must be done, be careful that the metal connection is not damaged.

If a hose clamp is broken or damaged, do not reuse it. Wire-type clamps usually weaken with age, so it is a good idea to replace them with screw-type clamps whenever a hose is removed.

Tools

A selection of good tools is a basic requirement for anyone who plans to maintain and repair his or her own vehicle. For the owner who has few tools, the initial investment might seem high, but when compared to the spiraling costs of professional auto maintenance and repair, it is a wise one.

To help the owner decide which tools are needed to perform the tasks detailed in this manual, the following tool lists are offered: *Maintenance and minor repair, Repair/overhaul* and *Special.*

The newcomer to practical mechanics should start off with the *maintenance and minor repair* tool kit, which is adequate for the simpler jobs performed on a vehicle. Then, as confidence and experience grow, the owner can tackle more difficult tasks, buying additional tools as they are needed. Eventually the basic kit will be expanded into the *repair and overhaul* tool set. Over a period of time, the experienced do-it-yourselfer will assemble a tool set complete enough for most repair and overhaul procedures and will add tools from the special category when it is felt that the expense is justified by the frequency of use.

Dial caliper

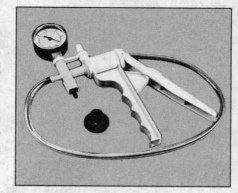

Hand-operated vacuum pump

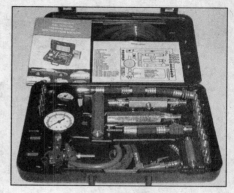

Fuel pressure gauge set

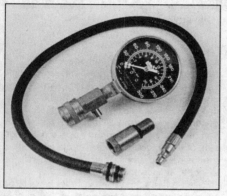

Compression gauge with spark plug hole adapter

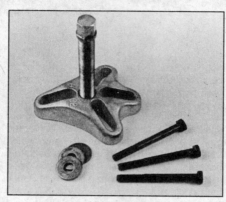

Damper/steering wheel puller

General purpose puller

Hydraulic lifter removal tool

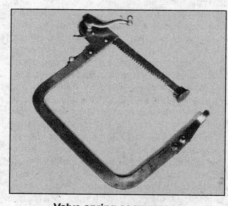

Valve spring compressor

Valve spring compressor

Ridge reamer

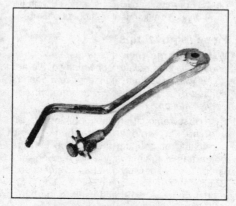

Piston ring groove cleaning tool

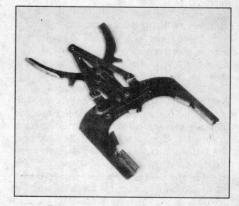

Ring removal/installation tool

Ring compressor

Cylinder hone

Brake hold-down spring tool

Torque angle gauge

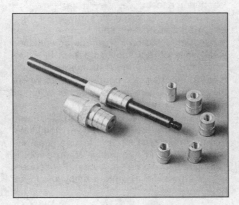

Clutch plate alignment tool

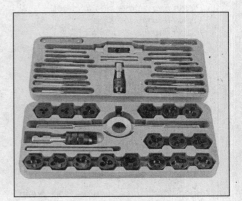

Tap and die set

Maintenance and minor repair tool kit

The tools in this list should be considered the minimum required for performance of routine maintenance, servicing and minor repair work. We recommend the purchase of combination wrenches (box-end and open-end combined in one wrench). While more expensive than open end wrenches, they offer the advantages of both types of wrench.

Combination wrench set (1/4-inch to 1 inch or 6 mm to 19 mm)
Adjustable wrench, 8 inch
Spark plug wrench with rubber insert
Spark plug gap adjusting tool
Feeler gauge set
Brake bleeder wrench
Standard screwdriver (5/16-inch x 6 inch)
Phillips screwdriver (No. 2 x 6 inch)
Combination pliers - 6 inch
Hacksaw and assortment of blades
Tire pressure gauge
Grease gun
Oil can
Fine emery cloth
Wire brush
Battery post and cable cleaning tool
Oil filter wrench
Funnel (medium size)
Safety goggles
Jackstands (2)
Drain pan

Note: *If basic tune-ups are going to be part of routine maintenance, it will be necessary to purchase a good quality stroboscopic timing light and combination tachometer/dwell meter. Although they are included in the list of special tools, it is mentioned here because they are absolutely necessary for tuning most vehicles properly.*

Repair and overhaul tool set

These tools are essential for anyone who plans to perform major repairs and are in addition to those in the maintenance and minor repair tool kit. Included is a comprehensive set of sockets which, though expensive, are invaluable because of their versatility, especially when various extensions and drives are available. We recommend the 1/2-inch drive over the 3/8-inch drive. Although the larger drive is bulky and more expensive, it has the capacity of accepting a very wide range of large sockets. Ideally, however, the mechanic should have a 3/8-inch drive set and a 1/2-inch drive set.

Socket set(s)
Reversible ratchet
Extension - 10 inch
Universal joint
Torque wrench (same size drive as sockets)
Ball peen hammer - 8 ounce
Soft-face hammer (plastic/rubber)
Standard screwdriver (1/4-inch x 6 inch)

Standard screwdriver (stubby - 5/16-inch)
Phillips screwdriver (No. 3 x 8 inch)
Phillips screwdriver (stubby - No. 2)
Pliers - vise grip
Pliers - lineman's
Pliers - needle nose
Pliers - snap-ring (internal and external)
Cold chisel - 1/2-inch
Scribe
Scraper (made from flattened copper tubing)
Centerpunch
Pin punches (1/16, 1/8, 3/16-inch)
Steel rule/straightedge - 12 inch
Allen wrench set (1/8 to 3/8-inch or 4 mm to 10 mm)
A selection of files
Wire brush (large)
Jackstands (second set)
Jack (scissor or hydraulic type)

Note: *Another tool which is often useful is an electric drill with a chuck capacity of 3/8-inch and a set of good quality drill bits.*

Special tools

The tools in this list include those which are not used regularly, are expensive to buy, or which need to be used in accordance with their manufacturer's instructions. Unless these tools will be used frequently, it is not very economical to purchase many of them. A consideration would be to split the cost and use between yourself and a friend or friends. In addition, most of these tools can be obtained from a tool rental shop on a temporary basis.

This list primarily contains only those tools and instruments widely available to the public, and not those special tools produced by the vehicle manufacturer for distribution to dealer service departments. Occasionally, references to the manufacturer's special tools are included in the text of this manual. Generally, an alternative method of doing the job without the special tool is offered. However, sometimes there is no alternative to their use. Where this is the case, and the tool cannot be purchased or borrowed, the work should be turned over to the dealer service department or an automotive repair shop.

> *Valve spring compressor*
> *Piston ring groove cleaning tool*
> *Piston ring compressor*
> *Piston ring installation tool*
> *Cylinder compression gauge*
> *Cylinder ridge reamer*
> *Cylinder surfacing hone*
> *Cylinder bore gauge*
> *Micrometers and/or dial calipers*
> *Hydraulic lifter removal tool*
> *Balljoint separator*
> *Universal-type puller*
> *Impact screwdriver*
> *Dial indicator set*
> *Stroboscopic timing light (inductive pick-up)*
> *Hand operated vacuum/pressure pump*
> *Tachometer/dwell meter*
> *Universal electrical multimeter*
> *Cable hoist*
> *Brake spring removal and installation tools*
> *Floor jack*

Buying tools

For the do-it-yourselfer who is just starting to get involved in vehicle maintenance and repair, there are a number of options available when purchasing tools. If maintenance and minor repair is the extent of the work to be done, the purchase of individual tools is satisfactory. If, on the other hand, extensive work is planned, it would be a good idea to purchase a modest tool set from one of the large retail chain stores. A set can usually be bought at a substantial savings over the individual tool prices, and they often come with a tool box. As additional tools are needed, add-on sets, individual tools and a larger tool box can be purchased to expand the tool selection. Building a tool set gradually allows the cost of the tools to be spread over a longer period of time and gives the mechanic the freedom to choose only those tools that will actually be used.

Tool stores will often be the only source of some of the special tools that are needed, but regardless of where tools are bought, try to avoid cheap ones, especially when buying screwdrivers and sockets, because they won't last very long. The expense involved in replacing cheap tools will eventually be greater than the initial cost of quality tools.

Care and maintenance of tools

Good tools are expensive, so it makes sense to treat them with respect. Keep them clean and in usable condition and store them properly when not in use. Always wipe off any dirt, grease or metal chips before putting them away. Never leave tools lying around in the work area. Upon completion of a job, always check closely under the hood for tools that may have been left there so they won't get lost during a test drive.

Some tools, such as screwdrivers, pliers, wrenches and sockets, can be hung on a panel mounted on the garage or workshop wall, while others should be kept in a tool box or tray. Measuring instruments, gauges, meters, etc. must be carefully stored where they cannot be damaged by weather or impact from other tools.

When tools are used with care and stored properly, they will last a very long time. Even with the best of care, though, tools will wear out if used frequently. When a tool is damaged or worn out, replace it. Subsequent jobs will be safer and more enjoyable if you do.

How to repair damaged threads

Sometimes, the internal threads of a nut or bolt hole can become stripped, usually from overtightening. Stripping threads is an all-too-common occurrence, especially when working with aluminum parts, because aluminum is so soft that it easily strips out.

Usually, external or internal threads are only partially stripped. After they've been cleaned up with a tap or die, they'll still work. Sometimes, however, threads are badly damaged. When this happens, you've got three choices:

1) *Drill and tap the hole to the next suitable oversize and install a larger diameter bolt, screw or stud.*
2) *Drill and tap the hole to accept a threaded plug, then drill and tap the plug to the original screw size. You can also buy a plug already threaded to the original size. Then you simply drill a hole to the specified size, then run the threaded plug into the hole with a bolt and jam nut. Once the plug is fully seated, remove the jam nut and bolt.*
3) *The third method uses a patented thread repair kit like Heli-Coil or Slimsert. These easy-to-use kits are designed to repair damaged threads in straight-through holes and blind holes. Both are available as kits which can handle a variety of sizes and thread patterns. Drill the hole, then tap it with the special included tap. Install the Heli-Coil and the hole is back to its original diameter and thread pitch.*

Regardless of which method you use, be sure to proceed calmly and carefully. A little impatience or carelessness during one of these relatively simple procedures can ruin your whole day's work and cost you a bundle if you wreck an expensive part.

Working facilities

Not to be overlooked when discussing tools is the workshop. If anything more than routine maintenance is to be carried out, some sort of suitable work area is essential.

It is understood, and appreciated, that many home mechanics do not have a good workshop or garage available, and end up removing an engine or doing major repairs outside. It is recommended, however, that the overhaul or repair be completed under the cover of a roof.

A clean, flat workbench or table of comfortable working height is an absolute necessity. The workbench should be equipped with a vise that has a jaw opening of at least four inches.

As mentioned previously, some clean, dry storage space is also required for tools, as well as the lubricants, fluids, cleaning solvents, etc. which soon become necessary.

Sometimes waste oil and fluids, drained from the engine or cooling system during normal maintenance or repairs, present a disposal problem. To avoid pouring them on the ground or into a sewage system, pour the used fluids into large containers, seal them with caps and take them to an authorized disposal site or recycling center. Plastic jugs, such as old antifreeze containers, are ideal for this purpose.

Always keep a supply of old newspapers and clean rags available. Old towels are excellent for mopping up spills. Many mechanics use rolls of paper towels for most work because they are readily available and disposable. To help keep the area under the vehicle clean, a large cardboard box can be cut open and flattened to protect the garage or shop floor.

Whenever working over a painted surface, such as when leaning over a fender to service something under the hood, always cover it with an old blanket or bedspread to protect the finish. Vinyl covered pads, made especially for this purpose, are available at auto parts stores.

Jacking and towing

Jacking

The jack supplied with the vehicle should only be used for raising the vehicle when changing a tire or placing jackstands under the frame. NEVER work under the vehicle or start the engine when the vehicle supported only by a jack.

The vehicle should be parked on level ground with the wheels blocked, the parking brake applied and the transmission in Park. If the vehicle is parked alongside the roadway, or in any other hazardous situation, turn on the emergency hazard flashers. If a tire is to be changed, loosen the lug nuts one-half turn before raising off the ground.

Place the jack under the vehicle in the indicated position (see illustrations). Operate the jack with a slow, smooth motion until the wheel is raised off the ground. Remove the lug nuts, pull off the wheel, install the spare and thread the lug nuts back on with the beveled side facing in. Tighten the lug nuts snugly, lower the vehicle until some weight is on the wheel, then tighten them completely in a criss-cross pattern and remove the jack.

Towing

Equipment specifically designed for towing should be used and attached to the main structural members of the vehicle. Optional tow hooks may be attached to the frame at both ends of the vehicle; they are intended for emergency use only, for rescuing a stranded vehicle. Do not use the tow hooks for highway towing. Stand clear when using tow straps or chains (they may break, causing serious injury.)

The manufacturer recommends that these vehicles be towed only by wheel-lift equipment or a flatbed car-carrier.

Safety is a major consideration when towing and all applicable state and local laws must be obeyed. In addition to a tow bar, a safety chain must be used for all towing.

Two-wheel drive vehicles may be towed with the rear wheels on a towing dolly with no mileage restriction (at posted highway speeds). If the front wheels are on the dolly, speed should be no more than 35 mph for no more than 50 miles, or damage may be done to the transmission.

Four-wheel drive vehicles with a transfer case selector switch on the instrument panel should be towed with the transfer case in Neutral. With the front end lifted, towing is not limited, but if the rear end is lifted and the front is on the ground, towing is restricted to a maximum of 50 miles distance.

Four-wheel drive vehicles without a transfer case selector switch on the instrument panel should only be towed from the front, with the front wheels raised or, preferably, on a flat-bed carrier.

If any vehicle is to be towed with the front wheels on the ground and the rear wheels raised, the ignition key must be turned to the OFF position to unlock the steering column and a steering wheel clamping device designed for towing must be used or damage to the steering column lock may occur.

Front jacking location - make sure the jack head securely engages the pocket in the frame

Rear jacking locations - the jack must be positioned directly under the axle tube

Booster battery (jump) starting

Observe these precautions when using a booster battery to start a vehicle:

a) *Before connecting the booster battery, make sure the ignition switch is in the Off position.*
b) *Turn off the lights, heater and other electrical loads.*
c) *Your eyes should be shielded. Safety goggles are a good idea.*
d) *Make sure the booster battery is the same voltage as the dead one in the vehicle.*
e) *The two vehicles MUST NOT TOUCH each other!*
f) *Make sure the transaxle is in Park (automatic).*
g) *If the booster battery is not a maintenance-free type, remove the vent caps and lay a cloth over the vent holes.*

Connect the red jumper cable to the positive (+) terminals of each battery **(see illustration)**.

Connect one end of the black jumper cable to the negative (-) terminal of the booster battery. The other end of this cable should be connected to a good ground on the vehicle to be started, such as a bolt or bracket on the body.

Start the engine using the booster battery, then, with the engine running at idle speed, disconnect the jumper cables in the reverse order of connection.

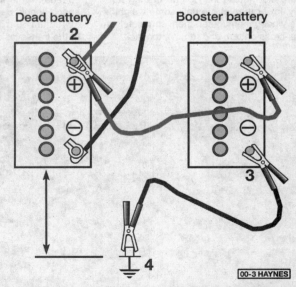

Make the booster battery cable connections in the numerical order shown (note that the negative cable of the booster battery is NOT attached to the negative terminal of the dead battery)

Automotive chemicals and lubricants

A number of automotive chemicals and lubricants are available for use during vehicle maintenance and repair. They include a wide variety of products ranging from cleaning solvents and degreasers to lubricants and protective sprays for rubber, plastic and vinyl.

Cleaners

Carburetor cleaner and choke cleaner is a strong solvent for gum, varnish and carbon. Most carburetor cleaners leave a dry-type lubricant film which will not harden or gum up. Because of this film it is not recommended for use on electrical components.

Brake system cleaner is used to remove brake dust, grease and brake fluid from the brake system, where clean surfaces are absolutely necessary. It leaves no residue and often eliminates brake squeal caused by contaminants.

Electrical cleaner removes oxidation, corrosion and carbon deposits from electrical contacts, restoring full current flow. It can also be used to clean spark plugs, carburetor jets, voltage regulators and other parts where an oil-free surface is desired.

Demoisturants remove water and moisture from electrical components such as alternators, voltage regulators, electrical connectors and fuse blocks. They are non-conductive and non-corrosive.

Degreasers are heavy-duty solvents used to remove grease from the outside of the engine and from chassis components. They can be sprayed or brushed on and, depending on the type, are rinsed off either with water or solvent.

Lubricants

Motor oil is the lubricant formulated for use in engines. It normally contains a wide variety of additives to prevent corrosion and reduce foaming and wear. Motor oil comes in various weights (viscosity ratings) from 0 to 50. The recommended weight of the oil depends on the season, temperature and the demands on the engine. Light oil is used in cold climates and under light load conditions. Heavy oil is used in hot climates and where high loads are encountered. Multi-viscosity oils are designed to have characteristics of both light and heavy oils and are available in a number of weights from 5W-20 to 20W-50.

Gear oil is designed to be used in differentials, manual transmissions and other areas where high-temperature lubrication is required.

Chassis and wheel bearing grease is a heavy grease used where increased loads and friction are encountered, such as for wheel bearings, balljoints, tie-rod ends and universal joints.

High-temperature wheel bearing grease is designed to withstand the extreme temperatures encountered by wheel bearings in disc brake equipped vehicles. It usually contains molybdenum disulfide (moly), which is a dry-type lubricant.

White grease is a heavy grease for metal-to-metal applications where water is a problem. White grease stays soft under both low and high temperatures (usually from -100 to +190-degrees F), and will not wash off or dilute in the presence of water.

Assembly lube is a special extreme pressure lubricant, usually containing moly, used to lubricate high-load parts (such as main and rod bearings and cam lobes) for initial start-up of a new engine. The assembly lube lubricates the parts without being squeezed out or washed away until the engine oiling system begins to function.

Silicone lubricants are used to protect rubber, plastic, vinyl and nylon parts.

Graphite lubricants are used where oils cannot be used due to contamination problems, such as in locks. The dry graphite will lubricate metal parts while remaining uncontaminated by dirt, water, oil or acids. It is electrically conductive and will not foul electrical contacts in locks such as the ignition switch.

Moly penetrants loosen and lubricate frozen, rusted and corroded fasteners and prevent future rusting or freezing.

Heat-sink grease is a special electrically non-conductive grease that is used for mounting electronic ignition modules where it is essential that heat is transferred away from the module.

Sealants

RTV sealant is one of the most widely used gasket compounds. Made from silicone, RTV is air curing, it seals, bonds, waterproofs, fills surface irregularities, remains flexible, doesn't shrink, is relatively easy to remove, and is used as a supplementary sealer with almost all low and medium temperature gaskets.

Anaerobic sealant is much like RTV in that it can be used either to seal gaskets or to form gaskets by itself. It remains flexible, is solvent resistant and fills surface imperfections. The difference between an anaerobic sealant and an RTV-type sealant is in the curing. RTV cures when exposed to air, while an anaerobic sealant cures only in the absence of air. This means that an anaerobic sealant cures only after the assembly of parts, sealing them together.

Thread and pipe sealant is used for sealing hydraulic and pneumatic fittings and vacuum lines. It is usually made from a Teflon compound, and comes in a spray, a paint-on liquid and as a wrap-around tape.

Chemicals

Anti-seize compound prevents seizing, galling, cold welding, rust and corrosion in fasteners. High-temperature ant-seize, usually made with copper and graphite lubricants, is used for exhaust system and exhaust manifold bolts.

Anaerobic locking compounds are used to keep fasteners from vibrating or working loose and cure only after installation, in the absence of air. Medium strength locking compound is used for small nuts, bolts and screws that may be removed later. High-strength locking compound is for large nuts, bolts and studs which aren't removed on a regular basis.

Oil additives range from viscosity index improvers to chemical treatments that claim to reduce internal engine friction. It should be noted that most oil manufacturers caution against using additives with their oils.

Gas additives perform several functions, depending on their chemical makeup. They usually contain solvents that help dissolve gum and varnish that build up on carburetor, fuel injection and intake parts. They also serve to break down carbon deposits that form on the inside surfaces of the combustion chambers. Some additives contain upper cylinder lubricants for valves and piston rings, and others contain chemicals to remove condensation from the gas tank.

Miscellaneous

Brake fluid is specially formulated hydraulic fluid that can withstand the heat and pressure encountered in brake systems. Care must be taken so this fluid does not come in contact with painted surfaces or plastics. An opened container should always be resealed to prevent contamination by water or dirt.

Weatherstrip adhesive is used to bond weatherstripping around doors, windows and trunk lids. It is sometimes used to attach trim pieces.

Undercoating is a petroleum-based, tar-like substance that is designed to protect metal surfaces on the underside of the vehicle from corrosion. It also acts as a sound-deadening agent by insulating the bottom of the vehicle.

Waxes and polishes are used to help protect painted and plated surfaces from the weather. Different types of paint may require the use of different types of wax and polish. Some polishes utilize a chemical or abrasive cleaner to help remove the top layer of oxidized (dull) paint on older vehicles. In recent years many non-wax polishes that contain a wide variety of chemicals such as polymers and silicones have been introduced. These non-wax polishes are usually easier to apply and last longer than conventional waxes and polishes.

Conversion factors

Length (distance)
Inches (in)	X	25.4	= Millimeters (mm)	X 0.0394	= Inches (in)
Feet (ft)	X	0.305	= Meters (m)	X 3.281	= Feet (ft)
Miles	X	1.609	= Kilometers (km)	X 0.621	= Miles

Volume (capacity)
Cubic inches (cu in; in³)	X	16.387	= Cubic centimeters (cc; cm³)	X 0.061	= Cubic inches (cu in; in³)
Imperial pints (Imp pt)	X	0.568	= Liters (l)	X 1.76	= Imperial pints (Imp pt)
Imperial quarts (Imp qt)	X	1.137	= Liters (l)	X 0.88	= Imperial quarts (Imp qt)
Imperial quarts (Imp qt)	X	1.201	= US quarts (US qt)	X 0.833	= Imperial quarts (Imp qt)
US quarts (US qt)	X	0.946	= Liters (l)	X 1.057	= US quarts (US qt)
Imperial gallons (Imp gal)	X	4.546	= Liters (l)	X 0.22	= Imperial gallons (Imp gal)
Imperial gallons (Imp gal)	X	1.201	= US gallons (US gal)	X 0.833	= Imperial gallons (Imp gal)
US gallons (US gal)	X	3.785	= Liters (l)	X 0.264	= US gallons (US gal)

Mass (weight)
Ounces (oz)	X	28.35	= Grams (g)	X 0.035	= Ounces (oz)
Pounds (lb)	X	0.454	= Kilograms (kg)	X 2.205	= Pounds (lb)

Force
Ounces-force (ozf; oz)	X	0.278	= Newtons (N)	X 3.6	= Ounces-force (ozf; oz)
Pounds-force (lbf; lb)	X	4.448	= Newtons (N)	X 0.225	= Pounds-force (lbf; lb)
Newtons (N)	X	0.1	= Kilograms-force (kgf; kg)	X 9.81	= Newtons (N)

Pressure
Pounds-force per square inch (psi; lbf/in²; lb/in²)	X	0.070	= Kilograms-force per square-centimeter (kgf/cm²; kg/cm²)	X 14.223	= Pounds-force per square inch (psi; lbf/in²; lb/in²)
Pounds-force per square inch (psi; lbf/in²; lb/in²)	X	0.068	= Atmospheres (atm)	X 14.696	= Pounds-force per square inch (psi; lbf/in²; lb/in²)
Pounds-force per square inch (psi; lbf/in²; lb/in²)	X	0.069	= Bars	X 14.5	= Pounds-force per square inch (psi; lbf/in²; lb/in²)
Pounds-force per square inch (psi; lbf/in²; lb/in²)	X	6.895	= Kilopascals (kPa)	X 0.145	= Pounds-force per square inch (psi; lbf/in²; lb/in²)
Kilopascals (kPa)	X	0.01	= Kilograms-force per square centimeter (kgf/cm²; kg/cm²)	X 98.1	= Kilopascals (kPa)

Torque (moment of force)
Pounds-force inches (lbf in; lb in)	X	1.152	= Kilograms-force centimeter (kgf cm; kg cm)	X 0.868	= Pounds-force inches (lbf in; lb in)
Pounds-force inches (lbf in; lb in)	X	0.113	= Newton meters (Nm)	X 8.85	= Pounds-force inches (lbf in; lb in)
Pounds-force inches (lbf in; lb in)	X	0.083	= Pounds-force feet (lbf ft; lb ft)	X 12	= Pounds-force inches (lbf in; lb in)
Pounds-force feet (lbf ft; lb ft)	X	0.138	= Kilograms-force meters (kgf m; kg m)	X 7.233	= Pounds-force feet (lbf ft; lb ft)
Pounds-force feet (lbf ft; lb ft)	X	1.356	= Newton meters (Nm)	X 0.738	= Pounds-force feet (lbf ft; lb ft)
Newton meters (Nm)	X	0.102	= Kilograms-force meters (kgf m; kg m)	X 9.804	= Newton meters (Nm)

Vacuum
Inches mercury (in. Hg)	X	3.377	= Kilopascals (kPa)	X 0.2961	= Inches mercury
Inches mercury (in. Hg)	X	25.4	= Millimeters mercury (mm Hg)	X 0.0394	= Inches mercury

Power
Horsepower (hp)	X	745.7	= Watts (W)	X 0.0013	= Horsepower (hp)

Velocity (speed)
Miles per hour (miles/hr; mph)	X	1.609	= Kilometers per hour (km/hr; kph)	X 0.621	= Miles per hour (miles/hr; mph)

Fuel consumption*
Miles per gallon, Imperial (mpg)	X	0.354	= Kilometers per liter (km/l)	X 2.825	= Miles per gallon, Imperial (mpg)
Miles per gallon, US (mpg)	X	0.425	= Kilometers per liter (km/l)	X 2.352	= Miles per gallon, US (mpg)

Temperature
Degrees Fahrenheit = (°C x 1.8) + 32

Degrees Celsius (Degrees Centigrade; °C) = (°F - 32) x 0.56

*It is common practice to convert from miles per gallon (mpg) to liters/100 kilometers (l/100km), where mpg (Imperial) x l/100 km = 282 and mpg (US) x l/100 km = 235

DECIMALS to MILLIMETERS

Decimal	mm	Decimal	mm
0.001	0.0254	0.500	12.7000
0.002	0.0508	0.510	12.9540
0.003	0.0762	0.520	13.2080
0.004	0.1016	0.530	13.4620
0.005	0.1270	0.540	13.7160
0.006	0.1524	0.550	13.9700
0.007	0.1778	0.560	14.2240
0.008	0.2032	0.570	14.4780
0.009	0.2286	0.580	14.7320
		0.590	14.9860
0.010	0.2540		
0.020	0.5080		
0.030	0.7620		
0.040	1.0160	0.600	15.2400
0.050	1.2700	0.610	15.4940
0.060	1.5240	0.620	15.7480
0.070	1.7780	0.630	16.0020
0.080	2.0320	0.640	16.2560
0.090	2.2860	0.650	16.5100
		0.660	16.7640
0.100	2.5400	0.670	17.0180
0.110	2.7940	0.680	17.2720
0.120	3.0480	0.690	17.5260
0.130	3.3020		
0.140	3.5560		
0.150	3.8100		
0.160	4.0640	0.700	17.7800
0.170	4.3180	0.710	18.0340
0.180	4.5720	0.720	18.2880
0.190	4.8260	0.730	18.5420
		0.740	18.7960
0.200	5.0800	0.750	19.0500
0.210	5.3340	0.760	19.3040
0.220	5.5880	0.770	19.5580
0.230	5.8420	0.780	19.8120
0.240	6.0960	0.790	20.0660
0.250	6.3500		
0.260	6.6040		
0.270	6.8580	0.800	20.3200
0.280	7.1120	0.810	20.5740
0.290	7.3660	0.820	21.8280
		0.830	21.0820
0.300	7.6200	0.840	21.3360
0.310	7.8740	0.850	21.5900
0.320	8.1280	0.860	21.8440
0.330	8.3820	0.870	22.0980
0.340	8.6360	0.880	22.3520
0.350	8.8900	0.890	22.6060
0.360	9.1440		
0.370	9.3980		
0.380	9.6520		
0.390	9.9060	0.900	22.8600
0.400	10.1600	0.910	23.1140
0.410	10.4140	0.920	23.3680
0.420	10.6680	0.930	23.6220
0.430	10.9220	0.940	23.8760
0.440	11.1760	0.950	24.1300
0.450	11.4300	0.960	24.3840
0.460	11.6840	0.970	24.6380
0.470	11.9380	0.980	24.8920
0.480	12.1920	0.990	25.1460
0.490	12.4460	1.000	25.4000

FRACTIONS to DECIMALS to MILLIMETERS

Fraction	Decimal	mm	Fraction	Decimal	mm
1/64	0.0156	0.3969	33/64	0.5156	13.0969
1/32	0.0312	0.7938	17/32	0.5312	13.4938
3/64	0.0469	1.1906	35/64	0.5469	13.8906
1/16	0.0625	1.5875	9/16	0.5625	14.2875
5/64	0.0781	1.9844	37/64	0.5781	14.6844
3/32	0.0938	2.3812	19/32	0.5938	15.0812
7/64	0.1094	2.7781	39/64	0.6094	15.4781
1/8	0.1250	3.1750	5/8	0.6250	15.8750
9/64	0.1406	3.5719	41/64	0.6406	16.2719
5/32	0.1562	3.9688	21/32	0.6562	16.6688
11/64	0.1719	4.3656	43/64	0.6719	17.0656
3/16	0.1875	4.7625	11/16	0.6875	17.4625
13/64	0.2031	5.1594	45/64	0.7031	17.8594
7/32	0.2188	5.5562	23/32	0.7188	18.2562
15/64	0.2344	5.9531	47/64	0.7344	18.6531
1/4	0.2500	6.3500	3/4	0.7500	19.0500
17/64	0.2656	6.7469	49/64	0.7656	19.4469
9/32	0.2812	7.1438	25/32	0.7812	19.8438
19/64	0.2969	7.5406	51/64	0.7969	20.2406
5/16	0.3125	7.9375	13/16	0.8125	20.6375
21/64	0.3281	8.3344	53/64	0.8281	21.0344
11/32	0.3438	8.7312	27/32	0.8438	21.4312
23/64	0.3594	9.1281	55/64	0.8594	21.8281
3/8	0.3750	9.5250	7/8	0.8750	22.2250
25/64	0.3906	9.9219	57/64	0.8906	22.6219
13/32	0.4062	10.3188	29/32	0.9062	23.0188
27/64	0.4219	10.7156	59/64	0.9219	23.4156
7/16	0.4375	11.1125	15/16	0.9375	23.8125
29/64	0.4531	11.5094	61/64	0.9531	24.2094
15/32	0.4688	11.9062	31/32	0.9688	24.6062
31/64	0.4844	12.3031	63/64	0.9844	25.0031
1/2	0.5000	12.7000	1	1.0000	25.4000

Safety first!

Regardless of how enthusiastic you may be about getting on with the job at hand, take the time to ensure that your safety is not jeopardized. A moment's lack of attention can result in an accident, as can failure to observe certain simple safety precautions. The possibility of an accident will always exist, and the following points should not be considered a comprehensive list of all dangers. Rather, they are intended to make you aware of the risks and to encourage a safety conscious approach to all work you carry out on your vehicle.

Essential DOs and DON'Ts

DON'T rely on a jack when working under the vehicle. Always use approved jackstands to support the weight of the vehicle and place them under the recommended lift or support points.

DON'T attempt to loosen extremely tight fasteners (i.e. wheel lug nuts) while the vehicle is on a jack - it may fall.

DON'T start the engine without first making sure that the transmission is in Neutral (or Park where applicable) and the parking brake is set.

DON'T remove the radiator cap from a hot cooling system - let it cool or cover it with a cloth and release the pressure gradually.

DON'T attempt to drain the engine oil until you are sure it has cooled to the point that it will not burn you.

DON'T touch any part of the engine or exhaust system until it has cooled sufficiently to avoid burns.

DON'T siphon toxic liquids such as gasoline, antifreeze and brake fluid by mouth, or allow them to remain on your skin.

DON'T inhale brake lining dust - it is potentially hazardous (see *Asbestos* below).

DON'T allow spilled oil or grease to remain on the floor - wipe it up before someone slips on it.

DON'T use loose fitting wrenches or other tools which may slip and cause injury.

DON'T push on wrenches when loosening or tightening nuts or bolts. Always try to pull the wrench toward you. If the situation calls for pushing the wrench away, push with an open hand to avoid scraped knuckles if the wrench should slip.

DON'T attempt to lift a heavy component alone - get someone to help you.

DON'T *rush or take unsafe shortcuts to finish a job.*

DON'T allow children or animals in or around the vehicle while you are working on it.

DO wear eye protection when using power tools such as a drill, sander, bench grinder, etc. and when working under a vehicle.

DO keep loose clothing and long hair well out of the way of moving parts.

DO make sure that any hoist used has a safe working load rating adequate for the job.

DO get someone to check on you periodically when working alone on a vehicle.

DO carry out work in a logical sequence and make sure that everything is correctly assembled and tightened.

DO keep chemicals and fluids tightly capped and out of the reach of children and pets.

DO remember that your vehicle's safety affects that of yourself and others. If in doubt on any point, get professional advice.

Steering, suspension and brakes

These systems are essential to driving safety, so make sure you have a qualified shop or individual check your work. Also, compressed suspension springs can cause injury if released suddenly - be sure to use a spring compressor.

Airbags

Airbags are explosive devices that can **CAUSE** injury if they deploy while you're working on the vehicle. Follow the manufacturer's instructions to disable the airbag whenever you're working in the vicinity of airbag components.

Asbestos

Certain friction, insulating, sealing, and other products - such as brake linings, brake bands, clutch linings, torque converters, gaskets, etc. - may contain asbestos or other hazardous friction material. Extreme care must be taken to avoid inhalation of dust from such products, since it is hazardous to health. If in doubt, assume that they do contain asbestos.

Fire

Remember at all times that gasoline is highly flammable. Never smoke or have any kind of open flame around when working on a vehicle. But the risk does not end there. A spark caused by an electrical short circuit, by two metal surfaces contacting each other, or even by static electricity built up in your body under certain conditions, can ignite gasoline vapors, which in a confined space are highly explosive. Do not, under any circumstances, use gasoline for cleaning parts. Use an approved safety solvent.

Always disconnect the battery ground (-) cable at the battery before working on any part of the fuel system or electrical system. Never risk spilling fuel on a hot engine or exhaust component. It is strongly recommended that a fire extinguisher suitable for use on fuel and electrical fires be kept handy in the garage or workshop at all times. Never try to extinguish a fuel or electrical fire with water.

Fumes

Certain fumes are highly toxic and can quickly cause unconsciousness and even death if inhaled to any extent. Gasoline vapor falls into this category, as do the vapors from some cleaning solvents. Any draining or pouring of such volatile fluids should be done in a well ventilated area.

When using cleaning fluids and solvents, read the instructions on the container carefully. Never use materials from unmarked containers.

Never run the engine in an enclosed space, such as a garage. Exhaust fumes contain carbon monoxide, which is extremely poisonous. If you need to run the engine, always do so in the open air, or at least have the rear of the vehicle outside the work area.

The battery

Never create a spark or allow a bare light bulb near a battery. They normally give off a certain amount of hydrogen gas, which is highly explosive.

Always disconnect the battery ground (-) cable at the battery before working on the fuel or electrical systems.

If possible, loosen the filler caps or cover when charging the battery from an external source (this does not apply to sealed or maintenance-free batteries). Do not charge at an excessive rate or the battery may burst.

Take care when adding water to a non maintenance-free battery and when carrying a battery. The electrolyte, even when diluted, is very corrosive and should not be allowed to contact clothing or skin.

Always wear eye protection when cleaning the battery to prevent the caustic deposits from entering your eyes.

Household current

When using an electric power tool, inspection light, etc., which operates on household current, always make sure that the tool is correctly connected to its plug and that, where necessary, it is properly grounded. Do not use such items in damp conditions and, again, do not create a spark or apply excessive heat in the vicinity of fuel or fuel vapor.

Secondary ignition system voltage

A severe electric shock can result from touching certain parts of the ignition system (such as the spark plug wires) when the engine is running or being cranked, particularly if components are damp or the insulation is defective. In the case of an electronic ignition system, the secondary system voltage is much higher and could prove fatal.

Hydrofluoric acid

This extremely corrosive acid is formed when certain types of synthetic rubber, found in some O-rings, oil seals, fuel hoses, etc. are exposed to temperatures above 750-degrees F (400-degrees C). The rubber changes into a charred or sticky substance containing the acid. *Once formed, the acid remains dangerous for years. If it gets onto the skin, it may be necessary to amputate the limb concerned.*

When dealing with a vehicle which has suffered a fire, or with components salvaged from such a vehicle, wear protective gloves and discard them after use.

Troubleshooting

Contents

This section provides an easy reference guide to the more common problems that may occur during the operation of your vehicle. These problems and possible causes are grouped under various components or systems; i.e. Engine, Cooling System, etc., and also refer to the Chapter and/or Section that deals with the problem.

Remember that successful troubleshooting is not a mysterious black art practiced only by professional mechanics. It's simply the result of a bit of knowledge combined with an intelligent, systematic approach to the problem. Always work by a process of elimination, starting with the simplest solution and working through to the most complex - and never overlook the obvious. Anyone can forget to fill the gas tank or leave the lights on overnight, so don't assume that you are above such oversights.

Finally, always get clear in your mind why a problem has occurred and take steps to ensure that it doesn't happen again. If the electrical system fails because of a poor connection, check all other connections in the system to make sure that they don't fail as well. If a particular fuse continues to blow, find out why - don't just go on replacing fuses. Remember, failure of a small component can often be indicative of potential failure or incorrect functioning of a more important component or system.

Engine

1 Engine will not rotate when attempting to start

1 Battery terminal connections loose or corroded. Check the cable terminals at the battery. Tighten the cable or remove corrosion as necessary.
2 Battery discharged or faulty. If the cable connections are clean and tight on the battery posts, turn the key to the On position and switch on the headlights and/or windshield wipers. If they fail to function, the battery is discharged.
3 Automatic transmission not completely engaged in Park or Neutral or clutch pedal not completely depressed.
4 Broken, loose or disconnected wiring in the starting circuit. Inspect all wiring and connectors at the battery, starter solenoid and ignition switch.
5 Starter motor pinion jammed in flywheel ring gear. If manual transmission, place transmission in gear and rock the vehicle to manually turn the engine. Remove starter and inspect pinion and flywheel at earliest convenience (Chapter 5).
6 Starter solenoid faulty (Chapter 5).
7 Starter motor faulty (Chapter 5).
8 Ignition switch faulty (Chapter 12).

2 Engine rotates but will not start

1 Fuel tank empty, fuel filter plugged or fuel line restricted.
2 Fault in the fuel injection system (Chapter 4).
3 Battery discharged (engine rotates slowly). Check the operation of electrical components as described in the previous Section.
4 Battery terminal connections loose or corroded (see previous Section).
5 Fuel pump faulty (Chapter 4).
6 Excessive moisture on, or damage to, ignition components (see Chapter 5).
7 Worn, faulty or incorrectly gapped spark plugs (Chapter 1).
8 Broken, loose or disconnected wiring in the starting circuit (see previous Section).
9 Broken, loose or disconnected wires at the ignition coils (Chapter 5).

3 Starter motor operates without rotating engine

1 Starter pinion sticking. Remove the starter (Chapter 5) and inspect.
2 Starter pinion or flywheel teeth worn or broken. Remove the flywheel/driveplate access cover and inspect.

4 Engine hard to start when cold

1 Discharged or low battery. Check as described in Section 1.
2 Fault in the fuel or ignition systems (Chapters 4 and 5).
3 Injector(s) leaking (Chapter 4).

5 Engine hard to start when hot

1 Air filter clogged (Chapter 1).
2 Fault in the fuel or ignition systems (Chapters 4 and 5).
3 Fuel not reaching the injectors (see Chapter 4).
4 Low cylinder compression (Chapter 2B).
5 Malfunctioning EVAP system (Chapter 6).

6 Starter motor noisy or excessively rough in engagement

1 Pinion or flywheel gear teeth worn or broken. Remove the cover at the rear of the engine (if equipped) and inspect.
2 Starter motor mounting bolts loose or missing.

7 Engine starts but stops immediately

1 Fault in the fuel or ignition systems (Chapters 4 and 5).
2 Vacuum leak at the gasket surfaces of the intake manifold or throttle body. Make sure all mounting bolts/nuts are tightened securely and all vacuum hoses connected to the manifold are positioned properly and in good condition.
3 Restricted intake or exhaust systems (Chapter 4).

8 Engine lopes while idling or idles erratically

1 Vacuum leakage. Check the mounting bolts/nuts at the throttle body and intake manifold for tightness. Make sure all vacuum hoses are connected and in good condition. Use a stethoscope or a length of fuel hose held against your ear to listen for vacuum leaks while the engine is running. A hissing sound will be heard. A soapy water solution will also detect leaks.
2 Fault in the fuel or ignition systems (Chapters 4 and 5).
3 Plugged PCV valve or hose (see Chapters 1 and 6).
4 Air filter clogged (Chapter 1).
5 Fuel pump not delivering sufficient fuel to the fuel injectors (see Chapter 4).
6 Leaking head gasket. Perform a compression check (Chapter 2B).
7 Camshaft lobes worn (Chapter 2).

9 Engine misses at idle speed

1 Spark plugs worn, fouled or not gapped properly (Chapter 1).
2 Fault in the fuel or ignition systems (Chapters 4 and 5).
3 Vacuum leaks at intake manifold or hose connections. Check as described in Section 8.
4 Uneven or low cylinder compression. Check compression as described in Chapter 2B.

10 Engine misses throughout driving speed range

1 Fuel filter clogged and/or impurities in the fuel system (Chapter 1).
2 Faulty or incorrectly gapped spark plugs (Chapter 1).
3 Fault in the fuel or ignition systems (Chapters 4 and 5).

4   Faulty emissions system components (Chapter 6).
5   Low or uneven cylinder compression pressures. Remove the spark plugs and test the compression with a gauge (Chapter 2B).
6   Vacuum leaks at the throttle body, intake manifold or vacuum hoses (see Section 8).

11 Engine stalls

1   Fuel filter clogged and/or water and impurities in the fuel system (Chapter 1).
2   Fault in the fuel system or sensors (Chapters 4 and 6).
3   Faulty emissions system components (Chapter 6).
4   Faulty or incorrectly gapped spark plugs (Chapter 1).
5   Vacuum leak at the throttle body, intake manifold or vacuum hoses. Check as described in Section 8.

12 Engine lacks power

1   Fault in the fuel or ignition systems (Chapters 4 and 5).
2   Faulty or incorrectly gapped spark plugs (Chapter 1).
3   Faulty coils (Chapter 5).
4   Brakes binding (Chapter 1).
5   Automatic transmission fluid level incorrect (Chapter 1).
6   Clutch slipping (Chapter 8).
7   Fuel filter clogged and/or impurities in the fuel system (Chapter 1).
8   Emissions control system not functioning properly (Chapter 6).
9   Use of substandard fuel. Fill the tank with the proper fuel.
10   Low or uneven cylinder compression pressures. Test with a compression tester, which will detect leaking valves and/or a blown head gasket (Chapter 2B).
11   Restriction in the intake or exhaust system (Chapter 4).

13 Engine backfires

1   Emissions system not functioning properly (Chapter 6).
2   Fault in the fuel or ignition systems (Chapters 4 and 5).
3   Faulty secondary ignition system (Chapters 1 and 5).
4   Fuel injection system not functioning properly (Chapter 4).
5   Vacuum leak at the throttle body, intake manifold or vacuum hoses. Check as described in Section 8.
6   Valves sticking (Chapter 2).

14 Pinging or knocking engine sounds during acceleration or uphill

1   Incorrect grade of fuel. Fill the tank with fuel of the proper octane rating.
2   Fault in the fuel or ignition systems (Chapters 4 and 5).
3   Improper spark plugs. Check the plug type against the VECI label located in the engine compartment. Also check the plugs for damage (Chapter 1).
4   Faulty emissions system (Chapter 6).
5   Vacuum leak. Check as described in Section 9.

15 Engine diesels (continues to run) after switching off

1   Fault in the fuel or ignition systems (Chapters 4 and 5).
2   Excessive engine operating temperature. Probable causes of this are a low coolant level (see Chapter 1), malfunctioning thermostat, clogged radiator or faulty water pump (see Chapter 3).

Engine electrical system

16 Battery will not hold a charge

1   Alternator drivebelt defective or not adjusted properly (Chapter 1).
2   Electrolyte level low or battery discharged (Chapter 1).
3   Battery terminals loose or corroded (Chapter 1).
4   Alternator not charging properly (Chapter 5).
5   Loose, broken or faulty wiring in the charging circuit (Chapter 5).
6   Short in the vehicle wiring causing a continuous drain on the battery (Chapter 12).
7   Battery defective internally.

17 Alternator light fails to go out

1   Fault in the alternator or charging circuit (Chapter 5).
2   Alternator drivebelt defective or not properly adjusted (Chapter 1).

18 Alternator light fails to come on when key is turned on

1   Instrument cluster warning light bulb defective (Chapter 12).
2   Alternator faulty (Chapter 5).
3   Fault in the instrument cluster printed circuit, dashboard wiring or bulb holder (Chapter 12).

Fuel system

19 Excessive fuel consumption

1   Dirty or clogged air filter element (Chapter 1).
2   Emissions system not functioning properly (Chapter 6).
3   Fault in the fuel or ignition systems (Chapters 4 and 5).
4   Low tire pressure or incorrect tire size (Chapter 1).
5   Restricted exhaust system (Chapter 4).

20 Fuel leakage and/or fuel odor

1   Leak in a fuel feed or vent line (Chapter 4).
2   Tank overfilled. Fill only to automatic shut-off.
3   Evaporative emissions system canister clogged (Chapter 6).
4   Vapor leaks from system lines or injectors (Chapter 4).

Cooling system

21 Overheating

1   Insufficient coolant in the system (Chapter 1).
2   Water pump drivebelt defective or not adjusted properly (Chapter 1).
3   Radiator core blocked or radiator grille dirty and restricted (see Chapter 3).
4   Thermostat faulty (Chapter 3).
5   Fan blades broken or cracked (Chapter 3).
6   Radiator cap not maintaining proper pressure. Have the cap pressure tested by a gas station or repair shop.
7   Fault in electrical circuit for cooling fans (Chapter 3).

22 Overcooling

1   Thermostat faulty (Chapter 3).
2   Inaccurate temperature gauge (Chapter 12).
3   Fault in electrical circuit for cooling fans (Chapter 3).

23 External coolant leakage

1   Deteriorated or damaged hoses or loose clamps. Replace hoses and/or tighten the clamps at the hose connections (Chapter 1).
2   Water pump seals defective. If this is the case, water will drip from the weep hole in the water pump body (Chapter 3).
3   Leakage from the radiator core or side tank(s). This will require the radiator to be professionally repaired (see Chapter 3 for removal procedures).

4   Engine drain plug(s) leaking (Chapter 1) or water jacket core plugs leaking (see Chapter 2B).
5   Leakage at the heater core. Signs of leakage should show up on interior carpeting (Chapter 3).

24   Internal coolant leakage

Note: *Internal coolant leaks can usually be detected by examining the oil. Check the dipstick and inside of the valve cover for water deposits and an oil consistency like that of a milkshake.*
1   Leaking cylinder head gasket. Have the cooling system pressure tested.
2   Cracked cylinder bore or cylinder head. Remove the head(s) and inspect (Chapter 2).
3   Leaking intake manifold gasket (Chapter 2).

25   Coolant loss

1   Too much coolant in the system (Chapter 1).
2   Coolant boiling away due to overheating (see Section 15).
3   External or internal leakage (see Sections 23 and 24).
4   Faulty radiator cap. Have the cap pressure tested.

26   Poor coolant circulation

1   Inoperative water pump. A quick test is to pinch the top radiator hose closed with your hand while the engine is idling, then let it loose. You should feel the surge of coolant if the pump is working properly.
2   Restriction in the cooling system. Drain, flush and refill the system (Chapter 1). If necessary, remove the radiator (Chapter 3) and have it reverse flushed.
3   Water pump drivebelt defective or not adjusted properly (Chapter 1).
4   Thermostat sticking (Chapter 3).
5   Drivebelt incorrectly routed, causing the pump to turn backward (Chapter 1).

Clutch

27   Fails to release (pedal pressed to the floor - shift lever does not move freely in and out of Reverse)

1   Leak in the clutch hydraulic system. Check the master cylinder, release cylinder and lines (Chapters 1 and 8).

2   Clutch plate warped or damaged (Chapter 8).
3   Broken release bearing (Chapter 8).

28   Clutch slips (engine speed increases with no increase in vehicle speed)

1   Clutch plate oil-soaked or lining worn. Remove clutch (Chapter 8) and inspect.
2   Clutch plate not seated. It may take 30 or 40 normal starts for a new one to seat.
3   Pressure plate worn (Chapter 8).

29   Grabbing (chattering) as clutch is engaged

1   Oil on clutch plate lining. Remove (Chapter 8) and inspect. Correct any leakage source.
2   Worn or loose engine or transmission mounts. These units move slightly when the clutch is released. Inspect the mounts and bolts (Chapter 2).
3   Worn splines on clutch plate hub. Remove the clutch components (Chapter 8) and inspect.
4   Warped pressure plate or flywheel. Remove the clutch components and inspect.

30   Squeal or rumble with clutch fully engaged (pedal released)

Release bearing binding on transmission bearing retainer. Remove clutch components (Chapter 8) and check release cylinder and release bearing assembly. Remove any burrs or nicks; clean and relubricate before installing.

31   Squeal or rumble with clutch fully disengaged (pedal depressed)

1   Worn, defective or broken release bearing (Chapter 8).
2   Worn or broken pressure plate springs (or diaphragm fingers) (Chapter 8).

32   Clutch pedal stays on floor when disengaged

1   Release bearing binding, or a fault in the hydraulic system (Chapter 8).
2   Clutch master cylinder faulty (Chapter 8).

Manual transmission

Note: *All the following references are in Chapter 7A, unless noted.*

33   Noisy in Neutral with engine running

1   Input shaft bearing worn.
2   Damaged main drive gear bearing.
3   Worn countershaft bearings.
4   Worn or damaged countershaft endplay shims.

34   Noisy in all gears

1   Any of the above causes, and/or:
2   Insufficient lubricant (see the checking procedures in Chapter 1).

35   Noisy in one particular gear

1   Worn, damaged or chipped gear teeth for that particular gear.
2   Worn or damaged synchronizer for that particular gear.

36   Slips out of high gear

1   Transmission loose on clutch housing.
2   Dirt between the transmission case and engine or misalignment of the transmission.

37   Difficulty in engaging gears

1   Clutch not releasing completely (Chapter 8).
2   Loose or damaged shifter. Make a thorough inspection, replacing parts as necessary.

38   Oil leakage

1   Excessive amount of lubricant in the transmission (see Chapter 1 for correct checking procedures). Drain lubricant as required.
2   Transmission oil seal in need of replacement.

Automatic transmission

Note: *Due to the complexity of the automatic transmission, it's difficult for the home mechanic to properly diagnose and service this component. For problems other than the following, the vehicle should be taken to a dealer service department or a transmission shop.*

39 General shift mechanism problems

1   Chapter 7B deals with checking and adjusting the shift cable on automatic transmissions. Common problems that may be attributed to poorly adjusted cable are:

a) *Engine starting in gears other than Park or Neutral.*
b) *Indicator on shifter pointing to a gear other than the one actually being selected.*
c) *Vehicle moves when in Park.*

2   Refer to Chapter 7A to adjust the linkage.
3   Problem with the electronic shift solenoid. Check for Diagnostic Trouble Codes (Chapter 6).

40 Transmission will not downshift with accelerator pedal pressed to the floor

Transmission pressure control solenoid valve faulty. Check for Diagnostic Trouble Codes (Chapter 6).

41 Transmission slips, shifts rough, is noisy or has no drive in forward or reverse gears

1   Of the many probable causes for the above problems, the home mechanic should be concerned with only one possibility - fluid level.
2   Before taking the vehicle to a repair shop, check the level and condition of the fluid as described in Chapter 1. Correct fluid level as necessary or change the fluid and filter if needed. If the problem persists, have a professional diagnose the probable cause.
3   If the transmission shifts late and the shifts are harsh, suspect a faulty transmission pressure control solenoid valve. Check for Diagnostic Trouble Codes (Chapter 6).

42 Fluid leakage

1   Automatic transmission fluid is a deep red color. Fluid leaks should not be confused with engine oil, which can easily be blown by airflow to the transmission.
2   To pinpoint a leak, first remove all built-up dirt and grime from around the transmission. Degreasing agents and/or steam cleaning will achieve this. With the underside clean, drive the vehicle at low speeds so airflow will not blow the leak far from its source. Raise the vehicle and determine where the leak is coming from. Common areas of leakage are:

a) **Pan:** *Tighten the mounting bolts and/or replace the pan gasket as necessary (see Chapter 1).*

b) **Filler pipe:** *Replace the rubber seal where the pipe enters the transmission case.*
c) **Transmission oil lines:** *Tighten the connectors where the lines enter the transmission case and/or replace the lines.*
d) **Vent pipe:** *Transmission overfilled and/or water in fluid (see checking procedures, Chapter 1).*
e) **Speed sensor connector:** *Replace the O-ring where the vehicle speed sensor enters the transmission case (Chapter 6).*

Transfer case

43 Transfer case will not shift into the desired range

1   Speed may be too great to permit engagement. Stop the vehicle and shift into the desired range.
2   Insufficient or incorrect grade of lubricant. Drain and refill the transfer case with the specified lubricant (Chapter 1).
3   Worn or damaged internal components. Disassembly and overhaul of the transfer case, by a qualified shop, may be necessary.
4   Fault in the electrical system of the front axle or transfer case. Check for Diagnostic Trouble Codes (Chapter 6).

44 Transfer case noisy in all gears

Insufficient or incorrect grade of lubricant. Drain and refill (Chapter 1).

45 Noisy or jumps out of four-wheel drive Low range

1   Transfer case not fully engaged. Stop the vehicle, shift into Neutral and then engage 4L.
2   Shift fork cracked, inserts worn or fork binding on the rail. Disassemble and repair as necessary (Chapter 7C).
3   Fault in the electrical system of the front axle or transfer case. Check for Diagnostic Trouble Codes (Chapter 6).

46 Lubricant leaks from the vent or output shaft seals

1   Transfer case is overfilled. Drain to the proper level (Chapter 1).
2   Vent is clogged or jammed closed. Clear or replace the vent.
3   Output shaft seal incorrectly installed or damaged. Replace the seal and check contact surfaces for nicks and scoring.

Driveshaft

47 Oil leak at seal end of driveshaft

Defective transmission or transfer case oil seal. See Chapter 7 for replacement procedures. While this is done, check the splined yoke for burrs or a rough condition that may be damaging the seal. Burrs can be removed with crocus cloth or a fine whetstone.

48 Knock or clunk when the transmission is under initial load (just after transmission is put into gear)

1   Loose or disconnected rear suspension components. Check all mounting bolts, nuts and bushings (see Chapter 10).
2   Loose driveshaft bolts. Inspect all bolts and nuts and tighten them to the specified torque.
3   Worn or damaged universal joint bearings. Check for wear (see Chapter 8).

49 Metallic grinding sound consistent with vehicle speed

Pronounced wear in the universal joint bearings. Check as described in Chapter 8.

50 Vibration

Note: *Before assuming that the driveshaft is at fault, make sure the tires are perfectly balanced and perform the following test.*

1   Install a tachometer inside the vehicle to monitor engine speed as the vehicle is driven. Drive the vehicle and note the engine speed at which the vibration (roughness) is most pronounced. Now shift the transmission to a different gear and bring the engine speed to the same point.
2   If the vibration occurs at the same engine speed (rpm) regardless of which gear the transmission is in, the driveshaft is NOT at fault since the driveshaft speed varies.
3   If the vibration decreases or is eliminated when the transmission is in a different gear at the same engine speed, refer to the following probable causes.
4   Bent or dented driveshaft. Inspect and replace as necessary (see Chapter 8).
5   Undercoating or built-up dirt, etc. on the driveshaft. Clean the shaft thoroughly and recheck.
6   Worn universal joint bearings. Remove and inspect (see Chapter 8).
7   Driveshaft and/or companion flange out of balance. Check for missing weights on the shaft. Remove the driveshaft (see Chapter 8) and reinstall 180-degrees from original position, then retest. Have the driveshaft professionally balanced if the problem persists.

Axles

51 Noise

1   Road noise. No corrective procedures available.
2   Tire noise. Inspect tires and check tire pressures (Chapter 1).
3   Rear wheel bearings worn or damaged (Chapter 8).

52 Vibration

See probable causes under *Driveshaft*. Proceed under the guidelines listed for the driveshaft. If the problem persists, check the rear wheel bearings by raising the rear of the vehicle and spinning the rear wheels by hand. Listen for evidence of rough (noisy) bearings. Remove and inspect (see Chapter 8).

53 Oil leakage

1   Pinion seal damaged (see Chapter 8).
2   Axleshaft oil seals damaged (see Chapter 8).
3   Differential inspection cover leaking. Tighten the bolts or replace the gasket as required (see Chapter 8).

Driveaxles (4WD)

54 Clicking noise on turns

Worn or damaged outboard CV joints (Chapter 8).

55 Shudder or vibration during acceleration

1   Excessive toe-in. Have alignment checked.
2   Incorrect spring heights (Chapter 10).
3   Worn or damaged inboard or outboard CV joints (Chapter 8).
4   Sticking inboard CV joint assembly (Chapter 8).

56 Vibration at highway speeds

1   Out-of-balance front wheels and/or tires (Chapters 1 and 10).
2   Out-of-round front tires (Chapters 1 and 10).
3   Worn CV joints (Chapter 8).

Brakes

Note: *Before assuming that a brake problem exists, make sure that the tires are in good condition and inflated properly (see Chap-*

ter 1), *that the front-end alignment is correct and that the vehicle is not loaded with weight in an unequal manner.*

57 Vehicle pulls to one side during braking

1   Defective, damaged or oil contaminated disc brake pads on one side. Inspect as described in Chapter 9.
2   Excessive wear of brake pad material or disc on one side. Inspect and correct as necessary.
3   Loose or disconnected front suspension components. Inspect and tighten all bolts to the specified torque (Chapter 10).
4   Defective brake caliper assembly. Remove the caliper and inspect for a stuck piston or other damage (Chapter 9).
5   Inadequate lubrication of front brake caliper slide pins. Remove caliper and lubricate slide pins (Chapter 9).

58 Noise (high-pitched squeal or grinding sound with the brakes applied)

1   Disc brake pads worn out. The noise comes from the wear sensor rubbing against the disc (does not apply to all vehicles) or the actual pad backing plate itself if the material is completely worn away. Replace the pads with new ones immediately (Chapter 9). If the pad material has worn completely away, the brake discs should be inspected for damage as described in Chapter 9.
2   Linings contaminated with dirt or grease. Replace pads.
3   Incorrect linings. Replace with correct linings.
4   Drum brake shoes worn out. Replace shoes (Chapter 9).

59 Excessive brake pedal travel

1   Partial brake system failure. Inspect the entire system (Chapter 9) and correct as required.
2   Insufficient fluid in the master cylinder. Check (Chapter 1), add fluid and bleed the system if necessary (Chapter 9).

60 Brake pedal feels spongy when depressed

1   Air in the hydraulic lines. Bleed the brake system (Chapter 9).
2   Faulty flexible hoses. Inspect all system hoses and lines. Replace parts as necessary.
3   Master cylinder mounting bolts/nuts loose.
4   Master cylinder defective (Chapter 9).

61 Excessive effort required to stop vehicle

1   Power brake booster not operating properly (see check in Chapter 1, replacement in Chapter 9).
2   Excessively worn pads. Inspect and replace if necessary (Chapter 9).
3   One or more caliper pistons seized or sticking. Inspect and rebuild as required (Chapter 9).
4   Brake pads contaminated with oil or grease. Inspect and replace as required (Chapter 9).
5   New pads or shoes installed and not yet seated. It will take a while for the new material to seat against the disc or drum.

62 Pedal travels to the floor with little resistance

1   Little or no fluid in the master cylinder reservoir caused by leaking caliper piston(s), loose, damaged or disconnected brake lines. Inspect the entire system and correct as necessary.
2   Worn master cylinder seals (Chapter 9).

63 Brake pedal pulsates during brake application

1   Caliper improperly installed. Remove and inspect (Chapter 9).
2   Disc(s) defective. Remove (Chapter 9) and check for excessive lateral runout and parallelism. Have the discs resurfaced or replace them with new ones (as a pair).
3   Rear brake drums out-of-round. Have the drums resurfaced or replace them as a set.

Suspension and steering systems

64 Vehicle pulls to one side

1   Tire pressures uneven or tires mismatched (Chapter 1).
2   Defective tire (Chapter 1).
3   Excessive wear in suspension or steering components (Chapter 10).
4   Front end in need of alignment.
5   Front brakes dragging. Inspect the brakes as described in Chapter 9.

65 Shimmy, shake or vibration

1   Tire or wheel out-of-balance or out-of-round. Have professionally balanced.
2   Loose, worn or out-of-adjustment front wheel bearings (Chapter 1).
3   Shock absorbers and/or suspension components worn or damaged (Chapter 10).

66   Excessive pitching and/or rolling around corners or during braking

1   Defective shock absorbers. Replace as a set (Chapter 10).
2   Broken or weak springs and/or suspension components. Inspect as described in Chapters 1 and 10.

67   Excessively stiff steering

1   Lack of fluid in power steering fluid reservoir (Chapter 1).
2   Incorrect tire pressures (Chapter 1).
3   Lack of lubrication at steering joints (see Chapter 1).
4   Front end out of alignment.
5   Lack of power assistance (see Section 69).

68   Excessive play in steering

1   Loose front wheel bearings (Chapters 1 and 10).
2   Excessive wear in suspension or steering components (Chapter 10).
3   Steering gear damaged (Chapter 10).

69   Lack of power assistance

1   Steering pump drivebelt faulty or not adjusted properly (Chapter 1).
2   Fluid level low (Chapter 1).
3   Hoses or lines restricted. Inspect and replace parts as necessary.
4   Air in power steering system. Bleed the system (Chapter 10).

70   Excessive tire wear (not specific to one area)

1   Incorrect tire pressures (Chapter 1).
2   Tires out-of-balance. Have professionally balanced.
3   Wheels damaged. Inspect and replace as necessary.
4   Suspension or steering components excessively worn (Chapter 10).

71   Excessive tire wear on outside edge

1   Inflation pressures incorrect (Chapter 1).
2   Excessive speed in turns.

3   Front-end alignment incorrect. Have the front end professionally aligned.
4   Suspension arm bent or twisted (Chapter 10).

72   Excessive tire wear on inside edge

1   Inflation pressures incorrect (Chapter 1).
2   Front-end alignment incorrect. Have the front end professionally aligned.
3   Loose or damaged steering components (Chapter 10).

73   Tire tread worn in one place

1   Tires out-of-balance.
2   Damaged or buckled wheel. Inspect and replace if necessary.
3   Defective tire (Chapter 1).

Notes

Chapter 1
Tune-up and routine maintenance

Contents

Specifications

Recommended lubricants and fluids
Note: *Listed here are manufacturer recommendations at the time this manual was written. Manufacturers occasionally upgrade their fluid and lubricant specifications, so check with your local auto parts store for current recommendations.*

Engine oil	API "certified for gasoline engines"
Viscosity	SAE 5W-30

Recommended lubricants and fluids

Fuel	Unleaded gasoline, 87-octane minimum
Automatic transmission fluid	DEXRON VI automatic transmission fluid
Transfer Case	GM synchromesh transmission fluid
Differential (front and rear)	SAE 75W-90 Synthetic Axle Lubricant
Power steering fluid	GM power steering fluid, or equivalent
Brake fluid	DOT 3 brake fluid
Clutch reservoir fluid	DOT 3 brake fluid
Engine coolant	50/50 mixture of DEX-COOL coolant and de-mineralized water
Parking brake mechanism grease	White lithium-based grease NLGI no. 2
Chassis lubrication grease	NLGI Grade 2 GC or GC-LB chassis grease
Hood, door and trunk hinge lubricant	Lubriplate lubricant aerosol spray
Door hinge and check spring grease	NLGI no. 2 multi-purpose grease or equivalent
Key lock cylinder lubricant	Graphite spray
Hood latch assembly lubricant	NLGI no. 2 multi-purpose grease or equivalent
Door latch lubricant	NLGI no. 2 multi-purpose grease or equivalent

Capacities*

Engine oil (including filter)
  Four-cylinder engine .... 5.0 quarts
  Five-cylinder engine .... 6.0 quarts
Automatic transmission
  Fluid and filter change.. 5.0 quarts
  From dry, including torque converter................................... 11 quarts
Manual transmission
  2WD .... 2.3 quarts
  4WD .... 2.4 quarts
Differential
  Front (4WD models).. 3.2 pints
  Rear .... 3.4 to 3.8 pints
Transfer case... 1.4 to 2.0 quarts
Cooling system
  Four-cylinder engine .... 10.4 quarts
  Five-cylinder engine .... 10.6 quarts

*All capacities approximate. Add as necessary to bring to appropriate level.

Brakes

Disc brake pad wear limit .... 3/32 inch
Drum brake shoe wear limit.. 1/16 inch

Ignition system

Spark plug type
  2004 through 2006.. ACDelco 41-981 or equivalent
  2007 and later models.. ACDelco 41-103 or equivalent
Spark plug gap .... 0.042 inch
Firing order
  Four-cylinder engine 1-3-4-2
  Five-cylinder engine 1-3-5-4-2

Torque specifications   **Ft-lbs** (unless otherwise indicated)

Note: *One foot-pound (ft-lb) of torque is equivalent to 12 inch-pounds (in-lbs) of torque. Torque values below approximately 15 ft-lbs are expressed in inch-pounds, since most foot-pound torque wrenches are not accurate at these smaller values.*

Engine oil drain plug 19
Automatic transmission fluid pan bolts .... 120 in-lbs
Drivebelt tensioner bolt.. 37
Manual transmission drain/fill plugs...................................... 27
Differential drain/fill plugs, front and rear............................. 24
Transfer case drain/fill plugs... 29
Spark plugs... 156 in-lbs
Wheel lug nuts.. 103

INLINE 4-CYLINDER

24027-1a-HAYNES

INLINE 5-CYLINDER

24027-1b-HAYNES

Cylinder locations

Chevrolet Colorado and GMC Canyon maintenance schedule

The following maintenance intervals are based on the assumption that the vehicle owner will be doing the maintenance or service work, as opposed to having a dealer service department do the work. These are the minimum maintenance intervals recommended by the factory for vehicles that are driven daily. If you wish to keep your vehicle in peak condition at all times, you may wish to perform some of these procedures even more often. Because frequent maintenance enhances the efficiency, performance and resale value of your car, we encourage you to do so. If you drive in dusty areas, tow a trailer, idle or drive at low speeds for extended periods or drive for short distances (less than four miles) in below freezing temperatures, shorter intervals are also recommended.

When the vehicle is new, follow the maintenance schedule to the letter, record the maintenance performed in your owners manual and keep all receipts to protect the new vehicle warranty. In many cases the initial maintenance check is done at no cost to the owner (check with your dealer service department for more information).

Every 250 miles or weekly, whichever comes first

Check the engine oil level (Section 4)
Check the coolant level (Section 4)
Check the windshield washer fluid level (Section 4)
Check the brake fluid level (Section 4)
Check the tires and tire pressures (Section 5)

Every 3000 miles or 3 months, whichever comes first

All items listed above, plus . . .
Check the power steering fluid level (Section 6)
Check the automatic transmission fluid level (Section 7)
Change the engine oil and filter (Section 8)

Every 6000 miles or 6 months, whichever comes first

All items listed above, plus . . .
Check the seat belts (Section 9)
Inspect the windshield wiper blades (Section 10)
Check and service the battery (Section 11)
Check the engine drivebelt (Section 12)
Inspect underhood hoses (Section 13)
Check the cooling system (Section 14)
Rotate the tires (Section 15)
Check the lubricant level in the front (4WD) and rear axles (Section 16)

Every 15,000 miles or 12 months, whichever comes first

All items listed above, plus . . .
Lubricate the chassis (Section 17)
Check the fuel system (Section 18)
Check the brake system (Section 19)*
Check the exhaust system (Section 20)
Check the manual transmission lubricant level (Section 21)
Check the transfer case lubricant level (4WD) (Section 22)

Every 30,000 miles or 30 months, whichever comes first

All items listed above, plus . . .
Change the brake fluid (Section 23)
Replace the air filter (Section 24)
Replace the fuel filter on 2004 and 2005 models (Section 25)
Replace the spark plugs (non-platinum type) (Section 26)
Check the steering, suspension and driveaxle boots (Section 27)
Change the automatic transmission fluid and filter (Section 28)**

Every 60,000 miles or 48 months, whichever comes first

Manual transmission lubricant change (Section 29)
Change the transfer case lubricant (Section 30)
Change the differential lubricant (Section 31)*

Every 100,000 miles or 60 months, whichever comes first

Replace the spark plugs (platinum type) (Section 26)
Service the cooling system (drain, flush and refill) (Section 32)

* *This item is affected by "severe" operating conditions, as described below. If the vehicle is operated under severe conditions, perform all maintenance indicated with an asterisk (*) at half the indicated intervals. Severe conditions exist if you mainly operate the vehicle . . .*
in dusty areas
towing a trailer
idling for extended periods
driving at low speeds when outside temperatures remain below freezing and most trips are less than four miles long
** *Perform this procedure at half the recommended interval if operated under one or more of the following conditions:*
in heavy city traffic where the outside temperature regularly reaches 90-degrees F or higher in hilly or mountainous terrain
frequent trailer towing
if the vehicle has been driven through deep water

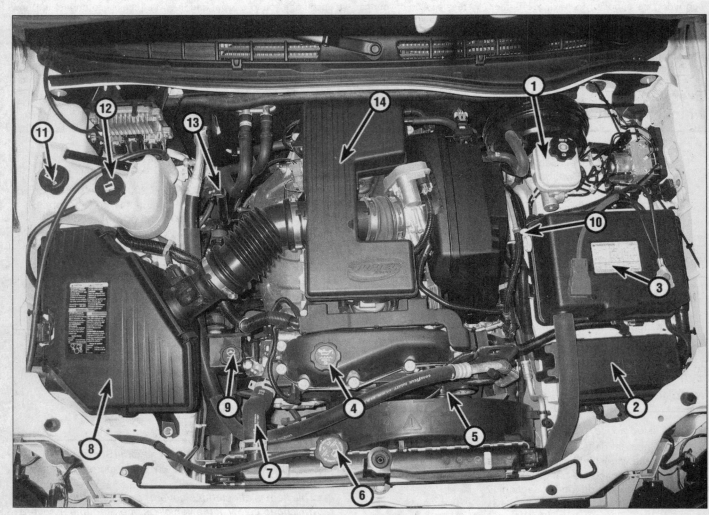

Engine compartment components

1	Brake fluid reservoir	6	Radiator cap	11	Windshield washer fluid reservoir
2	Underhood fuse/relay box	7	Upper radiator hose	12	Coolant reservoir
3	Battery	8	Air filter housing	13	Automatic transmission fluid dipstick
4	Engine oil filler cap	9	Power steering fluid reservoir	14	Spark plugs (underneath air intake
5	Drivebelt	10	Engine oil dipstick		resonator)

Typical engine compartment underside components

1	Stabilizer bar	5	Lower control arm bushing	9	Automatic transmission fluid pan
2	Lower radiator hose	6	Brake caliper	10	Exhaust pipe
3	Engine oil drain plug	7	Tie-rod end	11	Shock absorber/coil spring assembly
4	Engine oil filter	8	Steering gear boot	12	Lower balljoint

Typical rear underside components

1	Leaf spring	4	Drum brake	7	Muffler
2	Shock absorber	5	Fuel tank	8	Spring shackles
3	Differential drain plug	6	Rear universal joint		

2 Introduction

This Chapter is designed to help the home mechanic maintain the Chevrolet Colorado and GMC Canyon with the goals of maximum performance, economy, safety and reliability in mind.

Included is a master maintenance schedule, followed by procedures dealing specifically with each item on the schedule. Visual checks, adjustments, component replacement and other helpful items are included. Refer to the accompanying illustrations of the engine compartment and the underside of the vehicle for the locations of various components.

Servicing your vehicle in accordance with the mileage/time maintenance schedule and the step-by-step procedures will result in a planned maintenance program that should produce a long and reliable service life. Keep in mind that it's a comprehensive plan, so maintaining some items but not others at the specified intervals will not produce the same results.

As you service your vehicle, you will discover that many of the procedures can - and should - be grouped together because of the nature of the particular procedure you're performing or because of the close proximity of two otherwise unrelated components to one another.

For example, if the vehicle is raised for chassis lubrication, you should inspect the exhaust, suspension, steering and fuel systems while you're under the vehicle. When you're rotating the tires, it makes good sense to check the brakes since the wheels are already removed. Finally, let's suppose you have to borrow or rent a torque wrench. Even if you only need it to tighten the spark plugs, you might as well check the torque of as many critical fasteners as time allows.

The first step in this maintenance program is to prepare yourself before the actual work begins. Read through all the procedures you're planning to do, then gather up all the parts and tools needed. If it looks like you might run into problems during a particular job, seek advice from a mechanic or an experienced do-it-yourselfer.

Owner's Manual and VECI label information

Your vehicle Owner's Manual was written for your year and model and contains very specific information on component locations, specifications, fuse ratings, part numbers, etc. The Owner's Manual is an important resource for the do-it-yourselfer to have; if one was not supplied with your vehicle, it can generally be ordered from a dealer parts department.

Among other important information, the Vehicle Emissions Control Information (VECI) label contains specifications and procedures for tune-up adjustments (if applicable) and, in some instances, spark plugs (see Chapter 6 for more information on the VECI label). The information on this label is the exact mainte-

nance data recommended by the manufacturer. This data often varies by intended operating altitude, local emissions regulations, month of manufacture, etc.

This Chapter contains procedural details, safety information and more ambitious maintenance intervals than you might find in the manufacturer's literature. However, you may also find procedures and specifications in your Owner's Manual or VECI label that differ with what's printed here. In these cases, the Owner's Manual or VECI label can be considered correct, since it is specific to your particular vehicle.

3 Tune-up general information

The term tune-up is used in this manual to represent a combination of individual operations rather than one specific procedure that will maintain a gasoline engine in proper tune.

If, from the time the vehicle is new, the routine maintenance schedule is followed closely and frequent checks are made of fluid levels and high wear items, as suggested throughout this manual, the engine will be kept in relatively good running condition and the need for additional work will be minimized.

More likely than not, however, there may be times when the engine is running poorly due to lack of regular maintenance. This is even more likely if a used vehicle, which has not received regular and frequent maintenance checks, is purchased. In such cases, an engine tune-up will be needed outside of the regular routine maintenance intervals.

The first step in any tune-up or diagnostic procedure to help correct a poor running engine is a cylinder compression check. A compression check (see Chapter 2B) will help determine the condition of internal engine components and should be used as a guide for tune-up and repair procedures. If, for instance, the compression check indicates serious internal engine wear, a conventional tune-up won't improve the performance of

4.2 The engine oil dipstick is located along the right side of the engine

the engine and would be a waste of time and money. Because of its importance, the compression check should be done by someone with the right equipment and the knowledge to use it properly.

The following procedures are those most often needed to bring a generally poor running engine back into a proper state of tune.

Minor tune-up

Check all engine-related fluids (Section 4)
Clean, inspect and test the battery (Section 11)
Check and adjust the drivebelt (Section 12)
Check all underhood hoses (Section 13)
Check the cooling system (Section 14)
Check the air filter (Section 24)

Major tune-up

All items listed under Minor tune-up, plus . . .

Replace the air filter (Section 24)
Replace the spark plugs (Section 26)
Check the ignition system (Chapter 5)
Check the charging system (Chapter 5)

4 Fluid level checks (every 250 miles or weekly)

Note: *The following are fluid level checks to be done on a 250 mile or weekly basis. Additional fluid level checks can be found in specific maintenance procedures that follow. Regardless of intervals, be alert to fluid leaks under the vehicle, which would indicate a fault to be corrected immediately.*

1   Fluids are an essential part of the lubrication, cooling, brake and windshield washer systems. Because the fluids gradually become depleted and/or contaminated during normal operation of the vehicle, they must be periodically replenished. See *Recommended lubricants and fluids* at the beginning of this Chapter before adding fluid to any of the following components. **Note:** *The vehicle must be on level ground when fluid levels are checked.*

Engine oil

Refer to illustrations 4.2, 4.4 and 4.6

2   The engine oil level is checked with a dipstick that extends through a tube and into the oil pan at the bottom of the engine **(see illustration)**.

3   The oil level should be checked before the vehicle has been driven, or about 5 minutes after the engine has been shut off. If the oil is checked immediately after driving the vehicle, some of the oil will remain in the upper engine components, resulting in an inaccurate reading on the dipstick.

4   Pull the dipstick out of the tube and wipe all the oil from the end with a clean rag or paper towel. Insert the clean dipstick all the way back into the tube, then pull it out again. Note the oil at the end of the dipstick. Add oil as necessary to keep the level between the L

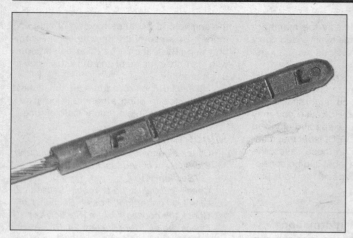

4.4 The oil level must be maintained between the marks at all times - it takes one quart of oil to raise the level from the L mark to the F mark

4.6 Oil is added to the engine after unscrewing the oil filler cap - always make sure the area around the opening is clean before removing the cap to prevent dirt from contaminating the engine

and F marks or within the SAFE zone on the dipstick **(see illustration)**.

5   Do not overfill the engine by adding too much oil since this may result in oil-fouled spark plugs, oil leaks or oil seal failures.

6   Oil is added to the engine after unscrewing a cap from the valve cover **(see illustration)**. A funnel will help to reduce spills.

7   Checking the oil level is an important preventive maintenance step. A consistently low oil level indicates oil leakage through damaged seals, defective gaskets or past worn rings or valve guides. If the oil looks milky or has water droplets in it, the cylinder head gasket(s) may be blown or the head(s) or block may be cracked. The engine should be checked immediately. The condition of the oil should also be checked. Whenever you check the oil level, slide your thumb and index finger up the dipstick before wiping off the oil. If you see small dirt or metal particles clinging to the dipstick, the oil should be changed (see Section 8).

Engine coolant

Refer to illustration 4.9

Warning 1: *Do not allow antifreeze to come in contact with your skin or painted surfaces of the vehicle. Rinse off spills immediately with plenty of water. Antifreeze is highly toxic if ingested. Never leave antifreeze lying around in an open container or in puddles on the floor; children and pets are attracted by its sweet smell and may drink it. Check with local authorities on disposing of used anti-freeze. Many communities have collection centers that will see that antifreeze is disposed of safely.*

Warning 2: *Never remove the radiator cap when the engine is warm.*

Caution 1: *Never mix green-colored ethylene glycol antifreeze and orange-colored "DEX-COOL" silicate-free coolant because doing so will destroy the efficiency of the "DEX-COOL" coolant which is designed to last for 100,000 miles or five years.*

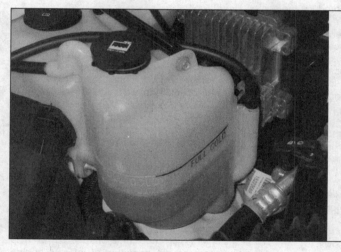

4.9 The coolant reservoir is located on the right side of the engine compartment

Caution 2: *Before mixing water with antifreeze, check the antifreeze container carefully. Some manufacturers pre-mix antifreeze to the proper 50/50 ratio, making the addition of water unnecessary.*

Note: *Non-toxic antifreeze is now manufactured and available at auto parts stores, but even this type should be disposed of properly.*

8   All vehicles covered by this manual are equipped with a coolant reservoir, located at the right side of the engine compartment, and connected by hoses to the radiator.

9   The coolant level in the reservoir should be checked regularly. When the engine is cold, the coolant level should be at or slightly above the COLD mark on the reservoir **(see illustration)**. Once the engine has warmed up, the level should be at or near the HOT mark. If it isn't, add coolant to the reservoir. To add coolant simply flip open the cap and add a 50/50 mixture of "DEX-COOL" coolant and water (see the **Cautions** at the beginning of this Section).

10   Drive the vehicle and recheck the coolant level. If only a small amount of coolant is required to bring the system up to the proper

level, water can be used. However, repeated additions of water will dilute the antifreeze and water solution. In order to maintain the proper ratio of antifreeze and water, always top up the coolant level with the correct mixture. An empty plastic milk jug or bleach bottle makes an excellent container for mixing coolant. Do not use rust inhibitors or additives.

11   If the coolant level drops consistently, there may be a leak in the system. Inspect the radiator, hoses, filler cap, drain plugs and water pump (see Section 14). If no leaks are noted, have the pressure cap tested by a service station.

12   If you have to remove the radiator cap, wait until the engine has cooled completely, then wrap a thick cloth around the cap and slowly unscrew it. If coolant or steam escapes, let the engine cool down longer, then remove the cap.

13   Check the condition of the coolant as well. It should be relatively clear. If it is brown or rust colored, the system should be drained, flushed and refilled. Even if the coolant appears to be normal, the corrosion inhibitors wear out, so it must be replaced at the speci-

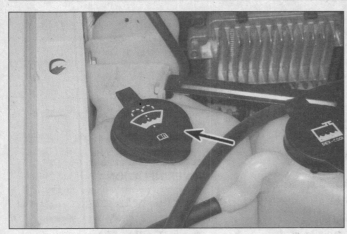

4.14 The windshield washer tank is also located on the right side of the engine compartment, next to the coolant reservoir

4.19 Never let the brake fluid level drop below the MIN mark

fied intervals. If the system is filled with standard green coolant/water, it must be flushed and replaced more frequently than if the original "DEX-COOL" coolant is retained.

Windshield washer fluid

Refer to illustration 4.14

14 Fluid for the windshield washer system is located in a plastic reservoir in the right side of the engine compartment **(see illustration)**.
15 In milder climates, plain water can be used in the reservoir, but it should be kept no more than 2/3 full to allow for expansion if the water freezes. In colder climates, use windshield washer system antifreeze, available at any auto parts store, to lower the freezing point of the fluid. Mix the antifreeze with water in accordance with the manufacturer's directions on the container. **Caution:** *Don't use cooling system antifreeze - it will damage the vehicle's paint.*
16 To help prevent icing in cold weather, warm the windshield with the defroster before using the washer.

Battery electrolyte

17 These vehicles are equipped with a battery which is permanently sealed (except for vent holes) and has no filler caps. Water doesn't have to be added to these batteries at any time. If a maintenance-type battery is installed, the caps on the top of the battery should be removed periodically to check for a low electrolyte level. This check is most critical during the warm summer months. Add only distilled water to any battery.

Brake and clutch fluid

Refer to illustration 4.19

18 The brake master cylinder is mounted on the upper left of the engine compartment firewall. The clutch fluid reservoir is located to the left of the brake master cylinder.
19 The translucent plastic reservoir allows the fluid inside to be checked without removing the cap **(see illustration)**. Be sure to wipe the top of the reservoir cap with a clean rag

to prevent contamination of the brake system before removing the cover.
20 When adding fluid, pour it carefully into the reservoir to avoid spilling it on surrounding painted surfaces. Be sure the specified fluid is used, since mixing different types of brake fluid can cause damage to the system. See *Recommended lubricants and fluids* at the front of this Chapter or your owner's manual. **Warning:** *Brake fluid can harm your eyes and damage painted surfaces, so use extreme caution when handling or pouring it. Do not use brake fluid that has been standing open or is more than one year old. Brake fluid absorbs moisture from the air. Moisture in the system can cause a dangerous loss of brake performance.*
21 At this time, the fluid and master cylinder can be inspected for contamination. The system should be drained and refilled if deposits, dirt particles or water droplets are seen in the fluid.
22 After filling the reservoir to the proper level, make sure the cover or cap is on tight to prevent fluid leakage.
23 The brake fluid level in the master cylinder will drop slightly as the pads at the front wheels wear down during normal operation. If the master cylinder requires repeated additions to keep it at the proper level, it's an indi-

cation of leakage in the brake system, which should be corrected immediately. Check all brake lines and connections (see Section 19 for more information).
24 If, upon checking the master cylinder fluid level, you discover one or both reservoirs empty or nearly empty, the brake system should be bled and thoroughly inspected (see Chapter 9).

5 Tire and tire pressure checks (every 250 miles or weekly)

Refer to illustrations 5.2, 5.3, 5.4a, 5.4b and 5.8

1 Periodic inspection of the tires may spare you the inconvenience of being stranded with a flat tire. It can also provide you with vital information regarding possible problems in the steering and suspension systems before major damage occurs.
2 The original tires on this vehicle are equipped with 1/2-inch wide wear bands that will appear when tread depth reaches 1/16-inch, at which point the tires can be considered worn out. Tread wear can be monitored with a simple, inexpensive device known as a tread depth indicator **(see illustration)**.

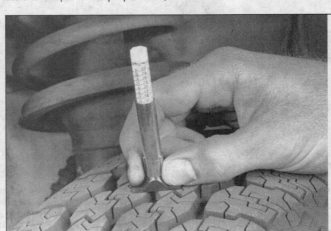

5.2 Use a tire tread depth indicator to monitor tire wear - they are available at auto parts stores and service stations and cost very little

UNDERINFLATION

CUPPING

Cupping may be caused by:
- Underinflation and/or mechanical irregularities such as out-of-balance condition of wheel and/or tire, and bent or damaged wheel.
- Loose or worn steering tie-rod or steering idler arm.
- Loose, damaged or worn front suspension parts.

OVERINFLATION

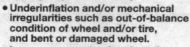

INCORRECT TOE-IN OR EXTREME CAMBER

FEATHERING DUE TO MISALIGNMENT

5.3 This chart will help you determine the condition of the tires and the probable cause(s) of abnormal wear

3   Note any abnormal tread wear (see illustration). Tread pattern irregularities such as cupping, flat spots and more wear on one side than the other are indications of front end alignment and/or balance problems. If any of these conditions are noted, take the vehicle to a tire shop or service station to correct the problem.

4   Look closely for cuts, punctures and embedded nails or tacks. Sometimes a tire will hold air pressure for a short time or leak down very slowly after a nail has embedded itself in the tread. If a slow leak persists, check the valve stem core to make sure it's tight (see illustration). Examine the tread for an object that may have embedded itself in the tire or for a "plug" that may have begun to leak (radial tire punctures are repaired with a plug that's installed in a puncture). If a puncture is suspected, it can be easily verified by spraying a solution of soapy water onto the puncture area (see illustration). The soapy solution will bubble if there's a leak. Unless the puncture is unusually large, a tire shop or service station can usually repair the tire.

5   Carefully inspect the inner sidewall of each tire for evidence of brake fluid leakage. If you see any, inspect the brakes immediately.

6   Correct air pressure adds miles to the lifespan of the tires, improves mileage and enhances overall ride quality. Tire pressure cannot be accurately estimated by looking at a tire, especially if it's a radial. A tire pressure gauge is essential. Keep an accurate gauge in the vehicle. The pressure gauges attached to the nozzles of air hoses at gas stations are often inaccurate.

7   Always check tire pressure when the tires are cold. Cold, in this case, means the

5.4a If a tire loses air on a steady basis, check the valve stem core first to make sure it's snug (special inexpensive wrenches are commonly available at auto parts stores)

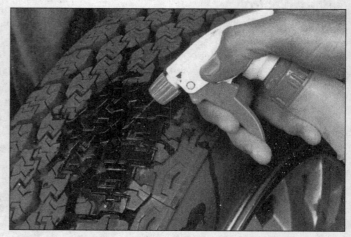

5.4b If the valve stem core is tight, raise the corner of the vehicle with the low tire and spray a soapy water solution onto the tread as the tire is turned slowly - leaks will cause small bubbles to appear

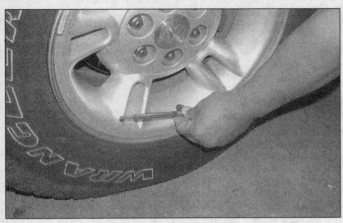

5.8 To extend the life of the tires, check the air pressure at least
once a week with an accurate gauge (don't forget the spare!)

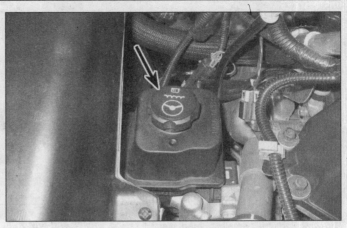

6.2 The power steering fluid reservoir is located on the
right side of the engine

vehicle has not been driven over a mile in the three hours preceding a tire pressure check. A pressure rise of four to eight pounds is not uncommon once the tires are warm.

8   Unscrew the valve cap protruding from the wheel or hubcap and push the gauge firmly onto the valve stem **(see illustration)**. Note the reading on the gauge and compare the figure to the recommended tire pressure shown on the placard on the driver's side door pillar. Be sure to reinstall the valve cap to keep dirt and moisture out of the valve stem mechanism. Check all four tires and, if necessary, add enough air to bring them up to the recommended pressure.

9   Don't forget to keep the spare tire inflated to the specified pressure (refer to your owner's manual or the tire sidewall).

6   Power steering fluid level check (every 3000 miles or 3 months)

Refer to illustrations 6.2 and 6.6

1   Unlike manual steering, the power steering system relies on fluid which may, over a period of time, require replenishing.

2   On all models, the fluid reservoir for the power steering pump is located on the pump body at the front of the engine, next to the air filter housing **(see illustration)**.

3   For the check, the front wheels should be pointed straight ahead and the engine should be off.

4   Use a clean rag to wipe off the reservoir cap and the area around the cap. This will help prevent any foreign matter from entering the reservoir during the check.

5   Twist off the cap and check the temperature of the fluid at the end of the dipstick with your finger.

6   Wipe off the fluid with a clean rag, reinsert the dipstick, then withdraw it and read the fluid level. The fluid should be at the proper level, depending on whether it was checked hot or cold **(see illustration)**. Never allow the fluid level to drop below the lower mark on the dipstick.

7   If additional fluid is required, pour the specified type directly into the reservoir, using a funnel to prevent spills.

8   If the reservoir requires frequent fluid additions, all power steering hoses, hose connections, steering gear and the power steering pump should be carefully checked for leaks.

7   Automatic transmission fluid level check (every 3000 miles or 3 months)

Refer to illustrations 7.3 and 7.6

1   The automatic transmission fluid level should be carefully maintained. Low fluid level can lead to slipping or loss of drive, while overfilling can cause foaming and loss of fluid.

2   With the parking brake set, start the engine, then move the shift lever through all the gear ranges, ending in Park. The fluid level must be checked with the vehicle level and the engine running at idle. **Note:** *Incorrect fluid level readings will result if the vehicle has just been driven at high speeds for an extended period, in hot weather in city traffic, or if it has been pulling a trailer. If any of these conditions apply, wait until the fluid has cooled (about 30 minutes).*

3   With the transmission at normal operating temperature, remove the dipstick from the filler tube. The dipstick is located at the rear of the engine compartment on the passenger's side **(see illustration)**.

4   Wipe the fluid from the dipstick with a

6.6 The power steering fluid dipstick has marks on it
so the fluid can be checked hot or cold

7.3 The automatic transmission dipstick is located at the
right rear of the engine compartment - flip up the
handle before pulling out the dipstick

clean rag and push it back into the filler tube until the cap seats.

5   Pull the dipstick out again and note the fluid level.

6   If the fluid is warm, the level should be in the area between the COLD and HOT ranges **(see illustration)**. If it's hot, the level should be in the crosshatched area in the HOT range. If additional fluid is required, add it directly into the tube using a funnel. It takes about one pint to raise the level from the COLD range to the HOT range with a hot transmission, so add the fluid a little at a time and keep checking the level until it's correct.

7   The condition of the fluid should also be checked along with the level. If the fluid at the end of the dipstick is a dark reddish-brown color, or if it smells burned, it should be changed. If you are in doubt about the condition of the fluid, purchase some new fluid and compare the two for color and smell.

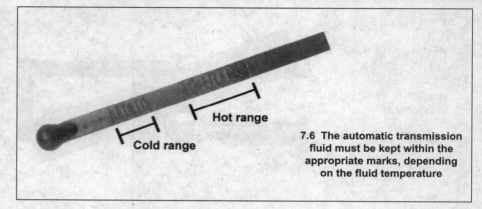

7.6 The automatic transmission fluid must be kept within the appropriate marks, depending on the fluid temperature

8   Engine oil and filter change (every 3000 miles or 3 months)

Refer to illustrations 8.3, 8.9, 8.14 and 8.18

Note: *These vehicles are equipped with an oil life indicator system that illuminates a light on the instrument panel when the system deems it necessary to change the oil. A number of factors are taken into consideration to determine when the oil should be considered "worn out." Generally, this system will allow the vehicle to accumulate more miles between oil changes than the traditional 3000 mile interval, but we believe that frequent oil changes are "cheap insurance" and will prolong engine life. If you do decide not to change your oil every 3000 miles and rely on the oil life indicator instead, make sure you don't exceed 10,000 miles before the oil is changed, regardless of what the oil life indicator shows.*

1   Frequent oil changes are the most important preventive maintenance procedures that can be done by the home mechanic. As engine oil ages, it becomes diluted and contaminated, which leads to premature engine wear.

2   Although some sources recommend oil filter changes every other oil change, we feel that the minimal cost of an oil filter and the relative ease with which it is installed dictate that a new filter be installed every time the oil is changed.

3   Gather together all necessary tools and materials before beginning this procedure **(see illustration)**.

4   You should have plenty of clean rags and newspapers handy to mop up any spills. Access to the underside of the vehicle may be improved if the vehicle can be lifted on a hoist, driven onto ramps or supported by jackstands. **Warning**: *Do not work under a vehicle that is supported only by a jack.*

5   If this is your first oil change, familiarize yourself with the locations of the oil drain plug and the oil filter.

6   Warm the engine to normal operating temperature. If the new oil or any tools are needed, use this warm-up time to gather everything necessary for the job. The correct type of oil for your application can be found in *Recommended lubricants and fluids* at the beginning of this Chapter.

7   With the engine oil warm (warm engine oil will drain better and more built-up sludge will be removed with it), raise and support the vehicle. Make sure it's safely supported!

8   Remove the under-vehicle splash shield. Move all necessary tools, rags and newspapers under the vehicle. Set the drain pan under the drain plug. Keep in mind that the oil will initially flow from the pan with some force; position the pan accordingly.

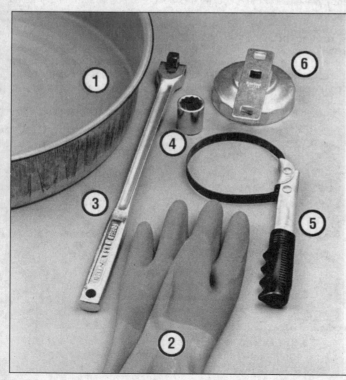

8.3 These tools are required when changing the engine oil and filter

1   **Drain pan** - *It should be fairly shallow in depth, but wide to prevent spills*

2   **Rubber gloves** - *When removing the drain plug and filter, you will get oil on your hands (the gloves will prevent burns)*

3   **Breaker bar** - *Sometimes the oil drain plug is tight, and a long breaker bar is needed to loosen it*

4   **Socket** - *To be used with the breaker bar or a ratchet (must be the correct size to fit the drain plug - six-point preferred)*

5   **Filter wrench** - *This is a metal band-type wrench, which requires clearance around the filter to be effective*

6   **Filter wrench** - *This type fits on the bottom of the filter and can be turned with a ratchet or breaker bar (different-size wrenches are available for different types of filters)*

8.9 Use a proper size box-end wrench or socket to remove the oil drain plug and avoid rounding it off

8.14 Since the oil filter is on very tight, you'll need a special wrench for removal - DO NOT use the wrench to tighten the new filter

9   Being careful not to touch any of the hot exhaust components, use a wrench to remove the drain plug near the bottom of the oil pan (see illustration). Depending on how hot the oil is, you may want to wear gloves while unscrewing the plug the final few turns.

10   Allow the oil to drain into the pan. It may be necessary to move the pan as the oil flow slows to a trickle.

11   After all the oil has drained, wipe off the drain plug with a clean rag. Small metal particles may cling to the plug and would immediately contaminate the new oil.

12   Clean the area around the drain plug opening and reinstall the plug. Tighten the plug securely with the wrench. If a torque wrench is available, use it to tighten the plug to the torque listed in this Chapter's Specifications.

13   Move the drain pan into position under the oil filter.

14   Use the oil filter wrench to loosen the oil filter (see illustration).

15   Completely unscrew the old filter. Be careful; it's full of oil. Empty the oil inside the filter into the drain pan, then lower the filter.

16   Compare the old filter with the new one to make sure they're the same type.

17   Use a clean rag to remove all oil, dirt and sludge from the area where the oil filter mounts to the engine. Check the old filter to make sure the rubber gasket isn't stuck to the engine. If the gasket is stuck to the engine (use a flashlight if necessary), remove it.

18   Apply a light coat of clean oil to the rubber gasket on the new oil filter (see illustration).

19   Attach the new filter to the engine, following the tightening directions printed on the filter canister or packing box. Most filter manufacturers recommend against using a filter wrench due to the possibility of overtightening and damage to the seal.

20   Remove all tools, rags, etc. from under the vehicle, being careful not to spill the oil in the drain pan, then lower the vehicle.

21   Move to the engine compartment and locate the oil filler cap.

22   Pour the fresh oil through the filler opening. Use a funnel to prevent spills.

23   Refer to the engine oil capacity in this Chapter's Specifications and add the proper amount of fresh oil into the engine. Wait a few minutes to allow the oil to drain into the pan, then check the level on the oil dipstick (see Section 4 if necessary). If the oil level is above the upper mark, start the engine and allow the new oil to circulate.

24   Run the engine for only about a minute and then shut it off. Immediately look under the vehicle and check for leaks at the oil pan drain plug and around the oil filter.

25   With the new oil circulated and the filter now completely full, recheck the level on the dipstick and add more oil as necessary.

26   During the first few trips after an oil change, make it a point to check frequently for leaks and proper oil level.

27   The old oil drained from the engine cannot be reused in its present state and should be disposed of. Check with your local auto parts store, disposal facility or environmental agency to see if they will accept the oil for recycling. After the oil has cooled it can be drained into a container (capped plastic jugs, topped bottles, milk cartons, etc.) for transport to one of these disposal sites. Don't dispose of the oil by pouring it on the ground or down a drain!

Oil Life Monitor

28   The Oil Life Monitor is a function of the PCM that tracks engine operating temperature and rpm. If the PCM determines that your engine's oil has been used long enough, an indicator that shows "OIL LIFE" will light on the instrument panel.

29   When you change your engine oil and filter, whether you change it at the interval recommended in this Chapter or only when the

8.18 Lubricate the oil filter gasket with clean engine oil before installing the filter on the engine

light comes on, you will have to reset the system to make the indicator go out.

30   Your vehicle is equipped with a Driver Information Center (DIC) on the instrument panel, which displays the OIL LIFE light, among other information. To reset the engine oil life system, turn the ignition key to the On position (engine off). Push in on the reset stem and release it, repeating this until the OIL LIFE light is illuminated. When the DIC switches back and forth from OIL LIFE to RESET hold the stem in until you hear a succession of beeps. The Monitor is now reset.

9   Seat belt check (every 6000 miles or 6 months)

1   Check seat belts, buckles, latch plates and guide loops for obvious damage and signs of wear.

2   Where the seat belt receptacle bolts to the floor of the vehicle, check that the bolts are secure.

3   See if the seat belt reminder light comes on when the key is turned to the Run or Start position. A chime should also sound.

10   Wiper blade inspection and replacement (every 6000 miles or 6 months)

Refer to illustration 10.3

1   The windshield wiper blade elements should be checked periodically for cracks and deterioration.

2   Lift the wiper blade assembly away from the glass.

3   Press the release lever and slide the blade assembly out of the hook in the end of the wiper arm **(see illustration)**.

4   Squeeze the two rubber prongs at the end of the blade element, then slide the element out of the frame. **Note:** *These elements can be replaced by hand, without pliers.*

5   Compare the new element with the old for length, design, etc. Some replacement elements come in a three-piece design (two metal strips, one on either side of the rubber) that is held together by several small plastic sleeves. Keep the sleeves in place on this design until you start sliding the element into the frame. Remove each of the plastic sleeves as needed when they reach the frame.

6   Slide the new element into the frame, notched end last and secure the clips into the notches of the frame.

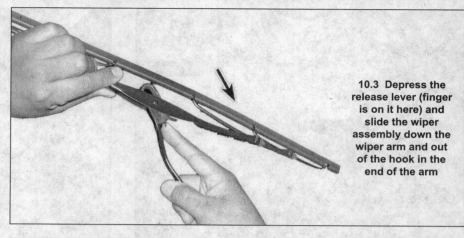

10.3 Depress the release lever (finger is on it here) and slide the wiper assembly down the wiper arm and out of the hook in the end of the arm

7   Reinstall the blade assembly on the arm, wet the windshield and test for proper operation.

11   Battery check, maintenance and charging (every 6000 miles or 6 months)

Refer to illustrations 11.1, 11.5, 11.7a, 11.7b and 11.7c

Warning: *Certain precautions must be followed when checking and servicing the battery. Hydrogen gas, which is highly flammable, is always present in the battery cells, so keep lighted tobacco and all other open flames and sparks away from the battery. The electrolyte inside the battery is actually dilute sul-furic acid, which will cause injury if splashed on your skin or in your eyes. It will also ruin clothes and painted surfaces. When removing the battery cables, always detach the negative cable first and hook it up last!*

1   A routine preventive maintenance program for the battery in your vehicle is the only way to ensure quick and reliable starts. But before performing any battery maintenance, make sure that you have the proper equipment necessary to work safely around the battery **(see illustration)**.

2   There are also several precautions that should be taken whenever battery maintenance is performed. Before servicing the battery, always turn the engine and all accessories off and disconnect the cable from the negative terminal of the battery.

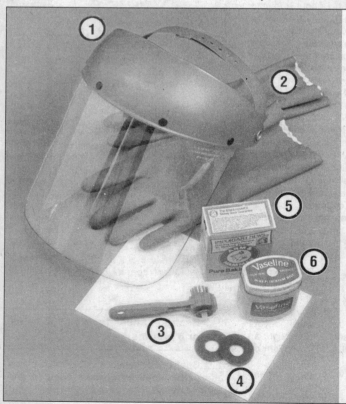

11.1 Tools and materials required for battery maintenance

*1   **Face shield/safety goggles** - When removing corrosion with a brush, the acidic particles can easily fly up into your eyes*

*2   **Rubber gloves** - Another safety item to consider when servicing the battery - remember that's acid inside the battery!*

*3   **Battery terminal/cable cleaner** - This wire brush cleaning tool will remove all traces of corrosion from the battery posts and cable clamps*

*4   **Treated felt washers** - Placing one of these on each post, directly under the cable clamps, will help prevent corrosion*

*5   **Baking soda** - A solution of baking soda and water can be used to neutralize corrosion*

*6   **Petroleum jelly** - A layer of this on the battery posts will help prevent corrosion*

3   The battery produces hydrogen gas, which is both flammable and explosive. Never create a spark, smoke or light a match around the battery. Always charge the battery in a ventilated area.

4   Electrolyte contains poisonous and corrosive sulfuric acid. Do not allow it to get in your eyes, on your skin or on your clothes. Never ingest it. Wear protective safety glasses when working near the battery. Keep children away from the battery.

5   Note the external condition of the battery. If the positive terminal and cable clamp on your vehicle's battery is equipped with a rubber protector, make sure that it's not torn or damaged. It should completely cover the terminal. Look for any corroded or loose connections, cracks in the case or cover or loose hold-down clamps. Also check the entire length of each cable for cracks and frayed conductors **(see illustration)**.

6   If corrosion, which looks like white, fluffy deposits is evident, particularly around the terminals, the battery should be removed for cleaning. Loosen the cable bolts with a wrench, being careful to remove the ground cable first, and slide them off the terminals. Then remove the hold-down clamp and lift the battery from the engine compartment.

7   Clean the cable ends thoroughly with a battery brush or a terminal cleaner and a solution of warm water and baking soda. Wash the terminals and the side of the battery case with the same solution but make sure that the solution doesn't get into the battery. When cleaning the cables, terminals and battery case, wear safety goggles and rubber gloves to prevent any solution from coming in contact with your eyes or hands. Wear old clothes too - even diluted, sulfuric acid splashed onto clothes will burn holes in them. If the terminals have been corroded, clean them up with a terminal cleaner **(see illustrations)**. Thoroughly wash all cleaned areas with plain water.

8   Make sure that the battery tray is in good condition and the hold-down clamp is tight. If the battery is removed from the tray, make sure no parts remain in the bottom of the tray when the battery is reinstalled. When reinstalling the hold-down clamp bolts, do not overtighten them.

9   Any metal parts of the vehicle damaged by corrosion should be covered with a zinc-based primer, then painted.

10   Information on removing and installing the battery can be found in Chapter 5. Information on jump starting can be found at the front of this manual. For more detailed battery checking procedures, refer to the Haynes Automotive Electrical Manual.

Charging

Warning: *When batteries are being charged, hydrogen gas, which is very explosive and flammable, is produced. Do not smoke or allow open flames near a charging or a recently charged battery. Wear eye protection when near the battery during charging. Also, make sure the charger is unplugged before connecting or disconnecting the battery from the charger.*
Caution: *The manufacturer recommends the battery be removed from the vehicle for charging because the gas that escapes during this procedure can damage the paint. Fast charging with the battery cables connected can result in damage to the electrical system.*

11   Slow-rate charging is the best way to restore a battery that's discharged to the point where it will not start the engine. It's also a good way to maintain the battery charge in a vehicle that's only driven a few miles between starts. Maintaining the battery charge is particularly important in the winter when the battery must work harder to start the engine and electrical accessories that drain the battery are in greater use.

12   It's best to use a one or two-amp battery charger (sometimes called a "trickle" charger). They are the safest and put the least strain on the battery. They are also the least expensive. For a faster charge, you can use a higher amperage charger, but don't use one rated more than 1/10th the amp/hour rating of the battery. Rapid boost charges that claim to restore the power of the battery in one to

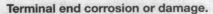

Terminal end corrosion or damage.

Insulation cracks.

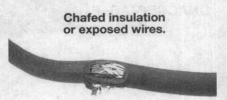

Chafed insulation or exposed wires.

Burned or melted insulation.

11.5 Typical battery cable problems

two hours are hardest on the battery and can damage batteries not in good condition. This type of charging should only be used in emergency situations.

13   The average time necessary to charge a battery should be listed in the instructions that come with the charger. As a general rule, a

11.7a A tool like this one (available at auto parts stores) is used to clean the side-terminal type battery-cable contact area

11.7b Use the brush side of the tool to finish the job

11.7c Regardless of the type of tool used on the battery and cables, a clean, shiny surface should be the result

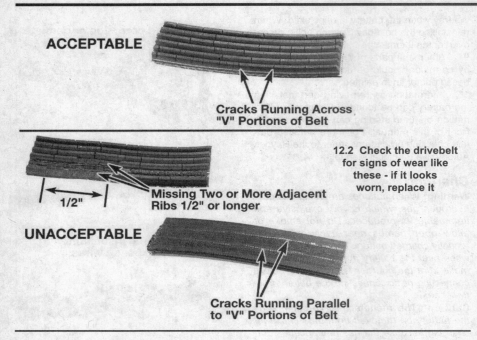

ACCEPTABLE

Cracks Running Across
"V" Portions of Belt

1/2"

Missing Two or More Adjacent
Ribs 1/2" or longer

UNACCEPTABLE

Cracks Running Parallel
to "V" Portions of Belt

**12.2 Check the drivebelt
for signs of wear like
these - if it looks
worn, replace it**

to check the charge. A fully charged battery should read 12.5 volts or higher.

19   Further information on the battery and jump-starting can be found in Chapter 5 and at the front of this manual.

12   Drivebelt and tensioner check and replacement (every 6000 miles or 6 months)

Refer to illustrations 12.2, 12.4, 12.5 and 12.7

1   A serpentine drivebelt is located at the front of the engine and plays an important role in the overall operation of the engine and its components. Due to its function and material make up, the belt is prone to wear and should be periodically inspected. The serpentine belt drives the alternator, power steering pump, water pump and air conditioning compressor.

2   With the engine off, open the hood and use your fingers (and a flashlight, if necessary), to move along the belt checking for cracks and separation of the belt plies. Also check for fraying and glazing, which gives the belt a shiny appearance **(see illustration)**. Both sides of the belt must be inspected.

3   Check the ribs on the underside of the belt. They should all be the same depth, with none of the surface uneven.

4   The tension of the belt is maintained by a spring-loaded tensioner assembly and isn't adjustable. The belt should be replaced when the mark on the tensioner arm is lined up with the indexing mark on the tensioner body **(see illustration)**.

5   To replace the belt, rotate the tensioner clockwise to release belt tension **(see illustration)**.

6   Remove the belt from the tensioner and auxiliary components and slowly release the tensioner.

7   After verifying the new belt is the same length as the original belt route the new belt over the various pulleys, again rotating the

trickle charger will charge a battery in 12 to 16 hours.

14   Remove all the cell caps (if equipped) and cover the holes with a clean cloth to prevent spattering electrolyte. Disconnect the negative battery cable and hook the battery charger cable clamps up to the battery posts (positive to positive, negative to negative), then plug in the charger. Make sure it is set at 12-volts if it has a selector switch.

15   If you're using a charger with a rate higher than two amps, check the battery regularly during charging to make sure it doesn't overheat. If you're using a trickle charger, you can safely let the battery charge overnight after you've checked it regularly for the first couple of hours.

16   If the battery has removable cell caps, measure the specific gravity with a hydrometer every hour during the last few hours of

the charging cycle. Hydrometers are available inexpensively from auto parts stores - follow the instructions that come with the hydrometer. Consider the battery charged when there's no change in the specific gravity reading for two hours and the electrolyte in the cells is gassing (bubbling) freely. The specific gravity reading from each cell should be very close to the others. If not, the battery probably has a bad cell(s).

17   Some batteries with sealed tops have built-in hydrometers on the top that indicate the state of charge by the color displayed in the hydrometer window. Normally, a bright-colored hydrometer indicates a full charge and a dark hydrometer indicates the battery still needs charging.

18   If the battery has a sealed top and no built-in hydrometer, you can hook up a digital voltmeter across the battery terminals

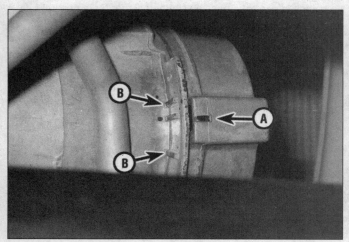

**12.4 The indexing mark (A) on the drivebelt's tensioner must
remain between the marks (B) on the tensioner assembly**

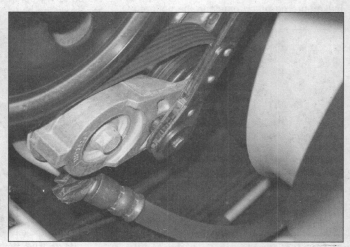

**12.5 Use a drivebelt tool to turn the tensioner clockwise
for belt removal (there may not be room for a standard
ratchet or breaker bar)**

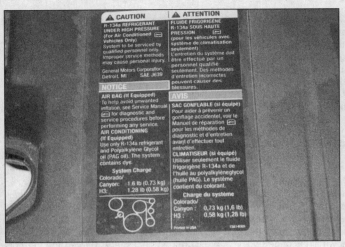

12.7 The drivebelt routing diagram is found on this decal at the radiator support

12.8 Drivebelt tensioner mounting bolt

tensioner to allow the belt to be installed, then release the belt tensioner. **Note:** *A drivebelt routing decal is located on the radiator support to help during drivebelt installation* **(see illustration).**

Tensioner replacement

Refer to illustration 12.8

8   To replace a damaged tensioner, remove the belt, then remove the tensioner mounting bolt **(see illustration).**

9   Installation is the reverse of the removal procedure. Tighten the mounting bolt to the torque listed in this Chapter's Specifications. **Note:** *Be certain to get the indexing dowel on the tensioner inserted into the hole provided on the tensioner mounting surface.*

---

13   Underhood hose check and replacement (every 6000 miles or 6 months)

Warning: *Replacement of air conditioning hoses must be left to a dealer service department or air conditioning shop that has the equipment to depressurize the system safely and recover the refrigerant. Never remove air conditioning components or hoses until the system has been depressurized.*

1   High temperatures in the engine compartment can cause the deterioration of the rubber and plastic hoses used for engine, accessory and emission systems operation. Periodic inspection should be made for cracks, loose clamps, material hardening and leaks. Information specific to the cooling system hoses can be found in Section 14.

2   Some, but not all, hoses are secured to their fittings with clamps. Where clamps are used, check to be sure they haven't lost their tension, allowing the hose to leak. If clamps aren't used, make sure the hose has not

expanded and/or hardened where it slips over the fitting, allowing it to leak.

Vacuum hoses

3   It's quite common for vacuum hoses, especially those in the emissions system, to be color-coded or identified by colored stripes molded into them. Various systems require hoses with different wall thickness, collapse resistance and temperature resistance. When replacing hoses, be sure the new ones are made of the same material.

4   Often the only effective way to check a hose is to remove it completely from the vehicle. If more than one hose is removed, be sure to label the hoses and fittings to ensure correct installation.

5   When checking vacuum hoses, be sure to include any plastic T-fittings in the check. Inspect the fittings for cracks and the hose where it fits over the fitting for distortion, which could cause leakage.

6   A small piece of vacuum hose (1/4-inch inside diameter) can be used as a stethoscope to detect vacuum leaks. Hold one end of the hose to your ear and probe around vacuum hoses and fittings, listening for the "hissing" sound characteristic of a vacuum leak. **Warning:** *When probing with the vacuum hose stethoscope, be very careful not to come into contact with moving engine components such as the drivebelt, cooling fan, etc.*

Fuel hose

Warning: *Gasoline is extremely flammable, so take extra precautions when you work on any part of the fuel system. Don't smoke or allow open flames or bare light bulbs near the work area, and don't work in a garage where a gas-type appliance (such as a water heater or clothes dryer) is present. Since gasoline is carcinogenic, wear fuel-resistant gloves when there's a possibility of being exposed to fuel, and, if you spill any fuel on your skin, rinse it off immediately with soap and water. Mop up*

any spills immediately and do not store fuel-soaked rags where they could ignite. When you perform any kind of work on the fuel system, wear safety glasses and have a Class B type fire extinguisher on hand. The fuel system is under pressure, so if any lines must be disconnected, the pressure in the system must be relieved first (see Chapter 4 for more information).

7   Check all rubber fuel lines for deterioration and chafing. Check especially for cracks in areas where the hose bends and just before fittings, such as where a hose attaches to the fuel filter and fuel injection unit.

8   High quality fuel line, specifically designed for high-pressure fuel injection applications, must be used for fuel line replacement. Never, under any circumstances, use regular fuel line, unreinforced vacuum line, clear plastic tubing or water hose for fuel lines.

9   Spring-type (pinch) clamps are commonly used on fuel lines. These clamps often lose their tension over a period of time, and can be "sprung" during removal. Replace all spring-type clamps with screw clamps whenever a hose is replaced.

Metal lines

10   Sections of metal line are routed along the frame, between the fuel tank and the engine. Check carefully to be sure the line has not been bent or crimped and no cracks have started in the line.

11   If a section of metal fuel line must be replaced, only seamless steel tubing should be used, since copper and aluminum tubing don't have the strength necessary to withstand normal engine vibration.

12   Check the metal brake lines where they enter the master cylinder and brake proportioning unit for cracks in the lines or loose fittings. Any sign of brake fluid leakage calls for an immediate and thorough inspection of the brake system.

14   Cooling system check (every 6000 miles or 6 months)

Refer to illustration 14.4

Warning: *Wait until the engine is completely cool before performing this procedure.*

Caution: *Never mix green-colored ethylene glycol anti-freeze and orange-colored "DEX-COOL" silicate-free coolant because doing so will destroy the efficiency of the "DEX-COOL" coolant which is designed to last for 100,000 miles or five years.*

1   Many major engine failures can be attributed to a faulty cooling system. If the vehicle is equipped with an automatic transmission, the cooling system also cools the transmission fluid and thus plays an important role in prolonging transmission life.

2   The cooling system must be checked with the engine cold. Do this before the vehicle is driven for the day or after it has been shut off for at least three hours.

3   Remove the radiator cap by slowly unscrewing it until it comes to a stop. If you

Check for a chafed area that could fail prematurely.

Check for a soft area indicating the hose has deteriorated inside.

Overtightening the clamp on a hardened hose will damage the hose and cause a leak.

Check each hose for swelling and oil-soaked ends. Cracks and breaks can be located by squeezing the hose.

14.4 Hoses, like drivebelts, have a habit of failing at the worst possible time - to prevent the inconvenience of a blown radiator or heater hose, inspect them carefully as shown here

hear any hissing sounds (indicating there is still pressure in the system), wait until it stops. If there is no hissing sound, depress the cap and continue unscrewing it. Thoroughly clean the cap, inside and out, with clean water. Also clean the filler neck on the radiator. All traces of corrosion should be removed. The coolant inside the coolant reservoir should be relatively transparent. If it is rust colored, the system should be drained and refilled (see Section 30). If the coolant level is not up to the top, add additional antifreeze/coolant mixture (see Section 4).

4   Carefully check the large upper and lower radiator hoses along with any smaller diameter heater hoses that run from the engine to the firewall. Inspect each hose along its entire length, replacing any hose that is cracked, swollen or shows signs of deterioration. Cracks may become more apparent if the hose is squeezed **(see illustration)**.

5   Make sure all hose connections are tight. A leak in the cooling system will usually show up as white or rust-colored deposits on the areas adjoining the leak. If wire-type clamps are used at the ends of the hoses, it may be wise to replace them with more secure, screw-type clamps.

6   Use compressed air or a soft brush to remove bugs, leaves, etc. from the front of the radiator or air conditioning condenser. Be careful not to damage the delicate cooling fins or cut yourself on them.

7   Every other inspection, or at the first indication of cooling system problems, have the cap and system pressure tested. If you don't have a pressure tester, most gas stations and repair shops will do this for a minimal charge.

15   Tire rotation (every 6000 miles or 6 months)

Refer to illustrations 15.2a and 15.2b

1   The tires should be rotated at the specified intervals and whenever uneven wear

is noticed.

2   Tires must be rotated in the recommended pattern **(see illustrations)**.

3   Refer to the information in *Jacking and towing* at the front of this manual for the proper procedures to follow when raising the vehicle and changing a tire. If the brakes are to be checked, don't apply the parking brake as stated. Make sure the tires are blocked to prevent the vehicle from rolling as it's raised.

4   Preferably, the entire vehicle should be raised at the same time. This can be done on a hoist or by jacking up each corner and then lowering the vehicle onto jack stands placed under the frame rails. Always use four jack stands and make sure the vehicle is safely supported.

5   After rotation, check and adjust the tire pressures as necessary. Tighten the lug nuts to the torque listed in this Chapter's Specifications.

16   Differential lubricant level check (every 6,000 miles or 6 months)

Refer to illustrations 16.2a and 16.2b

Note: *4WD vehicles have two differentials - one in the center of each axle. 2WD vehicles have one differential - in the center of the rear axle. On 4WD models, be sure to check the lubricant level in both differentials.*

1   The filler plug on all front and most rear differentials is a threaded metal type. If the vehicle is raised to gain access to the plug, be sure to support it safely on jackstands - DO NOT crawl under the vehicle when it's supported only by the jack. Be sure the vehicle is level or the check may not be accurate.

2   Remove the plug from the filler hole in the differential housing or cover **(see illustrations)**.

3   The lubricant level should be below the fill-plug opening by 1/2 inch. If not, use a pump or squeeze bottle to add the recommended lubricant until it just starts to run out of the

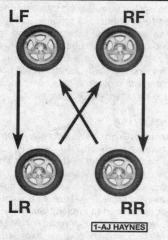

15.2a The recommended four-tire rotation pattern for non-directional radial tires

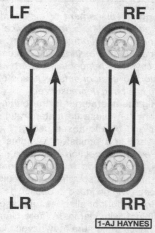

15.2b The recommended four-tire rotation pattern for directional radial tires

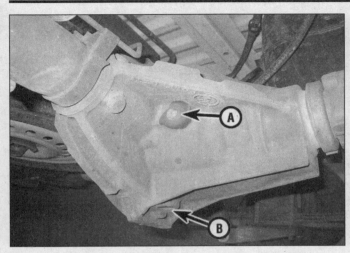

16.2a Remove the rear axle filler plug (A) to check the differential lubricant level - B is the differential drain plug

16.2b Remove the front (4WD) axle filler plug (A) to check the differential lubricant level - B is the drain plug (typical)

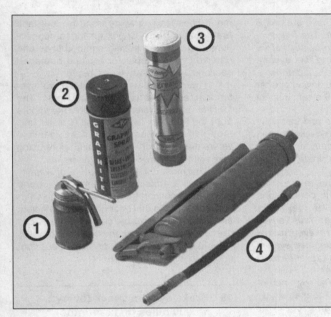

17.1 Materials required for chassis and body lubrication

1 *Engine oil* - *Light engine oil in a can like this can be used for door and hood hinges*
2 *Graphite spray* - *Used to lubricate lock cylinders*
3 *Grease* - *Grease, in a variety of types and weights, is available for use in a grease gun. Check the Specifications for your requirements*
4 *Grease gun* - *A common grease gun, shown here with a detachable hose and nozzle, is needed for chassis lubrication. After use, clean it thoroughly!*

opening. On some models a tag is located in the area of the plug which gives information regarding lubricant type.

4   Install the plug securely into the filler hole.

17 Chassis lubrication (every 15,000 miles or 12 months)

Refer to illustrations 17.1 and 17.2

1   Refer to *Recommended lubricants and fluids* at the front of this Chapter to obtain the necessary grease, etc. You'll also need a grease gun **(see illustration)**. If a suspension component has no grease fitting in place, this indicates the part is sealed and doesn't require periodic lubrication. Some components on 4WD models have fittings that aren't on 2WD versions, and vice versa.

2   Look under the vehicle and look for the presence of grease fittings **(see illustration)**.

3   For easier access under the vehicle, raise it with a jack and place jackstands under the frame. Make sure it's safely supported by the stands. If the wheels are to be removed at this interval for tire rotation or brake inspection, loosen the lug nuts slightly while the vehicle is still on the ground.

4   Before beginning, force a little grease out of the nozzle to remove any dirt from the end of the gun. Wipe the nozzle clean with a rag.

5   With the grease gun and plenty of clean rags, crawl under the vehicle and begin lubricating the components.

6   Wipe one of the grease fittings clean and push the nozzle firmly over it. Pump the gun until the component is completely lubricated. On balljoints, stop pumping when the rubber seal is firm to the touch. Do not pump too much grease into the fitting as it could rupture the seal. For all other suspension and steering

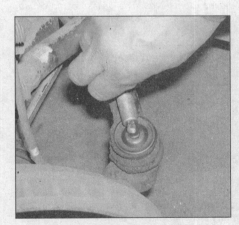

17.2 After cleaning the grease fitting, push the gun nozzle firmly into place and pump the grease into the component (usually about two pumps will be sufficient)

18.7 Inspect the fuel tank mounting straps and the various fuel and vapor lines

19.7a With the wheel off, check the thickness of the inner pad through the inspection hole in the caliper

components, continue pumping grease into the fitting until it oozes out of the joint between the two components. If it escapes around the grease gun nozzle, the fitting is clogged or the nozzle is not completely seated on the fitting. Resecure the gun nozzle to the fitting and try again. If necessary, replace the fitting with a new one.

7   Wipe the excess grease from the components and the grease fitting. Repeat the procedure for the remaining fittings.

8   Clean the fitting and pump grease into the driveline universal joints until the grease can be seen coming out of the contact points. The other U-joints are sealed and do not require lubrication. **Note:** *Most replacement driveshaft U-joints aren't permanently sealed, and are sold with grease fittings. If your U-joints have been replaced, make sure you include these fittings in your routine chassis lubrication.*

9   Also clean and lubricate the parking brake cable guides and levers. **Caution:** *Do not use chassis lubrication on the brake cables themselves. The grease could cause the cable housings to deteriorate.*

18   Fuel system check (every 15,000 miles or 12 months)

Refer to illustration 18.7

Warning: *Gasoline is extremely flammable, so take extra precautions when you work on any part of the fuel system. Don't smoke or allow open flames or bare light bulbs near the work area, and don't work in a garage where a gas-type appliance (such as a water heater or clothes dryer) is present. Since gasoline is carcinogenic, wear fuel-resistant gloves when there's a possibility of being exposed to fuel, and, if you spill any fuel on your skin, rinse it off immediately with soap and water. Mop up any spills immediately and do not store fuel-soaked rags where they could ignite. When you perform any kind of work on the fuel sys-*tem, wear safety glasses and have a Class B type fire extinguisher on hand. The fuel system is under constant pressure, so, before any lines are disconnected, the fuel system pressure must be relieved (see Chapter 4).*

1   If you smell gasoline while driving or after the vehicle has been sitting in the sun, inspect the fuel system immediately.

2   Remove the gas filler cap and inspect it for damage and corrosion. The gasket should have an unbroken sealing imprint. If the gasket is damaged or corroded, install a new cap.

3   Inspect the fuel feed and return lines for cracks. Make sure that the connections between the fuel lines and the fuel injection system are tight. **Warning:** *Your vehicle is fuel injected, so you must relieve the fuel system pressure before servicing fuel system components. The fuel system pressure relief procedure is outlined in Chapter 4.*

4   Where you see no external evidence of leaks, other indicators of fuel leakage may be fuel contaminated oil, or an excessively long crank time before engine start, followed by black smoke from the tailpipe immediately after starting.

5   Since some components of the fuel system - the fuel tank and part of the fuel feed and return lines, for example - are underneath the vehicle, they can be inspected more easily with the vehicle raised on a hoist. If that's not possible, raise the vehicle and support it on jack stands.

6   With the vehicle raised and safely supported, inspect the gas tank and filler neck for punctures, cracks and other damage. The connection between the filler neck and the tank is particularly critical. Sometimes a rubber filler neck will leak because of loose clamps or deteriorated rubber. Inspect all fuel tank mounting brackets and straps to be sure that the tank is securely attached to the vehicle. **Warning:** *Do not, under any circumstances, try to repair a fuel tank (except rubber components).*

7   Carefully check all rubber hoses and metal lines leading away from the fuel tank **(see illustration).** Check for loose connections, deteriorated hoses, crimped lines and other damage. Repair or replace damaged sections as necessary (see Chapter 4).

8   The evaporative emissions control system can also be a source of fuel odors. The function of the system is to store fuel vapors from the fuel tank in a charcoal canister until they can be routed to the intake manifold where they mix with incoming air before being burned in the combustion chambers.

9   The most common symptom of a faulty evaporative emissions system is a strong odor of fuel coming from the area of the charcoal canister. If a fuel odor has been detected, and you have already checked the areas described above, check the charcoal canister, located near the fuel tank, and the hoses connected to it (see Chapter 6).

19   Brake system check (every 15,000 miles or 12 months)

Warning: *The dust created by the brake system is harmful to your health. Never blow it out with compressed air and don't inhale any of it. An approved filtering mask should be worn when working on the brakes. Do not, under any circumstances, use petroleum-based solvents to clean brake parts. Use brake system cleaner only! Try to use non-asbestos replacement parts whenever possible.*

Note: *For detailed photographs of the brake system, refer to Chapter 9.*

1   In addition to the specified intervals, the brakes should be inspected every time the wheels are removed or whenever a defect is suspected.

2   Any of the following symptoms could indicate a potential brake system defect: The vehicle pulls to one side when the brake pedal is depressed; the brakes make squealing or dragging noises when applied; brake pedal travel is excessive; the pedal pulsates; or

19.7b The outer pad is more easily checked at the edge of the caliper

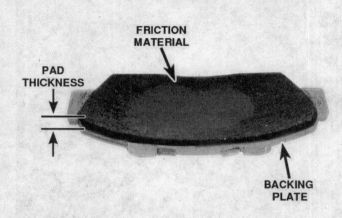

19.9 If a more precise measurement of pad thickness is necessary, remove the pads and measure the remaining friction material

brake fluid leaks, usually onto the inside of the tire or wheel.

3   Loosen the wheel lug nuts.

4   Raise the vehicle and support it securely on jackstands.

5   Remove the wheels (see *Jacking and towing* at the front of this book, or your owner's manual, if necessary).

Disc brakes

Refer to illustrations 19.7a, 19.7b, 19.9 and 19.11

6   There are two pads (an outer and an inner) in each caliper. The pads are visible with the front wheels removed.

7   Check the pad thickness by looking at each end of the caliper and through the inspection window in the caliper body **(see illustrations)**. If the lining material is less than the thickness listed in this Chapter's Specifications, replace the pads. **Note:** *Keep in mind that the lining material is riveted or bonded to a metal backing plate and the metal portion is not included in this measurement.*

8   If it is difficult to determine the exact thickness of the remaining pad material by the above method, or if you are at all concerned about the condition of the pads, remove the caliper(s), then remove the pads from the calipers for further inspection (refer to Chapter 9).

9   Once the pads are removed from the calipers, clean them with brake cleaner and re-measure them with a ruler or a vernier caliper **(see illustration)**.

10   Measure the disc thickness with a micrometer to make sure that it still has service life remaining. If any disc is thinner than the specified minimum thickness, replace it (refer to Chapter 9). Even if the disc has service life remaining, check its condition. Look for scoring, gouging and burned spots. If these conditions exist, remove the disc and have it resurfaced (see Chapter 9).

11   Before installing the wheels, check all brake lines and hoses for damage, wear, deformation, cracks, corrosion, leakage, bends and twists, particularly in the vicinity

of the rubber hoses at the calipers **(see illustration)**. Check the clamps for tightness and the connections for leakage. Make sure that all hoses and lines are clear of sharp edges, moving parts and the exhaust system. If any of the above conditions are noted, repair, reroute or replace the lines and/or fittings as necessary (see Chapter 9).

Drum brakes

Refer to illustrations 19.13 and 19.15

12   Refer to Chapter 9 and remove the rear brake drums.

13   Check the thickness of the lining on each brake shoe **(see illustration)**. If the lining is less than the thickness listed in this Chapter's Specifications, replace the brake shoes. **Note:** *Keep in mind that the lining material is riveted or bonded to a metal backing plate and the metal portion is not included in this measurement.* Also replace the brake shoes if the lining is cracked, glazed, or contaminated by grease, oil, or brake fluid (see Chapter 9).

19.11 Check along the brake hoses and at each fitting for deterioration, cracks and leakage

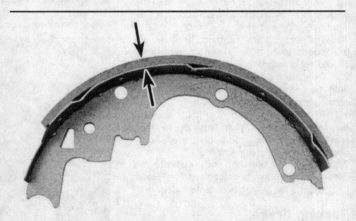

19.13 If the lining is bonded to the brake shoe, measure the lining thickness from the outer surface to the metal shoe, as shown here; if the lining is riveted to the shoe, measure from the lining outer surface to the rivet head

19.15 Carefully peel back the wheel cylinder boots and check for leaking fluid indicating that the cylinder must be replaced

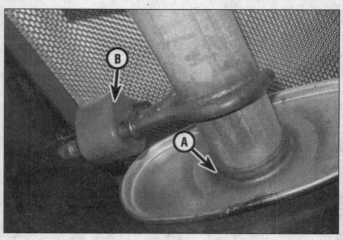

20.2a Inspect the muffler (A) for signs of deterioration, and all hangers (B)

14   Check the shoe return springs and the adjusting mechanism for damage, deterioration, and incorrect installation. Worn or damaged springs may let the brake linings drag on the drums and wear prematurely.

15   Carefully pull back the wheel cylinder boots and check for leakage **(see illustration)**. Replace the cylinder if you find brake fluid behind a boot (see Chapter 9).

16   Inspect the brake drums for cracks, scoring, deep scratches, and hard spots caused by overheating. Remove small imperfections with emery cloth. Take the drums to a machine shop to be refinished if they are deeply scratched or scored. Replace the drums if they are cracked, overheated, of worn beyond the maximum diameter cast on their outer surfaces. (see Chapter 9).

17   Refer to Chapter 9 and reinstall the drums.

Brake booster check

18   Sit in the driver's seat and perform the following sequence of tests.

19   With the brake fully depressed, start the engine - the pedal should move down a little when the engine starts.

20   With the engine running, depress the brake pedal several times - the travel distance should not change.

21   Depress the brake, stop the engine and hold the pedal in for about 30 seconds - the pedal should neither sink nor rise.

22   Restart the engine, run it for about a minute and turn it off. Then firmly depress the brake several times - the pedal travel should decrease with each application.

23   If your brakes do not operate as described, the brake booster has failed. Refer to Chapter 9 for the replacement procedure.

Parking brake

24   One method of checking the parking brake is to park the vehicle on a steep hill with the parking brake set and the transmission in Neutral (be sure to stay in the vehicle for this

check). If the parking brake cannot prevent the vehicle from rolling, it's in need of attention (see Chapter 9).

20   Exhaust system check (every 15,000 miles or 12 months)

Refer to illustrations 20.2a and 20.2b

1   With the engine cold (at least three hours after the vehicle has been driven), check the complete exhaust system from the manifold to the end of the tailpipe. Be careful around the catalytic converter, which may be hot even after three hours. The inspection should be done with the vehicle on a hoist to permit unrestricted access. If a hoist isn't available, raise the vehicle and support it securely on jackstands.

2   Check the exhaust pipes and connections for signs of leakage and/or corrosion indicating a potential failure. Make sure that all brackets and hangers are in good condition and tight **(see illustrations)**.

3   Inspect the underside of the body for holes, corrosion, open seams, etc. which may

20.2b Inspect all flanged joints for signs of exhaust gas leakage

allow exhaust gasses to enter the passenger compartment. Seal all body openings with silicone sealant or body putty.

4   Rattles and other noises can often be traced to the exhaust system, especially the hangers, mounts and heat shields. Try to move the pipes, mufflers and catalytic converter. If the components can come in contact with the body or suspension parts, secure the exhaust system with new brackets and hangers.

21   Manual transmission lubricant level check (every 15,000 miles or 12 months)

1   The manual transmission does not have a dipstick. To check the fluid level, raise the vehicle and support it securely on jackstands. On the side of the transmission housing, you will see a plug. Remove it. If the lubricant level is correct, it should be up to the lower edge of the hole.

2   If the transmission needs more lubricant (if the level is not up to the hole), use a syringe or a gear oil pump to add more. Stop filling the transmission when the lubricant begins to run out the hole.

3   Install the plug and tighten it securely. Drive the vehicle a short distance, then check for leaks.

22   Transfer case lubricant level check (4WD models) (every 15,000 miles or 12 months)

Refer to illustration 22.1

1   The transfer case lubricant level is checked by removing the upper plug located at the rear of the case **(see illustration)**.

2   After removing the plug, reach inside the hole. The lubricant level should be just at the bottom of the hole. If not, add the appropriate lubricant through the opening.

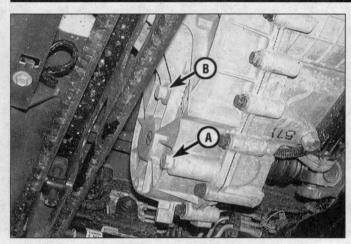

22.1 The drain plug (A) and fill plug (B) are on the rear cover of the transfer case (typical)

24.3a Loosen the screws and lift the air filter housing cover off

23 Brake fluid change (every 30,000 miles or 24 months)

Warning: *Brake fluid can harm your eyes and damage painted surfaces, so use extreme caution when handling or pouring it. Do not use brake fluid that has been standing open or is more than one year old. Brake fluid absorbs moisture from the air. Excess moisture can cause a dangerous loss of braking effectiveness.*

1 At the specified intervals, the brake fluid should be drained and replaced. Since the brake fluid may drip or splash when pouring it, place plenty of rags around the master cylinder to protect any surrounding painted surfaces.
2 Before beginning work, purchase the specified brake fluid (see *Recommended lubricants and fluids* at the beginning of this Chapter).
3 Remove the cap from the master cylinder reservoir.
4 Using a hand suction pump or similar device, withdraw the fluid from the master cylinder reservoir.
5 Add new fluid to the master cylinder until it rises to the line indicated on the reservoir.
6 Bleed the brake system as described in Chapter 9 at all four brakes until new and

uncontaminated fluid is expelled from the bleeder screw. Be sure to maintain the fluid level in the master cylinder as you perform the bleeding process. If you allow the master cylinder to run dry, air will enter the system.
7 Refill the master cylinder with fluid and check the operation of the brakes. The pedal should feel solid when depressed, with no sponginess. **Warning:** *Do not operate the vehicle if you are in doubt about the effectiveness of the brake system.*

24 Air filter replacement (every 30,000 miles or 24 months)

Refer to illustrations 24.3a and 24.3b

1 At the specified intervals, the air filter element should be replaced with a new one.
2 On all models, the air filter is housed in a black plastic box mounted on the right side of the engine compartment. Attached to the intake tube on some models is a plastic gauge that measures the airflow through the filter and indicates when the filter should be changed. If you drive in conditions that are particularly dusty, the gauge may indicate the need for a filter change before the normally-recommended mileage interval.

3 Snap open the clips and pull the housing cover up, then remove the air filter element from the housing **(see illustrations)**. Wipe out the inside of the air filter housing with a clean rag.
4 While the cover is off, be careful not to drop anything down into the air filter housing.
5 When installing the new filter element, align the tangs on the filter with the matching retainers on the lower half of the filter housing.
6 Installation is the reverse of removal.

25 Fuel filter replacement (2004 and 2005 models) (every 30,000 miles or 30 months)

Refer to illustration 25.5
Warning: *Gasoline is extremely flammable, so take extra precautions when you work on any part of the fuel system. Don't smoke or allow open flames or bare light bulbs near the work area, and don't work in a garage where a gas-type appliance (such as a water heater or clothes dryer) is present. Since gasoline is carcinogenic, wear fuel-resistant gloves when there's a possibility of being exposed to fuel, and, if you spill any fuel on your skin, rinse it off immediately with soap and water. Mop up any spills immediately and do not store fuel-soaked rags where they could ignite. The fuel system is under constant pressure, so, if any fuel lines are to be disconnected, the fuel pressure in the system must be relieved first (see Chapter 4 for more information). When you perform any kind of work on the fuel system, wear safety glasses and have a Class B type fire extinguisher on hand.*
Note: *2006 and later models do not have a replaceable fuel filter. They have a filter in the fuel pump module inside the fuel tank, but replacement is not a scheduled maintenance item.*
1 Relieve the fuel system pressure (see Chapter 4), then disconnect the cable from the negative terminal of the battery.

24.3b With the cover removed, pull the filter element from its retainers in the lower housing

2   Raise the vehicle and support it securely on jackstands.

3   The fuel filter is mounted in a bracket at the fuel tank.

4   Use compressed air or carburetor cleaner to clean any dirt surrounding the fuel inlet and outlet line fittings.

5   There are quick-connect fittings at each end of the filter, requiring finger pressure or a needle-nose pliers to remove **(see illustration)**. **Note:** *Have some rags or a small container to catch or wipe up extra gasoline that will spill from the filter assembly.*

6   Pry out the two locking tabs on the bracket that secure the filter element. Don't bend the tabs any more than is necessary to slide the filter element out.

7   Installation is the reverse of removal.

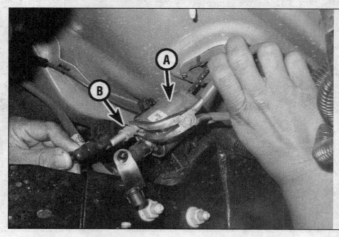

25.5 When changing the fuel filter (A), carefully squeeze the clips (B) to disconnect the fittings

26   Spark plug replacement (see maintenance schedule for service intervals)

Refer to illustrations 26.2, 26.5a, 26.5b, 26.7, 26.8, 26.9 and 26.10

1   The spark plugs are threaded into the top of the cylinder head. For access, you'll have to remove the air intake resonator and the ignition coils.

2   In most cases, the tools necessary for spark plug replacement include a spark plug socket which fits onto a ratchet (spark plug sockets are padded inside to prevent damage to the porcelain insulators on the new plugs), various extensions and a gap gauge to check and adjust the gaps on the new plugs **(see illustration)**. A torque wrench should be used to tighten the new plugs.

3   The best approach when replacing the spark plugs is to purchase the new ones in advance, adjust them to the proper gap and

replace them one at a time. When buying the new spark plugs, be sure to obtain the correct plug type for your particular engine. This information can be found in your owner's manual and the Specifications at the front of this Chapter.

4   Allow the engine to cool completely before attempting to remove any of the plugs. While you're waiting for the engine to cool, check the new plugs for defects and adjust the gaps.

5   The gap is checked by inserting the prop-

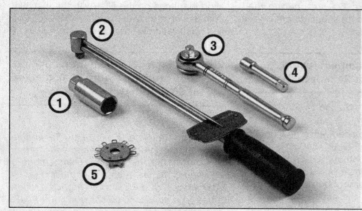

26.2 Tools required for changing spark plugs

1   *Spark plug socket - This will have special padding inside to protect the spark plug's porcelain insulator*

2   *Torque wrench - Although not mandatory, using this tool is the best way to ensure the plugs are tightened properly*

3   *Ratchet - Standard hand tool to fit the spark plug socket*

4   *Extension - Depending on model and accessories, you may need special extensions and universal joints to reach one or more of the plugs*

5   *Spark plug gap gauge - This gauge for checking the gap comes in a variety of styles. Make sure the gap for your engine is included*

26.5a The manufacturer recommends using a wire-type gauge to check the spark plug gap - if the wire doesn't slide between the electrodes with a slight drag, adjustment is required

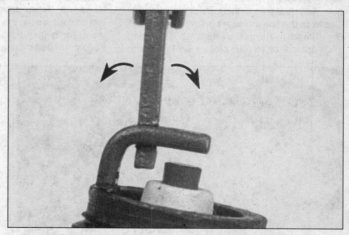

26.5b To change the gap, bend the side electrode only, and be very careful not to crack or chip the porcelain insulator surrounding the center electrode

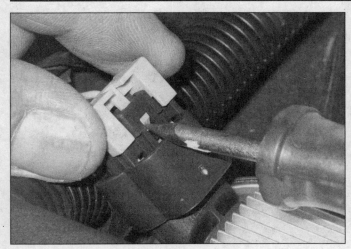

26.7 Use a pointed tool to depress the tab while pulling up the locking part of the ignition coil connector, then disconnect the electrical connector

26.8 Use a socket and extension to unscrew the spark plugs - various length extensions and perhaps a flex-joint may be required to reach some plugs

er-thickness gauge between the electrodes at the tip of the plug **(see illustration)**. The gap between the electrodes should be the same as the one specified on the Emissions Control Information label or in this Chapter's Specifications. The wire should just slide between the electrodes with a slight amount of drag. If the gap is incorrect, use the adjuster on the gauge body to bend the curved side electrode slightly until the proper gap is obtained **(see illustration)**. If the side electrode is not exactly over the center electrode, bend it with the adjuster until it is. Check for cracks in the porcelain insulator (if any are found, the plug should not be used). **Note:** *Manufacturers recommend using a tapered thickness gauge when checking platinum-type spark plugs. Other types of gauges may scrape the thin platinum coating from the electrodes, thus dramatically shortening the life of the plugs.*

6   Remove the air intake resonator (see Chapter 4).

7   With access to the ignition coils, pull up the locking tab on each coil and disconnect the electrical connector **(see illustration)**. Remove the bolt holding each coil to the valve cover and withdraw the coil/spark plug boot.

8   If compressed air is available, use it to blow any dirt or foreign material away from the spark plug hole. The idea here is to eliminate the possibility of debris falling into the cylinder as the spark plug is removed. Use a socket and extension to remove the spark plugs **(see illustration)**.

9   Compare the spark plug with the chart on the inside back cover of this manual to get an indication of the general running condition of the engine. Before installing the new plugs, it is a good idea to apply a thin coat of anti-seize compound to the threads **(see illustration)**. Do not get any on the electrodes.

10   Thread one of the new plugs into the hole until you can no longer turn it with your fingers, then tighten it with a torque wrench (if available) or the ratchet. It's a good idea to slip a short length of rubber hose over the end of the plug to use as a tool to thread it into place **(see illustration)**. The hose will grip the

plug well enough to turn it, but will start to slip if the plug begins to cross-thread in the hole - this will prevent damaged threads and the accompanying repair costs.

11   Attach the plug boot to the coil then the coil onto the spark plug.

12   Repeat the procedure for the remaining spark plugs, then install the ignition coils and air intake resonator.

27   Suspension, steering and driveaxle boot check (every 30,000 miles or 30 months)

Note: *The steering and suspension components should be checked periodically. Worn or damaged suspension and steering components can result in excessive and abnormal tire wear, poor ride quality and vehicle handling and reduced fuel economy. For detailed illustrations of the steering and suspension components, refer to Chapter 10.*

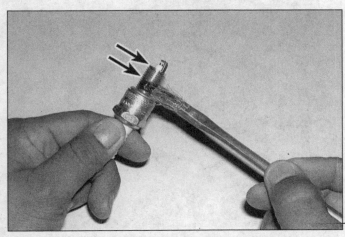

26.9 Apply a thin coat of anti-seize compound to the spark plug threads, being careful not to get any near the lower threads

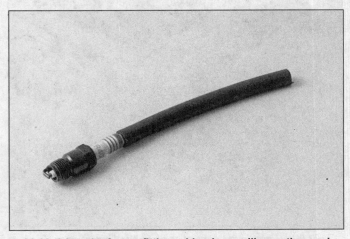

26.10 A length of snug-fitting rubber hose will save time and prevent damaged threads when installing the spark plugs

27.6 Check for signs of fluid leakage at this point on shock absorbers (2WD front shock module shown)

27.9a Examine the mounting points for the upper . . .

Shock absorber check

Refer to illustration 27.6

1   Park the vehicle on level ground, turn the engine off and set the parking brake. Check the tire pressures.

2   Push down at one corner of the vehicle, then release it while noting the movement of the body. It should stop moving and come to rest in a level position within one or two bounces.

3   If the vehicle continues to move up-and-down or if it fails to return to its original position, a worn or weak shock absorber is probably the reason.

4   Repeat the above check at each of the three remaining corners of the vehicle.

5   Raise the vehicle and support it securely on jack stands.

6   Check the shock absorbers for evidence of fluid leakage **(see illustration)**. A light film of fluid is no cause for concern. Make sure that any fluid noted is from the shocks and not from some other source. If leakage is noted, replace the shocks as a set.

7   Check the shocks to be sure that they are securely mounted and undamaged. Check the upper mounts for damage and wear. If damage or wear is noted, replace the shocks as a set (front or rear).

8   If the shocks must be replaced, refer to Chapter 10 for the procedure.

Steering and suspension check

Refer to illustrations 27.9a, 27.9b, 27.9c and 27.11

9   Visually inspect the steering and suspension components (front and rear) for damage and distortion. Look for damaged seals, boots and bushings and leaks of any kind. Examine the bushings where the control arms meet the chassis **(see illustrations)**.

10   Clean the lower end of the steering knuckle. Have an assistant grasp the lower edge of the tire and move the wheel in-and-out while you look for movement at the steering knuckle-to-control arm balljoint. If there

is any movement the suspension balljoint(s) must be replaced.

11   Grasp each front tire at the front and rear edges, push in at the front, pull out at the rear and feel for play in the steering system components. If any freeplay is noted, check the idler arm and the tie-rod ends for looseness **(see illustration)**.

12   On vehicles equipped with air suspension, inspect the air springs for physical damage as well as checking the air lines for cracks and leaks.

13   Additional steering and suspension system information and illustrations can be found in Chapter 10.

Driveaxle boot check (4WD models)

Refer to illustration 27.15

14   The driveaxle boots are very important because they prevent dirt, water and foreign material from entering and damaging the constant velocity (CV) joints. Oil and grease can cause the boot material to deteriorate prema-

27.9b . . . and lower control arms on the front suspension

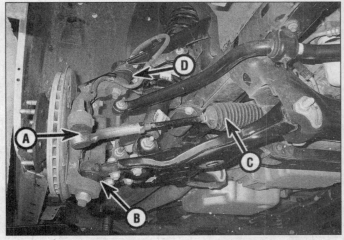

27.9c Inspect the tie-rod ends (A), the lower balljoints (B), the steering gear boots (C) and the upper balljoints (D)

27.11 With the steering wheel in the locked position and the vehicle raised, grasp the front tire as shown and try to move it back-and-forth - if any play is noted, check the steering gear mounts and tie-rod ends for looseness

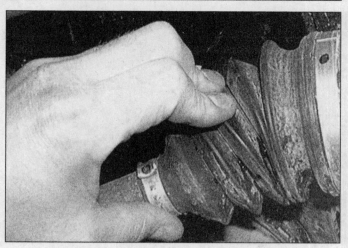

27.15 Inspect the inner and outer driveaxle boots on 4WD models for loose clamps, cracks or signs of leaking lubricant (inner boot shown)

turely, so it's a good idea to wash the boots with soap and water. Because it constantly pivots back and forth following the steering action of the front hub, the outer CV boot wears out sooner and should be inspected regularly.

15   Inspect the boots for tears and cracks as well as loose clamps **(see illustration)**. If there is any evidence of cracks or leaking lubricant, they must be replaced as described in Chapter 8.

28   Automatic transmission fluid and filter change (every 30,000 miles or 30 months)

Refer to illustrations 28.5a, 28.5b, 28.10, 28.11 and 28.12

1   At the specified intervals, the transmission fluid should be drained and replaced.

Since the fluid will remain hot long after driving, perform this procedure only after the engine has cooled down completely.

2   Before beginning work, purchase the specified transmission fluid (see *Recommended lubricants and fluids* at the front of this Chapter) and a new filter and pan gasket.

3   Other tools necessary for this job include a floor jack, jackstands to support the vehicle in a raised position, a drain pan capable of holding at least eight quarts, newspapers and clean rags.

4   Raise the vehicle and support it securely on jackstands.

5   Place the drain pan underneath the transmission pan. Loosen all the pan bolts, remove all but the front bolts and allow the pan to tilt and drain fluid into pan, then remove the final bolts **(see illustration)**. **Note:** *On some models the shift cable bracket must be removed to allow the fluid pan to be lowered* **(see illustration)**.

6   If your vehicle does not have a drain plug it will be necessary to remove all the bolts except the ones in each corner, then slowly remove the front pan bolts allowing fluid to drain as the bolts are removed.

7   Remove the transmission pan mounting bolts, then carefully pry the transmission pan loose with a screwdriver. **Warning:** *There is still some transmission fluid in the pan.*

8   Carefully clean the gasket surface of the transmission to remove all traces of the old gasket and sealant.

9   Clean the pan with solvent and dry it with compressed air, if available. **Note:** *Some models are equipped with magnets in the transmission pan to catch metal debris. Clean the magnet thoroughly. A small amount of metal material is normal at the magnet. If there is considerable debris, consult a dealer or transmission specialist.*

10   Remove the filter from the valve body

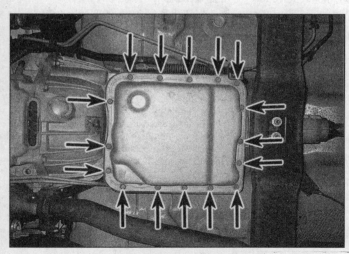

28.5a Drain the transmission fluid by removing the pan bolts and the pan

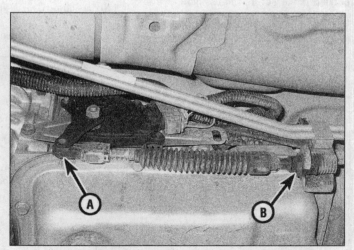

28.5b Disconnect the shift cable end from the ballstud (A), then remove the two bolts securing the shift cable bracket to the transmission (B) (this allows room to access the fluid pan bolts)

28.10 Remove the filter from the transmission by pulling it straight down

28.11 Use a seal removal tool to remove the transmission filter seal from the valve body, then replace it with a new seal - be careful not to scratch the aluminum cavity

inside the transmission **(see illustration)**. **Note:** *Be very careful not to gouge the delicate aluminum gasket surface on the valve body.*

11   Install a new seal and filter. On many replacement filters, the seal is attached to the filter to simplify installation **(see illustration)**.

12   Make sure the gasket surface on the transmission pan is clean, then install a new gasket on the pan **(see illustration)**. Put the pan in place against the transmission and install all of the bolts. Working around the pan, tighten each bolt a little at a time to the torque listed in this Chapter's Specifications.

13   Reinstall the components removed for access to the pan bolts. Refer to Chapter 7B for adjustment of the shift cable.

14   Lower the vehicle and add approximately three quarts of the specified type of automatic transmission fluid through the filler tube (see Section 7).

15   With the transmission in Park and the parking brake set, run the engine at a fast idle, but don't race it.

16   Move the gear selector through each range and back to Park, then let the engine

idle for a few minutes. Check the fluid level. It will probably be low. Add enough fluid to bring the level to the proper mark on the dipstick. Add fluid a little at a time, and be careful not to overfill the transmission.

17   Check under the vehicle for leaks during the first few trips. Check the fluid level again when the transmission is hot (see Section 7).

29   Manual transmission lubricant change (every 60,000 miles or 48 months)

1   The fluid should be drained immediately after the vehicle has been driven. Hot fluid is more effective than cold fluid at removing built up sediment.

2   After the vehicle has been driven to warm up the fluid, raise it and place it on jackstands for access to the drain plug.

3   Remove the filler plug, then remove the drain plug(s) and drain the fluid (see Section 21).

4   Reinstall the drain plug(s) and tighten to

the torque listed in this Chapter's Specifications.

5   Add new fluid until it begins to run out of the filler hole. See *Recommended lubricants and fluids* for the specified lubricant type.

30   Transfer case lubricant change (4WD models) (every 60,000 miles or 48 months)

1   This procedure should be performed after the vehicle has been driven so the lubricant will be warm and therefore will flow out of the transfer case more easily.

2   Raise the vehicle and support it securely on jackstands.

3   Remove the filler plug from the case **(see illustration 22.1)**.

4   Remove the drain plug from the lower part of the case and allow the lubricant to drain completely.

5   After the case is completely drained, carefully clean and install the drain plug. Tighten the plug to the torque listed in this Chapter's Specifications.

6   Fill the case with the specified lubricant until it is level with the lower edge of the filler hole.

7   Install the filler plug and tighten it to the torque listed in this Chapter's Specifications.

8   Drive the vehicle for a short distance and recheck the lubricant level. In some instances a small amount of additional lubricant will have to be added.

31   Differential lubricant change (every 60,000 miles or 48 months)

1   This procedure should be performed after the vehicle has been driven, so the lubricant will be warm and therefore will flow out of the differential more easily.

28.12 Clean the transmission pan, position the magnet back in place, and install the new pan gasket

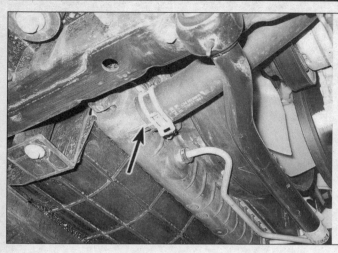

32.3 The cooling system on these vehicles is drained by detaching the lower radiator hose from the radiator

2   Raise the vehicle and support it securely on jackstands. You'll be draining the lubricant by removing the drain plug, so move a drain pan, rags, newspapers and wrenches under the vehicle.

3   Remove the fill plug **(see illustration 16.2a** [rear differential] or **16.2b** [front differential]). Now remove the drain plug and allow the lubricant to drain into the pan, then clean and reinstall the drain plug. Tighten the plug to the torque listed in this Chapter's Specifications.

4   Use a hand pump, syringe or squeeze bottle to fill the differential housing with the specified lubricant until it's level with the bottom of the fill-plug hole. If using synthetic axle lubricant, the level should be below the fill-plug opening by 1/2-inch. **Note:** On some models with limited-slip differentials, a special additive may be required (look for a tag secured by one of the differential cover bolts).

5   Install the fill plug and tighten it to the torque listed in this Chapter's Specifications.

---

32   Cooling system servicing (draining, flushing and refilling) (every 100,000 miles or 60 months)

Warning 1: *Wait until the engine is completely cool before beginning this procedure.*
Warning 2: *Do not allow antifreeze to come in contact with your skin or painted surfaces of the vehicle. Rinse off spills immediately with plenty of water. Antifreeze is highly toxic if ingested. Never leave antifreeze lying around in an open container or in puddles on the floor; children and pets are attracted by its sweet smell and may drink it. Check with local authorities on disposing of used anti-freeze.*

Many communities have collection centers that will see that antifreeze is disposed of safely. Antifreeze is flammable under certain conditions - be sure to read the precautions on the container.
Caution 1: *Never mix green-colored ethylene glycol antifreeze and orange-colored "DEX-COOL" silicate-free coolant because doing so will destroy the efficiency of the "DEX-COOL" coolant, which is designed to last for 100,000 miles or five years.*
Caution 2: *Before mixing water with antifreeze, check the antifreeze container carefully. Some manufacturers pre-mix antifreeze to the proper 50/50 ratio, making the addition of water unnecessary.*
Note: *Non-toxic coolant is available at local auto parts stores. Although the coolant is non-toxic when fresh, proper disposal is still required.*

Draining

Refer to illustration 32.3

1   Periodically, the cooling system should be drained, flushed and refilled to replenish the antifreeze mixture and prevent formation of rust and corrosion, which can impair the performance of the cooling system and cause engine damage. When the cooling system is serviced, all hoses and the surge tank cap should be checked and replaced if necessary.

2   Apply the parking brake and block the wheels. **Warning:** *If the vehicle has just been driven, wait several hours to allow the engine to cool down before beginning this procedure.* Detach the coolant air bleed hose from the throttle body.

3   Move a large container under the radiator drain to catch the coolant. Loosen the hose clamp on the lower radiator hose, slide the hose back and allow the coolant to begin to drain **(see illustration)**. Remove the radiator cap.

4   While the coolant is draining, check the condition of the radiator hoses, heater hoses and clamps (refer to Section 14 if necessary).

5   Replace any damaged clamps or hoses. Reconnect the lower radiator hose and reattach the coolant air bleed hose to the throttle body.

Flushing

6   Fill the cooling system with clean water, following the *Refilling* procedure (see Step 12).
7   Start the engine and allow it to reach normal operating temperature, then rev up the engine a few times.
8   Turn the engine off and allow it to cool completely, then drain the system as described earlier.
9   Repeat Steps 6 through 8 until the water being drained is free of contaminants.
10   In severe cases of contamination or clogging of the radiator, remove the radiator (see Chapter 3) and have a radiator repair facility clean and repair it if necessary.
11   Many deposits can be removed by the chemical action of a cleaner available at auto parts stores. Follow the procedure outlined in the manufacturer's instructions. **Note:** *When the coolant is regularly drained and the system refilled with the correct antifreeze/water mixture, there should be no need to use chemical cleaners or descalers.*

Refilling

12   Reconnect the lower radiator hose to the radiator and install the clamp. Detach the air bleed hose from the throttle body.
13   Place the heater temperature control in the maximum heat position.
14   Be sure to use the proper coolant listed in this Chapter's Specifications. Slowly fill the radiator until it's full, then install the radiator cap.
15   Fill the coolant reservoir with the same mixture up to the FULL COLD mark, then install the cap on the reservoir.
16   Connect the air bleed hose to the throttle body.
17   Start the engine and run it at 2,000 rpm until normal operating temperature is reached, then let the engine speed down to idle for about three minutes.
18   Turn the engine off and allow it to cool completely.
19   With the engine completely cool, remove the radiator cap and add coolant if necessary. Reinstall the cap and add coolant, as necessary, to the coolant reservoir.
20   Check the cooling system for leaks.

Notes

Chapter 2 Part A
Engines

Contents

Specifications

General

2006 and earlier models

Four-cylinder engine
Displacement	170 cubic inches (2.8 liters)
Bore and stroke	3.66 x 4.02 inches
Compression Ratio	10:1
Cylinder numbers (front-to-rear)	1-2-3-4
Firing order	1-3-4-2

Five-cylinder engine
Displacement	212 cubic inches (3.5 liters)
Bore and stroke	3.66 x 4.02 inches
Compression Ratio	10:1
Cylinder numbers (front-to-rear)	1-2-3-4-5
Firing order	1-3-5-4-2

2007 and later models

Four-cylinder engine
Displacement	178 cubic inches (2.9L)
Bore and stroke	3.76 x 4.02 inches
Compression ratio	10.3:1
Cylinder numbers (front-to-rear)	1-2-3-4
Firing order	1-3-4-2

Five-cylinder engine
Displacement	223 cubic inches (3.7L)
Bore and stroke	3.76 x 4.02 inches
Compression ratio	10.3:1
Cylinder numbers (front-to-rear)	1-2-3-4-5
Firing order	1-3-5-4-2

Camshaft

Journal diameter
Exhaust, journal no. 1	1.1794 to 1.1804 inch
Exhaust journals 2 through 7 and all intake journals	1.0612 to 1.0622 inch
Journal-to-bore clearance	0.0015 to 0.0033 inch

Endplay
Intake	0.0020 to 0.0079 inch
Exhaust	0.0017 to 0.0084 inch

INLINE 4-CYLINDER

24027-1a-HAYNES

INLINE 5-CYLINDER

24027-1b-HAYNES

Cylinder locations

Cylinder head
Warpage limit.. 0.003 inch per 6 inches

Exhaust manifold
Warpage limit.. 0.003 inch

Torque specifications   Ft-lbs (unless otherwise indicated)

Note: *One foot-pound (ft-lb) of torque is equivalent to 12 inch-pounds (in-lbs) of torque. Torque values below approximately 15 ft-lbs are expressed in inch-pounds, since most foot-pound torque wrenches are not accurate at these smaller values.*

Camshaft cap bolts..	106 in-lbs
Camshaft sprocket bolt	
Intake	
Step 1	15
Step 2	Tighten an additional 100-degrees
Exhaust (camshaft actuator)	
Step 1	18
Step 2	Tighten an additional 135-degrees
Cylinder head bolts (in sequence - **see illustrations 9.13a and 9.13b**)	
Four-cylinder engine	
Step 1 Tighten bolts 1 through 10..................................	22
Step 2	Tighten the same bolts in sequence an additional 155-degrees
Step 3 Tighten short bolts (11 and 12)...........................	62 in-lbs plus an additional 60-degrees
Step 4 Tighten long bolt 13......................................	62 in-lbs plus an additional 120-degrees
Five-cylinder engine	
Step 1 Tighten bolts 1 through 12..................................	22
Step 2	Tighten the same bolts in sequence an additional 155-degrees
Step 3 Tighten end bolts (13 and 14)............................	62 in-lbs plus an additional 60-degrees
Step 4 Tighten long bolt 15......................................	62 in-lbs plus an additional 120-degrees
Cylinder head access hole plugs..	44 in-lbs
Crankshaft pulley bolt	
Step 1..	110
Step 2..	Tighten bolts an additional 180-degrees (1/2-turn)
Timing chain	
Tensioner shoe bolt...	18
Lower chain guide bolts...	156 inch-lbs
Tensioner bolts..	18
Upper chain guide bolts	89 inch-lbs
Intake manifold bolts..	89 in-lbs
Exhaust manifold bolts (repeat three times)......................	15
Driveplate-to-crankshaft bolts	
Step 1..	30
Step 2..	Tighten an additional 45-degrees
Front cover bolts	
7mm center bolt	71 in-lbs
All other mounting bolts..	89 in-lbs
Rear main oil seal housing bolts..	89 in-lbs
Oil pan mounting bolts	
Sides	18
Ends	89 in-lbs
Oil pump cover bolts..	89 in-lbs
Oil pump relief valve plug	124 in-lbs
Engine mount-to-block bolts...	37
Engine mount-to-frame through-bolts.................................	63
Valve cover bolts	89 in-lbs

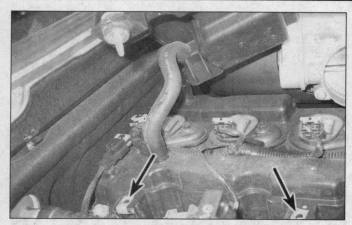

3.2 Pry up the resonator box until its pins come loose from the clips

4.5 Carefully pry open the cover over the engine harness and set the harness aside

1   General information

This Chapter is devoted to in-vehicle repair procedures for the inline four-cylinder engine and the inline five-cylinder engine. These two engines are of a modular design, in which a high percentage of the components are exactly the same. The only major difference between them is the number of cylinders. These engines utilize a cast aluminum block with the cylinders arranged in a straight line. The dual overhead camshaft, aluminum cylinder head is equipped with four valves per cylinder. Roller-type rocker arms actuate the valves through direct contact with the camshaft, while hydraulic lash adjusters take up the play between the cam lobes, rocker arms and valves. The oil pump is located in the front cover and is driven directly from the crankshaft. The oil pan is made of cast aluminum. The crankshaft is made of nodular iron, and the pistons are of a full floating design. Connecting rods are made from forged powdered metal.

To positively identify this engine, count the number of spark plug coils, or locate the Vehicle Identification Number (VIN) on the left front corner of the instrument panel. The VIN is visible from the outside of the vehicle through the windshield. The eighth character in the sequence is the engine designation:

2004 through 2006
  8 = 2.8L four-cylinder engine
  6 = 3.5L five-cylinder engine
2007 and later
  9 = 2.9L four-cylinder engine
  E = 3.7L five-cylinder engine

2   Repair operations possible with the engine in the vehicle

Many major repair operations can be accomplished without removing the engine from the vehicle.

Clean the engine compartment and the exterior of the engine with some type of pressure washer before any work is done. It will make the job easier and help keep dirt out of the internal areas of the engine. Do not direct high-pressure spray towards any electrical connector. Many of these are low voltage computer circuits and water may be forced past the seal, then causing a false reading, damage to the sensor or corrosion to occur.

Remove the hood, if necessary, to improve access to the engine as repairs are performed (see Chapter 11 if necessary).

If vacuum, exhaust, oil or coolant leaks develop, indicating a need for gasket or seal replacement, the repairs can generally be made with the engine in the vehicle. The intake and exhaust manifold gaskets, front cover gasket, oil pan gasket, crankshaft oil seals and cylinder head gasket are all accessible with the engine in place.

Exterior engine components, such as the intake and exhaust manifolds, the oil pan and oil pump, the water pump, the starter motor, the alternator, the distributor and the fuel system components can be removed for repair with the engine in place.

3   Intake manifold - removal and installation

Refer to illustration 3.2

Removal

1   Disconnect the cables from the negative and positive terminals of the battery then remove the battery and battery box (see Chapter 5).
2   Remove the air intake hose from the air cleaner resonator box over the valve cover, then pry up the resonator box from the clips at the right side of the valve cover (see illustration).
3   Remove the throttle body (see Chapter 4).
4   Disconnect the electrical harnesses from their brackets and the MAP sensor connector.
5   Remove the MAP sensor bracket.
6   Disconnect the crankcase vent hose from its ports on the manifold and valve cover.
7   Remove the engine harness bracket. To access the lower engine harness, support the vehicle on jackstands and remove the left front wheel and inner fender liner (see Chapter 11).
8   Remove the alternator (see Chapter 5).
9   Disconnect the vacuum hose from the power brake booster. On 2007 and later models, remove the oil dipstick and dipstick tube.
10   Loosen the left front wheel lug nuts, then raise the front of the vehicle and support it securely on jackstands. Remove the left front wheel and refer to Chapter 11 and remove the plastic inner fender liner.
11   Working through the fenderwell opening, remove the lower wiring harness bracket, then the intake manifold bolts and remove the manifold.
12   Remove the old gasket, then clean and inspect the intake manifold for damage, cracks and warping.

Installation

13   Install a new gasket in the intake manifold (no sealant is required).
14   Installation is the reverse of removal. Tighten the intake manifold bolts, a little at a time, to the torque listed in this Chapter's Specifications. Work from the middle bolts out to the ends of the manifold.

4   Valve cover - removal and installation

Refer to illustrations 4.5 and 4.7

Removal

1   Disconnect the cable from the negative terminal of the battery.
2   Remove the intake manifold (see Section 3).
3   From the valve cover, disconnect the electrical connectors for the engine coolant temperature sensor and the heated oxygen sensor.
4   Remove the mounting bolt for the fuel pressure regulator on 2004 and 2005 models.
5   Disconnect the injector connectors then carefully unclip the engine electrical harness from the valve cover (see illustration).

4.7 Front valve cover bolt locations (there are six total in front) - make sure all perimeter bolts are removed before attempting to remove the cover

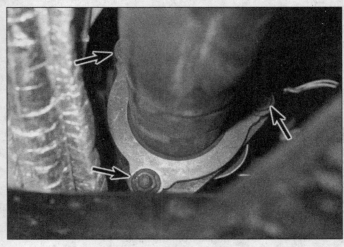

5.3 Access the exhaust pipe bolts/nuts from underneath the vehicle

6   Remove the ignition coils (see Chapter 5). On 2007 and later models, remove the bolt securing the ground wire at the valve cover.

7   Remove the valve cover bolts and valve cover **(see illustration)**.

8   Clean and inspect the valve cover for cracks.

Installation

9   Install new ignition coil seals, if necessary (see Chapter 5), and a new valve cover seal.

10   Installation is the reverse of removal.

11   Tighten the valve cover bolts to the torque listed in this Chapter's Specifications. Tighten the ignition coil bolts to the torque listed in the Chapter 5 Specifications.

5   Exhaust manifold - removal and installation

Removal

Refer to illustrations 5.3, 5.5 and 5.6

Warning: *Use caution when working around the exhaust manifolds; the sheet metal heat shields can be sharp on the edges. Also, the engine should be cold when this procedure is performed.*

1   Disconnect the cable from the negative terminal of the battery.

2   Raise the vehicle and support it securely on jackstands.

3   Working under the vehicle, apply penetrating oil to the exhaust pipe-to-manifold studs and nuts (they're usually rusty) **(see illustration)**.

4   Wait a little while and let the penetrating oil soak in, then remove the nuts retaining the exhaust pipe to the manifold.

5   Remove the oxygen sensor (see Chapter 6). Remove the heat shield nuts, then remove the heat shield **(see illustration)**.

6   Remove the exhaust manifold bolts and

5.5 Exhaust manifold heat shield nuts (typical)

detach the manifold from the cylinder head **(see illustration)**.

7   Remove the exhaust manifold gasket and clean the mating surfaces on the cylinder head and manifold.

Installation

8   Check the manifold for cracks and make sure the bolt threads are clean and undamaged. The manifold and cylinder head mating surfaces must be clean before the manifolds are reinstalled - use a gasket scraper to

remove all carbon deposits. Check the manifold for warpage using a straightedge and feeler gauges. If it exceeds the limit listed in this Chapter's Specifications, have the manifold resurfaced or replace it with a new one.

9   Install a new gasket.

10   Install the manifold on the cylinder head, apply heat-resistant thread locking compound to the bolt threads then start the bolts by hand.

11   Tighten the bolts in three passes starting from the center bolt and working your way to

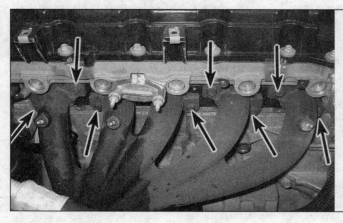

5.6 Exhaust manifold bolt locations (not all bolts are visible in this photo)

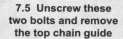
7.5 Unscrew these two bolts and remove the top chain guide

7.6a The exhaust camshaft actuator is retained by this Allen bolt

the ends, to the torque listed in this Chapter's Specifications.

12   The remaining installation steps are the reverse of removal.

13   Start the engine and check for exhaust leaks.

6   Front cover - removal and installation

Warning: *The engine must be completely cool before beginning this procedure.*

Removal

1   Drain the engine coolant (see Chapter 1).

2   Remove the drivebelt (see Chapter 1).

3   Remove the fan and fan shroud (see Chapter 3).

4   Remove the water pump (see Chapter 3) and the power steering pump (see Chapter 10).

5   Remove the crankshaft pulley (see Section 11).

6   Remove the oil pan (see Section 16).

7   Remove the front cover bolts, beginning with the 7 mm bolt in the center of the cover.

8   Install two bolts in the jackscrew holes on the front cover and evenly tighten the bolts until the cover comes off.

9   Remove the oil pump from the front cover, if necessary (see Section 12).

10   Clean the cover sealing area with solvent, remove all old gasket material, and

inspect the cover for nicks and damage in the sealing area. **Note:** *Do not use any powerdriven gasket removal tools such as wire wheels and cleaning disks, as this will damage the cover.*

Installation

11   Align the oil pump and the crankshaft splines (this will require you to temporarily install the cover without the sealant).

12   Remove the cover and apply a 3/16-inch bead of RTV sealant to the cover sealing area and the three bolt hole areas on the inside of the cover.

13   Make two alignment studs by cutting the heads from two bolts two inches long with the same thread as the front cover bolts. Use a hacksaw to cut a screwdriver slot in the head of these alignment bolts and install them through the front cover in the second hole up from the bottom on each side.

14   Slide the front cover in place, making sure the oil pump and crankshaft splines remain in alignment. Temporarily install the crankshaft pulley and center the seal on it to align the front cover.

15   Install the remaining front cover bolts within 10 minutes of applying the sealant. Tighten them to the torque listed in this Chapter's Specifications. Remove the two alignment bolts and install/tighten the two cover bolts there, then install/tighten the center cover bolt last.

16   The remainder of installation is the reverse of removal. Add engine oil and cool-

ant (see Chapter 1), start the engine and check for leaks.

7   Timing chain, sprockets and tensioner - replacement

Note: *A special camshaft holding tool (GM# J-44221 or equivalent) is required for this procedure.*

Removal

**** CAUTION ****
The timing system is complex. Severe engine damage will occur if you make any mistakes. Do not attempt this procedure unless you are highly experienced with this type of repair. If you are at all unsure of your abilities, consult an expert. Double-check all your work and be sure everything is correct before you attempt to start the engine.

Refer to illustrations 7.5, 7.6a, 7.6b, 7.7 and 7.8

1   Position the engine at Top Dead Center for cylinder number one (see Chapter 2B). Remove the valve cover (see Section 4) and the engine front cover (see Section 6). Check that the word "Delphi" on the exhaust camshaft is parallel to the valve cover mounting surface at the front of the cylinder head.

2   Refer to Chapter 6 and remove the intake and exhaust camshaft position sensors.

3   Collapse the timing chain tensioner and insert a drill bit or golf tee into the hole to hold it in place.

4   Install the camshaft holding tool to the rear of the camshafts.

5   Remove the top chain guide **(see illustration)**.

6   Remove the exhaust camshaft position actuator **(see illustration)**. When loosening the bolt, hold the camshaft stationary by placing a wrench on the hex cast into the camshaft **(see illustration)**.

7.6b To prevent the camshafts from turning while loosening the sprocket bolts, place a wrench on these hexes cast into the shafts

7.7 Intake camshaft sprocket bolt

7.8 Use a hex bit to remove these two access plugs from the front of the cylinder head

7   Remove the intake camshaft sprocket **(see illustration)**, then unhook the chain from the crankshaft sprocket and remove the chain. When loosening the sprocket bolt, hold the camshaft stationary by placing a wrench on the hex cast into the camshaft, just like in the previous step.

8   Remove the two access hole plugs from the front of the cylinder head **(see illustration)**.

9   Remove the timing chain tensioner shoe bolt (right) and the timing chain guide bolt (left) then remove the guide and shoe. Remove the tensioner (if it is being replaced).

10   Remove the crankshaft sprocket.

Installation

** CAUTION **
Before starting the engine, carefully rotate the crankshaft by hand through at least two full revolutions (use a socket

and breaker bar on the crankshaft pulley center bolt). If you feel any resistance, STOP! There is something wrong - most likely, valves are contacting the pistons. You must find the problem before proceeding. Check your work and see if any updated repair information is available.

Refer to illustrations 7.14, 7.23a and 7.23b
Note 1: *Every seventh timing chain link is darkened to identify the alignment links.*
Note 2: *Use NEW bolts when installing the camshaft sprockets.*

11   If removed, install the tensioner and tighten it to the torque listed in this Chapter's Specifications.

12   Install the chain guide and shoe and tighten the bolts to the torque listed in this Chapter's Specifications.

13   Install the two access plugs and tighten

them to the torque listed in this Chapter's Specifications.

14   Check to make sure cylinder number 1 is still at Top Dead Center; the lobes at the front of the camshafts will be pointing up and the flats on the back of each camshaft will be facing up **(see illustration)**.

15   Install the crankshaft sprocket, then place the chain on the intake sprocket making sure to align the mark on the sprocket with a darkened link.

16   Feed the chain through the cylinder head and onto the crankshaft sprocket making sure the mark on the crankshaft sprocket is aligned with a darkened link.

17   Install the intake sprocket on to the intake camshaft. **Note:** *It may be necessary to loosen the holding tool to allow slight movement of the camshaft to aid in sprocket-to-camshaft pin alignment. Retighten the holding tool.*

18   Lift up the timing chain and guide the exhaust camshaft actuator into place, making sure the mark on the actuator sprocket is

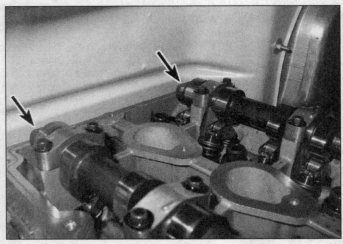

7.14 When the engine is at Top Dead Center for cylinder number one (on the compression stroke), the flats at the rear ends of the camshafts will be facing up, parallel with the top of the cylinder head (the camshaft holding tool engages these flats)

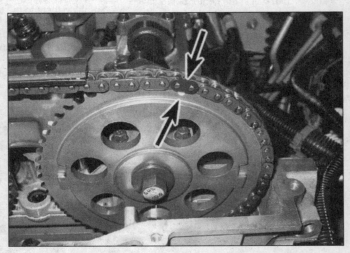

7.23a When the timing chain is properly installed (with the engine at TDC for cylinder number one on the compression stroke) the mark on the intake camshaft sprocket will be aligned with a darkened link . . .

7.23b . . . and the mark on the exhaust camshaft actuator will be aligned with a darkened link (the mark on the crankshaft sprocket will also be aligned with a dark link)

8.2 Correct timing mark alignment prior to camshaft sprocket removal

aligned with a darkened link.

19   Install the exhaust camshaft actuator onto the exhaust camshaft, but do not fully tighten the bolt. **Note:** *It may be necessary to loosen the holding tool to allow slight movement of the camshaft to aid in sprocket-to-camshaft pin alignment. Retighten the holding tool.*

20   Rotate the exhaust camshaft actuator clockwise (as you are facing it) until it stops. **Caution:** *The actuator must be installed in the full advance position (clockwise) or engine damage will occur. Tighten the bolt to the torque listed in this Chapter's Specifications, while keeping the actuator held clockwise.*

21   Tighten the intake camshaft sprocket bolt to the torque listed in this Chapter's Specifications.

22   Remove the drill bit or tee in the tensioner, then remove the camshaft holding tool.

23   Check the timing mark alignment **(see illustrations)**.

24   The remainder of the installation is the reverse of removal.

---

8   Camshafts, rocker arms and lash adjusters - removal and installation

Note: *A special camshaft holding tool (GM# J-44221 or equivalent) is required for this procedure.*

Removal

Refer to illustration 8.2

Note: *After removing the cam sprocket do not rotate the crankshaft or incorrect timing and engine damage can occur.*

1   Remove the valve cover (see Section 4). Also remove the spark plugs (it'll make the engine easier to rotate - see Chapter 1).

2   Rotate the engine until the sprocket alignment marks are each aligned with a dark

chain link **(see illustration)**, and the flats at the rear of the camshafts are facing up **(see illustration 7.14)**.

3   Following the procedure described in Section 7, remove the camshaft sprocket bolts, then carefully remove the sprockets from the camshafts. **Caution:** *Do not remove the sprockets from the chain, and be sure to suspend the sprockets and chain to prevent the bottom of the chain from coming off the crankshaft sprocket.*

4   Check the camshaft caps for markings; if there are none, mark them with paint prior to removal to insure they are installed in the exact location they were prior to disassembly.

5   Remove the camshaft cap bolts, a little at a time, until they can be removed, then remove the camshafts. Keep the shafts separated so you don't get them mixed up. The rocker arms and lash adjusters can now be lifted out, if necessary. Keep these parts laid out in order, too, since they must all be returned to their original locations if they're going to be re-used.

Inspection

Refer to illustrations 8.7 and 8.8

6   After the camshafts have been removed from the engine, cleaned with solvent and dried, inspect each camshaft for:

a) Scored camshaft journals
b) Check the camshaft lobes for heat discoloration, score marks, chipped areas, pitting and uneven wear
c) Damaged camshaft sprocket locator pin slots
d) Damaged threads

7   Measure the bearing journals with a micrometer to determine if they are excessively worn or out-of-round **(see illustration)**.

8   Compare the camshaft lobe height by measuring each lobe with a micrometer **(see illustration)**. Measure each of the intake lobes and write the measurements and relative positions down on a piece of paper. Then measure of each of the exhaust lobes and record the measurements and relative positions also. This will let you compare all of the intake lobes to

8.7 Measure the outside diameter of each camshaft journal and the inside diameter of each bearing to determine the oil clearance measurement

8.8 Measuring cam lobe height with a micrometer - make sure you move the micrometer to get the highest reading

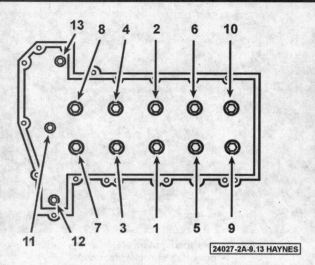

9.13a Cylinder head bolt tightening sequence -
four-cylinder engine

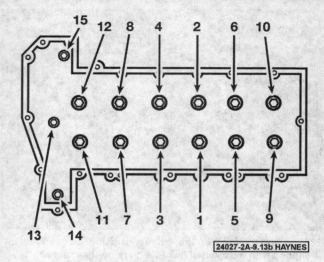

9.13b Cylinder head bolt tightening sequence -
five-cylinder engine

one another and all of the exhaust lobes to one another. If the difference between the lobes exceeds 0.005 inch the camshaft should be replaced. Do not compare intake lobe heights to exhaust lobe heights; only compare intake lobes to intake lobes and exhaust lobes to exhaust lobes.

Installation

9   If removed, soak the lash adjusters and rocker arms in clean engine oil, then install the lash adjusters and rocker arms in their original locations.
10   Completely coat the camshaft with clean engine oil. Place the camshafts in their correct locations in the cylinder head.
11   Install the camshaft holding tool.
12   Install all the camshaft caps to their original locations and hand tighten them.
13   Working from center out, evenly tighten the caps to the torque listed in this Chapter's Specifications.
14   Remove the holding fixture.
15   Place the sprockets onto the camshafts and tighten the bolts to the torque listed in this Chapter's Specifications.
16   Using a large breaker bar and a socket placed on the crankshaft pulley bolt, rotate the crankshaft 720-degrees (two full revolutions) and re-check the sprocket and chain alignment; the darkened links must align with the sprocket marks **(see illustration 8.2)**. If you feel any resistance while turning the crankshaft, stop immediately and find out what the problem is.
17   Install the spark plugs (see Chapter 1) and the valve cover (see Section 4).

9   Cylinder head - removal and installation

Warning: *Wait until the engine is completely cool before beginning this procedure.*

Removal

1   Drain the engine coolant (see Chapter 1).
2   Remove the valve cover (see Section 4).
3   Remove the exhaust manifold (see Section 5).
4   Remove the timing chain and sprockets (see Section 7). **Caution:** *Don't allow the camshafts to rotate once the timing chain has been removed.*
5   Unscrew the cylinder head bolts (13 on the four-cylinder engine, 15 on the five-cylinder engine), working in the reverse order of the tightening sequence **(see illustration 9.13a or 9.13b)**. Discard the bolts - new ones must be used when installing the cylinder head.
6   Lift the cylinder head off the engine. **Caution:** *The cylinder head is heavy! Have an assistant help you do this. If the cylinder head is stuck, don't pry between the block and the head - instead, pry on a casting protrusion or use a wood block and a hammer to jar it loose.*
7   Remove the cylinder head gasket.
8   Clean the surfaces of the engine block and cylinder head, taking care not to gouge the aluminum or lose the two alignment dowel pins. These aluminum surfaces should be cleaned with solvents only, do not use abrasive materials.
9   Check the surface of the engine block and the cylinder head with a precision straightedge and feeler gauges and compare the readings with the Specifications in this Chapter.

Installation

Refer to illustrations 9.13a and 9.13b
Note 1: *It is important that number 1 cylinder is at top dead center.*
Note 2: *Use NEW cylinder head bolts.*
10   Place a new head gasket on the engine block making sure the dowel pins are in the correct locations.

11   Place the cylinder head on the engine block.
12   Install *new* cylinder head bolts and hand tighten them.
13   Tighten the cylinder head bolts in sequence **(see illustrations)** to the torque listed in this Chapter's Specifications.
14   The remaining assembly is the reverse of removal.
15   Change the engine oil and filter and replace the coolant (see Chapter 1).

10   Valves - servicing

1   Because of the complex nature of the job and the special tools and equipment needed, servicing of the valves, the valve seats and the valve guides, commonly known as a valve job, should be done by a professional.
2   The automotive machine shop, will remove the valves and springs, recondition or replace the valves and valve seats, recondition the valve guides, check and replace the valve springs, spring retainers or rotators and keepers (as necessary), replace the valve seals with new ones, reassemble the valve components and make sure the installed spring height is correct. The cylinder head gasket surface will also be resurfaced if it's warped. Note that some cylinder heads have a minimum resurfacing height (similar to a brake rotor or drum). If they're resurfaced past the minimum height they'll have to be replaced.
3   After the valve job has been performed by a professional, the head will be in like-new condition. When the head is returned, be sure to clean it again before installation on the engine to remove any metal particles and abrasive grit that may still be present from the valve service or head resurfacing operations. Use compressed air, if available, to blow out all the oil holes, bolt holes and coolant passages.

11 Crankshaft front oil seal - replacement

Caution: *It is extremely important to avoid damaging the crankshaft threads. If the alternative setup described below does not readily remove the pulley, STOP. Obtain the special tools or have the work performed by a technician who does have the special tools. Be extremely careful not to damage the crankshaft end surface or the engine front cover.*

Note 1: *Special tools required: puller (GM # J-44226 or equivalent), crankshaft end protector (GM # J-41816-2 or equivalent), pulley installer (J-41478 or equivalent) and seal installer (GM # J-44218 or equivalent). An alternative to these tools would be a three-jaw puller, a deep socket that just fits into the nose of the crankshaft and bottoms-out in the hole (for the puller screw to bear down against), and a press tool that threads into the end of the crankshaft and pushes the pulley into place.*

Note 2: *Due to its design, the crank pulley has no keyway and can correctly be installed in any position on the crankshaft. A new shim should be used each time the pulley is removed.*

Removal

Refer to illustration 11.3

1   Remove the radiator (see Chapter 3).
2   Remove the drivebelt (see Chapter 1).
3   Remove the torque converter access plug in the oil pan **(see illustration)**; it will be necessary to have an assistant hold the flywheel from moving by using a large screwdriver braced against the ring gear as you loosen the pulley bolt.
4   Remove the crankshaft pulley bolt and install the crankshaft end protector.
5   Attach the puller and remove the pulley and pulley shim. **Caution:** *If you attempt to remove the pulley with a three-jaw puller, make sure the jaws of the puller grab the hub of the pulley only, not the outer circumference. Additionally, you'll have to insert an object such as a deep socket that is a close fit in the hole in the end of the crankshaft and bottoms-out in the hole; this is for the puller screw to*

push against. Never attempt to remove a crank pulley with a puller screw bearing down on the end of the crankshaft, since the threads in the end of the crankshaft will most likely be destroyed.
6   Using an appropriate tool, pry the oil seal out (notice the slots in the cover to access the outer edge of the seal).

Installation

7   Inspect the pulley for nicks and groves in the seal contact area. Also check the grooved drivebelt area on the circumference of the pulley for damage.
8   Lubricate the outside of the oil seal. **Note:** *Unless specified by the seal manufacturer, do not lubricate the inside area that comes in contact with the crankshaft; it must be installed dry or the seal will leak.*
9   Using a seal installation tool, drive the seal into the front cover until it is seated.
10   Install a new pulley shim and slide it against the crankshaft sprocket.
11   Raise the vehicle and support it securely on jackstands.
12   Place the pulley on the crankshaft and push it into place until it is seated using the installer tool. **Caution:** *Don't try to drive it on with a hammer.*
13   Remove the installer tool and install the pulley washer and bolt. While an assistant braces a screwdriver in the ring gear teeth, tighten the bolt to the torque listed in this Chapter's Specifications.
14   The remainder of the installation is the reverse of removal.

12 Oil pump and relief valve - replacement

1   Remove the front cover (see Section 6).
2   Remove the oil pump cover and mark the gear orientation for assembly.
3   Remove the gears.
4   Remove the oil pump relief plug, relief valve and spring.
5   Install the new relief valve and spring, tightening the plug to the torque listed in this Chapter's Specifications.

6   Install the new oil pump in the same orientation as the original gears.
7   Install the oil pump cover and tighten the screws to the torque listed in this Chapter's Specifications.
8   Reinstall the front cover.

13 Driveplate/flywheel - removal and installation

Removal

1   Raise the vehicle and support it securely on jackstands, then refer to Chapter 7A or 7B and remove the transmission.
2   Mark the relationship between the driveplate and the crankshaft with a marking pen, then remove the bolts that secure the driveplate to the crankshaft. If the crankshaft turns, wedge a screwdriver in the ring gear teeth to jam the driveplate or flywheel.
3   Remove the driveplate from the crankshaft. **Caution:** *When removing a flywheel, wear gloves to protect your fingers - the edges of the ring gear teeth may be sharp.*
4   Clean the driveplate to remove grease and oil. Inspect the surface for cracks, and check for cracked and broken ring gear teeth. Lay the driveplate on a flat surface to check for warpage.
5   Clean and inspect the mating surfaces of the driveplate and the crankshaft. If the rear main oil seal is leaking, replace it before reinstalling the driveplate.

Installation

6   Position the driveplate against the crankshaft. Be sure to align the marks made during removal. Note that some engines have an alignment dowel or staggered bolt holes to ensure correct installation. Before installing the bolts, apply thread-locking compound to the threads and place the retaining ring (if equipped) in position on the driveplate. **Note:** *Use only NEW bolts.*
7   Wedge a screwdriver through the ring gear teeth to keep the driveplate from turning as you tighten the bolts in a criss-cross pattern to the torque listed in this Chapter's Specifications.
8   If the front pump seal/O-ring in the automatic transmission is leaking, now would be a very good time to replace it.
9   The remainder of installation is the reverse of the removal procedure.

14 Rear main oil seal - replacement

Removal

1   Remove the transmission (see Chapter 7A or 7B).
2   Remove the driveplate or flywheel (see Section 13).
3   Inspect the oil seal, as well as the oil pan, engine block surface and oil seal housing for

11.3 To prevent the crankshaft from turning when removing the crankshaft pulley bolt, remove this plug and wedge a screwdriver in the ring gear teeth to jam the driveplate

signs of leakage. Sometimes an oil pan gasket leak can appear to be a rear oil seal leak.

4   Remove the rear main seal housing bolts, plus the two bolts retaining the oil pan to the rear main seal housing.

5   Install two bolts into the jackscrew holes provided in the housing. Carefully tighten each screw a little bit until the housing separates from the block, then remove the housing.

6   Remove the rear main oil seal from the housing. Inspect the crankshaft for nicks, grooves and damage.

Installation

7   Clean and inspect the oil seal housing.
8   Lubricate the outer seal surface with a film of engine oil. **Note:** *Unless specified by the seal manufacturer do not lubricate the inside area that comes in contact with the crankshaft, it must be installed dry or the seal will leak. Install the seal into the housing (make sure the lips of the seal point toward the engine) and carefully push it into place. A special aftermarket tool may be available at your local auto parts store. The tool just fits the diameter of the seal and, used with a hammer, drives the seal in.* **Note:** *Do not drive it in any further than the original seal was installed.*

9   Apply a 3/16-inch bead of RTV sealant to the housing-to-engine block mating surface.
10   Push the housing onto the block, making sure the lips of the seal slide over the rear of the crankshaft and don't fold under.
11   Install the bolts and tighten them to the torque listed in this Chapter's Specifications.
12   Install the driveplate (see Section 13).
13   Install the transmission (see Chapter 7).

15 Oil level tube - removal and installation

1   Remove the dipstick.
2   Release the clamp securing the fuel

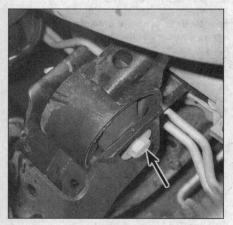

17.11 Remove the engine mount through-bolt

hoses and oil dipstick tube to the bracket on the intake manifold.

3   Remove the oil level tube mounting bolt.
4   Twist and pull the dipstick tube out of the oil pan.
5   Installation is the reverse of removal. Use a new O-ring at the block end of the tube, and lubricate it with engine oil.

16 Oil pan - removal and installation

Removal

1   Remove the oil level tube (see Section 15).
2   Loosen the front wheel lug nuts. Raise the front of the vehicle and support it securely on jackstands, then remove the front wheels.
3   Remove the under-vehicle splash shield.
4   On 2WD models, remove the steering gear (see Chapter 11). On 4WD models, remove only the mounting bolts and pull the steering gear downward.
5   If you're working on a 4WD model, disconnect the front driveshaft from the differential companion flange and secure it out of the way with a piece of wire or rope (see Chapter 8).
6   Drain the engine oil (see Chapter 1).
7   Free the transmission cooler lines from the clip on the side of the engine.
8   If you're working on a 4WD model, unbolt the differential carrier bushing-to-frame bolts and pull it downward.
9   Remove the bolts securing the oil pan to the transmission bellhousing, then remove the oil pan-to-engine block bolts.
10   Install two oil pan bolts in the jackscrew holes at the rear of the oil pan. Carefully and evenly tighten the bolts until the oil pan releases from the block.
11   Clean the pan and the bottom of the block with solvent. **Note:** *Do not use any power-driven gasket removal tools such as wire wheels and cleaning disks, as this will damage the components.*
12   Inspect the oil pan for nicks and cracks in the sealing areas. Also inspect the oil drain hole threads for damage.

Installation

13   Apply a 1/4-inch bead of RTV sealant to the pan) in the sealing area. **Note:** *The pan must be installed within ten minutes of sealant application.*
14   Place the oil pan on the block and start the bolts. Tighten the pan-to-transmission bellhousing bolts first, then tighten the oil pan-to-engine block bolts. Tighten the bolts to the torque listed in this Chapter's Specifications.
15   The remainder of installation is the reverse of removal. Be sure to tighten all fasteners to the torque values listed in the relevant Chapters.
16   Change the engine oil filter and fill the

crankcase with the correct type and amount of oil (see Chapter 1).

17 Engine mounts - check and replacement

1   Engine mounts seldom require attention, but broken or deteriorated mounts should be replaced immediately or the added strain placed on the driveline components may cause damage.

Check

2   During the check, the engine must be raised slightly to remove the weight from the mounts.
3   Raise the vehicle and support it securely on jackstands, then position the jack under the engine oil pan. Place a large block of wood between the jack head and the oil pan, then carefully raise the engine just enough to take the weight off the mounts. Do not use the jack to support the entire weight of the engine.
4   Check the mounts to see if the rubber is cracked, hardened or separated from the metal plates. Sometimes the rubber will split right down the center. Rubber preservative or WD-40 can be applied to the mounts to slow deterioration.
5   Check for relative movement between the mount plates and the engine or frame (use a large screwdriver or pry bar to attempt to move the mounts). If movement is noted, check the tightness of the mount fasteners first before condemning the mounts. Usually when engine mounts are broken, they are very obvious as the engine will easily move away from the mount when pried or under load.

Replacement

Refer to illustration 17.11

6   Disconnect the cable from the negative terminal of the battery.
7   Raise the vehicle and support it securely on jackstands, then remove both front wheels.
8   Place a block of wood on top of a floor jack, position the floor jack under the oil pan.
9   If you're replacing the left-side engine mount, remove the intermediate steering shaft.
10   Raise the engine enough to take the weight off the engine mounts.
11   Remove the engine mount through-bolt **(see illustration)**.
12   Raise the engine until the engine mount is clear of the frame bracket. Remove the mount-to-block bolts.
13   Twist the mount around until it comes free.
14   Installation is the reverse of removal. Use non-hardening thread-locking compound on the mount fasteners and be sure to tighten them to the torque listed in this Chapter's Specifications.

Chapter 2 Part B
General engine overhaul procedures

Contents

Specifications

General
2004 through 2006
Displacement
Four-cylinder engine ... 170 cubic inches (2.8L)
Five-cylinder engine ... 212 cubic inches (3.5L)
Compression ratio ... 10.0:1
2007 and later
Displacement
Four-cylinder engine ... 178 cubic inches (2.9L)
Five-cylinder engine ... 223 cubic inches (3.7L)
Compression ratio ... 10.3:1
Cylinder compression pressure
Minimum ... 150 psi
Typical ... 215 psi
Lowest allowable between cylinders ... 70 percent of the highest reading
Oil pressure (minimum warm engine) ... 12 psi @ 1200 rpm

Torque specifications*
Ft-lbs (unless otherwise indicated)

Note: *One foot-pound (ft-lb) of torque is equivalent to 12 inch-pounds (in-lbs) of torque. Torque values below approximately 15 ft-lbs are expressed in inch-pounds, since most foot-pound torque wrenches are not accurate at these smaller values.*

Connecting rod cap bolts or nuts
Step one ... 18
Step two ... Turn an additional 110-degrees
Main bearing cap bolts
Step one ... 18
Step two ... Turn an additional 180-degrees
Balance shaft
Retainer bolts
Left balance shaft retainer bolts ... 89 in-lbs
Right balance shaft retainer bolts ... 106 in-lbs
Chain guide mounting bolts ... 89 in-lbs
Chain tensioner mounting bolts ... 89 in-lbs

* **Note:** *Refer to Part A for additional torque specifications.*

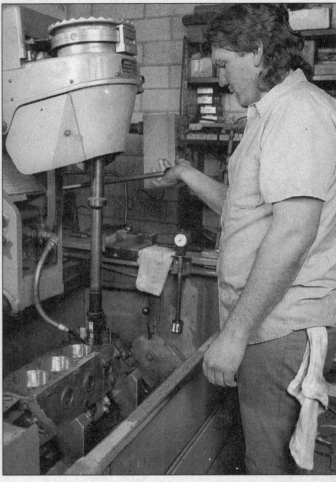

1.2 An engine block being bored. An engine rebuilder will use special machinery to recondition the cylinder bores

1.3 If the cylinders are bored, the machine shop will normally hone the engine on a machine like this

1   General information - engine overhaul

Refer to illustrations 1.2, 1.3, 1.4, 1.5, 1.6 and 1.7

Included in this portion of Chapter 2 are general information and diagnostic testing procedures for determining the overall mechanical condition of your engine.

The information ranges from advice concerning preparation for an overhaul and the purchase of replacement parts and/or components to detailed, step-by-step procedures covering removal and installation.

The following Sections have been written to help you determine whether your engine needs to be overhauled and how to remove and install it once you've determined it needs to be rebuilt. For information concerning in-vehicle engine repair, see Chapter 2A.

The Specifications included in this Part are general in nature and include only those necessary for testing the oil pressure and checking the engine compression. Refer to Chapter 2A for additional engine Specifications.

It's not always easy to determine when, or if, an engine should be completely overhauled, because a number of factors must be considered.

High mileage is not necessarily an indication that an overhaul is needed, while low mileage doesn't preclude the need for an overhaul. Frequency of servicing is probably the most important consideration. An engine that's had regular and frequent oil and filter changes, as well as other required maintenance, will most likely give many thousands of miles of reliable service. Conversely, a neglected engine may require an overhaul very early in its service life.

Excessive oil consumption is an indication that piston rings, valve seals and/or valve guides are in need of attention. Make sure that oil leaks aren't responsible before deciding that the rings and/or guides are bad. Perform a cylinder compression check to determine the extent of the work required (see Section 3). Also check the vacuum readings under various conditions (see Section 3).

Check the oil pressure with a gauge installed in place of the oil pressure sending unit and compare it to this Chapter's Specifi-

cations (see Section 2). If it's extremely low, the bearings and/or oil pump are probably worn out.

Loss of power, rough running, knocking or metallic engine noises, excessive valve train noise and high fuel consumption rates may also point to the need for an overhaul, especially if they're all present at the same time. If a complete tune-up doesn't remedy the situation, major mechanical work is the only solution.

An engine overhaul involves restoring the internal parts to the specifications of a new engine. During an overhaul, the piston rings are replaced and the cylinder walls are reconditioned (rebored and/or honed) **(see illustrations 1.2 and 1.3)**. If a rebore is done by an automotive machine shop, new oversize pistons will also be installed. The main bearings, connecting rod bearings and camshaft bearings are generally replaced with new ones and, if necessary, the crankshaft may be reground to restore the journals **(see illustration 1.4)**. Generally, the valves are serviced as well, since they're usually in less-than-perfect condition at this point. While the engine is being overhauled, other compo-

1.4 A crankshaft having a main bearing journal ground

1.5 A machinist checks for a bent connecting rod using specialized equipment

nents, such as the starter and alternator, can be rebuilt as well. The end result should be a like new engine that will give many trouble free miles. **Note:** *Critical cooling system components such as the hoses, drivebelt, thermostat and water pump should be replaced with new parts when an engine is overhauled. The radiator should be checked carefully to ensure that it isn't clogged or leaking (see Chapter 3). If you purchase a rebuilt engine or short block, some rebuilders will not warranty their engines unless the radiator has been professionally flushed. Also, we don't recommend overhauling the oil pump - always install a new one when an engine is rebuilt.*

Overhauling the internal components on today's engines is a difficult and time-consuming task which requires a significant amount of specialty tools and is best left to a professional engine rebuilder **(see illustrations 1.5, 1.6 and 1.7)**. A competent engine rebuilder will handle the inspection of your old parts and offer advice concerning the reconditioning or replacement of the original engine, never purchase parts or have machine work done on other components until the block has been thoroughly inspected by a profes-

sional machine shop. As a general rule, time is the primary cost of an overhaul, especially since the vehicle may be tied up for a minimum of two weeks or more. Be aware that some engine builders only have the capability to rebuild the engine you bring them while other rebuilders have a large inventory of rebuilt exchange engines in stock. Also be aware that many machine shops could take as much as two weeks time to completely rebuild your engine depending on shop workload. Sometimes it makes more sense to simply exchange your engine for another engine that's already rebuilt to save time.

2   Oil pressure check

Refer to illustration 2.2

1   Low engine oil pressure can be a sign of an engine in need of rebuilding. A "low oil pressure" indicator (often called an "idiot light") is not a test of the oiling system. Such indicators only come on when the oil pressure is dangerously low. Even an original pressure

gauge in the instrument panel is only a relative indication, although it's much better for driver information than a Warning light. An accurate test can only be performed with a mechanical (not electrical) oil pressure gauge. When used in conjunction with an accurate tachometer, the engine's oil pressure performance can be compared to the manufacturer's Specifications for that year and model.

2   Locate the oil pressure indicator sending unit **(see illustration)**.

3   Remove the oil pressure sending unit and install a fitting that will allow you to directly connect your hand-held, mechanical oil pressure gauge. Use Teflon tape or sealant on the threads of the adapter and the fitting on the end of your gauge's hose.

4   Connect an accurate tachometer to the engine, according to the tachometer manufacturer's instructions.

5   Check the oil pressure with the engine running (full operating temperature) at the specified engine speed, and compare it to this Chapter's Specifications. If it's extremely low, the bearings and/or oil pump are probably worn out.

1.6 A bore gauge being used to check the main bearing bore

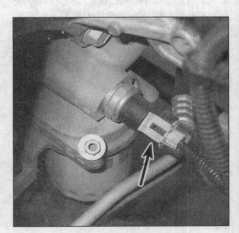

1.7 Uneven piston wear like this indicates a bent connecting rod

2.2 The oil pressure sending unit is located above the oil filter

3.5 A compression gauge with a threaded fitting for the spark plug hole is preferred over the type that requires hand pressure to maintain the seal

3.17 An inexpensive vacuum gauge can tell you a lot about an engine's condition

3   Compression check and vacuum gauge diagnostic checks

Compression check

Refer to illustration 3.5

1   A compression check will tell you what mechanical condition the upper end (pistons, rings, valves, head gaskets) of your engine is in. Specifically, it can tell you if the compression is down due to leakage caused by worn piston rings, defective valves and seats or a blown head gasket. **Note:** *The engine must be at normal operating temperature and the battery must be fully charged for this check.*

2   Begin by cleaning the area around the ignition coils before you remove them (compressed air should be used, if available). The idea is to prevent dirt from getting into the cylinders as the compression check is being done.

3   Remove all of the ignition coils and spark plugs from the engine (see Chapters 5 and 1, respectively).

4   The fuel pump circuit should be disabled by removing the fuel pump relay (it's located in the underhood fuse/relay box - see Chapter 4, **illustration 3.3**).

5   Install the compression gauge in the number one spark plug hole **(see illustration)**.

6   Crank the engine over at least four compression strokes and watch the gauge. The compression should build up quickly in a healthy engine. Low compression on the first stroke, followed by gradually increasing pressure on successive strokes, indicates worn piston rings. A low compression reading on the first stroke, which doesn't build up during successive strokes, indicates leaking valves or a blown head gasket (a cracked head could also be the cause). Deposits on the undersides of the valve heads can also cause low compression. Record the highest gauge reading obtained.

7   Repeat the procedure for the remaining cylinders and compare the results to this Chapter's Specifications.

8   Add some engine oil (about three squirts from a plunger-type oil can) to each cylinder, through the spark plug hole, and repeat the test.

9   If the compression increases after the oil is added, the piston rings are definitely worn. If the compression doesn't increase significantly, the leakage is occurring at the valves or head gasket. Leakage past the valves may be caused by burned valve seats and/or faces or warped, cracked or bent valves.

10   If two adjacent cylinders have equally-low compression, there's a strong possibility that the head gasket between them is blown. The appearance of coolant in the combustion chambers or the crankcase would verify this condition.

11   If one cylinder is slightly lower than the others, and the engine has a rough idle, a worn lobe on the camshaft could be the cause.

12   If the compression is unusually high, the combustion chambers are probably coated with carbon deposits. If that's the case, the cylinder head(s) should be removed and decarbonized.

13   If compression is way down or varies greatly between cylinders, it would be a good idea to have a leak-down test performed by an automotive repair shop. This test will pinpoint exactly where the leakage is occurring and how severe it is.

Vacuum gauge diagnostic checks

Refer to illustrations 3.17 and 3.19

14   A vacuum gauge provides valuable information about the condition of internal engine components. You can check for worn rings or cylinder walls, leaking head or intake manifold gaskets, restricted exhaust, stuck or burned valves, weak valve springs, improper ignition or valve timing and ignition problems.

15   Unfortunately, vacuum gauge readings are easy to misinterpret, so they should be used in conjunction with other tests to confirm the diagnosis.

16   Both the absolute readings and the rate of needle movement are important for accurate interpretation. Most gauges measure vacuum in inches of mercury (in-Hg). The following references to vacuum assume the diagnosis is being performed at sea level. As elevation increases (or atmospheric pressure decreases), the reading will decrease. For every 1,000 foot increase in elevation above approximately 2000 feet, the gauge readings will decrease about one inch of mercury.

17   Connect the vacuum gauge directly to intake manifold vacuum, not to ported (throttle body) vacuum **(see illustration)**. Be sure no hoses are left disconnected during the test or false readings will result.

18   Before you begin the test, allow the engine to warm up completely. Block the wheels and set the parking brake. With the transmission in Park or Neutral, start the engine and allow it to run at normal idle speed. **Warning:** *Always keep your hands, loose clothing and tools clear of the fan and do not stand in front of the vehicle or in line with the fan when the engine is running.*

19   Read the vacuum gauge; an average, healthy engine should normally produce about 17 to 22 inches of vacuum with a fairly steady needle **(see illustration)**. Refer to the following vacuum gauge readings and what they indicate about the engine's condition:

a)   *A low steady reading usually indicates a leaking gasket between the intake manifold and throttle body, a leaky vacuum hose, late ignition timing or incorrect camshaft timing. Check ignition timing with a timing light and eliminate all other possible causes, utilizing the tests provided in this Chapter before you remove the timing chain cover to check the timing marks.*

b) If the reading is three to eight inches below normal and it fluctuates at that low reading, suspect an intake manifold gasket leak at an intake port or a faulty fuel injector.

c) If the needle has regular drops of about two-to-four inches at a steady rate, the valves are probably leaking. Perform a compression check or leak-down test to confirm this.

d) An irregular drop or down-flick of the needle can be caused by a sticking valve or an ignition misfire. Perform a compression check or leak-down test and read the spark plugs.

e) A rapid vibration of about four inches Hg vibration at idle combined with exhaust smoke indicates worn valve guides. Perform a leak-down test to confirm this. If the rapid vibration occurs with an increase in engine speed, check for a leaking intake manifold gasket or head gasket, weak valve springs, burned valves or ignition misfire.

f) A slight fluctuation, say one inch up and down, may mean ignition problems. Check all the usual tune-up items and, if necessary, run the engine on an ignition analyzer.

g) If there is a large fluctuation, perform a compression or leak-down test to look for a weak or dead cylinder or a blown head gasket.

h) If the needle moves slowly through a wide range, check for a clogged PCV system, incorrect idle fuel mixture, carburetor/throttle body or intake manifold gasket leaks.

i) Check for a slow return after revving the engine by quickly snapping the throttle open until the engine reaches about 2,500 rpm and let it shut. Normally the reading should drop to near zero, rise above normal idle reading (about 5 in.-Hg over) and then return to the previous idle reading. If the vacuum returns slowly and doesn't peak when the throttle is snapped shut, the rings may be worn. If there is a long delay, look for a restricted exhaust system (often the muffler or catalytic converter). An easy way to check this is to temporarily disconnect the exhaust ahead of the suspected part and re-test.

4 Top Dead Center (TDC) for number one piston - locating

1 Top Dead Center (TDC) is the highest point in the cylinder that each piston reaches as it travels up the cylinder bore. Each piston reaches TDC on the compression stroke and again on the exhaust stroke, but TDC generally refers to piston position on the compression stroke.

2 Positioning the piston(s) at TDC is an essential part of certain procedures such as

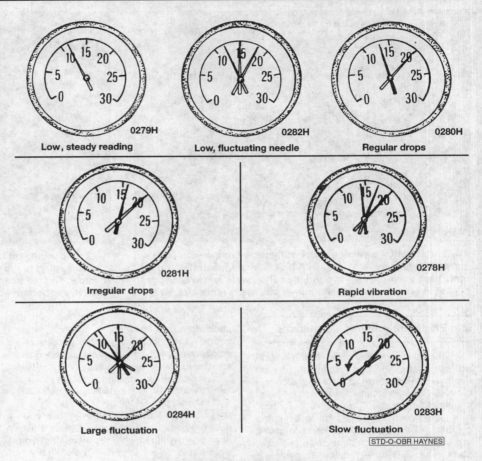

3.19 Typical vacuum gauge readings

timing chain/sprocket removal.

3 Before beginning this procedure, be sure to place the transmission in Park and apply the parking brake or block the rear wheels. Also, disconnect the cable from the negative terminal of the battery, then remove the spark plugs (see Chapter 1).

4 In order to bring any piston to TDC, the crankshaft must be turned using one of the methods outlined below. When looking at the front of the engine, normal crankshaft rotation is clockwise. The preferred method is to turn the crankshaft with a socket and ratchet attached to the bolt threaded into the front of the crankshaft. Turn the bolt in a clockwise direction.

5 Install a compression gauge into the number one spark plug hole **(see illustration 3.5)**. Rotate the crankshaft as described in Step 4 until air pressure begins to register on the gauge. Air pressure at the spark plug hole indicates that the cylinder has started the compression stroke. Once the compression stroke has begun, TDC for the number one cylinder is obtained when the piston reaches the top of the cylinder on the compression stroke. Remove the gauge.

6 To bring the piston to the top of the cylinder, insert a long screwdriver into the number

one spark plug hole until it touches the top of the piston. **Note:** *Make sure to wrap the tip of the screwdriver with tape to avoid scratching the top of the piston and the cylinder walls. Use the screwdriver (as a feeler gauge) to tell where the top of the piston is located in the cylinder while slowly rotating the crankshaft. As the piston rises the screwdriver will be pushed out. The point at which the screwdriver stops moving outward is TDC.* **Note:** *Always hold the screwdriver upright while the engine is being rotated so that the screwdriver will not get wedged as the piston travels upward.*

7 If you go past TDC, rotate the crankshaft counterclockwise until the piston is approximately one inch below TDC, then slowly rotate the crankshaft clockwise again until TDC is reached. **Note:** *The only method to locate the exact position of TDC number 1 is with the use of a degree wheel on the crankshaft vibration damper and a positive stop threaded into the spark plug hole, as you would use in the process of degreeing a camshaft.*

8 After the number one piston has been positioned at TDC on the compression stroke, TDC for any of the remaining pistons can be located by repeating the procedure described above and following the firing order.

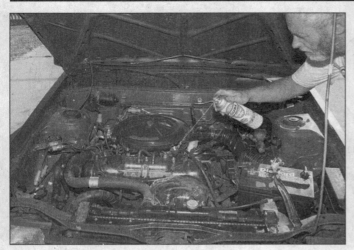

6.1 After tightly wrapping water-vulnerable components, use a spray cleaner on everything, with particular concentration on the greasiest areas, usually around the valve cover and lower edges of the block. If one section dries out, apply more cleaner

6.2 Depending on how dirty the engine is, let the cleaner soak in according to the directions and then hose off the grime and cleaner. Get the rinse water down into every area you can get at; then dry important components with a hair dryer or paper towels

5   Engine rebuilding alternatives

The do-it-yourselfer is faced with a number of options when performing an engine overhaul. The decision to replace the engine block, piston/connecting rod assemblies and crankshaft depends on a number of factors, with the number one consideration being the condition of the block. Other considerations are cost, access to machine shop facilities, parts availability, time required to complete the project and the extent of prior mechanical experience on the part of the do-it-yourselfer.

Some of the rebuilding alternatives include:

Individual parts - If the inspection procedures reveal that the engine block and most engine components are in reusable condition, purchasing individual parts may be the most economical alternative. The block, crankshaft and piston/connecting rod assemblies should all be inspected carefully. Even if the block shows little wear, the cylinder bores should be surface-honed.

Crankshaft kit - This rebuild package consists of a reground crankshaft and a matched set of pistons and connecting rods. The pistons will already be installed on the connecting rods. Piston rings and the necessary bearings will be included in the kit. These kits are commonly available for standard cylinder bores, as well as for engine blocks that have been bored to a regular oversize.

Short block - A short block consists of an engine block with renewed crankshaft and piston/connecting rod assemblies already installed. All new bearings are incorporated and all clearances will be correct. The existing cylinder head(s), camshaft, valve train components and external parts can be bolted to the short block with little or no machine shop work necessary.

Long block - A long block consists of a short block plus an oil pump, oil pan, cylinder heads, valve covers, camshaft and valve train components, timing sprockets, timing chain and timing cover. All components are installed with new bearings, seals and gaskets incorporated throughout. The installation of manifolds and external parts is all that is necessary.

Used engine assembly - While overhaul provides the best assurance of a like-new engine, used engines available from wrecking yards and importers are often a very simple and economical solution. Many used engines come with warranties, but always give any engine a thorough diagnostic check-out before purchase. Check compression, vacuum and also for signs of oil leakage. If possible, have the seller run the engine, ether in the vehicle or on a test stand so you can be sure it runs smoothly with no knocking or other noises.

Give careful thought to which alternative is best for you and discuss the situation with local automotive machine shops, auto parts dealers or parts store countermen before ordering or purchasing replacement parts.

6   Engine removal - methods and precautions

Refer to illustrations 6.1, 6.2, 6.3 and 6.4

If you've decided that an engine must be removed for overhaul or major repair work, several preliminary steps should be taken.

Locating a suitable place to work is extremely important. Adequate work space, along with storage space for the vehicle, will be needed. If a shop or garage isn't available, at the very least a flat, level, clean work surface made of concrete or asphalt is required.

Cleaning the engine compartment and engine before beginning the removal procedure will help keep your tools and your hands clean (see illustrations 6.1 and 6.2).

An engine hoist or A-frame will also be necessary. Make sure the equipment is rated in excess of the combined weight of the engine and accessories. Safety is of primary importance, considering the potential hazards involved in lifting the engine out of the vehicle.

If the engine is being removed by a novice, a helper should be available. Advice and aid from someone more experienced would also be helpful. There are many instances when one person cannot simultaneously per-

6.3 Get an engine hoist that's strong enough to easily lift your engine in and out of the engine compartment; an adapter, like the one shown here, can be used to change the angle of the engine as it's being removed or installed

6.4 Get an engine stand sturdy enough to firmly support the engine while you're working on it. Stay away from three-wheeled models; they have a tendency to tip over more easily, so get a four-wheeled unit

form all of the operations required when lifting the engine out of the vehicle.

Plan the operation ahead of time. Arrange for or obtain all of the tools and equipment you'll need prior to beginning the job **(see illustrations 6.3 and 6.4)**. Some of the equipment necessary to perform engine removal and installation safely and with relative ease are (in addition to an engine hoist) a heavy duty floor jack, complete sets of wrenches and sockets as described in the front of this manual, wooden blocks and plenty of rags and cleaning solvent for mopping up spilled oil, coolant and gasoline. If the hoist must be rented, make sure that you arrange for it in advance and perform all of the operations possible without it beforehand. This will save you money and time.

Plan for the vehicle to be out of use for quite a while. A machine shop will be required to perform some of the work that the do-it-yourselfer can't accomplish without special equipment. These shops often have a busy schedule, so it would be a good idea to consult them before removing the engine in order to accurately estimate the amount of time required to rebuild or repair components that

may need work.

Always be extremely careful when removing and installing the engine. Serious injury can result from careless actions. Plan ahead, take your time and a job of this nature, although major, can be accomplished successfully.

7   Engine - removal and installation

Warning 1: *The air conditioning system is under high pressure. Do not loosen any hose fittings or remove any components until after the system has been discharged. Air conditioning refrigerant must be properly discharged into an EPA-approved recovery/recycling unit at a dealer service department or an automotive air conditioning repair facility. Always wear eye protection when disconnecting air conditioning system fittings.*

Warning 2: *Gasoline is extremely flammable, so take extra precautions when you work on any part of the fuel system. Don't smoke or allow open flames or bare light bulbs near the work area, and don't work in a garage where a gas-type appliance (such as a water heater or*

a clothes dryer) is present. Since gasoline is carcinogenic, wear fuel-resistant gloves when there's a possibility of being exposed to fuel, and, if you spill any fuel on your skin, rinse it off immediately with soap and water. Mop up any spills immediately and do not store fuel-soaked rags where they could ignite. The fuel system is under constant pressure, so, if any fuel lines are to be disconnected, the fuel pressure in the system must be relieved first (see Chapter 4 for more information). When you perform any kind of work on the fuel system, wear safety glasses and have a Class B type fire extinguisher on hand.

Warning 3: *The models covered by this manual are equipped with airbags. Always disable the airbag system before working in the vicinity of any airbag system components to avoid the possibility of accidental deployment of the airbag(s), which could cause personal injury (see Chapter 12).*

Removal

Refer to illustrations 7.5a, 7.5b, 7.6, 7.19, 7.21, 7.25a, 7.25b and 7.27

1   Have the air conditioning system discharged and the refrigerant recovered by an air conditioning specialist.

2   Refer to Chapter 4 and relieve the fuel system pressure, then disconnect the cable from the negative terminal of the battery.

3   Cover the fenders and cowl and remove the hood (see Chapter 11). Special pads are available to protect the fenders, but an old bedspread or blanket will also work.

4   Remove the air cleaner assembly (see Chapter 4). Drain the cooling system (see Chapter 1).

5   Label the vacuum lines, emissions system hoses, wiring connectors, ground straps and fuel lines, to ensure correct reinstallation, then detach them **(see illustrations)**. If there's any possibility of confusion, make a sketch of the engine compartment and clearly label the lines, hoses and wires. Detach the wiring harness brackets from the engine and set the engine wiring harness aside. **Note:** *Some components will be easier to disconnect once the vehicle is raised and supported by jackstands.*

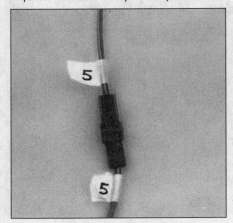

7.5a Label both ends of each wire before unplugging the connector

7.5b There are a number of ground straps, brackets and electrical connectors attached to the engine block (left rear of the engine shown)

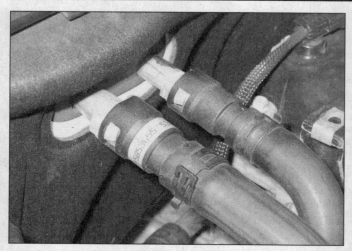

7.6 Be sure to disconnect the heater hoses at the firewall - push in the tabs to release the quick-connect fittings

7.19 Mark the torque converter to the driveplate, then remove the bolts

6   Label and detach all coolant hoses from the engine. The heater hoses, however, should be detached at the heater core tubes on the firewall **(see illustration)**.

7   Remove the MAP sensor (see Chapter 4).

8   Remove the throttle body (see Chapter 4). Refer to Chapter 5 and remove the battery, the battery box and the alternator.

9   Disconnect the air conditioning lines at the condenser and accumulator (see the **Warning** at the beginning of this Section).

10   Remove the radiator (see Chapter 3).

11   Remove the drivebelt (see Chapter 1) and the power steering pump mounting bolts (see Chapter 10), then wire the pump aside.

12   Disconnect the transmission fill tube bracket nut from the engine.

13   On 4WD models, disconnect the front axle electrical connector.

14   Remove the bolt holding the transmission line/fuel line bracket to the side of the engine and transmission, then move the lines away from the powertrain.

15   Remove the PCM (see Chapter 6).

16   Raise the vehicle and support it securely on jackstands. Working under the vehicle, drain the engine oil (see Chapter 1).

17   If the vehicle is a 4WD model, remove the front driveshaft and remove the two differential carrier bushing-to-frame bolts, then push the differential forward and secure it there (see Chapter 8).

18   Disconnect the exhaust pipe from the manifold (see Chapter 2A), then slide the pipe to the rear.

19   Remove the torque converter access cover, mark the torque converter to the driveplate, then remove the torque converter bolts **(see illustration)**.

20   Support the transmission with a floor jack. **Note:** *Place a block of wood between the jack and transmission oil pan.*

21   On 2WD models, remove the center portion of the front crossmember **(see illustration)**.

22   There are four bolts at the top of the bellhousing. To access these bolts for removal, remove the transmission crossmember and lower the transmission just enough to reach the bolts. Unclip the engine harness from two of the bolts and remove all four bolts, then raise the transmission and reinstall the crossmember using only two bolts.

23   Remove the remaining bellhousing bolts.

24   Lower the vehicle and loosen the upper engine mount throughbolts. Reposition the jack under the vehicle to support the transmission.

25   Attach an engine sling or a length of chain to the lifting bracket at the left front of the engine **(see illustration)**. Attach the other end of the chain to the right rear of the engine; remove an exhaust manifold bolt and, using a longer bolt of the same size and thread pitch as the original, attach the chain to the cylinder head **(see illustration)**. **Caution:** *DO NOT lift the engine by the intake manifold.* Lift the

7.21 Remove the bolts securing the center portion of the crossmember (2WD models)

7.25a Connect the engine lifting chain to the lifting hook at the front of the engine . . .

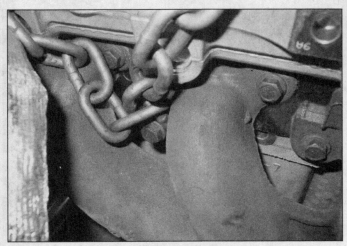

7.25b . . . and to the cylinder head at the right rear of the engine (use a bolt that is longer than the original exhaust manifold bolt and a washer, if necessary). As an alternative, you can wrap the chain around one of the manifold runners and bolt it together

7.27 Pull the engine forward as far as possible to clear the transmission and the cowl, then lift the engine high enough to clear the body

engine by the block or the cylinder head only.

26   Roll the hoist into position and connect the sling to it. Take up the slack in the sling or chain, but don't lift the engine. **Warning:** *DO NOT place any part of your body under the engine when it's supported only by a hoist or other lifting device.*

27   Raise the engine slightly. Carefully work it forward to separate it from the transmission. If you're working on a vehicle with an automatic transmission, be sure the torque converter stays in the transmission (clamp a pair of vise-grips to the housing to keep the converter from sliding out). Slowly raise the engine out of the engine compartment **(see illustration)**. Check carefully to make sure nothing is hanging up.

28   Remove the flywheel/driveplate and mount the engine on an engine stand.

Installation

29   Install the driveplate on the engine (see Chapter 2A). Check the engine and transmission mounts. If they're worn or damaged, replace them.

30   Carefully lower the engine into the engine compartment - make sure the engine mounts line up.

31   Guide the torque converter into the crankshaft following the procedure outlined in Chapter 7A.

32   Install the transmission-to-engine bolts and tighten them securely. **Caution:** *DO NOT use the bolts to force the transmission and engine together!*

33   Reinstall the remaining components in the reverse order of removal.

34   Add coolant, oil, power steering and transmission fluid as needed (see Chapter 1).

35   Run the engine and check for leaks and proper operation of all accessories, then install the hood and test drive the vehicle.

36   Have the air conditioning system

recharged and leak tested by the shop that discharged it.

8   Engine overhaul - disassembly sequence

1   It's much easier to disassemble and work on the engine if it's mounted on a portable engine stand. A stand can often be rented quite cheaply from an equipment rental yard. Before the engine is mounted on a stand, the flywheel/driveplate should be removed from the engine.

2   If a stand isn't available, it's possible to disassemble the engine with it blocked up on the floor. Be extra careful not to tip or drop the engine when working without a stand.

3   If you're going to obtain a rebuilt engine, all external components must come off first to be transferred to the replacement engine, just as they will if you're doing a complete engine overhaul yourself. These include:

Alternator and brackets
Emissions control components
Thermostat and housing cover
Water pump
Fuel injection components
Intake/exhaust manifold
Oil filter
Engine mounts
Driveplate

Note: *When removing the external components from the engine, pay close attention to details that may be helpful or important during installation. Note the installed position of gaskets, seals, spacers, pins, brackets, washers, bolts and other small items.*

4   If you're obtaining a short block, which consists of the engine block, crankshaft, pistons and connecting rods all assembled, then the cylinder head, oil pan and oil pump

will have to be removed as well. See *Engine rebuilding alternatives* for additional information regarding the different possibilities to be considered.

5   If you're planning a complete overhaul, the engine must be disassembled and the internal components removed in the following order:

Valve cover
Intake and exhaust manifolds
Timing chain cover
Oil pan
Oil pump
Timing chain and sprockets
Camshaft
Cylinder head
Piston/connecting rod assemblies
*Rear main oil seal retainer and
     balance shafts*
Crankshaft and main bearings

6   Before beginning the disassembly and overhaul procedures, make sure the following items are available. Also, refer to Section 11 for a list of tools and materials needed for engine reassembly.

Common hand tools
*Small cardboard boxes or plastic
     bags for storing parts*
Gasket scraper
Ridge reamer
Crankshaft balancer puller
Micrometers
Telescoping gauges
Dial-indicator set
Valve spring compressor
Cylinder surfacing hone
Piston ring groove-cleaning tool
Electric drill motor
Tap and die set
Wire brushes
Oil gallery brushes
Cleaning solvent

9.1 Before you try to remove the pistons, use a ridge reamer to remove the raised material (ridge) from the top of the cylinders

9.3 Checking the connecting rod endplay (side clearance) (typical)

9   Pistons and connecting rods - removal and installation

Removal

Refer to illustrations 9.1 and 9.3

Note: *Prior to removing the piston/connecting rod assemblies, remove the cylinder head and oil pan (see Chapter 2A).*

1   Use your fingernail to feel if a ridge has formed at the upper limit of ring travel (about 1/4-inch down from the top of each cylinder). If carbon deposits or cylinder wear have produced ridges, they must be completely removed with a special tool **(see illustration)**. Follow the manufacturer's instructions provided with the tool. Failure to remove the ridges before attempting to remove the piston/connecting rod assemblies may result in piston breakage.

2   After the cylinder ridges have been removed, turn the engine so the crankshaft is facing up.

3   Before the main bearing caps and connecting rods are removed, check the connecting rod endplay with feeler gauges. Slide them between the first connecting rod and the crankshaft throw until the play is removed **(see illustration)**. Repeat this procedure for each connecting rod. The endplay is equal to the thickness of the feeler gauge(s). Check with an automotive machine shop for the endplay service limit (a typical endplay limit should measure between 0.005 to 0.015 inch). If the play exceeds the service limit, new connecting rods will be required. If new rods (or a new crankshaft) are installed, the endplay may fall under the minimum allowable. If it does, the rods will have to be machined to restore it. If necessary, consult an automotive machine shop for advice.

4   Check the connecting rods and caps for identification marks. If they aren't plainly marked, use paint or marker to clearly identify each rod and cap (1, 2, 3, etc., depending on the cylinder they're associated with). **Caution:** *Do not use a punch and hammer to mark the connecting rods or they may be damaged.*

5   Loosen each of the connecting rod cap bolts 1/2-turn at a time until they can be removed by hand. **Note:** *New connecting rod cap bolts must be used when reassembling the engine, but save the old bolts for use when checking the connecting rod bearing oil clearance.*

6   Remove the number one connecting rod cap and bearing insert. Don't drop the bearing insert out of the cap.

7   Remove the bearing insert and push the connecting rod/piston assembly out through the top of the engine. Use a wooden or plastic hammer handle to push on the upper bearing surface in the connecting rod. If resistance is felt, double-check to make sure that all of the ridge was removed from the cylinder.

8   Repeat the procedure for the remaining cylinders.

9   After removal, reassemble the connecting rod caps and bearing inserts in their respective connecting rods and install the cap bolts finger tight. Leaving the old bearing inserts in place until reassembly will help prevent the connecting rod bearing surfaces from being accidentally nicked or gouged.

10   The pistons and connecting rods are now ready for inspection and overhaul at an automotive machine shop.

Piston ring installation

Refer to illustrations 9.13, 9.14, 9.15, 9.19a, 9.19b and 9.22

11   Before installing the new piston rings, the ring end gaps must be checked. It's assumed that the piston ring side clearance has been checked and verified correct.

12   Lay out the piston/connecting rod assemblies and the new ring sets so the ring sets will be matched with the same piston and cylinder during the end gap measurement and engine assembly.

13   Insert the top (number one) ring into the first cylinder and square it up with the cylinder walls by pushing it in with the top of the piston **(see illustration)**. The ring should be near

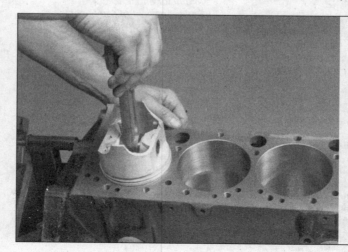

9.13 Install the piston ring into the cylinder then push it down into position using a piston so the ring will be square in the cylinder

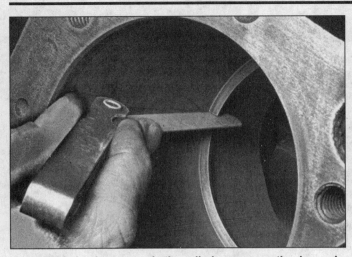

9.14 With the ring square in the cylinder, measure the ring end gap with a feeler gauge

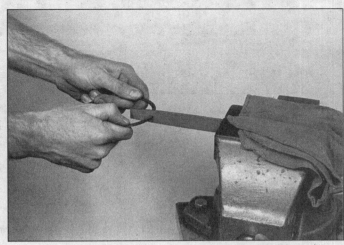

9.15 If the ring end gap is too small, clamp a file in a vise as shown and file the piston ring ends - be sure to remove all raised material

the bottom of the cylinder, at the lower limit of ring travel.

14   To measure the end gap, slip feeler gauges between the ends of the ring until a gauge equal to the gap width is found **(see illustration)**. The feeler gauge should slide between the ring ends with a slight amount of drag. A typical ring gap should fall between 0.010 and 0.020 inch for compression rings and up to 0.030 inch for the oil ring steel rails. If the gap is larger or smaller than specified, double-check to make sure you have the correct rings before proceeding.

15   If the gap is too small, it must be enlarged or the ring ends may come in contact with each other during engine operation, which can cause serious damage to the engine. If necessary, increase the end gaps by filing the ring ends very carefully with a fine file. Mount the file in a vise equipped with soft jaws, slip the ring over the file with the ends contacting the file face and slowly move the ring to

remove material from the ends. When performing this operation, file only by pushing the ring from the outside end of the file towards the vise **(see illustration)**.

16   Excess end gap isn't critical unless it's greater than 0.040 inch. Again, double-check to make sure you have the correct ring type.

17   Repeat the procedure for each ring that will be installed in the first cylinder and for each ring in the remaining cylinders. Remember to keep rings, pistons and cylinders matched up.

18   Once the ring end gaps have been checked/corrected, the rings can be installed on the pistons.

19   The oil control ring (lowest one on the piston) is usually installed first. It's composed of three separate components. Slip the spacer/expander into the groove **(see illustration)**. If an anti-rotation tang is used, make sure it's inserted into the drilled hole in the ring groove. Next, install the upper side rail

in the same manner **(see illustration)**. Don't use a piston ring installation tool on the oil ring side rails, as they may be damaged. Instead, place one end of the side rail into the groove between the spacer/expander and the ring land, hold it firmly in place and slide a finger around the piston while pushing the rail into the groove. Finally, install the lower side rail.

20   After the three oil ring components have been installed, check to make sure that both the upper and lower side rails can be rotated smoothly inside the ring grooves.

21   The number two (middle) ring is installed next. It's usually stamped with a mark that must face up, toward the top of the piston. Do not mix up the top and middle rings, as they have different cross-sections. **Note:** *Always follow the instructions printed on the ring package or box - different manufacturers may require different approaches.*

22   Use a piston ring installation tool and make sure the identification mark is facing

9.19a Installing the spacer/expander in the oil ring groove

9.19b DO NOT use a piston ring installation tool when installing the oil control ring side-rails

ENGINE BEARING ANALYSIS

Debris

Babbitt bearing embedded with debris from machinings

Microscopic detail of debris

Microscopic detail of gouges

Overplated copper alloy bearing gouged by cast iron debris

Aluminum bearing embedded with glass beads

Microscopic detail of glass beads

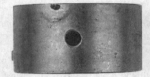 

Damaged lining caused by dirt left on the bearing back

Misassembly

Result of a lower half assembled as an upper - blocking the oil flow

Excessive oil clearance is indicated by a short contact arc

Polished and oil-stained backs are a result of a poor fit in the housing bore

Result of a wrong, reversed, or shifted cap

Overloading

Damage from excessive idling which resulted in an oil film unable to support the load imposed

Damaged upper connecting rod bearings caused by engine lugging; the lower main bearings (not shown) were similarly affected

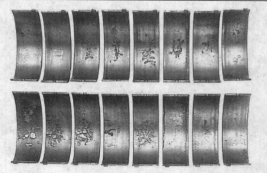

The damage shown in these upper and lower connecting rod bearings was caused by engine operation at a higher-than-rated speed under load

Misalignment

A warped crankshaft caused this pattern of severe wear in the center, diminishing toward the ends

A poorly finished crankshaft caused the equally spaced scoring shown

A tapered housing bore caused the damage along one edge of this pair

A bent connecting rod led to the damage in the "V" pattern

Lubrication

Result of dry start: The bearings on the left, farthest from the oil pump, show more damage

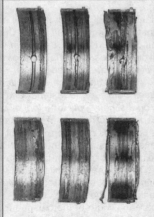

Result of a low oil supply or oil starvation

Severe wear as a result of inadequate oil clearance

Corrosion

Microscopic detail of corrosion

Corrosion is an acid attack on the bearing lining generally caused by inadequate maintenance, extremely hot or cold operation, or inferior oils or fuels

Microscopic detail of cavitation

Example of cavitation - a surface erosion caused by pressure changes in the oil film

Damage from excessive thrust or insufficient axial clearance

Bearing affected by oil dilution caused by excessive blow-by or a rich mixture

9.22 Use a piston ring installation tool to install the number 2 and the number 1 (top) rings - be sure the directional mark on the piston ring(s) is facing toward the top of the piston

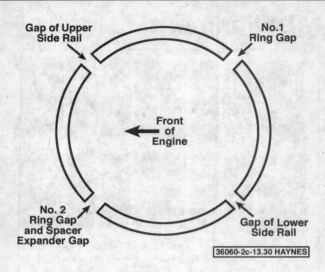

9.30 Position the piston ring end gaps as shown

the top of the piston, then slip the ring into the middle groove on the piston **(see illustration)**. Don't expand the ring any more than necessary to slide it over the piston.

23   Install the number one (top) ring in the same manner. Make sure the mark is facing up. Be careful not to confuse the number one and number two rings.

24   Repeat the procedure for the remaining pistons and rings.

Installation

25   Before installing the piston/connecting rod assemblies, the cylinder walls must be perfectly clean, the top edge of each cylinder bore must be chamfered, and the crankshaft must be in place.

26   Remove the cap from the end of the number one connecting rod (refer to the marks made during removal). Remove the original bearing inserts and wipe the bearing surfaces of the connecting rod and cap with a clean, lint-free cloth. They must be kept spotlessly clean.

Connecting rod bearing oil clearance check

Refer to illustrations 9.30, 9.35, 9.37 and 9.41

27   Clean the back side of the new upper bearing insert, then lay it in place in the connecting rod.

28   Make sure the tab on the bearing fits into the recess in the rod. Don't hammer the bearing insert into place and be very careful not to nick or gouge the bearing face. Don't lubricate the bearing at this time.

29   Clean the back side of the other bearing insert and install it in the rod cap. Again, make sure the tab on the bearing fits into the recess in the cap, and don't apply any lubricant. It's critically important that the mating surfaces of the bearing and connecting rod are perfectly clean and oil free when they're assembled.

30   Position the piston ring gaps at 90-

degree intervals around the piston as shown **(see illustration)**.

31   Lubricate the piston and rings with clean engine oil and attach a piston ring compressor to the piston. Leave the skirt protruding about 1/4-inch to guide the piston into the cylinder. The rings must be compressed until they're flush with the piston.

32   Rotate the crankshaft until the number one connecting rod journal is at BDC (bottom dead center) and apply a liberal coat of engine oil to the cylinder walls.

33   With the mark on top of the piston facing the front (timing chain end) of the engine, gently insert the piston/connecting rod assembly into the number one cylinder bore and rest the bottom edge of the ring compressor on the engine block.

34   Tap the top edge of the ring compressor to make sure it's contacting the block around its entire circumference.

35   Gently tap on the top of the piston with the end of a wooden or plastic hammer handle **(see illustration)** while guiding the end of the connecting rod into place on the crankshaft journal. The piston rings may try to pop out of the ring compressor just before entering the cylinder bore, so keep some downward pressure on the ring compressor. Work slowly, and if any resistance is felt as the piston enters the cylinder, stop immediately. Find out what's hanging up and fix it before proceeding. Do not, for any reason, force the piston into the cylinder - you might break a ring and/or the piston.

36   Once the piston/connecting rod assembly is installed, the connecting rod bearing oil clearance must be checked before the rod cap is permanently installed.

37   Cut a piece of the appropriate size Plastigage slightly shorter than the width of the connecting rod bearing and lay it in place on the number one connecting rod journal, parallel with the journal axis **(see illustration)**.

38   Clean the connecting rod cap bearing

9.35 Use a plastic or wooden hammer handle to push the piston into the cylinder

face and install the rod cap. Make sure the mating mark on the cap is on the same side as the mark on the connecting rod **(see illustration 9.4)**.

39   Install the old rod bolts, at this time, and tighten them to the torque listed in this Chapter's Specifications. **Note***: Use a thin-wall socket to avoid erroneous torque readings that can result if the socket is wedged between the rod cap and the bolt. If the socket tends to wedge itself between the fastener and the cap, lift up on it slightly until it no longer contacts the cap. DO NOT rotate the crankshaft at any time during this operation.*

40   Remove the fasteners and detach the rod cap, being very careful not to disturb the Plastigage. Discard the cap bolts at this time as they cannot be reused. **Note:** *You MUST use new connecting rod bolts.*

41   Compare the width of the crushed Plastigage to the scale printed on the Plastigage envelope to obtain the oil clearance **(see illustration)**. The connecting rod oil clearance is usually about 0.001 to 0.002 inch. Consult an automotive machine shop for the clearance

9.37 Place Plastigage on each connecting rod bearing journal parallel to the crankshaft centerline

9.41 Use the scale on the Plastigage package to determine the bearing oil clearance - be sure to measure the widest part of the Plastigage and use the correct scale; it comes with both standard and metric scales

specified for the rod bearings on your engine.
42   If the clearance is not as specified, the bearing inserts may be the wrong size (which means different ones will be required). Before deciding that different inserts are needed, make sure that no dirt or oil was between the bearing inserts and the connecting rod or cap when the clearance was measured. Also, recheck the journal diameter. If the Plastigage was wider at one end than the other, the journal may be tapered. If the clearance still exceeds the limit specified, the bearing will have to be replaced with an undersize bearing. **Caution:** *When installing a new crankshaft always use a standard size bearing.*

Final installation

43   Carefully scrape all traces of the Plastigage material off the rod journal and/or bearing face. Be very careful not to scratch the bearing - use your fingernail or the edge of a plastic card.
44   Make sure the bearing faces are perfectly clean, then apply a uniform layer of clean moly-base grease or engine assembly lube to both of them. You'll have to push the piston into the cylinder to expose the face of the bearing insert in the connecting rod.
45   **Caution:** *Install new connecting rod cap bolts. Do NOT reuse old bolts - they have stretched and cannot be reused. Slide the connecting rod back into place on the journal, install the rod cap, install the nuts or new bolts and tighten them to the torque listed in this Chapter's Specifications. Again, work up to the torque in three steps.*
46   Repeat the entire procedure for the remaining pistons/connecting rods.
47   The important points to remember are:
a) *Keep the back sides of the bearing inserts and the insides of the connecting rods and caps perfectly clean when assembling them.*
b) *Make sure you have the correct piston/ rod assembly for each cylinder.*

c) *The mark on the piston must face the front of the engine.*
d) *Lubricate the cylinder walls liberally with clean oil.*
e) *Lubricate the bearing faces when installing the rod caps after the oil clearance has been checked.*

48   After all the piston/connecting rod assemblies have been correctly installed, rotate the crankshaft a number of times by hand to check for any obvious binding.
49   As a final step, check the connecting rod endplay again.
50   Compare the measured endplay to the tolerance listed in this Chapter's Specifications to make sure it's acceptable. If it was correct before disassembly and the original crankshaft and rods were reinstalled, it should still be correct. If new rods or a new crankshaft were installed, the endplay may be inadequate. If so, the rods will have to be removed and taken to an automotive machine shop for resizing.

10 Crankshaft - removal and installation

Removal

Refer to illustrations 10.1 and 10.3
Note: *The crankshaft can be removed only after the engine has been removed from the vehicle. It's assumed that the driveplate, crankshaft pulley, oil pan, timing chain and piston/connecting rod assemblies have already been removed. The rear main oil seal retainer must be unbolted and separated from the block before proceeding with crankshaft removal (see Chapter 2A).*
1   Before the crankshaft is removed, measure the endplay. Mount a dial indicator with the indicator in line with the crankshaft and just touching the end of the crankshaft as shown **(see illustration)**.
2   Pry the crankshaft all the way to the rear and zero the dial indicator. Next, pry the crankshaft to the front as far as possible and check

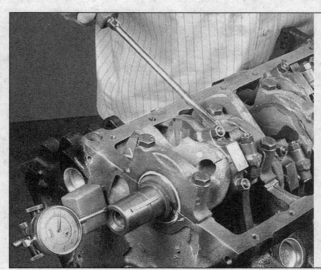

10.1 Checking crankshaft endplay with a dial indicator

COMMON ENGINE OVERHAUL TERMS

B

Backlash - The amount of play between two parts. Usually refers to how much one gear can be moved back and forth without moving gear with which it's meshed.

Bearing Caps - The caps held in place by nuts or bolts which, in turn, hold the bearing surface. This space is for lubricating oil to enter.

Bearing clearance - The amount of space left between shaft and bearing surface. This space is for lubricating oil to enter.

Bearing crush - The additional height which is purposely manufactured into each bearing half to ensure complete contact of the bearing back with the housing bore when the engine is assembled.

Bearing knock - The noise created by movement of a part in a loose or worn bearing.

Blueprinting - Dismantling an engine and reassembling it to EXACT specifications.

Bore - An engine cylinder, or any cylindrical hole; also used to describe the process of enlarging or accurately refinishing a hole with a cutting tool, as to bore an engine cylinder. The bore size is the diameter of the hole.

Boring - Renewing the cylinders by cutting them out to a specified size. A boring bar is used to make the cut.

Bottom end - A term which refers collectively to the engine block, crankshaft, main bearings and the big ends of the connecting rods.

Break-in - The period of operation between installation of new or rebuilt parts and time in which parts are worn to the correct fit. Driving at reduced and varying speed for a specified mileage to permit parts to wear to the correct fit.

Bushing - A one-piece sleeve placed in a bore to serve as a bearing surface for shaft, piston pin, etc. Usually replaceable.

C

Camshaft - The shaft in the engine, on which a series of lobes are located for operating the valve mechanisms. The camshaft is driven by gears or sprockets and a timing chain. Usually referred to simply as the cam.

Carbon - Hard, or soft, black deposits found in combustion chamber, on plugs, under rings, on and under valve heads.

Cast iron - An alloy of iron and more than two percent carbon, used for engine blocks and heads because it's relatively inexpensive and easy to mold into complex shapes.

Chamfer - To bevel across (or a bevel on) the sharp edge of an object.

Chase - To repair damaged threads with a tap or die.

Combustion chamber - The space between the piston and the cylinder head, with the piston at top dead center, in which air-fuel mixture is burned.

Compression ratio - The relationship between cylinder volume (clearance volume) when the piston is at top dead center and cylinder volume when the piston is at bottom dead center.

Connecting rod - The rod that connects the crank on the crankshaft with the piston. Sometimes called a con rod.

Connecting rod cap - The part of the connecting rod assembly that attaches the rod to the crankpin.

Core plug - Soft metal plug used to plug the casting holes for the coolant passages in the block.

Crankcase - The lower part of the engine in which the crankshaft rotates; includes the lower section of the cylinder block and the oil pan.

Crank kit - A reground or reconditioned crankshaft and new main and connecting rod bearings.

Crankpin - The part of a crankshaft to which a connecting rod is attached.

Crankshaft - The main rotating member, or shaft, running the length of the crankcase, with offset throws to which the connecting rods are attached; changes the reciprocating motion of the pistons into rotating motion.

Cylinder sleeve - A replaceable sleeve, or liner, pressed into the cylinder block to form the cylinder bore.

D

Deburring - Removing the burrs (rough edges or areas) from a bearing.

Deglazer - A tool, rotated by an electric motor, used to remove glaze from cylinder walls so a new set of rings will seat.

E

Endplay - The amount of lengthwise movement between two parts. As applied to a crankshaft, the distance that the crankshaft can move forward and back in the cylinder block.

F

Face - A machinist's term that refers to removing metal from the end of a shaft or the face of a larger part, such as a flywheel.

Fatigue - A breakdown of material through a large number of loading and unloading cycles. The first signs are cracks followed shortly by breaks.

Feeler gauge - A thin strip of hardened steel, ground to an exact thickness, used to check clearances between parts.

Free height - The unloaded length or height of a spring.

Freeplay - The looseness in a linkage, or an assembly of parts, between the initial application of force and actual movement. Usually perceived as slop or slight delay.

Freeze plug - See Core plug.

G

Gallery - A large passage in the block that forms a reservoir for engine oil pressure.

Glaze - The very smooth, glassy finish that develops on cylinder walls while an engine is in service.

H

Heli-Coil - A rethreading device used when threads are worn or damaged. The device is installed in a retapped hole to reduce the thread size to the original size.

I

Installed height - The spring's measured length or height, as installed on the cylinder head. Installed height is measured from the spring seat to the underside of the spring retainer.

J

Journal - The surface of a rotating shaft which turns in a bearing.

K

Keeper - The split lock that holds the valve spring retainer in position on the valve stem.

Key - A small piece of metal inserted into matching grooves machined into two parts fitted together - such as a gear pressed onto a shaft - which prevents slippage between the two parts.

Knock - The heavy metallic engine sound, produced in the combustion chamber as a result of abnormal combustion - usually detonation. Knock is usually caused by a loose or worn bearing. Also referred to as detonation, pinging and spark knock. Connecting rod or main bearing knocks are created by too much oil clearance or insufficient lubrication.

L

Lands - The portions of metal between the piston ring grooves.

Lapping the valves - Grinding a valve face and its seat together with lapping compound.

Lash - The amount of free motion in a gear train, between gears, or in a mechanical assembly, that occurs before movement can begin. Usually refers to the lash in a valve train.

Lifter - The part that rides against the cam to transfer motion to the rest of the valve train.

M

Machining - The process of using a machine to remove metal from a metal part.

Main bearings - The plain, or babbit, bearings that support the crankshaft.

Main bearing caps - The cast iron caps, bolted to the bottom of the block, that support the main bearings.

O

O.D. - Outside diameter.

Oil gallery - A pipe or drilled passageway in the engine used to carry engine oil from one area to another.

Oil ring - The lower ring, or rings, of a piston; designed to prevent excessive amounts of oil from working up the cylinder walls and into the combustion chamber. Also called an oil-control ring.

Oil seal - A seal which keeps oil from leaking out of a compartment. Usually refers to a dynamic seal around a rotating shaft or other moving part.

O-ring - A type of sealing ring made of a special rubberlike material; in use, the O-ring is compressed into a groove to provide the sealing action.

Overhaul - To completely disassemble a unit, clean and inspect all parts, reassemble it with the original or new parts and make all adjustments necessary for proper operation.

P

Pilot bearing - A small bearing installed in the center of the flywheel (or the rear end of the crankshaft) to support the front end of the input shaft of the transmission.

Pip mark - A little dot or indentation which indicates the top side of a compression ring.

Piston - The cylindrical part, attached to the connecting rod, that moves up and down in the cylinder as the crankshaft rotates. When the fuel charge is fired, the piston transfers the force of the explosion to the connecting rod, then to the crankshaft.

Piston pin (or wrist pin) - The cylindrical and usually hollow steel pin that passes through the piston. The piston pin fastens the piston to the upper end of the connecting rod.

Piston ring - The split ring fitted to the groove in a piston. The ring contacts the sides of the ring groove and also rubs against the cylinder wall, thus sealing space between piston and wall. There are two types of rings: Compression rings seal the compression pressure in the combustion chamber; oil rings scrape excessive oil off the cylinder wall.

Piston ring groove - The slots or grooves cut in piston heads to hold piston rings in position.

Piston skirt - The portion of the piston below the rings and the piston pin hole.

Plastigage - A thin strip of plastic thread, available in different sizes, used for measuring clearances. For example, a strip of plastigage is laid across a bearing journal and mashed as parts are assembled. Then parts are disassembled and the width of the strip is measured to determine clearance between journal and bearing. Commonly used to measure crankshaft main-bearing and connecting rod bearing clearances.

Press-fit - A tight fit between two parts that requires pressure to force the parts together. Also referred to as drive, or force, fit.

Prussian blue - A blue pigment; in solution, useful in determining the area of contact between two surfaces. Prussian blue is commonly used to determine the width and location of the contact area between the valve face and the valve seat.

R

Race (bearing) - The inner or outer ring that provides a contact surface for balls or rollers in bearing.

Ream - To size, enlarge or smooth a hole by using a round cutting tool with fluted edges.

Ring job - The process of reconditioning the cylinders and installing new rings.

Runout - Wobble. The amount a shaft rotates out-of-true.

S

Saddle - The upper main bearing seat.

Scored - Scratched or grooved, as a cylinder wall may be scored by abrasive particles moved up and down by the piston rings.

Scuffing - A type of wear in which there's a transfer of material between parts moving against each other; shows up as pits or grooves in the mating surfaces.

Seat - The surface upon which another part rests or seats. For example, the valve seat is the matched surface upon which the valve face rests. Also used to refer to wearing into a good fit; for example, piston rings seat after a few miles of driving.

Short block - An engine block complete with crankshaft and piston and, usually, camshaft assemblies.

Static balance - The balance of an object while it's stationary.

Step - The wear on the lower portion of a ring land caused by excessive side and back-clearance. The height of the step indicates the ring's extra side clearance and the length of the step projecting from the back wall of the groove represents the ring's back clearance.

Stroke - The distance the piston moves when traveling from top dead center to bottom dead center, or from bottom dead center to top dead center.

Stud - A metal rod with threads on both ends.

T

Tang - A lip on the end of a plain bearing used to align the bearing during assembly.

Tap - To cut threads in a hole. Also refers to the fluted tool used to cut threads.

Taper - A gradual reduction in the width of a shaft or hole; in an engine cylinder, taper usually takes the form of uneven wear, more pronounced at the top than at the bottom.

Throws - The offset portions of the crankshaft to which the connecting rods are affixed.

Thrust bearing - The main bearing that has thrust faces to prevent excessive endplay, or forward and backward movement of the crankshaft.

Thrust washer - A bronze or hardened steel washer placed between two moving parts. The washer prevents longitudinal movement and provides a bearing surface for thrust surfaces of parts.

Tolerance - The amount of variation permitted from an exact size of measurement. Actual amount from smallest acceptable dimension to largest acceptable dimension.

U

Umbrella - An oil deflector placed near the valve tip to throw oil from the valve stem area.

Undercut - A machined groove below the normal surface.

Undersize bearings - Smaller diameter bearings used with re-ground crankshaft journals.

V

Valve grinding - Refacing a valve in a valve-refacing machine.

Valve train - The valve-operating mechanism of an engine; includes all components from the camshaft to the valve.

Vibration damper - A cylindrical weight attached to the front of the crankshaft to minimize torsional vibration (the twist-untwist actions of the crankshaft caused by the cylinder firing impulses). Also called a harmonic balancer.

W

Water jacket - The spaces around the cylinders, between the inner and outer shells of the cylinder block or head, through which coolant circulates.

Web - A supporting structure across a cavity.

Woodruff key - A key with a radiused backside (viewed from the side).

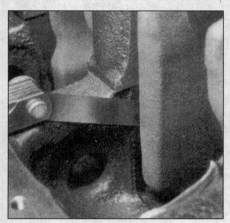

10.3 Checking crankshaft endplay with feeler gauges at the thrust-bearing journal

10.17 Place the Plastigage onto the crankshaft bearing journal as shown

10.21 Use the scale on the Plastigage package to determine the bearing oil clearance - be sure to measure the widest part of the Plastigage and use the correct scale; it comes with both standard and metric scales

the reading on the dial indicator. The distance traveled is the endplay. A typical crankshaft endplay will fall between 0.003 to 0.010 inch. If it is greater than that, check the crankshaft thrust surfaces for wear after it's removed. If no wear is evident, new main bearings should correct the endplay.

3   If a dial indicator isn't available, feeler gauges can be used. Gently pry the crankshaft all the way to the front of the engine. Slip feeler gauges between the crankshaft and the front face of the thrust bearing or washer to determine the clearance **(see illustration)**.

4   Loosen the main bearing cap bolts 1/4-turn at a time each, until they can be removed by hand.

5   Remove the main bearing cap stiffener, then check for marks on the main bearing caps indicating their positions. If there aren't any, number them from front to rear and also add an arrow to each one pointing to the front of the engine. Now remove the main bearing caps. Try not to drop the bearing inserts if they come out with the caps.

6   Carefully lift the crankshaft out of the engine. It's a good idea to have an assistant available, since the crankshaft is quite heavy and awkward to handle. With the bearing inserts in place inside the engine block and main bearing caps, reinstall the main bearing caps and stiffener onto the engine block and tighten the bolts finger tight. Make sure you install the main bearing caps in their proper positions and facing the proper direction.

Installation

7   Crankshaft installation is the first step in engine reassembly. It's assumed at this point that the engine block and crankshaft have been cleaned, inspected and repaired or reconditioned.

8   Position the engine block with the bottom facing up.

9   Remove the mounting bolts and lift off the stiffener and main bearing caps.

10   If they're still in place, remove the original bearing inserts from the block and from the main bearing caps. Wipe the bearing

surfaces of the block and main bearing caps with a clean, lint-free cloth. They must be kept spotlessly clean. This is critical for determining the correct bearing oil clearance.

Main bearing oil clearance check

Refer to illustrations 10.17 and 10.21

11   Without mixing them up, clean the back sides of the new upper main bearing inserts (with grooves and oil holes) and lay one in each main bearing saddle in the block. Each upper bearing has an oil groove and oil hole in it. **Caution:** *The oil holes in the block must line up with the oil holes in the upper bearing inserts.* Counting from the front, the thrust washer or thrust bearing insert must be installed in the number 3 crankshaft journal on four-cylinder 2.8L engines and the 4th journal on the 3.5L five-cylinder engine. Clean the back sides of the lower main bearing inserts and lay them in their corresponding locations in the main bearing caps. Make sure the tab on the bearing insert fits into the recess in the block or main bearing cap assembly. The upper bearings with the oil holes are installed into the engine block while the lower bearings without the oil holes are installed in the main bearing caps. **Caution:** *Do not hammer the bearing insert into place and don't nick or gouge the bearing faces. DO NOT apply any lubrication at this time.*

12   Clean the faces of the bearing inserts in the block and the crankshaft main bearing journals with a clean, lint-free cloth.

13   Check or clean the oil holes in the crankshaft, as any dirt here can go only one way - straight through the new bearings.

14   Once you're certain the crankshaft is clean, carefully lay it in position in the cylinder block.

15   Before the crankshaft can be permanently installed, the main bearing oil clearance must be checked.

16   Cut several strips of the appropriate size of Plastigage. They must be slightly shorter than the width of the main bearing journal.

17   Place one piece on each crankshaft

main bearing journal, parallel with the journal axis as shown **(see illustration)**.

18   Clean the faces of the bearing inserts in the main bearing cap assembly. Hold the bearing inserts in place and install the assembly onto the crankshaft and cylinder block. DO NOT disturb the Plastigage. Make sure you install the main bearing caps with the arrows facing the front of the engine, then install the stiffener.

19   Apply clean engine oil to all bolt threads prior to installation, then install all bolts finger-tight (see the old bolts for this). Tighten main bearing cap bolts working from the center outwards and alternating from side-to-side, progressing in steps, to the torque listed in this Chapter's Specifications. DO NOT rotate the crankshaft at any time during this operation.

20   Remove the bolts in the reverse order of the tightening sequence, remove the stiffener and carefully lift the main bearing caps straight up and off the block. Do not disturb the Plastigage or rotate the crankshaft.

21   Compare the width of the crushed Plastigage on each journal to the scale printed on the Plastigage envelope to determine the main bearing oil clearance **(see illustration)**. Check with an automotive machine shop for the oil clearance for your engine.

22   If the clearance is not as specified, the bearing inserts may be the wrong size (which means different ones will be required). Before deciding if different inserts are needed, make sure that no dirt or oil was between the bearing inserts and the cap assembly or block when the clearance was measured. If the Plastigage was wider at one end than the other, the crankshaft journal may be tapered. If the clearance still exceeds the limit specified, the bearing insert(s) will have to be replaced with an undersize bearing insert(s). **Caution:** *When installing a new crankshaft always install a standard bearing insert set.*

23   Carefully scrape all traces of the Plastigage material off the main bearing journals

and/or the bearing insert faces. Be sure to remove all residue from the oil holes. Use your fingernail or the edge of a plastic card - don't nick or scratch the bearing faces.

Final installation

24   Carefully lift the crankshaft out of the cylinder block.

25   Clean the bearing insert faces in the cylinder block, then apply a thin, uniform layer of moly-base grease or engine assembly lube to each of the bearing surfaces. Be sure to coat the thrust faces as well as the journal face of the thrust bearing.

26   Make sure the crankshaft journals are clean, then lay the crankshaft back in place in the cylinder block.

27   Clean the bearing insert faces and then apply the same lubricant to them. Clean the engine block and the main bearing caps thoroughly. The surfaces must be free of oil residue.

28   Install the main bearing caps and stiffener.

29   Prior to installation, apply clean engine oil to the threads of the new main bearing cap bolts, wiping off any excess, then install all bolts finger-tight.

30   Tighten the main bearing cap bolts, working from the center out and alternating from side-to-side, to the torque listed in this Chapter's Specifications.

31   Recheck crankshaft endplay with a feeler gauge or a dial indicator. The endplay should be correct if the crankshaft thrust faces aren't worn or damaged and if new bearings have been installed.

32   Rotate the crankshaft a number of times by hand to check for any obvious binding. It should rotate with a running torque of 50 in-lbs or less (without the pistons and connecting rods installed). If the running torque is too high, correct the problem at this time.

33   Install the new rear main oil seal in the rear main seal retainer (see Chapter 2A), but do not install the retainer until the balance shafts have been installed in the back of the block (see Section 12).

11   Engine overhaul - reassembly sequence

1   Before beginning engine reassembly, make sure you have all the necessary new parts, gaskets and seals as well as the following items on hand:

   Common hand tools
   A 1/2-inch drive torque wrench
   New engine oil
   Gasket sealant
   Thread locking compound

2   If you obtained a short block it will be necessary to install the cylinder head, the oil pump and pick-up tube, the water pump, the timing chain and front cover, the oil pan, the camshafts and the valve cover (see Chapter 2A). In order to save time and avoid

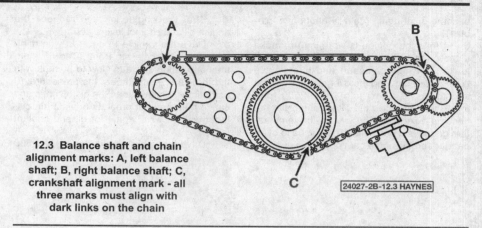

12.3 Balance shaft and chain alignment marks: A, left balance shaft; B, right balance shaft; C, crankshaft alignment mark - all three marks must align with dark links on the chain

problems, the external components must be installed in the following general order:

   Thermostat and housing cover
   Water pump
   Intake and exhaust manifolds
   Fuel injection components
   Emission control components
   Spark plug wires and spark plugs
   Ignition coils
   Oil filter
   Engine mounts and mount brackets
   Clutch and flywheel (manual transaxle)
   Driveplate (automatic transaxle)

12   Balance shafts - removal and installation

Removal

Refer to illustration 12.3

Note: *Balance shafts must be replaced as an assembly, with their retainers and sprockets. Do not disassemble them.*

1   Refer to Chapter 2A for removal of the crankshaft rear oil seal retainer, which is also the cover for the two balance shafts.

2   The balance shafts are driven by a chain, similar to a timing chain, which has a tensioner.

3   Before removing the balance shaft chain or tensioner, the engine must be turned so that three of the five dark links on the balance shaft chain are aligned with the marks on each balance shaft sprocket and the crankshaft sprocket. When aligned properly, the mark on the left balance shaft sprocket will be straight up (12 o'clock), the right sprocket's mark will be at 2:30, and the crankshaft sprocket mark will be at the 4:30 position **(see illustration)**. **Note:** *This alignment occurs only once in 11 rotations of the crankshaft.*

4   Remove the two bolts and the balance shaft chain tensioner.

5   Slip the chain from the crankshaft sprocket first, then the left balance shaft, followed by the right balance shaft.

6   Rotate each balance shaft and ensure that they rotate freely

7   Remove the bolts (one for the left shaft

retainer, two for the right shaft retainer) and withdraw each shaft straight out of the block.

Installation

8   Clean the balance shafts and lubricate them with clean engine oil, then insert them with their balance weights down.

9   Use NEW bolts when tightening the balance shaft retainer plates.

10   Align the timing marks **(see illustration 12.3)** and install the chain so that dark links align with each of the three marks. Put the chain over the left sprocket first, then the right, and finally over the crankshaft sprocket.

11   Depress the small lever on the chain tension and hold it down while collapsing the tensioner shoe, then release the lever. Insert a pin through the hole in the tensioner to retain the shoe in this position.

12   Install the chain tensioner and tighten the bolts to the Specifications in this Chapter. Take out the pin or drill bit used to hold the tensioner in the retracted position.

13   The remainder of installation is the reverse of the removal procedure.

13   Initial start-up and break-in after overhaul

Warning: *Have a fire extinguisher handy when starting the engine for the first time.*

1   Once the engine has been installed in the vehicle, double-check the engine oil and coolant levels.

2   With the spark plugs out of the engine and the ignition and fuel systems disabled (see Section 3), crank the engine until oil pressure registers on the gauge or the light goes out.

3   Install the spark plugs, coils and restore the ignition and fuel system functions.

4   Start the engine. It may take a few moments for the fuel system to build up pressure, but the engine should start without a great deal of effort.

5   After the engine starts, it should be allowed to warm up to normal operating temperature. Do not allow the engine to exceed a fast idle until the hydraulic lifters pump up and

become quiet again (usually about five minutes).

6   While the engine is warming up, make a thorough check for fuel, oil and coolant leaks. If a new camshaft and lifters have been installed during the overhaul, the engine should run at a fast idle (2000-2500 rpm) for 15 minutes after the lifters pump up and become quiet (keep an eye on the temperature gauge and don't allow the engine to overheat) to "break in" the cam and lifters.

7   Shut the engine off and recheck the engine oil and coolant levels.

8   Drive the vehicle to an area with minimum traffic, accelerate from 30 to 50 mph, then allow the vehicle to slow to 30 mph with the throttle closed. Repeat the procedure 10 or 12 times. This will load the piston rings and cause them to seat properly against the cylinder walls. Check again for oil and coolant leaks.

9   Drive the vehicle gently for the first 500 miles (no sustained high speeds) and keep a constant check on the oil level. It is not unusual for an engine to use oil during the break-in period.

10   At approximately 500 to 600 miles, change the oil and filter.

11   For the next few hundred miles, drive the vehicle normally. Do not pamper it or abuse it.

12   After 2000 miles, change the oil and filter again and consider the engine broken in.

Chapter 3
Cooling, heating and air conditioning systems

Contents

Specifications

General

Coolant capacity	
Four-cylinder engine	10.4 quarts
Five-cylinder engine	10.6 quarts
Radiator pressure cap rating	15 psi
Refrigerant type	R-134a
Refrigerant oil type	PAG
Oil capacity (total system)	4.0 oz
Refrigerant capacity...	1.6 pounds

Torque specifications

Ft-lbs (unless otherwise indicated)

Note: *One foot-pound (ft-lb) of torque is equivalent to 12 inch-pounds (in-lbs) of torque. Torque values below approximately 15 ft-lbs are expressed in inch-pounds, since most foot-pound torque wrenches are not accurate at these smaller values.*

Air conditioning compressor mounting bolts..	37
Cooling fan hub nut	41
Fan blade-to-clutch bolts	20
Thermostat housing bolts	89 in-lbs
Water pump attaching bolts..	89 in-lbs
Water pump pulley bolts...	18

1   General information

All vehicles covered by this manual employ a pressurized engine cooling system with thermostatically controlled coolant circulation. Coolant is drawn from the radiator by an impeller-type water pump mounted at the front of the block. The coolant is then circulated through the engine block where it passes around the individual cylinders. After exiting the cylinder block, the coolant then enters the cylinder head where it quenches the combustion chamber area. The coolant flows out of the cylinder head and into the thermostat where, depending on the coolant temperature, it is either blocked until the desired temperature is obtained or allowed to pass through the thermostat into the radiator.

During the coolant flow cycle some coolant is directed into the heater core for passenger compartment heating, and some coolant is directed to the throttle body to allow the throttle body to operate at a consistent temperature.

A wax pellet type thermostat is located in the thermostat housing on the engine. During warm up, the closed thermostat prevents coolant from circulating through the radiator. When the engine reaches normal operating temperature, the thermostat opens and allows hot coolant to travel through the radiator, where it is cooled before returning to the engine.

The cooling system is pressurized by the radiator cap, which contains a blow-off pressure valve and a vacuum atmospheric valve. By maintaining higher atmospheric pressure, it increases the boiling point of the coolant. If the coolant temperature goes above this increased boiling point, the extra pressure in the system forces the cap valve off its seat and allows excess pressure to escape the system.

The coolant reservoir serves as a holding tank that contains coolant which, as the engine cools, is drawn into the radiator, and when hot allows for normal coolant expansion out of the radiator into the coolant reservoir.

The heating system works by directing air through the heater core mounted in the dash and then to the interior of the vehicle by a system of ducts. Rear heating systems are equipped with a separate heater core located at the rear of the vehicle. Temperature is controlled by mixing heated air with fresh air, using a system of doors in the ducts, and a blower motor.

Air conditioning is standard on all models and consists of an evaporator core located under the dash, a condenser in front of the radiator, an accumulator in the engine compartment and a belt-driven compressor mounted at the front of the engine.

2   Antifreeze - general information

Refer to illustration 2.4

Warning: *Do not allow antifreeze to come in contact with your skin or painted surfaces of the vehicle. Rinse off spills immediately with plenty of water. Antifreeze is highly toxic if ingested. Never leave antifreeze lying around in an open container or in puddles on the floor; children and pets are attracted by its sweet smell and may drink it. Check with local authorities about disposing of used antifreeze. Many communities have collection centers that will see that antifreeze is disposed of safely. Never dump used anti-freeze on the ground or pour it into drains.*
Caution: *The manufacturer recommends using only DEX-COOL coolant for these systems. DEX-COOL is a long-lasting coolant designed for up to 100,000 miles or 5 years. Never mix green-colored ethylene glycol antifreeze and orange-colored DEX-COOL silicate-free coolant because doing so will destroy the efficiency of the DEX-COOL.*

The cooling system should be filled with a water/DEX-COOL based antifreeze solution which will prevent freezing down to at least -20-degrees F. It also provides protection against corrosion and increases the coolant boiling point.

The cooling system should be drained, flushed and refilled according to the vehicle maintenance schedule (see Chapter 1). The use of antifreeze solutions for periods of longer than recommended is likely to cause damage and encourage the formation of rust and scale in the system.

Before adding antifreeze, check all hose connections, because antifreeze tends to leak through very minute openings. Engines don't normally consume coolant, so if the level goes down, find the cause and correct it.

The exact mixture of antifreeze to water that you should use depends on the relative weather conditions. The mixture should contain at least 50-percent antifreeze, but should never contain more than 70-percent antifreeze. Consult the mixture ratio chart on the antifreeze container before adding coolant. Hydrometers are available at most auto parts stores to test the coolant **(see illustration)**. Always use antifreeze that meets the vehicle manufacturer's specifications. **Caution:** *Before mixing water with antifreeze, check the antifreeze container carefully. Some manufacturers pre-mix antifreeze to the proper 50/50 ratio, making the addition of water unnecessary.*

3   Thermostat - check and replacement

Note: *The thermostat is part of the thermostat housing and must be replaced as a unit.*

Check

1   Before assuming the thermostat is to blame for a cooling system problem, check the coolant level, drivebelt tension (see Chapter 1) and temperature gauge (or light) operation.
2   If the engine seems to be taking a long time to warm up (based on heater output or temperature gauge operation), the thermostat is probably stuck open. Replace the thermostat with a new one.
3   If the engine runs hot, use your hand to check the temperature of the lower radiator hose. If the hose isn't hot, but the engine is, the thermostat is probably stuck closed, preventing the coolant inside the engine from escaping to the radiator. Replace the thermostat. **Caution:** *Don't drive the vehicle without a thermostat. The computer may stay in open loop and emissions and fuel economy will suffer.*
4   If the lower radiator hose is hot, it means the coolant is flowing and the thermostat is open. Consult the *Troubleshooting* section at the front of this manual for cooling system diagnosis.

Replacement

Refer to illustrations 3.7 and 3.11
Warning: *The engine must be completely cool when this procedure is performed.*
5   Disconnect the cable from the negative terminal of the battery. Drain the cooling system. If the coolant is relatively new or in good condition, save it and reuse it. If it is to

2.4 An inexpensive hydrometer can be used to test the condition of your coolant

3.7 The thermostat housing is located on the left side of the engine, above the air conditioning compressor (one of the two bolts is visible here)

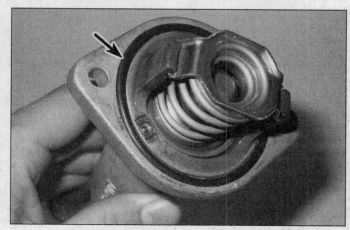

3.11 After the housing is cleaned, or a new thermostat/housing is used, a new O-ring should always be used

be replaced, see Section 2 for cautions about proper handling of used antifreeze.

6   Loosen the left front wheel lug nuts. Raise and support the vehicle on jackstands, then remove the left front wheel and fenderwell liner (see Chapter 11).

7   Follow the lower radiator hose to the engine to locate the thermostat housing. The thermostat housing is located below the alternator at the left-front of the block **(see illustration)**.

8   Loosen the hose clamp, then detach the radiator hose from the thermostat housing. If the hose sticks, grasp it near the end with a pair of adjustable pliers and twist it to break the seal, then pull it off. If the hose is old or deteriorated, cut it off and install a new one.

9   If the outer surface of the fitting that mates with the hose is deteriorated (corroded, pitted, etc.) it may be damaged further by hose removal. If it is, the thermostat housing will have to be replaced.

10   Remove the bolts and detach the thermostat housing. If the housing is stuck, tap it with a soft-face hammer to jar it loose. Be prepared for some coolant to spill as the gasket seal is broken.

11   Clean the mating surfaces on the engine and the thermostat housing. Install a new O-

ring in the groove in the housing **(see illustration)**.

12   Reattach the thermostat housing to the engine and tighten the bolts to the torque listed in this Chapter's Specifications.

13   The remaining steps are the reverse of the removal procedure. Now would be a good time to check and replace the hoses and clamps (see Chapter 1).

14   Refer to Chapter 1 and refill the cooling system, then run the engine and check carefully for leaks.

15   Repeat steps 1 through 4 to be sure the repairs corrected the previous problem(s).

4   Engine cooling fan and clutch - check

Warning: *Keep your hands, tools and clothing away from the fan. To avoid injury or damage DO NOT operate the engine with a damaged fan. Do not attempt to repair fan blades - replace a damaged fan with a new one.*

Check

Warning: *If the fan is damaged in any way, don't attempt to repair it. Replace the fan with a new one.*

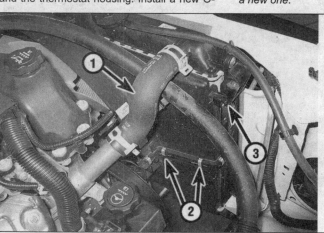

5.4 Remove the upper radiator hose (1), pry off the clips securing the upper and lower shrouds (2 indicates two of the clips), and pull the pin at each side of the upper shroud from its clip (3)

1   The vehicles covered by this manual are equipped with viscous fan clutches.

2   Remove the key from the ignition switch for safety purposes.

3   Begin the check with a visual inspection. With the engine cold, inspect the fan blades for cracks or damage; replace any fan that shows signs of either.

4   Wiggle the fan blade from side-to-side - there should be 1/4-inch or less play in the fan. Replace the clutch if play is excessive.

5   Inspect the clutch for signs of leakage and proper tightness to the water pump. Replace the clutch if leakage is present.

6   Turn the fan blades and note the resistance. There should be less resistance with a cold engine.

7   Drive the vehicle until the engine is warmed up. Shut it off and remove the key.

8   Turn the fan blades and again note the resistance. There should be a noticeable increase in resistance.

9   If the fan clutch fails this check or is locked up solid, replacement is indicated.

5   Engine cooling fan, clutch and shroud - removal and installation

Refer to illustrations 5.4, 5.5 and 5.6

Warning: *The engine must be completely cool when this procedure is performed.*

Note: *A special fan clutch wrench, available at most auto parts stores, is required.*

1   Partially drain the cooling system (see Chapter 1).

2   Remove the upper radiator hose from the radiator; be prepared for coolant spillage.

3   Unclip the air conditioning hoses from the fan shroud.

4   Remove the clips at the left and right junctures of the upper and lower fan shroud section, then pull the upper shroud from the clips at the side brackets **(see illustration)**.

5   Remove the fan clutch hub from the

5.5 A strap wrench can be used to immobilize the water pump pulley while loosening the fan clutch hub

5.6 Fan retaining bolts

water pump by turning it counterclockwise **(see illustration)**.

6   The fan can now be unbolted from the clutch, if necessary. Be sure to tighten the fan-to-clutch bolts to the torque listed in this Chapter's Specifications.

7   Installation is the reverse of removal. Tighten the fan hub nut to the torque listed in this Chapter's Specifications.

8   Check the coolant, adding as necessary to bring it to the appropriate level (see Chapter 1).

6   Radiator - removal and installation

Refer to illustrations 6.5 and 6.8

Warning: *The engine must be completely cool before beginning this procedure.*

Note: *The vehicles covered by this manual use spring-type radiator hose clamps. If you*

decide to reuse them, make sure that the hose is installed on a connection that is clean and dry. Don't try to reuse these clamps on aftermarket hoses. Replace them with conventional worm-drive type clamps.

1   Disconnect the cable from the negative terminal of the battery.

2   Drain the cooling system as described in Chapter 1, then remove the fan shroud, fan and clutch (see section 5)

3   Raise the vehicle and support it securely on jackstands.

4   Remove the lower radiator hose from the radiator.

5   On automatic transmission models, detach the transmission cooler lines from the radiator **(see illustration)**. To disconnect the lines from the radiator, simply unsnap the plastic collar from the quick-connect fitting, then remove the retaining clip and pull out the lines. Plug the ends of the lines to prevent fluid from leaking out after you disconnect them. Have a drip pan ready to catch any

spills. Always be sure to inspect the O-rings on the cooler lines before reinstallation. **Note:** *Do not remove the clips by pulling straight out. Hold one side in with your fingers while using a pick (with a bent tip) to pull the other side out, then rotate the clip off. Install clips the same way, not straight on.*

6   Lower the vehicle.

7   Remove the grille (see Chapter 11).

8   Remove the radiator mount bracket **(see illustration)** and the condenser mounting bolts (see Section 16).

9   Pull the condenser forward (away from the radiator), and remove the radiator.

10   Prior to installation of the radiator, replace any damaged radiator hoses and hose clamps.

11   Radiator installation is the reverse of removal. When installing the radiator, make sure that the radiator seats properly in the lower saddles and that the upper brackets are secure. Install the transmission cooler line retaining clips onto the quick-connect fitting

6.5 Unsnap the plastic collar, then remove the retaining clip from the quick-connect fitting to disconnect the transmission cooler lines (typical)

6.8 Radiator mount bracket

7.2 The weep hole is located on the bottom of the water pump (typical)

7.10 To remove the water pump pulley, prevent it from turning with a pin spanner (or a strap wrench wrapped around the pulley) and unscrew the bolts

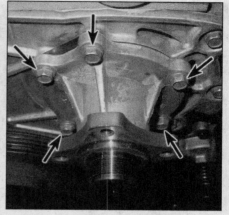

7.11 Water pump mounting bolts

before installing the lines, then snap the cooler lines into place on the quick connect fittings. Be sure to reinstall the plastic collars on the quick connect fittings as they lock the retaining clip in place. **Note:** *If the plastic collars don't easily fit over the retaining clips the quick disconnect fitting is not assembled correctly.*

12   After installation, refill the cooling system (see Chapter 1), then check the automatic transmission fluid level.

7   Water pump - check and replacement

Warning: *Wait until the engine is completely cool before starting this procedure.*

Check

Refer to illustration 7.2

1   Water pump failure can cause overheating and serious damage to the engine. There are three ways to check the operation of the water pump while it is installed on the engine. If any one of the following quick-checks indicates water pump problems, it should be replaced immediately.

2   A seal protects the water pump impeller shaft bearing from contamination by engine coolant. If this seal fails, a weep hole in the water pump snout will leak coolant **(see illustration)** (an inspection mirror can be used to look at the underside of the pump if the hole isn't on top). If the weep hole is leaking, shaft bearing failure will follow. Replace the water pump immediately.

3   The water pump impeller shaft bearing can also prematurely wear out. When the bearing wears out, it emits a high-pitched squealing sound. If such a noise is coming from the water pump during engine operation, the shaft bearing has failed - replace the water pump immediately. **Note:** *Do not confuse belt noise with bearing noise.*

4   To identify excessive bearing wear, remove the drivebelt (see Chapter 1), grasp the water pump pulley and try to force it up-and-down or from side-to-side. If the pulley can be moved either horizontally or vertically, the bearing is nearing the end of its service life. Replace the water pump.

5   It is possible for a water pump to be bad, even if it doesn't howl or leak water. Sometimes the fins on the back of the impeller can corrode away until the pump is no longer effective. The only way to check for this is to remove the pump for examination.

Replacement

Refer to illustrations 7.10 and 7.11

6   Disconnect the cable from the negative terminal of the battery.

7   Drain the coolant (see Chapter 1). Remove the air intake duct and resonator.

8   Remove the radiator shroud and fan/clutch assembly (see Section 5).

9   Remove the drivebelt (see Chapter 1).

10   Remove the water pump pulley **(see illustration).**

11   Unbolt the water pump **(see illustration).** It may be necessary to tap the pump with a soft-face hammer to break the gasket seal. Inspect the pump's impeller blades on the backside for corrosion. If any fins are missing or badly corroded, replace the pump with a new one.

12   Clean the sealing surfaces of all gasket material on both the water pump and block. Wipe the mating surfaces with a rag saturated with lacquer thinner or acetone.

13   Apply a thin layer of RTV sealant to both sides of the new gasket and install the gasket on the water pump.

14   Place the water pump in position and install the bolts finger tight. Use caution to ensure that the gasket doesn't slip out of position. Now tighten the bolts to the torque listed in this Chapter's Specifications.

15   Install the pulley and tighten the bolts to the torque listed in this Chapter's Specifications.

16   The remainder of the installation procedure is the reverse of removal.

17   Add coolant to the specified level (see Chapter 1), start the engine and check for the proper coolant level. Be sure to bleed the cooling system of air as described in Chapter 1. Also check for coolant leaks around the water pump and hoses.

8   Coolant temperature gauge sending unit - check and replacement

1   The coolant temperature indicator system is composed of a temperature gauge or warning light mounted in the dash and a coolant temperature sensor mounted on the engine. This coolant temperature sensor doubles as an information sensor for the fuel and engine control systems (see Chapter 6) and as a sending unit for the temperature gauge.

2   If an overheating indication occurs, check the coolant level in the system and then make sure the wiring between the gauge and the sending unit is secure and all fuses are intact.

3   Check the operation of the coolant temperature sensor (see Chapter 6). If the sensor is defective, replace it by following the procedure in that Chapter. **Note:** *A faulty sensor should set a diagnostic trouble code (DTC) and turn on the CHECK ENGINE light.*

4   If the coolant temperature sensor is good, have the temperature gauge checked by a dealer service department or other properly equipped repair shop. This test will require a scan tool to access the information as it is processed by the Powertrain Control Module (PCM).

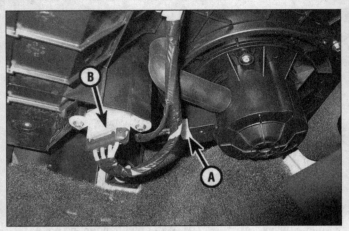

9.4 Backprobe the blower motor connector terminals (A) with a voltmeter. Check the running voltage in each of the fan speed switch positions - B is the blower motor resistor

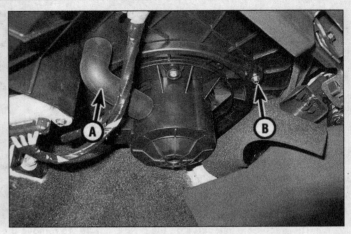

10.4 Blower motor vent tube (A) and one of the mounting screws (B)

9 Blower motor and circuit - check

Refer to illustration 9.4

Warning: *These models have airbags. Always disable the airbag system before working in the vicinity of any airbag system component to avoid the possibility of accidental deployment of the airbag, which could cause personal injury (see Chapter 12).*

1   Check the fuse (marked *climate control fan*) and all connections in the circuit for looseness and corrosion. Make sure the battery is fully charged. **Note:** *The heater/blower relay (marked IGN3/HVAC) and the blower fuse are located in the underhood fuse panel. The blower motor resistor is mounted in the HVAC housing under the right side of the instrument panel, close to the blower motor.*

2   With the transmission in Park, set the parking brake securely and turn the ignition switch to the Run position. It isn't necessary to start the vehicle.

3   Remove the right-side door sill plate and the plastic trim panel at the lower part of the hinge pillar. The panel is retained by clips - pull it straight out from the body. This provides access to the blower motor.

4   Backprobe the blower motor electrical connector with a voltmeter **(see illustration)**.

5   Move the blower switch through each of its positions and note the voltage readings. Changes in voltage indicate that the motor speeds will also vary as the switch is moved to the different positions.

6   If there is voltage present, but the blower motor does not operate, the blower motor is probably faulty. Disconnect the blower motor connector, then hook one side of the blower motor terminals to a chassis ground and the other to a fused source of battery voltage. If the blower doesn't operate, it is faulty.

7   If there was no voltage present at the blower motor, and the motor itself tested OK, follow the blower motor ground wire to the splice pack near the right front of the lower console. Check the ground terminal for con-tinuity to ground against the chassis metal. If no continuity exists, repair the ground circuit as necessary.

8   If the blower still doesn't operate properly, the resistor, control panel or related wiring is probably faulty.

10 Blower motor - removal and installation

Refer to illustration 10.4

Warning: *These models have airbags. Always disable the airbag system before working in the vicinity of any airbag system component to avoid the possibility of accidental deployment of the airbag, which could cause personal injury (see Chapter 12).*

1   Disconnect the negative cable from the battery (see Chapter 1).

2   Remove the door sill plate on the right side of the vehicle and pull out the plastic trim panel at the base of the right hinge pillar.

3   Disconnect the electrical connector from the blower motor.

4   Remove the blower motor screws and cooling tube **(see illustration)**.

5   Remove the blower motor and separate it from the cover.

6   If you're replacing the blower motor with a new one, remove the fan from the blower motor. The fan is pressed onto the blower motor shaft and can be pried off with two screwdrivers.

11 Heater and air conditioning control assembly - removal and installation

Refer to illustration 11.3

Warning: *These models have airbags. Always disable the airbag system before working in the vicinity of any airbag system component to avoid the possibility of accidental deploy-*ment of the airbag, which could cause personal injury (see Chapter 12).*

1   Disconnect the cable from the negative terminal of the battery.

2   Remove the center trim panel from the instrument panel, using a flat-bladed plastic trim tool (see Chapter 11)

3   Remove the control assembly retaining screws, then pull the unit from the dash **(see illustration)**. It can be pulled out just far enough to allow disconnecting the electrical connections and control cables from the control head. Use a small screwdriver to release the clips.

4   To install the control assembly, reverse the removal procedure.

12 Heater core - removal and installation

Refer to illustration 12.3

Warning 1: *These models have airbags. Always disable the airbag system before working in the vicinity of any airbag system component to avoid the possibility of accidental deployment of the airbag, which could*

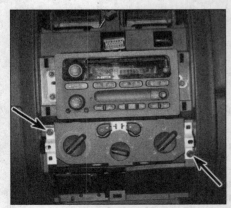

11.3 Remove the screws and pull the control assembly outward

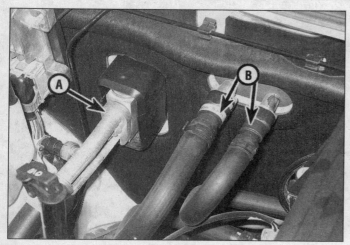

12.3 Remove the nut from the stud and disconnect the evaporator lines (A) at the firewall, then cap the fittings to prevent moisture from entering the system. The heater hoses are disconnected at the quick-connect fittings (B)

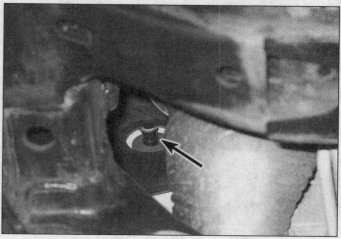

13.1 Check that the evaporator housing drain tube at the firewall is clear of any blockage - the view here is from below the vehicle, looking up at the right side of the firewall

cause personal injury (see Chapter 12).

Warning 2: *The air conditioning system is under high pressure. DO NOT loosen any fittings or remove any components until after the system has been discharged. Air conditioning refrigerant must be properly discharged into an EPA-approved container at a dealership service department or an automotive air conditioning facility. Always wear eye protection when disconnecting air conditioning system fittings.*

Warning 3: *Wait until the engine is completely cool before beginning the procedure.*

Note: *This is a difficult procedure for the home mechanic. There are a variety of fasteners, clips and electrical connectors to deal with, and requires a trained mechanic.*

1   Have the air conditioning system discharged by a dealership service department or an automotive air conditioning facility (see **Warning 2** above).

2   Disconnect the cable at the negative terminal of the battery.

3   Drain the cooling system (see Chapter 1), then remove the heater hoses and air conditioning lines from the fittings at the firewall **(see illustration)**. Be sure to plug the lines line to avoid coolant spillage and contamination of the air conditioning system.

4   Remove the instrument panel assembly (see Chapter 11).

5   Pull back the carpeting and remove the rear floor duct from the floor.

6   Remove the instrument panel carrier (see Chapter 11).

7   Remove the nuts securing the HVAC module to the firewall and withdraw the unit.

8   Remove the screw and clamp securing the heater core pipes and carefully pull out the heater core.

9   Installation is the reverse of removal.

Note: *When reinstalling the heater core, make sure any original insulating/sealing materials are in place around the heater core pipes and around the core.*

10   Refill the cooling system (see Chapter 1). Have the air conditioning system charged by the shop that discharged it.

11   Start the engine and check for proper operation.

---

13   Air conditioning and heating system - check and maintenance

Refer to illustration 13.1

Warning: *The air conditioning system is under high pressure. Do not loosen any hose fittings or remove any components until after the system has been discharged. Air conditioning refrigerant must be properly discharged into an EPA-approved recovery/recycling unit at a dealer service department or an automotive air conditioning repair facility. Always wear eye protection when disconnecting air conditioning system fittings.*

Caution 1: *All models covered by this manual use environmentally-friendly R-134A. Do not introduce any other refrigerant or refrigerant oils not compatible with R-134A refrigerant.*

Caution 2: *When replacing entire components, additional refrigerant oil should be added equal to the amount that is removed with the component being replaced. Be sure to read the can before adding any oil to the system, to make sure it is compatible with the R-134a system.*

1   The following maintenance checks should be performed on a regular basis to ensure that the air conditioning continues to operate at peak efficiency.

a) *Inspect the condition of the drivebelt. If it is worn or deteriorated, replace it (see Chapter 1).*

b) *Check the drivebelt tension (see Chapter 1).*

c) *Inspect the system hoses. Look for cracks, bubbles, hardening and deterioration. Inspect the hoses and all fittings*

for oil bubbles or seepage. If there is any evidence of wear, damage or leakage, replace the hose(s).

d) *Inspect the condenser fins for leaves, bugs and any other foreign material that may have embedded itself in the fins. Use a fin comb or compressed air to remove debris from the condenser.*

e) *Make sure the system has the correct refrigerant charge.*

f) *If you hear water sloshing around in the dash area or have water dripping on the carpet, check the evaporator housing drain tube* **(see illustration)** *and insert a piece of wire into the opening to check for blockage.*

2   It's a good idea to operate the system for about ten minutes at least once a month. This is particularly important during the winter months because long term non-use can cause hardening, and subsequent failure, of the seals. Note that using the Defrost function operates the compressor.

3   If the air conditioning system is not working properly, proceed to Step 6 and perform the general checks outlined below.

4   Because of the complexity of the air conditioning system and the special equipment necessary to service it, in-depth troubleshooting and repairs beyond checking the refrigerant charge and the compressor clutch operation are not included in this manual. However, simple checks and component replacement procedures are provided in this Chapter. For more complete information on the air conditioning system, refer to the *Haynes Automotive Heating and Air Conditioning Manual.*

5   The most common cause of poor cooling is simply a low system refrigerant charge. If a noticeable drop in system cooling ability occurs, one of the following quick checks will help you determine whether the refrigerant level is low. Should the system lose its cooling ability, the following procedure will help you pinpoint the cause.

13.18 A basic charging kit for 134a systems is available at most auto parts stores - it must say 134a (not R-12) and so must the can of refrigerant

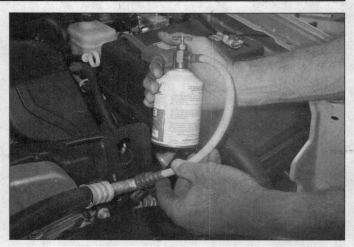

13.21 Attach the refrigerant kit to the low-side charging port - the cap may be marked with an "L"

Check

6   Warm the engine up to normal operating temperature.

7   Place the air conditioning temperature selector at the coldest setting and put the blower at the highest setting. Open the doors (to make sure the air conditioning system doesn't cycle off as soon as it cools the passenger compartment).

8   After the system reaches operating temperature, feel the two pipes connected to the evaporator at the firewall.

9   The pipe leading from the accumulator to the evaporator should be cold, and the evaporator outlet line (the tubing that leads back to the compressor) should be slightly warmer (about 3 to 10 degrees F warmer). If the evaporator outlet is considerably warmer than the inlet, or if the evaporator inlet isn't cold, the system needs a charge. Insert a thermometer in the center air distribution duct while operating the air conditioning system at its maximum setting - the temperature of the output air should be 35 to 40 degrees F below the ambient air temperature (down to approximately 40 degrees F). If the ambient (outside) air temperature is very high, say 110 degrees F, the duct air temperature may be as high as 60 degrees F, but generally the air conditioning is 35 to 40 degrees F cooler than the ambient air.

10   If the air isn't as cold as it used to be, the system probably needs a charge.

11   If the air is warm and the system doesn't seem to be operating properly check the operation of the compressor clutch.

12   Have an assistant switch the air conditioning On while you observe the front of the compressor. The clutch will make an audible click and the center of the clutch should rotate. If it doesn't, shut the engine off and disconnect the air conditioning system low pressure switch **(see illustration 13.22)**. Bridge the terminals of the connector with a jumper wire and turn the air conditioning On again. If it works now, the system pressure is too high or

too low. Have your system tested by a dealer service department or air conditioning shop.

13   If the clutch still didn't operate, check the appropriate fuses. Inspect the fuses in the interior fuse panel.

14   Remove the compressor clutch (A/C) relay from the engine compartment relay panel and test it (see Chapter 12). With the relay out and the ignition On, check for battery power at two of the relay terminals (refer to the wiring diagrams for wire color designations to determine which terminals to check). There should be battery power with the key On, at the terminals for the relay control and power circuits.

15   Using a jumper wire, connect the terminals in the relay box from the relay power circuit to the terminal that leads to the compressor clutch (refer to the wiring diagrams for wire color designations to determine which terminals to connect). Listen for the clutch to click as you make the connection. If the clutch doesn't respond, disconnect the clutch connector at the compressor and check for battery voltage at the compressor clutch connector. Check for continuity to ground on the black wire terminal of the compressor clutch connector. If power and ground are available and the clutch doesn't operate when connected, the compressor clutch is defective.

16   If the compressor clutch, relay and related circuits are good and the system is fully charged with refrigerant and the compressor does not operate under normal conditions, have the PCM and related circuits checked by a dealer service department or other properly equipped repair facility.

17   Further inspection or testing of the system is beyond the scope of the home mechanic and should be left to a professional.

Adding refrigerant

Refer to illustrations 13.18, 13.21 and 13.22

Caution: *Make sure any refrigerant, refrigerant oil or replacement component your purchase is designated as compatible with envi-*

ronmentally friendly R-134a systems.

18   Purchase an R-134a automotive charging kit at an auto parts store **(see illustration)**. A charging kit includes a can of refrigerant, a tap valve and a short section of hose that can be attached between the tap valve and the system low side service valve. **Warning:** *Never add more than one can of refrigerant to the system - you could overcharge the system.*

19   Hook up the charging kit by following the manufacturer's instructions. **Warning:** *DO NOT hook the charging kit hose to the system high side! The fittings on the charging kit are designed to fit only on the low side of the system.*

20   Back off the valve handle on the charging kit and screw the kit onto the refrigerant can, making sure first that the O-ring or rubber seal inside the threaded portion of the kit is in place. **Warning:** *Wear protective eyewear when dealing with pressurized refrigerant cans.*

21   Remove the dust cap from the low-side charging port and attach the quick-connect fitting on the kit hose **(see illustration)**.

22   Warm up the engine and turn on the air conditioning. Keep the charging kit hose away from the fan and other moving parts. **Note 1:** *The charging process requires the compressor to be running. If the clutch cycles off, you can put the air conditioning switch on High and leave the car doors open to keep the clutch on and compressor working.* **Note 2:** *The compressor can be kept on during the charging by removing the connector from the low pressure switch and bridging it with a paper clip or jumper wire during the procedure* **(see illustration)**.

23   Turn the valve handle on the kit until the stem pierces the can, then back the handle out to release the refrigerant. You should be able to hear the rush of gas. Add refrigerant to the low side of the system, keeping the can upright at all times, but shaking it occasionally. Allow stabilization time between each

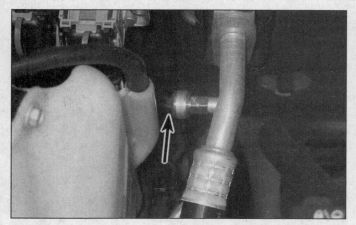

13.22 The air conditioning low pressure switch is located on a tube at the firewall - if the compressor will not stay engaged, disconnect the connector and bridge the terminals (on the harness side) with a jumper wire during the charging procedure

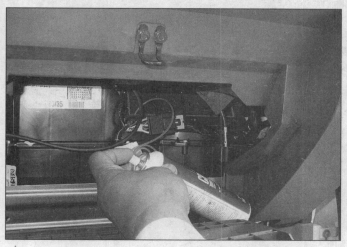

13.32 Spray the disinfectant at the evaporator core

addition. **Note:** *The charging process will go faster if you wrap the can with a hot-water-soaked shop rag to keep the can from freezing up.*

24 If you have an accurate thermometer, you can place it in the center air conditioning duct inside the vehicle and keep track of the output air temperature. A charged system that is working properly should cool down to approximately 40-degrees F. If the ambient (outside) air temperature is very high, say 110 degrees F, the duct air temperature may be as high as 60 degrees F, but generally the air conditioning is 30-40 degrees F cooler than the ambient air.

25 When the can is empty, turn the valve handle to the closed position and release the connection from the low-side port. Replace the dust cap.

26 Remove the charging kit from the can and store the kit for future use with the piercing valve in the UP position, to prevent inadvertently piercing the can on the next use.

Heating systems

27 If the carpet under the heater core is damp, or if antifreeze vapor or steam is coming through the vents, the heater core is leaking. Remove it (see Section 12) and install a new unit (most radiator shops will not repair a leaking heater core).

28 If the air coming out of the heater vents isn't hot, the problem could stem from any of the following causes:

a) *The thermostat is stuck open, preventing the engine coolant from warming up enough to carry heat to the heater core. Replace the thermostat (see Section 3).*

b) *There is a blockage in the system, preventing the flow of coolant through the heater core. Feel both heater hoses at the firewall. They should be hot. If one of them is cold, there is an obstruction in one of the hoses or in the heater core, or the heater control valve is shut. Detach the hoses and back flush the heater core*

with a water hose. If the heater core is clear but circulation is impeded, remove the two hoses and flush them out with a water hose.

c) *If flushing fails to remove the blockage from the heater core, the core must be replaced (see Section 12).*

Eliminating air conditioning odors

Refer to illustration 13.32

29 Unpleasant odors that often develop in air conditioning systems are caused by the growth of a fungus, usually on the surface of the evaporator core. The warm, humid environment there is a perfect breeding ground for mildew to develop.

30 The evaporator core on most vehicles is difficult to access, and dealerships have a lengthy, expensive process for eliminating the fungus by opening up the evaporator case and using a powerful disinfectant and rinse on the core until the fungus is gone. You can service your own system at home, but it takes something much stronger than basic household germ-killers or deodorizers.

31 Aerosol disinfectants for automotive air conditioning systems are available in most auto parts stores, but remember when shopping for them that the most effective treatments are also the most expensive. The basic procedure for using these sprays is to start by running the system in the RECIRC mode for ten minutes with the blower on its highest speed. Use the highest heat mode to dry out the system and keep the compressor from engaging by disconnecting the wiring connector at the compressor (see Section 15).

32 The disinfectant can usually comes with a long spray hose. Remove the passenger's side lower dash trim panel, then remove the small access cover from the HVAC housing. Point the nozzle inside the hole and to the left towards the evaporator core, and spray according to the manufacturer's recommendations **(see illustration)**. Try to cover the

whole surface of the evaporator core, by aiming the spray up, down and sideways. Follow the manufacturer's recommendations for the length of spray and waiting time between applications.

33 Once the evaporator has been cleaned, the best way to prevent the mildew from coming back again is to make sure your evaporator housing drain tube is clear **(see illustration 13.1)**.

Automatic heating and air conditioning systems

34 Some models are equipped with an optional automatic climate control system. This system has its own computer that receives inputs from various sensors in the heating and air conditioning system. This computer, like the PCM, has self-diagnostic capabilities to help pinpoint problems or faults within the system. Vehicles equipped with automatic heating and air conditioning systems are very complex and considered beyond the scope of the home mechanic. Vehicles equipped with automatic heating and air conditioning systems should be taken to dealer service department or other qualified facility for repair.

14 Air conditioning receiver/drier - removal and installation

Removal

Refer to illustration 14.2

Warning: *The air conditioning system is under high pressure. DO NOT loosen any fittings or remove any components until after the system has been discharged. Air conditioning refrigerant must be properly discharged into an EPA-approved container at a dealership service department or an automotive air conditioning repair facility. Always wear eye protection when disconnecting air conditioning system fittings.*

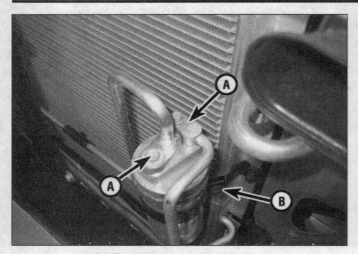

14.2 Receiver/drier mounting details

A   *Refrigerant line fitting bolts*
B   *Mounting bracket bolt*

15.8 Access the compressor mounting bolts from below or through the fenderwell (with the liner removed) - two lower mounting bolts shown

1   Have the air conditioning system discharged (see **Warning** above). Disconnect the cable from the negative terminal of the battery. Refer to Chapter 11 and remove the radiator grille.

2   Disconnect the refrigerant inlet and outlet lines **(see illustration)**. Remove the bolts and remove the fittings from the receiver/drier. Cap or plug the open lines immediately to prevent the entry of dirt or moisture.

3   Remove the clamp bolt on the mounting bracket and remove the receiver/drier assembly up and out of the engine compartment.

Installation

4   If you are replacing the receiver/drier with a new one, add one ounce of fresh refrigerant oil to the new unit (oil must be R-134a compatible).

5   Place the new accumulator/drier into position in the bracket, then position the accumulator and bracket on the mounting stud.

6   Install the inlet and outlet lines, using clean refrigerant oil on the new O-rings. Tighten the mounting bolt securely.

7   Install the pressure cycling switch and reattach the connector.

8   Connect the cable to the negative terminal of the battery.

9   Have the system evacuated, recharged and leak tested by the shop that discharged it.

15 Air conditioning compressor - removal and installation

Removal

Refer to illustration 15.8
Warning: *The air conditioning system is under high pressure. DO NOT loosen any fittings or remove any components until after the system has been discharged. Air conditioning refrigerant must be properly discharged into*

an EPA-approved container at a dealership service department or an automotive air conditioning repair facility. Always wear eye protection when disconnecting air conditioning system fittings.
Note: *The receiver/drier (see Section 14) and the expansion valve (orifice tube) (see Section 18) should be replaced whenever the compressor is replaced.*

1   Have the air conditioning system discharged (see **Warning** above).

2   Disconnect the cable from the negative terminal of the battery.

3   Clean the compressor thoroughly around the refrigerant line fittings.

4   Remove the drivebelt (see Chapter 1).

5   Remove the alternator (see Chapter 5).

6   Disconnect the electrical connector(s) from the air conditioning compressor.

7   Disconnect the suction and discharge blocks from the compressor. Both lines are mounted to the compressor with bolts. Plug the open fittings to prevent the entry of dirt and moisture, and discard the seals between the blocks and compressor.

8   Remove the compressor mounting bolts, then remove the compressor **(see illustration)**.

Installation

9   If a new compressor is being installed, pour the oil from the old compressor into a graduated container and add that exact amount of new refrigerant oil to the new compressor. Also follow any directions included with the new compressor. **Note:** *Some replacement compressors come with refrigerant oil in them. Follow the directions with the compressor regarding the draining of excess oil prior to installation.* **Caution:** *The oil used must be labeled as compatible with R-134a refrigerant systems.*

10   Installation is the reverse of disassembly. When installing the line fitting blocks to the compressor, use new seals lubricated with clean refrigerant oil, and tighten the bolts to

the torque listed in this Chapter's Specifications.

11   Reconnect the cable to the negative terminal of the battery.

12   Have the system evacuated, recharged and leak tested by the shop that discharged it.

16 Air conditioning condenser - removal and installation

Refer to illustration 16.6
Warning: *The air conditioning system is under high pressure. DO NOT loosen any fittings or remove any components until after the system has been discharged. Air conditioning refrigerant must be properly discharged into an EPA-approved container at a dealership service department or an automotive air conditioning repair facility. Always wear eye protection when disconnecting air conditioning system fittings.*
Note: *The receiver/drier should be replaced if the condenser was damaged, causing the system to be open for some time (see Section 14).*

1   Have the air conditioning system discharged (if equipped) at a dealer service department or service station. Drain the engine coolant (see Chapter 1).

2   Disconnect the cable from the negative terminal of the battery.

3   Disconnect the refrigerant lines from the condenser. Plug the open ends of the condenser and the disconnected refrigerant lines to prevent entry of dirt or moisture.

4   Remove the radiator grille (see Chapter 11) and the radiator (see Section 6).

5   Remove the receiver/drier (Section 14).

6   The condenser is mounted to the radiator. Remove the radiator/condenser assembly as a unit, then remove the bolts **(see illustration)** securing the condenser to the radiator.

7   Inspect the rubber insulator pads (on the

16.6 Location of the condenser mounting bolts

lower crossmember) on which the radiator sits. Replace them if they're dried or cracked.

8   If the original condenser will be reinstalled, store it with the line fittings on top to prevent oil from draining out. If a new condenser is being installed, pour one ounce of R-134a-compatible refrigerant oil into it prior to installation.

9   Reinstall the components in the reverse order of removal. Be sure the rubber pads are in place under the condenser.

10   Refill the cooling system (see Chapter 1).

11   Have the system evacuated, recharged and leak tested by the shop that discharged it.

17   Evaporator core - replacement

Warning 1: *Wait until the engine is completely cool before beginning the procedure.*
Warning 2: *The air conditioning system is*

under high pressure. DO NOT loosen any fittings or remove any components until after the system has been discharged. Air conditioning refrigerant must be properly discharged into an EPA-approved container at a dealership service department or an automotive air conditioning repair facility. Always wear eye protection when disconnecting air conditioning system fittings.

1   Have the air conditioning system discharged (see **Warning** above).

2   Drain the cooling system (see Chapter 1). Remove the HVAC module assembly (see Section 12).

3   Remove the screws securing the HVAC module halves.

4   Remove the mounting screws for the evaporator temperature sensor control module and set the module aside.

5   Separate the housing halves and remove the evaporator core. Use caution not to damage the seal.

6   If a new evaporator core is used, add 2

oz. of refrigerant oil to it.

7   The remaining installation is the reverse of removal.

8   Refill the cooling system (see Chapter 1).

9   Have the system evacuated, recharged and leak tested by the shop that discharged it.

18   Air conditioning expansion valve - removal and installation

Warning 1: *The air conditioning system is under high pressure. DO NOT loosen any fittings or remove any components until after the system has been discharged. Air conditioning refrigerant must be properly discharged into an EPA-approved container at a dealership service department or an automotive air conditioning repair facility. Always wear eye protection when disconnecting air conditioning system fittings.*
Warning 2: *The engine must be completely cool before beginning this procedure.*

1   Have the air conditioning system discharged (see **Warning** above).

2   Remove the two refrigerant lines from the block fitting at the firewall **(see illustration 12.3)**.

3   The expansion valve is actually part of the metal block the refrigerant lines attach to at the firewall. Remove the two bolts securing this block to the firewall and remove the block/expansion valve.

4   Installation is the reverse of removal. The expansion valve and block must be replaced as a unit. **Caution:** *Always use a new O-ring when installing the expansion (orifice) tube.*

5   Reinstall the refrigerant lines (using new seals) and tighten the nut securely, then have the system evacuated, recharged and leak-tested by the shop that discharged it.

Notes

Chapter 4
Fuel and exhaust systems

Contents

Specifications

General
Fuel pressure (key On, engine Off) .... 50 to 57 psi
Fuel injector resistance .... 11 to 14 ohms

Torque specifications   Ft-lbs (unless otherwise indicated)
Note: *One foot-pound (ft-lb) of torque is equivalent to 12 inch-pounds (in-lbs) of torque. Torque values below approximately 15 ft-lbs are expressed in inch-pounds, since most foot-pound torque wrenches are not accurate at these smaller values.*

Fuel pressure regulator screw (2004 and 2005 models) .... 71 in-lbs
Fuel rail mounting bolts .... 89 in-lbs
Fuel tank mounting strap bolts 24
Throttle body mounting bolts
  2004 through 2006 .... 80 in-lbs
  2007 and later .... 89 in-lbs

1 General information

Refer to illustration 1.1
Warning: *Gasoline is extremely flammable, so take extra precautions when you work on any part of the fuel system. Don't smoke or allow open flames or bare light bulbs near the work area, and don't work in a garage where a gas-type appliance (such as a water heater or a clothes dryer) is present. Since gasoline is carcinogenic, wear fuel-resistant gloves when there's a possibility of being exposed to fuel, and, if you spill any fuel on your skin, rinse it off immediately with soap and water. Mop*

up any spills immediately and do not store fuel-soaked rags where they could ignite. The fuel system is under constant pressure, so, if any fuel lines are to be disconnected, the fuel pressure in the system must be relieved first. When you perform any kind of work on the fuel system, wear safety glasses and have a Class B type fire extinguisher on hand.

All models covered by this manual are equipped with a Sequential Multi Port Fuel Injection (SFI) system **(see illustration)**. This system uses timed impulses to sequentially inject the fuel directly into the intake ports of each cylinder. The injectors are controlled by the Powertrain Control Module (PCM). The

PCM monitors various engine parameters and delivers the exact amount of fuel, in the correct sequence, into the intake ports.

All models are equipped with an electric fuel pump, mounted in the fuel tank. It is necessary to remove the fuel tank for access to the fuel pump. The fuel level sending unit is an integral component of the fuel pump module and it must be removed from the fuel tank in the same manner.

The 2004 and 2005 models have a conventional feed-and-return fuel system, in which fuel is delivered to the fuel rail at the engine under high pressure and the fuel pressure regulator is mounted at the fuel rail, excess

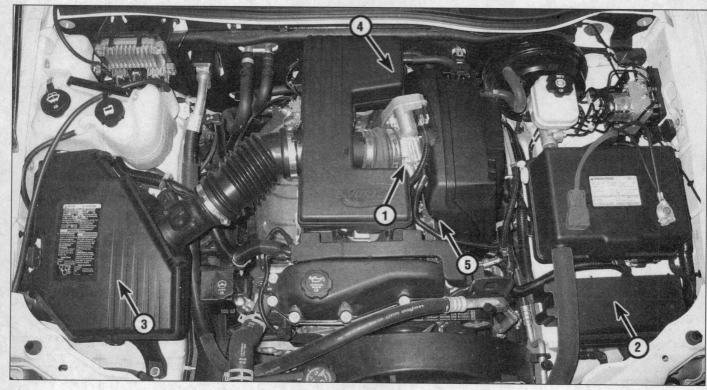

1.1 Typical fuel system components

1 Throttle body	3 Air filter housing	5 Fuel rail and injectors (not visible)
2 Fuel pump relay (inside underhood electrical center)	4 Air intake duct and resonator	

fuel is routed back to the fuel tank through a return line. On 2006 models, the system is "returnless," having the fuel pressure regulator mounted in the fuel pump module inside the tank, so there is no return fuel line. Not having heated fuel (from a long return line under the vehicle) return to the tank reduces evaporative emissions.

The exhaust system consists of an exhaust manifold, a catalytic converter, exhaust pipes and a muffler. Each of these components is replaceable. For further information regarding the catalytic converter, refer to Chapter 6.

2   Fuel pressure relief procedure

Warning: See the **Warning** in Section 1.
Note: After the fuel pressure has been relieved, it's a good idea to lay a shop towel over any fuel connection to be disassembled, to absorb the residual fuel that may leak out when servicing the fuel system.

1   Before servicing any fuel system component, you must relieve the fuel pressure to minimize the risk of fire or personal injury.
2   Remove the fuel filler cap - this will relieve any pressure built up in the tank.

3   Remove the fuel pump relay located in the underhood fuse box **(see illustration 3.3)**.
4   Start the engine and allow it to stall, then continue to crank the engine an additional 5 to 10 seconds.
5   Disconnect the negative battery cable from the battery.
6   Place shop towels around the fuel fitting to be disconnected to absorb any residual fuel that may spill out.

3   Fuel pump/fuel pressure - check

Warning: See the **Warning** in Section 1.

Preliminary check

Refer to illustration 3.3
1   If you suspect insufficient fuel delivery, first inspect all fuel lines to ensure that the problem is not simply a leak in a line. Be certain there is adequate fuel in the fuel tank before proceeding.
2   Set the parking brake and have an assistant turn the ignition switch to the ON position while you listen to the fuel pump (inside the fuel tank). You should hear a whirring sound,

lasting for approximately two seconds, indicating the fuel pump is operating. If the fuel pump is operating, proceed to the pressure check.
3   If there is no sound, turn the ignition key Off and remove the cover from the underhood electrical center. Check the fuse (#13, Fuel PMP) and the fuel pump relay **(see illustration)** (you can swap another same type relay in the fuse box with the fuel pump relay). If the fuse and relay are good, check the fuel pump relay control circuit from the electrical center to the PCM. If the circuit is good, have the PCM diagnosed by a dealer service department or other qualified repair shop.
4   If the pump does not run, disconnect the electrical connector from the fuel pump module at the fuel tank (see Section 5). Using a test light or voltmeter, check for power at the gray wire terminal of the harness connector. Using a continuity tester or ohmmeter, check for continuity to a good chassis ground at the black wire terminal. If power is not indicated on the gray wire terminal or the ground circuit is open, repair the wiring harness.
5   If power is present at the connector, the ground circuit is good and the fuel pump does not operate when connected, replace the fuel pump (see Section 7).

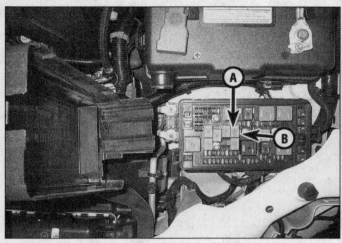

3.3 Fuel pump relay (A) and 15A Fuel PMP fuse (B) locations (refer to the diagram under the electrical center cover)

3.6 Fuel pressure test port location

Pressure check

Refer to illustration 3.6

Note: *In order to perform the fuel pressure test, you will need a fuel pressure gauge capable of measuring high fuel pressure. The fuel gauge must be equipped with the proper fitting required to attach it to the test port. To test the fuel pressure regulator on 2004 and 2005 models, a fuel shut off valve must be installed in the fuel return line with the necessary adapters.* (see illustration).

6   Relieve the fuel pressure (see Section 2). Remove the cap from the fuel pressure test port and attach a fuel pressure gauge **(see illustration)**.

7   Turn the ignition key On; the fuel pump should run for approximately two seconds then shut off. Note the pressure indicated on the gauge and compare your reading with the pressure listed in this Chapter's Specifications. Cycle the ignition key On and Off several times, if necessary, to obtain the highest reading.

2004 and 2005 models

8   If the fuel pressure is lower than specified, turn the ignition key Off and relieve the fuel system pressure (see Section 2). Install a fuel shut-off valve in the fuel return line and close the valve. **Caution 1:** *Do not pinch the flexible fuel line shut or damage to the fuel line may occur. Turn the ignition key On and note the fuel pressure.* **Caution 2:** *Do not allow the fuel pressure to rise above 75 psi or damage to the fuel system may occur.* If the fuel pressure is now above the specified pressure, replace the fuel pressure regulator (see Section 13). If the fuel pressure is lower than specified, check the fuel lines and the fuel filter for restrictions. If no restriction is found, remove the fuel pump module (see Section 7) and check the fuel strainer for restrictions, check the fuel flex pipe for leaks and check the fuel pump wiring for high resistance. If no problems are found, replace the fuel pump.

9   If the fuel pressure recorded in Step 7 is higher than specified, check the fuel return line for restrictions. If no restrictions are found, replace the fuel pressure regulator (see Section 13).

10   If the fuel pressure is within specifications, start the engine. With the engine running, the fuel pressure should be 3 to 10 psi below the pressure recorded in Step 7. If it isn't, remove the vacuum hose from the fuel pressure regulator and verify there is 12 to 14 in-Hg of vacuum present at the hose. If vacuum is not present at the hose, check the hose for a restriction or a broken hose. If vacuum is present, reconnect the hose to the fuel pressure regulator. If the fuel pressure regulator does not decrease the fuel pressure with vacuum applied, replace the fuel pressure regulator.

2006 and later models

11   Start the engine and check the pressure on the gauge, comparing your reading with the pressure listed in this Chapter's Specifications.

12   If the fuel pressure is not within specifications, check the following:

a) *If the pressure is lower than specified, check for a restriction in the fuel system (this includes the inlet strainer and the fuel filter at the fuel pump module). If no restrictions are found, replace the fuel pump module (see Section 7).*

b) *If the fuel pressure is higher than specified, replace the fuel pump module (see Section 7).*

All models

13   Turn the engine off and monitor the fuel pressure for five minutes. The fuel pressure should not drop more than 5 psi within five minutes. If it does, there is a leak in the fuel line, a fuel injector is leaking, the pressure regulator or the fuel pump module check valve is defective. To check for an internal leak at the pressure regulator on 2004 and 2005 models, simply disconnect the vacuum line and check for the presence of fuel; the line may be wet or fuel may run out of it.

14   Relieve the fuel pressure before removing the gauge (see Section 2).

4   Fuel lines and fittings - repair and replacement

Refer to illustrations 4.11a, 4.11b, 4.11c and 4.11d

Warning: *See the* **Warning** *in Section 1.*

1   Always relieve the fuel pressure before servicing fuel lines or fittings (see Section 2).

2   Metal fuel supply and vapor lines extend from the fuel tank to the engine compartment. The lines are secured to the underbody or frame with plastic retainers. Flexible hose connects the metal lines to the fuel tank, fuel filter and fuel rail. Fuel lines must be occasionally inspected for leaks or damage.

3   In the event of any fuel line damage, metal lines may be repaired with steel tubing of the same diameter, provided the correct fittings are used. Flexible lines, on the other hand, must be replaced with factory replacement parts; others may fail from the high pressures of this system. Never repair a damaged section of steel line with rubber hose and hose clamps.

4   If evidence of contamination is found in the system or fuel filter during disassembly, the line should be disconnected and blown out. Check the fuel strainer on the fuel pump module for damage and deterioration.

5   Don't route fuel line or hose within four inches of any part of the exhaust system or within ten inches of the catalytic converter. Fuel line must never be allowed to chafe against the engine, body or frame. A minimum of 1/4-inch clearance must be maintained around a fuel line.

6   When replacing a fuel line, remove all

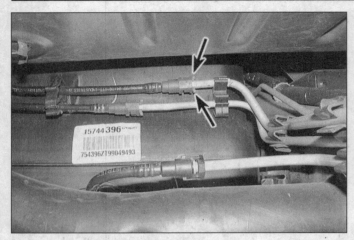

4.11a To disconnect a plastic collar two-tab type fitting, squeeze the two tabs together and pull the lines apart

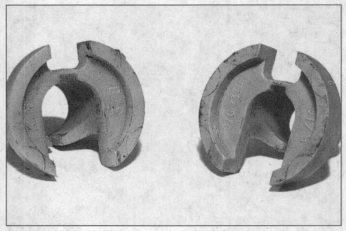

4.11b A special tool (available at most auto parts stores) is required to disconnect the metal collar type fitting

fasteners attaching the fuel line to the vehicle body.

7   Because fuel lines used on fuel-injected vehicles are under high pressure, they require special consideration.

Steel tubing

8   If replacement of a steel fuel line or emission line is called for, use genuine replacement parts or equivalent only.

9   Never use copper or aluminum tubing to replace steel tubing. These materials cannot withstand normal vehicle vibration.

10   Some fuel lines have threaded fittings with O-rings. Any time the fittings are loosened to service or replace components:

  a) Use a flare-nut wrench on the fitting nut and a backup wrench on the stationary portion of the fitting while loosening and tightening the fittings.

  b) Metal quick disconnect fittings require the use of a special tool GM#J37088-A or equivalent (available at most auto parts stores).

  c) Check all O-rings for cuts, cracks and deterioration. Replace any that appear hardened, worn or damaged.

  d) If the lines are replaced, always use original equipment parts, or parts that meet the original equipment standards.

Flexible hose

11   There are various methods of disconnecting the fittings, depending upon the type of quick-connect fitting installed on the fuel line **(see illustrations)**. Clean any debris from around the fitting. Disconnect the fitting and carefully remove the fuel line from the vehicle. **Caution:** The quick-connect fittings are not serviced separately. Do not attempt to repair these types of fuel lines in the event the fitting or line becomes damaged. Replace the entire fuel line as an assembly.

12   Installation is the reverse of removal with the following additions:

  a) Clean the quick-connect fittings with a lint-free cloth and apply clean engine oil the fittings.

  b) After connecting a quick-connect fitting, check the integrity of the connection by attempting to pull the lines apart.

  c) Use new O-rings at the threaded fittings (if equipped).

  d) Cycle the ignition key On and Off several times and check for leaks at the fitting, before starting the engine.

5   Fuel tank - removal and installation

Refer to illustrations 5.6 and 5.10

Warning: *See the* **Warning** *in Section 1.*
Note: *If necessary, clean the fuel tank and areas surrounding the fuel lines and hoses to prevent contaminating the fuel system.*

1   Remove the fuel tank filler cap to relieve fuel tank pressure.

2   Relieve the fuel system pressure (see Section 2).

3   Disconnect the cable from the negative battery terminal.

4.11c To disconnect a metal collar type fitting, remove the safety tether from the fitting . . .

4.11d . . . place the tool over the fuel line, insert it squarely into the fitting and pull the lines apart (the tool is not required to connect the lines)

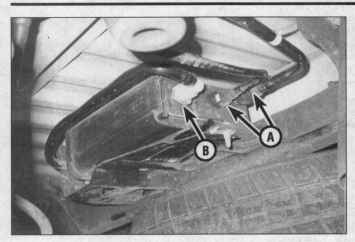

5.6 Evaporative emissions vapor canister lines (A)
and EVAP vent valve (B)

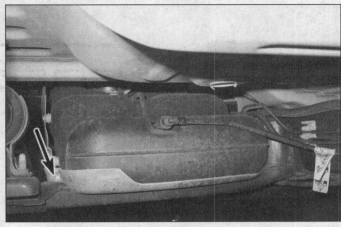

5.10 Remove the fuel tank strap bolts - front strap bolt shown

4   Using a siphoning kit (available at most auto parts stores), siphon the fuel into an approved gasoline container. **Warning:** *Do not start the siphoning action by mouth!*
5   Raise the vehicle and support it securely on jackstands. Refer to Chapter 11 and remove the left rear fenderwell liner.
6   Disconnect the fuel supply line (and return line on 2004 and 2005 models). On all models, disconnect the EVAP vapor lines from the vapor canister **(see illustration)**. **Note:** *See Section 4 for information on quick-connect fitting disconnection.*
7   Remove the fuel filler hose from the tank.
8   Disconnect the electrical connectors from the tank pressure sensor, fuel pump module and the EVAP vent valve.
9   Position a transmission jack under the fuel tank and support the tank.
10   There is one tank strap at the front that is over the tank, and one strap at the rear that goes under the tank. Unscrew the fuel tank strap bolts and remove the straps **(see illustration)**. **Caution:** *Do not bend the fuel tank straps.*

11   Lower the jack and remove the tank from the vehicle. An assistant would be helpful while doing this.
12   Installation is the reverse of removal.

6   Fuel tank cleaning and repair - general information

1   The fuel tanks installed in the vehicles covered by this manual are not repairable. If the fuel tank becomes damaged, it must be replaced.
2   Cleaning the fuel tank (due to fuel contamination) should be performed by a professional with the proper training to carry out this critical and potentially dangerous work. Even after cleaning and flushing, explosive fumes may remain inside the fuel tank.
3   If the fuel tank is removed from the vehicle, it should not be placed in an area where sparks or open flames could ignite the fumes coming out of the tank. Be especially careful inside a garage where a gas-type appliance is located.

7   Fuel pump module - removal and installation

Refer to illustrations 7.5 and 7.6
Warning: *See the* **Warning** *in Section 1.*
1   Relieve the fuel system pressure (see Section 2).
2   Disconnect the cable from the negative battery terminal.
3   Remove the fuel tank from the vehicle (see Section 5).
4   Disconnect the fuel lines and EVAP line from the fuel pump module.
5   Rotate the fuel pump module retaining ring counterclockwise until it's loose **(see illustration)**. A special tool (J45722) is useful for this operation. **Note:** *Some module retaining rings may be marked "Do Not Reuse," but the manufacturer says that the rings may be reused as long as they are not corroded, bent or otherwise damaged.*
6   Remove the fuel pump module from the tank **(see illustration)**. Angle the assembly slightly to avoid damaging the fuel level sending unit float. **Warning:** *Some fuel may remain*

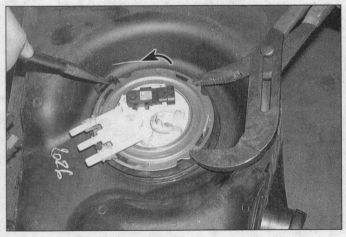

7.5 Release the locking tab and loosen the fuel pump module retaining ring by rotating it counterclockwise

7.6 Carefully remove the fuel pump module from the tank and drain the fuel from the reservoir

8.2 Fuel pump module terminal identification (module side)

1   *Ground*
2   *Fuel level sending unit signal*
3   *Low reference voltage*
4   *Fuel pump 12-volt supply (from fuel pump relay)*

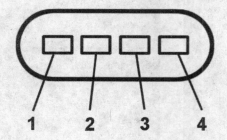

24027-4-8.2 HAYNES

in the module reservoir and spill as the module is removed. Have several shop towels ready and a drain pan nearby to place the module in.

7   The electric fuel pump is not serviced separately. In the event of failure, the complete assembly must be replaced. Transfer the fuel pressure sensor and fuel level sending unit to the new fuel pump module assembly, if necessary (see Section 8).

8   Clean the fuel tank sealing surface and install a new seal on the fuel pump module.

9   Install the fuel pump module, aligning the fuel line fittings with the fuel lines.

10   Press the fuel pump module down until seated and install the retaining ring. Make sure the retaining ring is fully seated and the locking tab is engaged with the slot.

11   The remainder of installation is the reverse of removal.

8   Fuel level sending unit - check and replacement

Warning: *See the* **Warning** *in Section 1.*

Check

Refer to illustration 8.2

1   Remove the fuel tank and the fuel pump module (see Sections 5 and 7).

2   Connect the probes of an ohmmeter to the two fuel level sensor terminals (2 and 3)

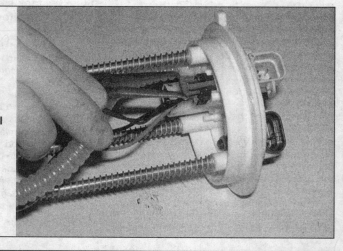

8.7 Disconnect the fuel pump/fuel level sending unit electrical connector from the fuel pump module

of the fuel pump module electrical connector **(see illustration)**.

3   Position the float in the down (empty) position and note the reading on the ohmmeter.

4   Move the float up to the full position while watching the meter.

5   If the fuel level sending unit resistance does not change smoothly as the float travels from empty to full, replace the fuel level sending unit assembly.

Replacement

Refer to illustrations 8.7, 8.8 and 8.9

6   Remove the fuel tank and the fuel pump module (see Sections 5 and 7).

7   Disconnect the fuel level sending unit electrical connector from the module cover **(see illustration)**.

8   Remove the sending unit retaining clip **(see illustration)**.

9   Pinch the tabs together and slide the fuel level sending unit off the module **(see illustration)**. Note the routing of the wiring for installation.

10   Installation is the reverse of removal.

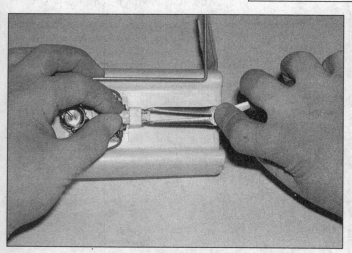

8.8 Remove the sending unit retaining clip

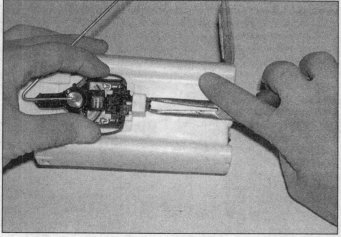

8.9 Pinch the tabs together and remove the fuel level sending unit from the module

9.2 Loosen the clamps (A and B) to remove the air intake hose - loosen clamp C to remove the resonator box from the engine

9.5 Pull up the air intake resonator box until its two pins release from the clips on the engine

9 Air filter housing and air intake resonator - removal and installation

Refer to illustrations 9.2 and 9.5

1   Disconnect the Mass Air Flow/IAT Sensor electrical connector at the air intake tube.
2   Release the clamps at each end of the duct and remove the duct from the air cleaner housing **(see illustration)**.
3   Remove the two bolts and one nut securing the air filter housing to the right fenderwell. On 2007 five-cylinder models and all 2008 models, disconnect the quick-connect fitting and remove the AIR hose from the air cleaner housing.
4   Remove the housing from the engine compartment.
5   If the resonator is to be removed for access to the throttle body or other repairs, disconnect the clamp at the throttle body **(see illustration 9.2)** and pull up the resonator from its clips **(see illustration)**.
6   Installation is the reverse of removal.

10 Fuel injection system - general information

The Sequential Multi Port Fuel Injection (SFI) system consists of three sub-systems: air intake, engine control and fuel delivery. The system uses a Powertrain Control Module (PCM) along with the sensors (Coolant Temperature Sensor, Throttle Position Sensor, Mass Airflow Sensor, oxygen Sensor, etc.) to determine the proper air/fuel ratio under all operating conditions.

The fuel injection system and the engine control system are closely linked in function and design. For additional information, refer to Chapter 6.

Air intake system

The air intake system consists of the air filter, the air intake ducts, the throttle body, and the intake manifold.

When the engine is idling, the air/fuel ratio is controlled by the idle air control system, which consists of the Powertrain Control Module (PCM) and the Idle Air Control valve. This idle air control regulates the amount of airflow past the throttle plate and into the intake manifold, thus increasing or decreasing the engine idle speed. The PCM receives information from the sensors (vehicle speed, coolant temperature, air conditioning, power steering mode etc.) and adjusts the idle according to the demands of the engine and driver. Refer to Chapter 6 for information on the Idle Air Control valve.

Emissions and engine control system

The emissions and engine control system is described in detail in Chapter 6.

Fuel delivery system

The fuel delivery system consists of these components: the fuel pump, the fuel pressure regulator, the fuel rail and the fuel injectors.

The fuel pump is an electric type. Fuel is drawn through an inlet screen into the pump, flows through the one-way valve, passes through the fuel filter and is delivered to the fuel rail and injectors. The pressure regulator maintains a constant fuel pressure to the injectors. On 2004 and 2005 models, the fuel pressure regulator is mounted on the fuel rail and sends excess fuel back to the fuel tank through the fuel return line. On 2006 models, the fuel pressure regulator is mounted in the fuel pump module at the tank, and there is no need for a return line from the engine.

The injectors are solenoid-actuated pintle types consisting of a solenoid, plunger, needle valve and housing. When current is applied to the solenoid coil, the needle valve raises and pressurized fuel sprays out the nozzle. The injection quantity is determined by the length of time the valve is open (the length of time during which current is supplied to the solenoid coils).

The fuel pump relay is located in the engine compartment electrical center. The PCM controls the relay by supplying battery voltage to the relay coil. When energized, the fuel pump relay connects battery voltage to the fuel pump. If the PCM senses there is NO signal from the camshaft or crankshaft sensors (as with the engine not running or cranking), the PCM will de-energize the relay.

11 Fuel injection system - check

Refer to illustrations 11.7a, 11.7b and 11.7c
Note: *The following procedure is based on the assumption that the fuel pressure is adequate (see Section 3).*

1   Check all electrical connectors that are related to the system. Check the ground wire connections for tightness. Loose connectors and poor grounds can cause many problems that resemble more serious malfunctions.
2   Check to see that the battery is fully charged, as the control unit and sensors depend on an accurate supply voltage in order to properly meter the fuel.
3   Check the air filter element - a dirty or partially blocked filter will severely impede performance and economy (see Chapter 1).
4   Check the related fuses. If a blown fuse is found, replace it and see if it blows again. If it does, search for a wire shorted to ground in the harness.
5   Check the air intake duct from the air filter housing to the throttle body for leaks, which will result in an excessively lean mixture. Also check the condition of all vacuum hoses connected to the intake manifold and/or throttle body.
6   Remove the air intake duct from the throttle body (see Section 9) and check for dirt, carbon or other residue build-up on the throttle bore and throttle plate. If it's dirty, clean it with carburetor cleaner spray, a toothbrush and a shop towel. **Caution:** *Do not use*

a solvent containing Methyl Ethyl Ketone or damage to the throttle body may occur.

7   Locate and disconnect the injector harness connector **(see illustration)** and measure the resistance of each injector by attaching an ohmmeter on the injector side of the disconnected harness, between terminal A and the corresponding injector terminals **(see illustration)**. Compare the measurements with the resistance values listed in this Chapter's Specifications. If the resistance of one of the injectors is way out of range (shorted or open), replace that injector.

8   Turn the ignition key On and check for battery voltage at the pink wire (terminal A) of the injector harness connector (on the engine harness side - the terminal that *corresponds* to terminal A in **illustration 11.7b or 11.7c**). If battery voltage is not present, check the fuel injector fuse and related wiring (see Chapter 12).

9   The remainder of the engine control system checks can be found in Chapter 6.

12 Throttle body - removal and installation

Refer to illustrations 12.3 and 12.4
Warning: *Wait until the engine is completely cool before beginning this procedure.*

1   Remove the air intake duct (see Section 9).

2   Disconnect the electrical connector and the evap canister purge line from the throttle body **(see illustration)**.

3   Remove the mounting bolts and remove the throttle body and gasket **(see illustration)**.

4   Remove all traces of old gasket material from the throttle body and intake manifold and install a new gasket. **Caution:** *Do not use solvent or a sharp tool to clean the throttle body gasket surface or damage to the throttle body may occur.*

5   Install the throttle body and tighten the bolts to the torque listed in this Chap-

11.7a Fuel injector harness connector

ter's Specifications.

6   The remainder of installation is the reverse of removal.

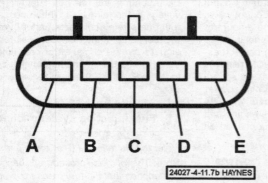

11.7b Terminal guide for the injector 8-way harness connector (injector side of connector, looking into unplugged connector, four-cylinder engine)

A Ignition voltage (pink)	D Injector 3 (pink/black)
B Injector 1 (black)	E Injector 4 (lt-blue/black)
C Injector 2 (lt-green/black)	

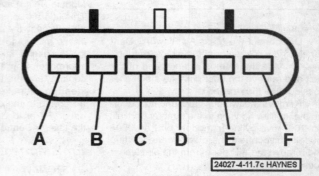

11.7c Terminal guide for the injector 8-way harness connector (injector side of connector, looking into unplugged connector, five-cylinder engine)

A Ignition voltage (pink)	D Injector 1 (black)
B Injector 4 (lt-blue/black)	E Injector 2 (lt-green/black)
C Injector 5 (black/white)	F Injector 3 (pink/black)

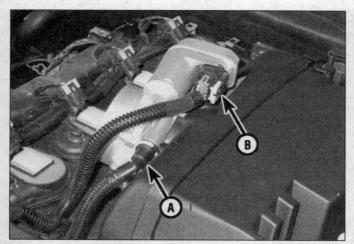

12.3 Disconnect the EVAP purge line (A) and the throttle body electrical connector (B)

12.4 Throttle body mounting bolts

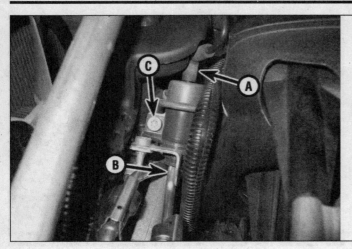

13.4 Fuel pressure regulator mounting details

A   *Vacuum line*
B   *Fuel return line*
C   *Mounting screw*

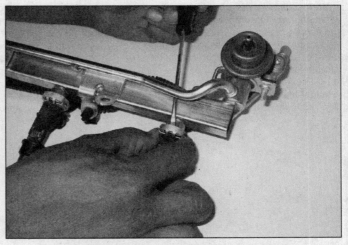

13.8 Lubricate the O-ring with clean engine oil

13   Fuel pressure regulator (2004 and 2005 models) - replacement

Refer to illustrations 13.4 and 13.8
Warning: *See the* **Warning** *in Section 1.*
1   Relieve the fuel system pressure (see Section 2).
2   Disconnect the cable from the negative battery terminal.
3   Clean any dirt and debris from around the fuel pressure regulator and fuel lines.
4   Disconnect the fuel pressure regulator vacuum line **(see illustration)**.
5   Disconnect the fuel return line (see Section 4) from the fuel rail and remove the retainer.
6   Remove the fuel pressure regulator mounting screws and remove the fuel pressure regulator. **Caution:** *Have a towel placed around the pressure regulator area to catch the fuel that will spill as the regulator is removed.*
7   Inspect the screen inside the fuel regulator for dirt or debris. If the screen is dirty, replace the fuel pressure regulator.
8   Install a new O-ring and lubricate it with

clean engine oil **(see illustration)**.
9   The remainder of installation is the reverse of removal.
10   Tighten the fuel pressure regulator screw to the torque listed in this Chapter's Specifications.

14   Fuel rail and injectors - removal and installation

Warning: *See the* **Warning** *in Section 1.*
Note: *When replacing components of the fuel rail/injector assembly, refer to the identification numbers on the fuel injectors. Fuel injectors are calibrated with different flow rates and must not be interchanged with injectors from a different application.*

Removal

Refer to illustrations 14.6 and 14.8
1   Relieve the fuel system pressure (see Section 2).
2   Disconnect the cable from the negative battery terminal.

3   Remove the intake manifold (see Chapter 2A).
4   Before proceeding, clean the fuel rail/fuel injector area with degreaser or other appropriate solvent, then blow dry with compressed air. **Caution:** *Wear eye protection.*
5   Disconnect the fuel pressure regulator vacuum line (2004 and 2005 models), the fuel injector harness connector **(see illustration 11.7a)** and the fuel line fitting(s) (see Section 4).
6   Remove the fuel rail attaching bolts and apply gentle and even outward pressure on the fuel rail to free it from the cylinder head **(see illustration)**.
7   Disconnect the electrical connector from the injector(s) to be removed.
8   Remove the retaining clip(s) and remove the injector(s) from the fuel rail assembly **(see illustration)**. Remove and discard the O-rings and seals. **Note:** *Whether you're replacing an injector or a leaking O-ring, it's a good idea to remove all the injectors from the fuel rail and replace all the O-rings (two per injector).*

Installation

9   Replace the injector O-rings. Apply a

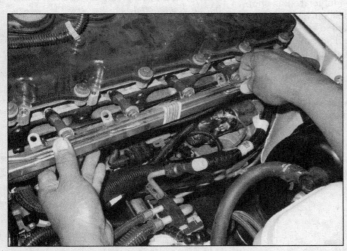

14.6 The fuel rail and injectors are removed as a unit, then the individual injectors can be serviced

14.8 The retaining clip must be removed prior to removing the injector

15.2a Inspect the exhaust system connections for leakage

15.2b Inspect the exhaust system rubber hangers for damage

light coat of clean engine oil to the O-rings and press the injector into the fuel rail until seated.

10   Install the injector retaining clips.

11   Inspect the cylinder head injector holes and clean them out if necessary, then lubricate the injector O-rings with clean engine oil.

12   The remainder of installation is the reverse of removal. Tighten the fuel rail mounting bolts to the torque listed in this Chapter's Specifications.

13   After installation is complete, turn the ignition switch to On, but don't operate the starter (this activates the fuel pump for about two seconds, which builds up fuel pressure in the fuel lines and the fuel meter body). Cycle the ignition On and Off several times, then check the fuel lines, fuel rail and injector for fuel leakage.

15   Exhaust system servicing - general information

Warning: *Inspection and repair of exhaust system components should be done only after enough time has elapsed after driving the vehicle to allow the system components to cool completely. Also, when working under the vehicle, make sure it is securely supported on jackstands.*

1   The exhaust system consists of the exhaust manifolds, catalytic converters, muffler, resonators, the tailpipe and all connecting pipes, brackets, hangers and clamps. The exhaust system is attached to the body with mounting brackets and rubber hangers. If any of the parts are improperly installed, excessive noise and vibration will be transmitted to the body.

Muffler and pipes

Refer to illustrations 15.2a and 15.2b

2   Conduct regular inspections of the exhaust system to keep it safe and quiet. Look for any damaged or bent parts, open seams, holes, loose connections, excessive corrosion or other defects which could allow exhaust fumes to enter the vehicle **(see illustrations)**. Also check the catalytic converter when you inspect the exhaust system (see below). Deteriorated exhaust system components should not be repaired; they should be replaced with new parts.

3   If the exhaust system components are extremely corroded or rusted together, welding equipment will probably be required to remove them. The convenient way to accomplish this is to have a muffler repair shop remove the corroded sections with a cutting torch. If, however, you want to save money by doing it yourself (and you don't have a welding outfit with a cutting torch), simply cut off the old components with a hacksaw. If you have compressed air, special pneumatic cutting chisels can also be used. If you do decide to tackle the job at home, be sure to wear safety goggles to protect your eyes from metal chips and work

gloves to protect your hands.

4   Here are some simple guidelines to follow when repairing the exhaust system:

a)   *Work from the back to the front when removing exhaust system components.*

b)   *Apply penetrating oil to the exhaust system component fasteners to make them easier to remove.*

c)   *Use new gaskets, hangers and clamps when installing exhaust systems components.*

d)   *Apply anti-seize compound to the threads of all exhaust system fasteners during reassembly.*

e)   *Be sure to allow sufficient clearance between newly installed parts and all points on the underbody to avoid overheating the floor pan and possibly damaging the interior carpet and insulation. Pay particularly close attention to the catalytic converter and heat shield.*

Catalytic converter

Warning: *The converter gets very hot during operation. Make sure it has cooled down before you touch it.*

Note: *See Chapter 6 for additional information on the catalytic converter.*

5   Periodically inspect the heat shield for cracks, dents and loose or missing fasteners.

6   Inspect the converter for cracks or other damage.

7   If the catalytic converter requires replacement, refer to Chapter 6.

Chapter 5
Engine electrical systems

Contents

Specifications

General
Battery voltage
Engine off .... 12.0 to 12.6 volts
Engine running .... 13.5 to 14.7 volts
Alternator output
2004 through 2007 .... 100 amps
2008
Four-cylinder engine .... 125 amps
Five-cylinder engine .... 145 amps

Torque specifications
Ft-lbs (unless otherwise indicated)
Alternator mounting bolts 37
Starter mounting bolt/nut 37
Ignition coil bolts .... 89 in-lbs

1   General information and precautions

General information
Refer to illustration 1.1

The engine electrical systems include all ignition, charging and starting components **(see illustration)**. Because of their engine-related functions, these components are discussed separately from body electrical devices such as the lights, the instruments, etc. (which are included in Chapter 12).

Precautions
Always observe the following precautions when working on the electrical system:

a) Be extremely careful when servicing engine electrical components. They are easily damaged if checked, connected or handled improperly.
b) Never leave the ignition switched on for long periods of time when the engine is not running.
c) Never disconnect the battery cables while the engine is running.
d) Maintain correct polarity when connecting battery cables from another vehicle during jump starting - see the "Booster battery (jump) starting" section at the front of this manual.
e) Always disconnect the negative battery cable before working on the electrical system.

It's also a good idea to review the safety-related information regarding the engine electrical systems located in the "Safety first!" section at the front of this manual, before beginning any operation included in this Chapter.

Battery disconnection
Several systems on the vehicle require battery power to be available at all times, either to ensure their continued operation (such as the clock) or to maintain control unit memories (such as that in the engine management system's Powertrain Control Module) which would be wiped out if the battery were to be disconnected. Therefore, whenever the battery is to be disconnected, first note the following to ensure that there are no unforeseen consequences of this action:

a) First, on any vehicle with power door locks, it is a wise precaution to remove the key from the ignition and to keep it with you, so that it does not get locked inside if the power door locks should engage accidentally when the battery is reconnected!
b) The engine management system's PCM will lose the information stored in its memory when the battery is disconnected. This includes idling and operating values, and any fault codes detected (see Chapter 6). Whenever the battery is disconnected, the information relating to idle speed control and other operating values will have to be re-programmed

1.1 Typical engine electrical system components

1 Ignition coils (under air intake resonator)	2 Underhood Electrical Center 3 Battery	4 Alternator

into the unit's memory. The PCM does this by itself, but until then, there may be surging, hesitation, erratic idle and a generally inferior level of performance. To allow the PCM to relearn these values, start the engine and run it as close to idle speed as possible until it reaches its normal operating temperature, then run it for approximately two minutes at 1200 rpm. Next, drive the vehicle as far as necessary - approximately 5 miles of varied driving conditions is usually sufficient - to complete the relearning process.

Devices known as "memory-savers" can be used to avoid some of the above problems. Precise details vary according to the device used. Typically, it is plugged into the cigarette lighter, and is connected by its own wires to a spare battery; the vehicle's own battery is then disconnected from the electrical system, leaving the "memory-saver" to pass sufficient current to maintain audio unit security codes and PCM memory values, and also to run permanently live circuits such as the clock, all the while isolating the battery in the event of a short-circuit occurring while work is carried out. **Warning 1:** *Some of these devices allow a considerable amount of current to pass, which can mean that many of the vehicle's systems are still operational when the main battery is disconnected. If a "memory-saver" is used, ensure that the circuit concerned is*

actually "dead" before carrying out any work on it! **Warning 2:** *If work is to be performed around any of the airbag system components, the battery must be disconnected and no "memory saver" can be used. If a memory saver is used, power will be supplied to the airbag system and personal injury may result if the airbag is accidentally deployed.*

2   Battery - emergency jump starting

Refer to the *Booster battery (jump) starting* procedure at the front of this manual.

3   Battery - check and replacement

Warning: *Hydrogen gas is produced by the battery, so keep open flames and lighted cigarettes away from it at all times. Always wear eye protection when working around a battery. Rinse off spilled electrolyte immediately with large amounts of water.*

Check

Refer to illustrations 3.2 and 3.3

1   The battery's surface charge must be removed before accurate voltage measurements can be made. Turn On the high beams for ten seconds, then turn them Off,

let the vehicle stand for two minutes. Remove the battery from the vehicle (see Steps 4 through 9).

2   Check the battery state of charge. Visually inspect the indicator eye on the top of the battery, if the indicator eye is clear, charge the battery as described in Chapter 1. Next perform an open voltage circuit test using a digital voltmeter **(see illustration)**. With the engine and all accessories Off, connect the

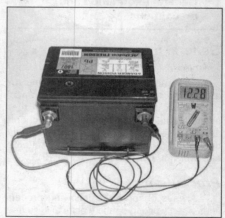

3.2 To test the open-circuit voltage of the battery, connect a voltmeter to the battery - a fully charged battery should measure at least 12.4 volts (depending on outside air temperature)

3.3 Connect a battery load tester to the battery and check the battery condition under load following the tool manufacturer's instructions

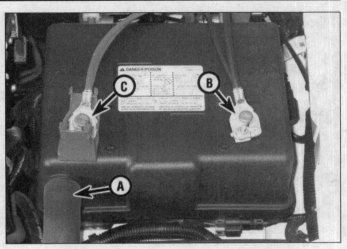

3.4 Disconnect the vent duct (A) from the battery cover, then disconnect the negative cable (B) followed by the positive cable (C)

negative probe of the voltmeter to the negative terminal of the battery and the positive probe to the positive terminal of the battery. The battery voltage should be 12.4 volts or more. If the battery is less than the specified voltage, charge the battery before proceeding to the next test. Do not proceed with the battery load test unless the battery charge is correct.

3   Perform a battery load test. An accurate check of the battery condition can only be performed with a load tester (available at most auto parts stores). This test evaluates the ability of the battery to operate the starter and other accessories during periods of heavy amperage draw (load). Connect a battery load-testing tool to the terminals (see illustration). Load test the battery according to the tool manufacturer's instructions. This tool increases the load demand (amperage draw) on the battery. Maintain the load on the battery for 15 seconds or less and observe that the battery voltage does not drop below 9.6 volts.

If the battery condition is weak or defective, the tool will indicate this condition immediately. Note: *Cold temperatures will cause the minimum voltage reading to drop slightly. Follow the chart given in the tool manufacturer's instructions to compensate for cold climates. Minimum load voltage for freezing temperatures (32-degrees F) should be approximately 9.1 volts.*

Replacement

Refer to illustrations 3.4, 3.7 and 3.8

4   Detach the vent duct from the battery cover, then disconnect the cable from the negative battery terminal (see illustration).
5   Disconnect the positive battery cable.
6   On vehicles equipped with an engine block heater, remove the heater cord retainer from the battery cover.
7   To remove the battery cover, depress the locking tabs on each side and lift it straight up (see illustration).

8   Remove the battery retainer nut and the retainer (see illustration).
9   Lift the battery straight up to remove it.
10   If corrosion is evident, remove the battery tray and use a baking soda/water solution to clean the corroded area to prevent further oxidation. Repaint the area as necessary using rust-resistant paint.
11   Clean and service the battery and cables (see Chapter 1).
12   If you are replacing the battery, make sure you purchase one that is identical to yours, with the same dimensions, amperage rating, cold cranking amps rating, etc. Make sure it is fully charged prior to installation in the vehicle.
13   Installation is the reverse of removal. Connect the positive cable first and the negative cable last.
14   After connecting the cables to the battery, apply a light coating of petroleum jelly or grease to the connections to help prevent corrosion.

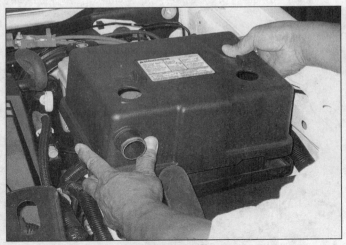

3.7 Depress the clips on each side of the battery cover, then lift the cover straight up

3.8 Remove the nut and retainer, then lift the battery out

4.4a One branch of the positive cable is connected to the underhood electrical center

4.4b Disconnect the lead from the alternator

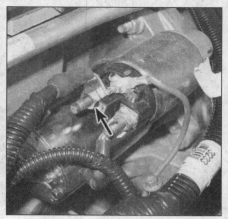

4.4c Disconnect the cable at the starter

4   Battery cables - replacement

Refer to illustrations 4.4a, 4.4b, 4.4c and 4.4d

1   Periodically inspect the entire length of each battery cable for damage, cracked or burned insulation and corrosion. Poor battery cable connections can cause starting problems and decreased engine performance.

2   Check the cable-to-terminal connections at the ends of the cables for cracks, loose wire strands and corrosion. The presence of white, fluffy deposits under the insulation at the cable terminal connection is a sign that the cable is corroded and should be replaced. Check the terminals for distortion, missing mounting bolts and corrosion.

3   When removing the cables, always disconnect the negative cable first and hook it up last or the battery may be shorted by the tool used to loosen the cable clamps. Even if only the positive cable is being replaced, be sure to disconnect the negative cable first (see Chapter 1 for further information regarding battery cable maintenance).

4   Disconnect the old cables from the battery, then disconnect them at the opposite end. Detach the cables from the starter solenoid, underhood electrical center and ground terminals, as necessary **(see illustrations)**. Note the routing of each cable to ensure correct installation.

5   If you are replacing either or both of the battery cables, take them with you when buying new cables. It is vitally important that you replace the cables with identical parts. Cables have characteristics that make them easy to identify: positive cables are usually red and larger in cross-section; ground cables are usually black and smaller in cross-section.

6   Clean the threads of the starter solenoid or ground connection with a wire brush to remove rust and corrosion. Apply a light coat of battery terminal corrosion inhibitor or petroleum jelly to the threads to prevent future corrosion.

7   Attach the cable to the terminal and tighten the mounting nut/bolt securely.

8   Before connecting a new cable to the battery, make sure that it reaches the battery without having to be stretched.

5   Ignition system - general information

All models are equipped with a distributorless ignition system. The ignition system consists of the battery, one ignition coil per cylinder, spark plug boot, spark plugs, camshaft position sensor, crankshaft position sensor and the Powertrain Control Module (PCM).

On all models, the PCM controls the ignition timing and spark advance characteristics for the engine. The ignition timing is not adjustable.

The ignition system is also equipped with a knock sensor to detect detonation, or spark knock (usually caused by the use of sub-standard fuel). The system uses a knock sensor in conjunction with the Powertrain Control Module (PCM) to control spark timing. If a knock signal is received, the PCM will retard the timing until the knock is eliminated. The knock sensor system allows the engine to use maximum spark advance without spark knock, which improves driveability and fuel economy.

6   Ignition system - check

Refer to illustration 6.4

Warning 1: *Because of the high voltage generated by the ignition system, extreme care should be taken whenever an operation is performed involving ignition components. This not only includes the ignition coil, but also related components and test equipment.*

Warning 2: *The following procedure requires the engine to be cranked during testing. Make sure the meter leads, loose clothing, long hair, etc. are away from the moving parts of the engine (drivebelt, cooling fan, etc.) before cranking the engine.*

1   Before proceeding with the ignition system, check the following items:

a) *Make sure the battery cable clamps, where they connect to the battery, are clean and tight.*

b) *Test the condition of the battery (see Section 3). If it does not pass all the tests, replace it with a new battery.*

c) *Check the ignition coil and ignition control module external wiring and connections.*

d) *Check the related fuses inside the underhood electrical center (see Chapter 12). If they're burned, determine the cause and repair the circuit.*

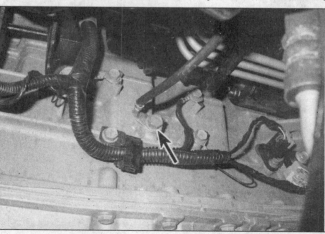

4.4d The negative cable is fastened to the engine block

6.4 To use a calibrated ignition tester, remove an ignition coil, connect the tester to the spark plug boot and clip the tester to a convenient ground, then crank the engine over

2   If the engine turns over but won't start or has a severe misfire, make sure there is sufficient secondary ignition voltage to fire the spark plugs.

3   Disable the fuel system by removing the fuel pump relay from the underhood electrical center (see Chapter 12).

4   Remove an ignition coil (see Section 7) from one of the spark plugs and attach a calibrated ignition system tester (available at most auto parts stores) to the spark plug boot. Connect the clip on the tester to a bolt or metal bracket on the engine **(see illustration)**. Crank the engine and watch the end of the tester to see if bright blue, well-defined sparks occur (weak spark or intermittent spark is the same as no spark).

5   If spark occurs, sufficient voltage is reaching the plug to fire it. Repeat the check at the remaining cylinders to verify that the ignition coil(s), spark plug boots and control systems are functioning properly. If the ignition system is operating properly the problem lies elsewhere; i.e., a mechanical or fuel system problem. However, the spark plugs may be fouled, so remove and check them as described in Chapter 1.

6   If none of the cylinders has spark, check the PCM I fuse in the underhood fuse box.

7   **Warning:** *The following tests require the engine to be cranked. Keep all loose clothing, hair, etc. away from the drivebelt and engine cooling fan as the starter is operated or seriously injury may result.* If no spark occurs at one or more cylinders, check for battery voltage to the ignition coils from the ignition switch. Attach a 12 volt test light to the battery negative (-) terminal or other good ground. Disconnect the electrical connector from one of the ignition coils and check for power at the pink wire terminal. Battery voltage should be available with the ignition key On. If there is no battery voltage present, check the wiring and/or circuit between the underhood electrical center and ignition coil connector (don't forget to check the fuses). Also check the

7.7 Pull up the engine harness conduit to access the first ignition coil

black wire terminal for continuity to battery ground. If there is battery voltage at the coil, but there is no spark from the coil, the coil, crankshaft position sensor, PCM or wiring are likely culprits.

8   Check for a trigger signal from the PCM. Attach the lead of a test light to the positive battery terminal and touch the probe of the test light to the ignition control circuit terminal of the coil electrical connector (it's the center terminal in the connector). Crank the engine. The test light should blink with the engine cranking if a trigger signal is present. Check each coil, if necessary. If a trigger signal is present at the coil, the power and ground circuits are good and there is no spark, replace the ignition coil. If a trigger signal is not present, check the crankshaft position sensor (see Chapter 6). If the crankshaft position sensor is good, check the circuits from the coil to the PCM. If the circuits are good, have the PCM checked by a dealer service department or other qualified repair shop.

7   Ignition coils - removal and installation

Refer to illustrations 7.7, 7.8, 7.9a, 7.9b and 7.10

1   Disconnect the cable from the negative battery terminal.

2   Remove the air intake duct and resonator from the throttle body (see Chapter 4).

3   The engine wiring harness crosses the valve cover in a large conduit, which must be removed to access the front coils. A number of electrical connectors must be disconnected.

4   From below the vehicle, disconnect the connector at the oil pressure sensor and unclip the harness from the oil filter adapter and the power steering pump.

5   Refer to Chapter 6 and disconnect the camshaft position sensor and camshaft position sensor actuator solenoid. Unclip these wires from the valve cover.

6   On top of the engine disconnect the ECT (Chapter 6), the fuel injector harness con-

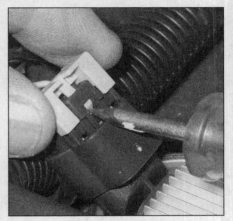

7.8 Disengage the connector lock then unplug the electrical connector

7.9a Unscrew the ignition coil mounting bolt . . .

7.9b . . . then pull the coil from the valve cover

nector (Chapter 4), and the oxygen sensor (Chapter 6).

7   Pop the engine harness conduit from its tabs on the valve cover **(see illustration)**.

8   Disconnect the electrical connector from the ignition coil **(see illustration)**.

9   Unscrew the ignition coil mounting bolt and remove the coil from the valve cover **(see illustrations)**.

10   Check the seals on the coils for cracks

7.10 Install new seal(s) on the ignition coil(s) if they are damaged or hardened

or other signs of damage, replacing them as necessary **(see illustration)**. Installation is otherwise the reverse of removal. Tighten the mounting bolt to the torque listed in this Chapter's Specifications.

8 Charging system - general information and precautions

The main components of the charging system are an alternator (with an integral voltage regulator), the battery and the wiring connecting the components. The components work together to supply electrical power for the electrical system and maintain the battery in a charged condition. The alternator is driven by the drivebelt at the front of the engine.

All models are equipped with an AD-244 alternator. AD type alternators should be considered non-serviceable and, if defective, exchanged as cores for new or rebuilt units. An identification number and amperage rating

is stamped on the alternator housing. Refer to these numbers to obtain the correct replacement alternator, if necessary.

The purpose of the voltage regulator is to limit the alternator voltage output to a preset value. This prevents power surges and circuit overloads during peak voltage output. On all models with which this manual is concerned, the voltage regulator is integral with the alternator.

The charging system doesn't ordinarily require periodic maintenance. However, the drivebelt, battery and wires and connections should be inspected at the intervals outlined in Chapter 1.

The instrument panel warning light should come on when the ignition key is turned to START, then go off immediately after the engine has started. If the warning light stays on or comes on when the engine is running, a charging system problem has occurred (see Section 9).

Be very careful when making electrical circuit connections to a vehicle equipped with an alternator and note the following:

a) *When reconnecting wires to the alternator from the battery, be sure to note the polarity.*
b) *Before using arc welding equipment to repair any part of the vehicle, disconnect the wires from the alternator and the battery terminals.*
d) *Always disconnect both battery leads before using a battery charger.*
e) *The alternator is turned by an engine drivebelt that could cause serious injury if your hands, hair or clothes become entangled in it with the engine running.*
f) *Because the alternator is connected directly to the battery, it could arc or cause a fire if overloaded or shorted out.*
g) *Wrap a plastic bag over the alternator and secure it with rubber bands before steam cleaning the engine.*

9 Charging system - check

Refer to illustration 9.2

Note: *These vehicles are equipped with an On-Board Diagnostic (OBD) system that is useful for detecting charging system problems. Refer to Chapter 6 for the list of diagnostic codes and procedures for obtaining the codes.*

1   If a malfunction occurs in the charging circuit, do not immediately assume that the alternator is causing the problem. First check the following items:

a) *The battery cables where they connect to the battery. Make sure the connections are clean and tight.*
b) *The battery electrolyte specific gravity (by observing the charge indicator on the battery). If it is low, charge the battery.*
c) *Check the external alternator wiring and connections.*
d) *Check the drivebelt condition and tension (see Chapter 1).*
e) *Check the alternator mounting bolts for tightness.*
f) *Run the engine and check the alternator for abnormal noise.*

2   Connect a voltmeter to the positive and negative battery terminals **(see illustration)**. Check the battery voltage with the engine off. It should be approximately 12.4 to 12.7 volts, if the battery is fully charged.

3   Start the engine and check the battery voltage again. It should now be greater than the voltage recorded in Step 2, but not more than 14.7 volts.

4   If the indicated voltage reading is less or more than the specified charging voltage, have the charging system checked at a dealer service department or other properly equipped repair facility. **Note:** *Many auto parts stores will bench test an alternator off the vehicle. Refer to your local auto parts store regarding their policy, many will perform this service free of charge.*

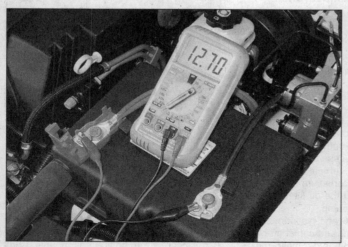

9.2 To measure battery voltage, attach the voltmeter leads to the battery terminals (engine OFF) - to measure charging voltage, start the engine

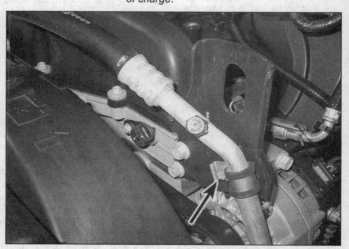

10.4 Unbolt and set aside the refrigerant hose, then remove the engine lifting bracket

10 Alternator - removal and installation

Refer to illustrations 10.4, 10.5a and 10.5b

1   Disconnect the cable from the negative battery terminal.

2   Remove the drivebelt (see Chapter 1).

3   Raise and support the vehicle and remove the left front wheel and fenderwell liner.

4   Unbolt the refrigerant line from the engine lifting bracket (do not disconnect the refrigerant line) and remove the engine lifting bracket **(see illustration)**. Disconnect the electrical connector at the air conditioning compressor, remove the compressor mounting bolts and lower the compressor for access to the alternator bolts (see Chapter 3). **Warning:** *The air conditioning system is under high pressure; do not disconnect the refrigerant hoses from the compressor.*

5   Move the electrical harness out of the way if necessary, then remove the alternator mounting bolts and the alternator **(see illustrations)**.

6   If you are replacing the alternator, take the old one with you when purchasing a replacement unit. Make sure the new/rebuilt unit looks identical to the old alternator. Look at the terminals - they should be the same in number, size and location as the terminals on the old alternator. Finally, look at the identification numbers - they will be stamped into the housing. Make sure the numbers are the same on both alternators.

7   Many new/rebuilt alternators do not have a pulley installed, so you may have to switch the pulley from the old unit to the new/rebuilt one. When buying an alternator, find out the shop's policy regarding pulleys; some shops will perform this service free of charge.

8   Installation is the reverse of removal. Tighten the mounting bolts to the torque listed in this Chapter's Specifications.

9   Install the drivebelt (see Chapter 1).

10 Check the charging voltage to verify proper operation of the alternator (see Section 9).

11 Starting system - general information and precautions

The starting system consists of the battery, ignition switch, starter relay, starter motor assembly and the wiring connecting the components.

The starter motor assembly is a permanent magnet, planetary gear drive starter motor. The starter motor assembly is serviced as a complete unit. If any component of the starter motor fails, including the solenoid, the entire assembly must be replaced.

When the ignition key is turned to the START position, the starter solenoid is actuated through the starter control circuit. The starter solenoid then connects the battery to the starter motor. The battery supplies the

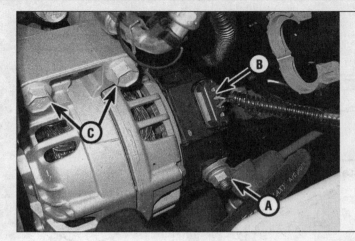

10.5a Alternator mounting details

A   *Positive battery connection*
B   *Electrical connector*
C   *Upper mounting bolts*

electrical energy to the starter motor, which does the actual work of cranking the engine.

Always observe the following precautions when working on the starting system:

a) *Excessive cranking of the starter motor can overheat it and cause serious damage. Never operate the starter motor for more than 15 seconds at a time without pausing to allow it to cool for at least two minutes.*

b) *The starter is connected directly to the battery and could arc or cause a fire if mishandled, overloaded or shorted.*

c) *Always detach the cable from the negative terminal of the battery before working on the starting system.*

12 Starter motor and circuit - check

Refer to illustration 12.4

1   If a malfunction occurs in the starting circuit, do not immediately assume that the starter is causing the problem. First, check the following items:

* *Make sure the battery cable clamps, where they connect to the battery, are clean and tight.*
* *Check the condition of the battery cables (see Section 4). Replace any defective battery cables with new parts.*
* *Test the condition of the battery (see Section 3). If it does not pass all the tests, replace it with a new battery.*
* *Check the starter motor wiring and connections.*
* *Check the starter motor mounting bolts for tightness.*
* *Check the related fuses in the engine compartment fuse box (see Chapter 12). If they're blown, determine the cause and repair the circuit.*
* *Check the ignition switch circuit for correct operation (see Chapter 12).*
* *Check the starter relay (located in the underhood electrical center) for proper operation (see Chapter 12).*
* *Check the operation of the Park/Neutral*

10.5b Alternator lower mounting bolt

position switch (see Chapter 7). These systems must operate correctly to provide battery voltage to the starter relay.

2   If the starter does not activate when the ignition switch is turned to the start position, check for battery voltage to the starter solenoid. This will determine if the solenoid is receiving the correct voltage from the starter relay. Install a 12-volt test light or a voltmeter to the starter solenoid terminal. While an assistant turns the ignition switch to the start position, observe the test light or voltmeter. The test light should shine brightly or battery voltage should be indicated on the voltmeter. If voltage is not available to the starter solenoid, check the fuses, ignition switch, starter relay and related wiring in series with the starting system. If voltage is available but there is no movement from the starter motor, remove the starter from the engine (see Section 13) and bench test the starter (see Step 4).

3   If the starter turns over slowly, check the starter cranking voltage and the current draw from the battery. This test must be performed with the starter assembly on the engine. Crank the engine over (for 10 seconds or less) and observe the battery voltage. It should not drop below 8.5 volts. Also, observe the current draw using an amp meter. Typically a starter amperage draw should not exceed 350 amps.

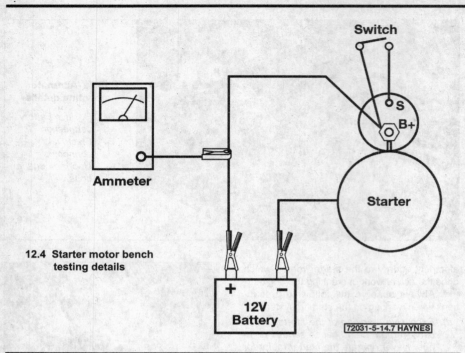

12.4 Starter motor bench testing details

sure to try and rotate the crankshaft pulley before proceeding. With the starter assembly mounted in a vise on the bench, install one jumper cable from the positive terminal of a test battery to the B+ terminal on the starter. Install another jumper cable from the negative terminal of the battery to the body of the starter **(see illustration)**. Install a starter switch and apply battery voltage to the solenoid S terminal (for 10 seconds or less) and observe the solenoid plunger, shift lever and overrunning clutch extend and rotate the pinion drive. If the pinion drive extends but does not rotate, the solenoid is operating but the starter motor is defective. If there is no movement but the solenoid clicks, the solenoid and/or the starter motor is defective. If the solenoid plunger extends and rotates the pinion drive, the starter assembly is operating properly.

13 Starter motor - removal and installation

Refer to illustrations 13.3 and 13.4

1   Disconnect the cable from the negative battery terminal.

2   Remove the intake manifold (see Chapter 2A).

3   Disconnect the electrical connections at the starter **(see illustration)**.

4   Remove the starter nut (top) and bolt (bottom) then remove the starter motor **(see illustration)**.

5   Installation is the reverse of removal. Tighten the starter mounting fasteners to the torque listed in this Chapter's Specifications.

If the starter motor amperage draw is excessive, have it tested by a dealer service department or other qualified repair shop. There are several conditions that may affect the starter cranking potential. The battery must be in good condition and the battery cold-cranking rating must not be underrated for the particular application. Be sure to check the battery specifications carefully. The battery terminals

and cables must be clean and not corroded. Also, in cases of extreme cold temperatures, make sure the battery and/or engine block is warmed before performing the tests.

4   If the starter is receiving voltage but does not activate, remove and check the starter motor assembly on the bench. Most likely the starter motor or solenoid is defective. In some rare cases, the engine may be seized so be

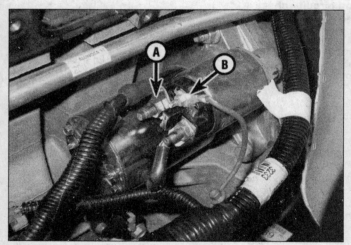

13.3 Remove the nuts and disconnect the battery cable (A) and the solenoid terminal nut and wire (B) from the starter motor

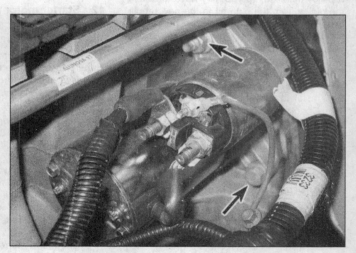

13.4 Remove the starter mounting nut and bolt

Chapter 6
Emissions and engine control systems

Contents

1.1 Typical emission and engine control system components

1 Manifold Absolute Pressure (MAP) sensor
2 Powertrain Control Module (PCM)
3 Throttle body
4 Camshaft Position (CMP) sensor
5 Vehicle Emissions Control Information (VECI) label
6 Intake Air Temperature (IAT) sensor

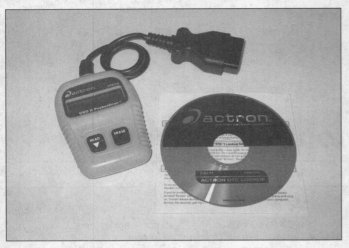

2.1 Simple code readers are an economical way to extract trouble codes when the CHECK ENGINE light comes on

2.2 Scanners like these from Actron and AutoXray are powerful diagnostic aids - they can tell you just about anything that you want to know about your engine management system

1   General information

Refer to illustration 1.1

To prevent pollution of the atmosphere from incompletely burned and evaporating gases, and to maintain good driveability and fuel economy, a number of emission control systems are incorporated **(see illustration)**. They include the:

*Electronic engine control system
Crankcase ventilation system
Evaporative emissions control system
Catalytic converter
Secondary Air injection system (2008
    models only)*

All of these systems are linked, directly or indirectly, to the emission control system.

The Sections in this Chapter include general descriptions, checking procedures within the scope of the home mechanic (when possible) and component replacement procedures for each of the systems listed above.

Before assuming that an emissions control system is malfunctioning, check the fuel and ignition systems carefully. The diagnosis of some emission control devices requires specialized tools, equipment and training. If checking and servicing become too difficult or if a procedure is beyond your ability, consult a dealer service department or other properly equipped repair facility. Remember, the most frequent cause of emissions problems is simply a loose or broken vacuum hose or wire, so always check the hose and wiring connections first.

This doesn't mean, however, that emission control systems are particularly difficult to maintain and repair. You can quickly and easily perform many checks and do most of the regular maintenance at home with common tune-up and hand tools. **Note:** *Because of a Federally mandated warranty which covers the emission control system components, check with your dealer about warranty coverage before working on any emissions-related systems. Once the warranty has expired, you may wish to perform some of the component checks and/or replacement procedures in this Chapter to save money.*

Pay close attention to any special precautions outlined in this Chapter. It should be noted that the illustrations of the various systems may not exactly match the system installed on the vehicle you're working on because of changes made by the manufacturer during production or from year-to-year.

A Vehicle Emissions Control Information (VECI) label is located in the engine compartment. This label contains important emissions specifications and adjustment information, as well as a vacuum hose schematic with emissions components identified. When servicing the engine or emissions systems, the VECI label in your particular vehicle should always be checked for up-to-date information.

2   On-Board Diagnostic (OBD) system and trouble codes

Diagnostic tool information

Refer to illustrations 2.1, 2.2 and 2.3

1   Hand-held scanners are handy for analyzing the engine management systems used on late-model vehicles. Because extracting the Diagnostic Trouble Codes (DTCs) from an engine management system is now the first step in troubleshooting many computer-controlled systems and components, even the most basic generic code readers are capable of accessing a computer's DTCs **(see illustration)**. More powerful scan tools can also perform many of the diagnostics once associated with expensive factory scan tools. If you're planning to obtain a generic scan tool for your vehicle, make sure that it's compatible with OBD-II systems. If you don't plan to purchase a code reader or scan tool and don't have access to one, you can have the codes extracted by a dealer service department or by an independent repair shop.

2   With the advent of the Federally mandated emission control system known as On-Board Diagnostics-II (OBD-II), specially designed scanners were developed. Several tool manufacturers have released OBD-II scan tools for the home mechanic **(see illustration)**.

3   A digital multimeter is necessary for checking fuel injection and emission related components **(see illustration)**. A digital volt-ohmmeter is preferred over the older style analog multimeter for several reasons. The analog multimeter cannot display the volts-ohms or amps measurement in hundredths and thousandths increments. When working with electronic circuits which are often

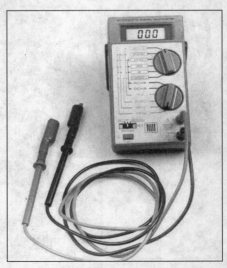

2.3 Digital multimeters can be used for testing all types of circuits; because of their high impedance, they are much more accurate than analog meters for measuring low-voltage computer circuits

very low voltage, this accurate reading is most important. Another good reason for the digital multimeter is the high impedance circuit. The digital multimeter is equipped with a high resistance internal circuitry (10 million ohms). Because a voltmeter is hooked up in parallel with the circuit when testing, it is vital that none of the voltage being measured should be allowed to travel the parallel path set up by the meter itself. This dilemma does not show itself when measuring larger amounts of voltage (9 to 12 volt circuits) but if you are measuring a low voltage circuit such as the oxygen sensor signal voltage, a fraction of a volt may be a significant amount when diagnosing a problem. However, there are several exceptions where using an analog voltmeter may be necessary to test certain sensors.

On-Board Diagnostic system general description

4   All models described in this manual are equipped with the second generation On-Board Diagnostic (OBD-II) system. The system consists of an on-board computer, known as the Powertrain Control Module (PCM), information sensors and output actuators.

5   The information sensors monitor various functions of the engine and send data to the PCM. Based on the data and the information programmed into the computer's memory, the PCM generates output signals to control various engine functions via control relays, solenoids and other output actuators. The PCM is specifically calibrated to optimize the emissions, fuel economy and driveability of the vehicle.

6   Because of a Federally mandated warranty which covers the emissions system components and because any owner-induced damage to the PCM, the sensors and/or the control devices may void the warranty, it isn't a good idea to attempt diagnosis or replacement of the system components while the vehicle is under warranty. Take the vehicle to a dealer service department if the PCM or a system component malfunctions.

Information sensors

7   **Accelerator pedal position (APP) sensor** - The APP sensor is mounted on the accelerator pedal assembly. The APP consists of two individual position sensors within one housing. There are two separate signal, low reference, and 5-volt reference circuits. Position sensor 1 voltage increases as the accelerator pedal is depressed. Position sensor 2 voltage decreases as the accelerator pedal is depressed. This sensor along with several others is needed for the Throttle Actuator Control System operation.

8   **Camshaft Position (CMP) sensor** - The Camshaft Position sensor provides information on camshaft position. The PCM uses this information, along with the crankshaft position sensor information, to control fuel injection

synchronization and variable valve timing.

9   **Crankshaft Position (CKP) sensor** - The Crankshaft Position sensor senses crankshaft position (TDC) during each engine revolution. The PCM uses this information to control ignition timing and fuel injection synchronization.

10   **Engine Coolant Temperature (ECT) sensor** - The Engine Coolant Temperature sensor monitors engine coolant temperature. The PCM uses this information to control fuel injection duration and ignition timing.

11   **Intake Air Temperature (IAT) sensor** - The Intake Air Temperature sensor monitors the temperature of the air entering the intake manifold. The PCM uses this information to control fuel injection duration.

12   **Knock Sensor (KS)** - The Knock Sensor is a piezoelectric element that detects the sound of engine detonation, or pinging. The PCM uses the input signal from the knock sensor to recognize detonation and retard spark advance to avoid engine damage.

13   **Manifold Absolute Pressure (MAP) sensor** - The Manifold Absolute Pressure sensor monitors intake manifold pressure and ambient barometric pressure. The PCM uses this input signal to determine engine load and adjust fuel injection duration accordingly.

14   **Mass Airflow (MAF) sensor** - The Mass Airflow Sensor measures the amount of air passing through the sensor body and ultimately entering the engine. The PCM uses this information to control fuel delivery.

15   **Oxygen (O2) sensor** - The oxygen sensors generate a voltage signal that varies with the varying oxygen content of the exhaust gas. The PCM uses this information to determine if the fuel system is running rich or lean and make adjustments accordingly.

16   **Throttle Position Sensor (TPS)** - The Throttle Position Sensor senses throttle movement and position. This signal enables the PCM to determine when the throttle is closed, in a cruise position, or wide open. The PCM uses this information to control fuel delivery and ignition timing. Note that the TPS on this vehicle is a integral part of the throttle body and must be replaced as a unit.

17   **Vehicle Speed Sensor (VSS)** - The Vehicle Speed Sensor provides information to the PCM to indicate vehicle speed.

18   **Miscellaneous PCM inputs** - In addition to the various sensors, the PCM monitors various switches and circuits to determine vehicle operating conditions. The switches and circuits include:

a) Air conditioning system
b) Battery voltage
c) Brake On/Off switch
d) Cruise control system
e) Engine oil level and pressure
f) EVAP system
g) Fuel level and fuel tank pressure
h) Ignition switch
i) Park/Neutral Position (PNP) switch
j) Sensor signal and ground circuits
k) Transmission controls

Output actuators

19   **Air conditioning clutch relay** - The PCM controls the operation of the air conditioning compressor clutch with the air conditioning clutch relay.

20   **Camshaft Position Actuator System** - The PCM pulses voltage to the cam position actuator solenoid to control the exhaust camshaft timing as required for optimal engine operation.

21   **Check Engine light** - The PCM will illuminate the Check Engine light if a malfunction in the electronic engine control system occurs.

22   **Cruise control operation** - The cruise control system operation is controlled by the PCM.

23   **EVAP canister purge and vent valve solenoids** - The evaporative emission canister purge and vent valve solenoids are operated by the PCM to purge the fuel vapor canister and route fuel vapor to the intake manifold for combustion.

24   **Fuel injectors** - The PCM opens the fuel injectors individually in firing order sequence. The PCM also controls the time the injector is held open (pulse width). The pulse width of the injector (measured in milliseconds) determines the amount of fuel delivered. For more information on the fuel delivery system and the fuel injectors, including injector replacement, refer to Chapter 4.

25   **Fuel pump relay** - The fuel pump relay is activated by the PCM with the ignition switch in the Start or Run position. When the ignition switch is turned on, the relay is activated to supply initial line pressure to the system. For more information on fuel pump check and replacement, refer to Chapter 4.

26   **Ignition coils/modules** - The PCM controls ignition timing through the ignition coils/modules depending on the engine operation conditions. Refer to Chapter 5 for more information on the ignition coils/modules.

Obtaining diagnostic trouble codes

Refer to illustration 2.28

Note: *The diagnostic trouble codes on all models can only be extracted from the Powertrain Control Module (PCM) using a specialized scan tool. Have the vehicle diagnosed by a dealer service department or other qualified automotive repair facility if the proper scan tool is not available.*

27   The PCM will illuminate the SERVICE ENGINE SOON light (also known as the Malfunction Indicator Lamp) on the dash if it recognizes a fault in the system. The light will remain illuminated until the problem is repaired and the code is cleared or the PCM does not detect any malfunction for several consecutive drive cycles.

28   The diagnostic codes for the On-Board Diagnostic (OBD) system can only be extracted from the PCM using a code reader or a scan tool. These tools are programmed

2.28 The diagnostic connector is typically located under the instrument panel

to interface with the OBD system by plugging into the diagnostic connector (see illustration). Code readers are only capable of reading trouble codes that have been stored in the PCM. On the other hand, the scan tool has the ability to diagnose in-depth driveability problems, and many scan tools allow freeze frame data to be retrieved from the PCM stored memory. Freeze frame data is an OBD-II PCM feature that records all related sensor and actuator activity on the PCM data stream whenever an engine control or emissions fault is detected and a trouble code is set. This ability to look at the circuit conditions and values when the malfunction occurs provides a valuable tool when trying to diagnose intermittent driveability problems. If the tool is not available and intermittent driveability problems exist, have the vehicle checked at a dealer service department or other qualified repair shop.

Clearing diagnostic trouble codes

29   After the system has been repaired, the codes must be cleared from the PCM memory. The preferred method is with a scan tool, but the PCM will turn off the CHECK ENGINE light if it senses the malfunction is gone in three successive ignition cycles. The code itself will be cleared by the PCM: A, after one start cycle if the code is a new one and the repair has been made; and B, an old trouble code will be cleared if the PCM senses there are no failure reports for 40 start cycles.

Diagnostic trouble code identification

30   The accompanying list of diagnostic trouble codes is a compilation of all the codes that may be encountered using a generic scan tool. Additional trouble codes may be obtainable with the use of the manufacturer specific scan tool. Not all codes pertain to all models and not all codes will illuminate the Service Engine Soon light when set. All models require a scan tool to access the diagnostic trouble codes.
Note: *The following list of OBD II trouble codes is a generic list applicable to all models equipped with an OBD II system, although not all codes apply to all models.*

Trouble Codes

Code	Possible Cause
P0013	Camshaft position - exhaust camshaft actuator circuit malfunction
P0014	Camshaft position - exhaust camshaft CMP performance
P0016	Crankshaft position/intake camshaft position, sensor correlation
P0017	Crankshaft position/exhaust camshaft position, sensor correlation
P0030	HO2S heater control circuit (sensor 1)
P0036	HO2S heater control circuit (sensor 2)
P0053	HO2S sensor 1, heater resistance
P0054	HO2S sensor 2, heater resistance
P0068	Throttle body airflow performance
P0101	Mass air flow or volume problem, IAT, MAF, or MAP
P0102	Mass air flow or volume air flow circuit, low input
P0103	Mass air flow or volume air flow circuit, high input
P0106	Manifold absolute pressure or barometric pressure circuit, range or performance problem
P0107	Manifold absolute pressure or barometric pressure circuit, low input
P0108	Manifold absolute pressure or barometric pressure circuit, high input
P0112	Intake air temperature circuit, low input
P0113	Intake air temperature circuit, high input
P0116	ECT sensor, circuit performance
P0117	Engine coolant temperature circuit, low input

Code	Possible Cause
P0118	Engine coolant temperature circuit, high input
P0120	Throttle position or pedal position sensor/switch circuit malfunction
P0121	Throttle position or pedal position sensor/switch circuit, range or performance problem
P0122	Throttle position or pedal position sensor/switch circuit, low input
P0123	Throttle position or pedal position sensor/switch circuit, high input
P0125	Insufficient coolant temperature for closed loop fuel control
P0128	Coolant thermostat (coolant temperature below thermostat regulating temperature)
P0130	O2 sensor circuit malfunction (sensor 1)
P0131	O2sensor circuit, low voltage (sensor 1)
P0132	O2 sensor circuit, high voltage (sensor 1)
P0133	O2 sensor circuit, slow response (sensor 1)
P0134	O2 sensor circuit - no activity detected (sensor 1)
P0135	O2 sensor heater circuit malfunction (sensor 1)
P0136	O2 sensor circuit malfunction (sensor 2)
P0137	O2 sensor circuit, low voltage (sensor 2)
P0138	O2 sensor circuit, high voltage (sensor 2)
P0140	O2 sensor circuit - no activity detected (sensor 2)
P0141	O2 sensor heater circuit malfunction (sensor 2)
P0171	System too lean
P0172	System too rich
P0201	Injector circuit malfunction - cylinder no. 1
P0202	Injector circuit malfunction - cylinder no. 2
P0203	Injector circuit malfunction - cylinder no. 3
P0204	Injector circuit malfunction - cylinder no. 4
P0205	Injector circuit malfunction - cylinder no. 5
P0218	Transmission overheating condition
P0220	Throttle position or pedal position sensor/switch B circuit malfunction
P0222	Throttle position or pedal position sensor/switch B circuit, low input
P0223	Throttle position or pedal position sensor/switch B circuit, high input
P0230	Fuel pump primary circuit malfunction
P0300	Random/multiple cylinder misfire detected
P0301	Misfire detected - cylinder number 1
P0302	Misfire detected - cylinder number 2

Trouble Codes (continued)

Code	Possible Cause
P0303	Misfire detected - cylinder number 3
P0304	Misfire detected - cylinder number 4
P0305	Misfire detected - cylinder number 5
P0315	Crankshaft position system - variation not learned
P0324	Knock sensor, module performance
P0325	Knock sensor no. 1 circuit malfunction (bank 1 or single sensor)
P0326	Knock sensor no. 1 circuit, range or performance problem (number 1 or single sensor)
P0327	Knock sensor no. 1 circuit, low input (number 1 or single sensor)
P0328	Knock sensor, circuit, high voltage
P0332	Knock sensor no. 2 circuit (if equipped), low input
P0335	Crankshaft position sensor A circuit malfunction
P0336	Crankshaft position sensor A circuit - range or performance problem
P0351	Ignition coil A primary or secondary circuit malfunction
P0352	Ignition coil B primary or secondary circuit malfunction
P0353	Ignition coil C primary or secondary circuit malfunction
P0354	Ignition coil D primary or secondary circuit malfunction
P0355	Ignition coil E, control circuit
P0365	Camshaft position sensor B circuit (bank 1)
P0366	Camshaft position sensor B circuit range/performance
P0411	Secondary Air Injection system, airflow incorrect
P0412	Secondary Air Injection system, solenoid control circuit
P0418	Secondary Air Injection system, pump control circuit
P0420	Catalyst system efficiency below threshold
P0442	Evaporative emission control system, small leak detected
P0443	Evaporative emission control system, purge control valve circuit malfunction
P0446	Evaporative emission control system, vent control circuit malfunction
P0449	Evaporative emission control system, vent valve/solenoid circuit malfunction
P0451	Evaporative emission control system, pressure sensor range or performance problem
P0452	Evaporative emission control system, pressure sensor low input
P0453	Evaporative emission control system, pressure sensor high input
P0455	Evaporative emission (EVAP) control system leak detected (no purge flow or large leak)
P0461	Fuel level sensor circuit, range or performance problem

Code	Possible Cause
P0462	Fuel level sensor circuit, low input
P0463	Fuel level sensor circuit, high input
P0464	Fuel level sensor circuit, intermittent
P0496	Evaporative emission system - high purge flow
P0502	Vehicle speed sensor circuit, low input
P0503	Vehicle speed sensor circuit, Intermittent, erratic or high input
P0506	Idle control system, rpm lower than expected
P0507	Idle control system, rpm higher than expected
P0520	Engine oil pressure sensor/switch circuit malfunction
P0532	A/C refrigerant pressure sensor, low input
P0533	A/C refrigerant pressure sensor, high input
P0562	System voltage low
P0563	System voltage high
P0564	Cruise control system, multi-function input signal
P0567	Cruise control system, Resume switch circuit
P0568	Cruise control system, Set switch circuit
P060D	APP system performance
P060E	PCM TP system performance
P0601	Internal control module, memory check sum error
P0602	Control module, programming error
P0603	Internal control module, keep alive memory (KAM) error
P0604	Internal control module, random access memory (RAM) error
P0606	PCM processor fault
P0607	Control module performance
P0615	Starter relay, control circuit
P0621	Generator lamp L, control circuit malfunction
P0622	Generator lamp F, control circuit malfunction
P0641	Sensor reference voltage A - circuit open
P0650	Malfunction indicator lamp (MIL), control circuit malfunction
P0651	Sensor reference voltage B - circuit open
P0700	Transmission Control Module, request for MIL light
P0705	Transmission range sensor, circuit malfunction (PRNDL input)
P0711	Transmission fluid temperature sensor circuit, range or performance problem

Trouble Codes (continued)

Code	Possible Cause
P0712	Transmission fluid temperature sensor circuit, low input
P0713	Transmission fluid temperature sensor circuit, high input
P0716	Transmission input speed sensor, circuit performance
P0717	Transmission input speed sensor, circuit low voltage
P0719	Torque converter/brake switch B, circuit low
P0724	Torque converter/brake switch B circuit, high
P0741	Torque converter clutch, circuit performance or stuck in off position
P0742	Torque converter clutch circuit, stuck in on position
P0748	Pressure control solenoid, electrical problem
P0751	Shift solenoid A, performance problem or stuck in off position
P0752	Shift solenoid A, stuck in on position
P0756	Shift solenoid B, performance problem or stuck in off position
P0757	Shift solenoid B, stuck in on position
P0787	Shift/timing solenoid, low
P0788	Shift/timing solenoid, high
P0806	Clutch Pedal Position sensor, circuit performance
P0807	Clutch Pedal Position sensor, circuit low voltage
P0808	Clutch Pedal Position sensor, circuit high voltage
P0851	Park/Neutral position switch, circuit low voltage
P0852	Park/Neutral position switch, circuit high voltage
P0856	Traction control input signal - malfunction
P0894	Transmission component slipping
P0961	Transmission line pressure control solenoid, system performance
P0973	Shift solenoid (SS) A - control circuit low
P0974	Shift solenoid (SS) A - control circuit high
P0976	Shift solenoid (SS) B - control circuit low
P0977	Shift solenoid (SS) B - control circuit high

3   Powertrain Control Module (PCM) - removal and installation

Refer to illustrations 3.3 and 3.4

Caution: *Avoid static electricity damage to the Powertrain Control Module (PCM) by* grounding yourself to the body of the vehicle before touching the PCM and using a special anti-static pad to store the PCM on, once it is removed.

Note 1: *Whenever the PCM is replaced with a new unit the PCM must be reprogrammed with special equipment. A crankshaft posi-* tion sensor variation relearn procedure and a vehicle anti-theft system password relearn procedure must be performed, as well. The following procedure pertains to removal and installation of the original PCM only. If the PCM must be replaced with a new unit, take the vehicle to a dealership service department

3.3 Disconnect the electrical connectors from the PCM

3.4 Pull up the clips and lift the PCM up and out of the bracket

or other properly equipped repair shop.
Note 2: *Whenever the battery is disconnected, stored operating parameters may be lost from the PCM causing the engine to run rough for a period of time while the PCM relearns the information.*

1   Disconnect the cable from the negative battery terminal.
2   The PCM is located in the right rear corner of the engine compartment, on the firewall. Clean any debris from around the PCM connectors.
3   Lift up the latches and disconnect the electrical connectors from the PCM **(see illustration)**.
4   Release the two upper mounting tabs and lift the PCM out of its bracket **(see illustration)**.
5   Installation is the reverse of removal. Make sure the lower tabs on the PCM fit into their slots at the bottom of the PCM mounting bracket.

4   Throttle Position Sensor (TPS) - replacement

1   The Throttle Position Sensor (TPS) is a variable potentiometer connected to the end of the throttle shaft inside the throttle body. By monitoring the output voltage from the TPS, the PCM can determine fuel delivery based on throttle valve angle. **Note:** *The TPS sensor works with the Throttle Actuator Control system (TAC) and the Accelerator Pedal Position (APP) sensor. The latter is actually two sensors in one housing. When there is a difference between the actual throttle position and the position sensed by the TPS, codes are set.*

Replacement

2   The Throttle Position Sensor is part of the throttle body and must be replaced as a unit. Refer to Chapter 4 for the throttle body replacement procedure.

5   Accelerator Pedal Position sensor (APP) - replacement

1   The Accelerator Pedal Position sensor (APP) contains two separate sensors that send an opposing voltage signal to the PCM. The PCM uses this voltage to calculate the throttle position requested by the vehicle driver. The APP sensor is one of the three major components of the Throttle Actuator Control (TAC) system, the other two major components being the throttle body and the PCM. This vehicle uses no throttle cable; instead, the PCM utilizes inputs from the driver and engine to determine the correct throttle opening at the throttle body.

Replacement

Refer to illustration 5.2
2   Disconnect the APP sensor electrical connector **(see illustration)**.
3   Unscrew the mounting nuts and remove the APP sensor/accelerator pedal assembly.
4   Installation is the reverse of removal.

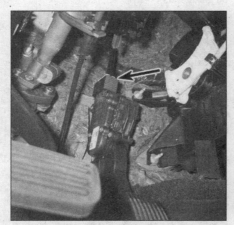

5.2 Accelerator Pedal Position (APP) sensor electrical connector

6   Manifold Absolute Pressure (MAP) sensor - replacement

1   The Manifold Absolute Pressure (MAP) sensor monitors the intake manifold pressure changes resulting from changes in engine load and speed and converts the information into a voltage output. The PCM receives information as a varying voltage signal from closed throttle (high vacuum) to wide open throttle (low vacuum). The PCM uses the MAP sensor to control fuel delivery and ignition timing.

Replacement

Refer to illustration 6.2
2   Disconnect the MAP sensor electrical connector **(see illustration)**.
3   Squeeze the sensor retainer tabs inward, then pull up to remove it.
4   Lift the sensor straight up to remove it.
5   Installation is the reverse of removal.

7   Mass Air Flow/ Intake Air temperature sensor (MAF/IAT) - replacement

1   The Intake Air Temperature (IAT) sensor is a thermistor (a resistor which varies the value of its resistance in accordance with temperature changes). The change in the resistance values will directly affect the voltage signal from the sensor to the PCM. As the sensor temperature INCREASES, the resistance values will DECREASE. As the sensor temperature DECREASES, the resistance values will INCREASE. The IAT is part of the Mass Air Flow sensor, which uses a hot-wire sensing element to measure the amount of air entering the engine. The air passing over the heated wire causes it to cool. The change in temperature is converted into an analog voltage signal to the PCM, which varies the fuel injector pulse width to match the airflow.

6.2 Unplug the MAP sensor electrical connector (A), squeeze the retainer tabs and remove the retainer (B), then pull the sensor straight up and out of the manifold

7.2 **MAF/IAT sensor is located on the intake air duct**

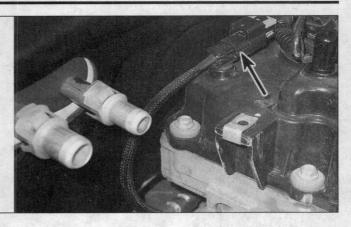

8.3 **Location of the Engine Coolant Temperature (ECT) sensor electrical connector . . .**

Replacement

Refer to illustration 7.2

2   The MAF/IAT is located on the intake air duct. Disconnect the sensor electrical connector **(see illustration)**.
3   Remove the two mounting screws and pull the sensor out from the air intake duct.
4   Installation is the reverse of removal.

8   Engine Coolant Temperature (ECT) sensor - replacement

1   The Engine Coolant Temperature (ECT) sensor is a thermistor (a resistor which varies the value of its resistance in accordance with temperature changes). The change in the resistance values will directly affect the voltage signal from the sensor to the PCM. As the sensor temperature INCREASES, the resistance values will DECREASE. As the sensor temperature DECREASES, the resistance values will INCREASE.

Replacement

Refer to illustrations 8.3 and 8.4

Warning: *Wait until the engine is completely cool before beginning this procedure.*
2   Drain the cooling system (see Chapter 1).
3   Disconnect the electrical connector from the sensor harness **(see illustration)**.
4   Carefully unscrew the sensor from the engine **(see illustration)**.
5   If the new sensor doesn't have a sealing compound on its threads, wrap the threads with Teflon sealing tape to prevent leakage.
6   Installation is the reverse of removal. Refill the cooling system by following the procedure described in Chapter 1.

9   Crankshaft Position (CKP) sensor - replacement

1   The Crankshaft Position (CKP) sensor provides the PCM with a crankshaft position

signal. The PCM uses the signal to determine the spark sequence (firing order) for each cylinder. The PCM also uses the signal to precisely control ignition timing and calculate engine speed (RPM). The signal is used by the Onboard Diagnostic system for misfire detection. The crankshaft position sensor is triggered by slots cut into a reluctor ring on the crankshaft. The sensor tip is positioned approximately 0.050 inch from the reluctor ring. As the notches pass the sensor the magnetic field is altered, producing a pulsating voltage. The ignition system will not operate if the PCM does not receive a crankshaft position sensor input.

Replacement

Refer to illustration 9.4

Note: *Whenever a crankshaft position sensor is disturbed, a Crankshaft Position Sensor variation learning procedure should be performed or a false misfire diagnostic trouble code may be set. If, after replacing the sensor a false diagnostic trouble code is set, take the vehicle to a dealership service department or other properly equipped repair shop for the procedure.*
2   Disconnect the cable from the negative battery terminal.
3   Raise the vehicle and support it securely on jackstands.

8.4 **. . . the sensor itself is threaded into the cylinder head at the right-rear**

4   The sensor is located at the left rear of the engine block. Disconnect the electrical connector from the sensor **(see illustration)**.
5   Remove the crankshaft position sensor mounting bolt and remove the sensor.
6   Installation is the reverse of removal. Be sure to install new O-rings on the sensor before installation, and lube the O-rings with engine oil.

10   Camshaft Position (CMP) sensor - replacement

1   The exhaust Camshaft Position (CMP) sensor is very similar in operation to the Crankshaft Position sensor, but it produces a signal pulse four (four-cylinder engine) or five (five-cylinder engine) times every exhaust camshaft revolution. Five-cylinder engines also have an intake CMP sensor, which produces one pulse-per-revolution of the camshaft.

Replacement

Refer to Illustrations 10.2a and 10.2b

2   Disconnect the electrical connector from the sensor **(see illustrations)**.
3   Remove the camshaft position sensor mounting bolt and withdraw the sensor from the cylinder head.

9.4 **The Crankshaft Position (CKP) sensor is located at the left rear of the engine block**

10.2a The exhaust Camshaft Position Sensor (CMP) is located at the right front corner of the cylinder head

10.2b There is a CMP sensor for the intake cam on five-cylinder engines only, near the front engine lifting bracket

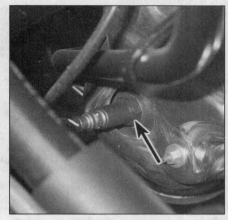

11.9a Location of the engine monitoring (pre-catalyst) oxygen sensor, at the bottom of the exhaust manifold

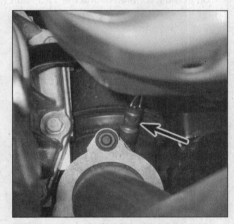

11.9b Location of the catalyst monitoring (post-catalyst) oxygen sensor, seen from below the vehicle

4   Installation is the reverse of removal. Be sure to install a new O-ring on the sensor before installation, and lubricate the O-ring with engine oil.

11 Oxygen sensor - replacement

Note: *All models are equipped with two oxygen sensors; one pre-converter oxygen sensor and one post-converter oxygen sensor.*

1   An oxygen sensor, in effect, measures the oxygen remaining in the exhaust gas after the combustion process. The leftover oxygen in the exhaust reacts with the elements inside the oxygen sensor to produce a voltage output that varies from 0.1 volt (high oxygen, lean mixture) to 0.9 volt (low oxygen, rich mixture). The pre-converter oxygen sensor is mounted in the exhaust manifold. The PCM monitors the varying voltage signal from the pre-converter oxygen sensor continuously to determine the required fuel injector pulse width, controlling the engine air/fuel ratio. A mixture ratio of 14.7 parts air to 1 part fuel is the ideal ratio for gasoline fuel to minimize exhaust emissions, as well as the best combination of fuel economy and engine performance. Based on oxygen sensor signals, the PCM tries to maintain this air/fuel ratio of 14.7:1 at all times.

2   The post-converter oxygen sensor (mounted in the exhaust system after the catalytic converter) has no effect on PCM control of the air/fuel ratio. However, the post-converter sensor operates in the same way, and the PCM uses the post-converter signal to monitor the efficiency of the catalytic converter. A post-converter oxygen sensor will produce a slower fluctuating voltage signal that reflects the lower oxygen content in the post-catalyst exhaust.

3   An oxygen sensor produces no voltage when it is below its normal operating temperature of about 600-degrees F. During this warm-up period, the PCM operates in an open-loop fuel control mode. It does not use the oxygen sensor signal as a feedback indication of residual oxygen in the exhaust. Instead, the PCM controls fuel metering based on the inputs of other sensors and its own programs. All oxygen sensors are equipped with a heating element, powered by fused ignition voltage, to heat the oxygen sensor to operating range as quickly as possible.

4   Proper operation of an oxygen sensor depends on four conditions:

a) *Electrical - The low voltages generated by the sensor require good, clean connections which should be checked whenever a sensor problem is suspected or indicated.*

b) *Outside air supply - The sensor needs air circulation to the internal portion of the sensor. Whenever the sensor is installed, make sure the air passages are not restricted.*

c) *Proper operating temperature - The PCM will not react to the sensor signal until the sensor reaches approximately 600-degrees F. This factor must be considered when evaluating the performance of the sensor.*

d) *Unleaded fuel - Unleaded fuel is essential for proper operation of the sensor.*

5   The PCM can detect several different oxygen sensor problems and set diagnostic trouble codes to indicate the specific fault (see Section 2). When an oxygen sensor fault occurs, the PCM will disregard the oxygen sensor signal voltage and revert to open-loop fuel control as described previously.

Replacement

Refer to illustrations 11.9a and 11.9b

6   The exhaust pipe contracts when cool, and the oxygen sensor may be hard to loosen when the engine is cold. To make sensor removal easier, start and run the engine for a minute or two; then shut it off. Be careful not to burn yourself during the following procedure. Also observe these guidelines when replacing an oxygen sensor.

a) *The sensor has a permanently attached pigtail and electrical connector that should not be removed from the sensor. Damage or removal of the pigtail or electrical connector can harm operation of the sensor.*

b) *Keep grease, dirt and other contaminants away from the electrical connector and the louvered end of the sensor.*

c) *Do not use cleaning solvents of any kind on the oxygen sensor.*

d) *Do not drop or roughly handle the sensor.*

e) *Do not attempt to repair any oxygen sensor wire, if the wire is damaged the sensor must be replaced.*

7   If replacing the post-converter oxygen sensor, raise the vehicle and support it securely on jackstands.

8   The pre-converter sensor can be replaced without raising the vehicle.

9   Locate the sensor (**see illustrations**), follow the leads to its electrical connector, then disconnect the electrical connector from the sensor.

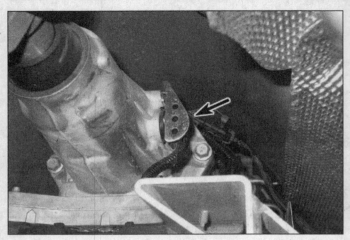

13.3 The Vehicle Speed Sensor is located on the right side of the extension housing on automatic transmission models (shown) - on manual transmissions the VSS is on the left side of the extension housing

14.2 Crankcase ventilation pipe (air intake resonator box removed for clarity)

10   Using a suitable wrench or specialized oxygen sensor socket, unscrew the sensor from the exhaust pipe.

11   Anti-seize compound must be used on the threads of the sensor to aid future removal. The threads of most new sensors will be coated with this compound. If not, be sure to apply anti-seize compound before installing the sensor.

12   Install the sensor and tighten it securely.

13   Reconnect the electrical connector to the sensor and lower the vehicle.

12   Knock sensor - replacement

1   The knock sensor detects abnormal vibration (spark knock or pinging) in the engine. The knock control system is designed to reduce spark knock during periods of heavy detonation. This allows the engine to use maximum spark advance to improve drive-ability. Knock sensors produce an AC output voltage that increases with the severity of the knock. The signal is fed into the PCM and the timing is retarded to compensate for the severe detonation.

Replacement

Warning: *The engine must be completely cool before beginning this procedure.*

2   Disconnect the cable from the negative battery terminal.

3   Raise the vehicle and place it securely on jackstands.

4   The knock sensor is located on the left side of the block, just rearward from the air-conditioning compressor. Access is best from below. Disconnect the electrical connector.

5   Remove the knock sensor bolt and sensor.

6   Installation is the reverse of removal. Tighten the sensor mounting bolt to 18 ft-lbs.

13   Vehicle Speed Sensor (VSS) - replacement

1   The Vehicle Speed Sensor (VSS) is a permanent magnet generator mounted on the transmission. The sensor is triggered by a toothed rotor on the transmission output shaft. As the output shaft rotates, the sensor produces an AC voltage, the frequency of which is proportional to vehicle speed. The PCM uses the sensor input signal for several different engine, transmission and radio control functions. The VSS signal also drives the speedometer on the instrument panel. A defective VSS can cause various driveability and transmission problems.

Replacement

Refer to illustration 13.3

2   Raise the vehicle and support it securely on jackstands.

3   Disconnect the electrical connector from the VSS **(see illustration)**. The sensor is located on the transmission extension housing (on the left side on manual transmissions, on the right side of automatic transmissions).

4   Remove the mounting bolt and withdraw the VSS from the transmission case.

5   Replace the sensor O-ring and lubricate it with clean transmission fluid.

6   Installation is the reverse of removal.

14   Crankcase ventilation system

Refer to illustration 14.2

1   When the engine is running, a certain amount of the gasses produced during combustion escape past the piston rings into the crankcase as blow-by gasses. The crankcase ventilation system is designed to reduce the resulting hydrocarbon emissions (HC) by

routing the gasses and vapors from the crankcase into the intake manifold and combustion chambers, where they are consumed during engine operation.

2   All models use a fixed-orifice (PCV) system. The main component of the Positive Crankcase Ventilation (PCV) system is the PCV pipe **(see illustration)**. Fresh air flows from the air intake duct through a vent tube into the engine. Crankcase vapors are drawn from the crankcase by the PCV pipe. Other than checking to see that the pipe is attached and has no cracks or leaks there is no other service or maintenance required.

15   Evaporative emissions control (EVAP) system

1   The fuel evaporative emissions control (EVAP) system absorbs fuel vapors from the fuel tank and, during engine operation, releases them into the engine intake system where they mix with the incoming air/fuel mixture. The main components of the evaporative emissions system are the canister (filled with activated charcoal to absorb fuel vapors), the purge valve, the vent valve, the fuel tank pressure sensor, the fuel tank and the vapor and purge lines.

2   After passing through a check valve, fuel tank vapor is carried through the vapor hose to the charcoal canister. The activated charcoal in the canister absorbs and stores the vapors. When a programmed set of conditions are met (engine running, warmed to a pre-set temperature, etc.), the PCM opens the purge valve and the vent valve. Fuel vapors from the canister are then drawn through the purge hose by intake manifold vacuum into the intake manifold and combustion chamber where they are consumed during normal engine operation.

15.10 The EVAP canister is located on the rear frame crossmember, near the spare tire

15.13 The EVAP purge valve/control solenoid is located on the left side of the engine block

3   The PCM regulates the rate of vapor flow from the canister to the intake manifold by controlling the duty cycle of the EVAP purge valve control solenoid. During cold running conditions and hot start time delay, the PCM does not energize the solenoid. After the engine has warmed up to the correct operating temperature, the PCM purges the vapors into the intake manifold according to the running conditions of the engine. The PCM will cycle (ON then OFF) the purge valve control solenoid about 5 to 10 times per second. The flow rate will be controlled by the pulse width, or length of time, the solenoid is allowed to be energized.

4   The system performs a self-diagnostic check when the engine is started cold. When the programmed conditions are met, the PCM opens the EVAP canister purge valve, leaving the vent valve closed. This action allows the engine to draw a vacuum on the entire EVAP system. Once the proper vacuum level is reached, the PCM closes the purge valve, sealing the system. The PCM then monitors the fuel tank pressure sensor voltage and sets a diagnostic code if a leak is detected.

5   The fuel tank pressure sensor operation is similar to the MAP sensor. The PCM supplies a 5-volt reference voltage and ground circuit to the sensor. The sensor returns a signal voltage to the PCM that varies according to the air pressure inside the fuel tank. When the air pressure inside the tank is equal to the outside air pressure (as with the fuel filler cap removed), the sensor output voltage is approximately 1.5 volts. With 14 in-Hg vacuum inside the tank the sensor output voltage is 4.5 volts. **Note:** *The evaporative emissions control system, like all emission control systems, is protected by a Federally-mandated warranty (5 years or 50,000 miles at the time this manual was written).*

Component replacement

6   All EVAP system hoses are equipped with quick-connect fittings. Before disconnecting a fitting, clean around the fitting and twist the fitting back-and-forth to loosen the seal. To disconnect a large hose fitting, squeeze the retainer tabs together and pull the fitting off the pipe. To disconnect a small hose fitting, push the locking tab in and pull the fitting off the pipe.

EVAP canister
Refer to illustration 15.10

7   The EVAP canister is attached to the crossmember near the spare tire.
8   Raise the vehicle and support it securely on jackstands.
9   Disconnect the electrical connector at the canister vent solenoid.
10   Disconnect the hoses from the canister **(see illustration)**.
11   Remove the bracket mounting bolt and remove the canister.
12   Installation is the reverse of removal.

Purge valve
Refer to illustration 15.13

13   The purge valve is mounted on the left side of the engine on a bracket ahead of the starter **(see illustration)**. It's easier to reach with the left fenderwell liner removed (see Chapter 11).
14   Disconnect the electrical connector.
15   Depress the locking tab and remove the quick-disconnect hose from the purge valve.
16   Remove the mounting bolt.
17   Remove the purge valve.
18   Installation is the reverse of removal.

Vent valve
Refer to illustration 15.19

19   The canister vent valve is mounted on a bracket at the EVAP canister **(see illustration)**.
20   Raise the vehicle and support it securely on jackstands. Refer to Chapter 11 and remove the left front fenderwell liner.
21   Disconnect the electrical connector.
22   Remove the hose from the vent valve.
23   Release the retainers and remove the vent valve from the bracket.
24   Installation is the reverse of removal.

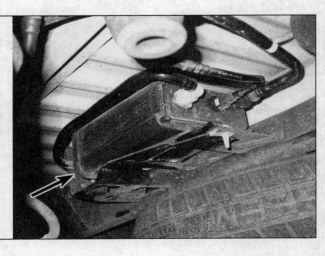

15.19 EVAP vent valve/control solenoid location - follow the hose around the canister to locate the valve/solenoid

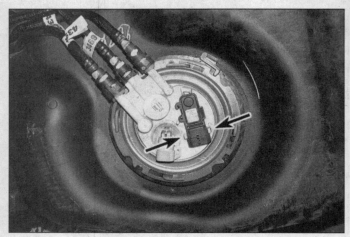

15.25 Fuel tank pressure sensor location - squeeze the sides of the retaining clip to free it

16.2 The camshaft position actuator solenoid is located at the right front corner of the cylinder head

Fuel tank pressure sensor

Refer to illustration 15.25

25   The fuel tank pressure sensor is located on the fuel pump module (see illustration).

26   Remove the fuel tank (see Chapter 4).

27   Disconnect the electrical connector from the fuel tank pressure sensor.

28   Release the retaining clip and remove the sensor from the top of the fuel pump module.

29   Installation is the reverse of removal.

16   Camshaft position actuator solenoid - replacement

1   The camshaft position actuator solenoid is sent a pulse-width modulated 12-volt signal from the PCM. The signal on-off time determines the amount of engine oil that flows through the Cam Phaser advance or retard passage. The Cam Phaser is attached to the exhaust camshaft and hydraulically advances or retards the camshaft. This continuous phasing of the exhaust camshaft results in a wider torque range and eliminates the need for an EGR valve.

Replacement

Refer to illustration 16.2

2   Disconnect the electrical connector from the camshaft position actuator solenoid (see illustration).

3   Remove the retaining bolt, then twist and pull the solenoid to remove it.

4   Clean any debris from the camshaft position actuator solenoid hole.

5   Installation is the reverse of removal. Be sure to install a new O-ring on the solenoid before installation, and lubricate the O-ring with engine oil.

17   Catalytic converter

Note: *Because of a Federally mandated warranty which covers emissions-related components such as the catalytic converter, check with a dealer service department before replacing the converter at your own expense.*

1   The catalytic converter is an emission control device added to the exhaust system to reduce pollutants from the exhaust gas stream. A three-way (reduction) catalyst design is used. The catalytic coating on the three-way catalyst contains platinum and rhodium, which lowers the levels of oxides of nitrogen (NOx) as well as hydrocarbons (HC) and carbon monoxide (CO).

2   The test equipment for a catalytic converter is expensive and highly sophisticated. If you suspect that the converter on your vehicle is malfunctioning, take it to a dealer or authorized emissions inspection facility for diagnosis and repair.

Replacement

Note: *Refer to the exhaust system servicing section in Chapter 4 for additional information.*

3   Raise the vehicle and support it securely on jackstands.

4   Remove the bolts and detach the catalytic converter header pipe from the exhaust manifold.

5   Remove the catalytic converter-to-muffler flange nuts and push the muffler back far enough for the studs to clear the converter flange.

6   Remove the catalytic converter and pipe assembly.

7   Clean the carbon deposits from the mounting flanges.

8   Installation is the reverse of removal.

18   Secondary Air Injection system

Note: *This system is only used on 2008 and later models.*

1   During cold warm-ups of the engine, the electrically-powered Secondary Air Injection pump delivers air into the exhaust manifolds to reduce emission and speed the warm-up of the catalytic converter. While it is operating, an exhaust-like sound is heard from the pump, though it may not be heard from inside the cab. Depending on how cold the ambient temperature is, the pump may only run for 5 to 60 seconds, and will not operate again until the next start-up.

2   The Secondary Air Injection pump is mounted to the crossmember at the lower right in the front of the engine compartment. A hose runs from the pump to the air filter housing, from which the pump draws filtered fresh air. A second hose from the pump is routed to the exhaust.

3   If a trouble code indicates the Secondary Air Injection pump is not operating, disconnect the electrical connector at the pump, disconnect the two hoses, and remove the nuts securing the pump to the bracket on the front crossmember.

4   Installation is the reverse of the removal procedure.

Chapter 7 Part A
Manual transmission

Contents

Specifications

General
Transmission lubricant type .... See Chapter 1

Torque specifications
	Ft-lbs
Shift tower-to-transmission bolts	15
Transmission mount-to-transmission bolts	44
Transmission mount nut	42
Transmission-to-engine bolts	37

1 General information

The vehicles covered by this manual are equipped with a manual or an automatic transmission. Information on the manual transmission is included in this Part of Chapter 7. Information on the automatic transmission can be found in Part B of this Chapter. Information on the transfer case is in Part C of this Chapter.

Vehicles equipped with a manual transmission use an Aisin AR5, five-speed transmission, with fifth gear being an overdrive gear.

Depending on the cost of having a transmission overhauled, it might be a better idea to replace it with a used or rebuilt unit. Your local dealer or transmission shop should be able to supply information concerning cost, availability and exchange policy. Regardless of how you decide to remedy a transmission problem, you can still save a lot of money by removing and installing the unit yourself.

2 Shift lever - removal and installation

1 Place the shift lever in Neutral.
2 Pull up on the front of the shifter boot to release the clips on the console, then remove the boot.
3 At the left side of the shift lever, near the bottom, remove the one setscrew and the shift lever.
4 If removing the shift control lever (the shaft the shift lever attaches to), remove the four bolts attaching the shift tower and shift lever assembly to the transmission.
5 If necessary, disassemble the shift lever assembly, clean the parts in solvent, blow everything dry with compressed air, coat all friction surfaces with clean multi-purpose grease and reassemble.
6 Installation is the reverse of removal. Use a thread-locking compound on the setscrew when reinstalling the shift lever. Be sure to tighten the shift tower bolts to the torque listed in this Chapter's Specifications.

3 Back-up light switch - check and replacement

1 The back-up light switch is located on the right side of the transmission, near the center of the transmission case.

Check
2 Turn the ignition key to the On position and move the shift lever to the Reverse position; the back-up lights should go on.
3 If the lights don't go on, check the back-up light fuse first (see Chapter 12). If the fuse is blown, trace the back-up light circuit for a short-circuit condition.
4 If the fuse is okay, raise the vehicle and support it securely on jackstands. Place the shifter in Reverse.
5 Working under the vehicle, unplug the back-up light switch electrical connector. Using an ohmmeter, check for continuity across the terminals of the switch. Continuity should exist. If not, replace the switch.

6   If the switch has continuity, check for voltage at the electrical connector; one of the two terminals should have battery voltage present with the ignition key in the On position. If no voltage is present, trace the circuit between the fuse block and the electrical connector for an open circuit condition.

7   If voltage is present, trace the back-up light circuit between the electrical connector and the back-up light bulbs for an open circuit condition. **Note:** *Although not very likely, the back-up light bulbs could both be burned out; don't rule out this possibility.*

Replacement

8   Raise the vehicle and support it securely on jackstands, if not already done.

9   Unplug the back-up light switch electrical connector.

10   Unscrew the back-up light switch from the transmission case.

11   Apply RTV sealant or Teflon tape to the threads of the new switch to prevent leakage. Install the switch in the transmission case and tighten it securely. Plug in the electrical connector.

12   Lower the vehicle and check the operation of the back-up lights.

4   Transmission - removal and installation

Removal

1   Disconnect the negative cable from the battery.

2   Shift the transmission into Neutral and remove the shift lever (see Section 2).

3   Raise the vehicle sufficiently to provide clearance to easily remove the transmission. Support the vehicle securely on jackstands.

4   Remove the skid plate, if equipped.

5   Disconnect the electrical connectors from the transmission and the oxygen sensor connectors.

6   If the transmission is going to be torn down, drain the lubricant (see Chapter 1).

7   Remove the driveshaft (see Chapter 8). Use a plastic bag to cover the end of the transmission to prevent fluid loss and contamination.

8   On 4WD models, remove the shift cable and vent hose from the transfer case.

9   Disconnect the clutch hydraulic line at the bellhousing, using a special tool to push back the quick-connect line. **Note:** *The hydraulic line has check-balls inside, so there is no need to plug the line once it is disconnected.*

10   Remove the starter motor (see Chapter 5).

11   Support the engine from above with an engine hoist, or place a jack (with a block of wood as an insulator) under the engine oil pan. The engine must remain supported at all times while the transmission is out of the vehicle.

12   Support the transmission with a jack - preferably a special jack made for this purpose. **Note:** *These jacks can be obtained at most equipment rental yards.* Safety chains will help steady the transmission on the jack.

13   The fuel lines are attached to the transmission with two brackets. Remove the mounting nuts to separate the brackets from the transmission.

14   Remove the exhaust pipe and exhaust pipe hanger from the transmission crossmember.

15   Remove the transmission mount nuts from below the crossmember.

16   Raise the engine slightly and remove the transmission crossmember.

17   Lower the jacks supporting the transmission and engine assembly.

18   Remove the bolts attaching the transmission to the engine.

19   Make a final check for any wiring or hoses connected to the transmission, then move the transmission and jack toward the rear of the vehicle until the transmission input shaft clears the splined-hub in the clutch disc. Keep the transmission level as this is done.

20   Once the input shaft is clear, lower the transmission slightly and remove it from under the vehicle.

21   While the transmission is removed, be sure to remove and inspect all clutch components (see Chapter 8). In most cases, new clutch components should be routinely installed if the transmission is removed.

Installation

22   Insert a small amount of multi-purpose grease into the pilot bearing in the crankshaft and lubricate the inner surface of the bearing. Also apply a light film of grease on the input shaft splines, input shaft bearing retainer and the release lever/bearing contact points (see Chapter 8).

23   Install the clutch components (see Chapter 8).

24   With the transmission secured to the jack as on removal, raise the transmission into position and carefully slide it forward, engaging the input shaft with the clutch plate hub. Do not use excessive force to install the transmission - if the input shaft does not slide into place, readjust the angle of the transmission so it is level and/or turn the input shaft so the splines engage properly with the clutch.

25   Install the transmission-to-engine bolts and tighten them to the torque listed in this Chapter's Specifications. **Caution:** *Don't use the bolts to draw the transmission to the engine. If the transmission doesn't slide forward easily and mate with the engine block, find out why before proceeding.* **Note:** *The two upper transmission-to-engine mounting bolts must go through the tabs on the coolant pipe at the back of the engine.*

26   Raise the transmission into place and install the mount.

27   Install the crossmember and carefully lower the transmission extension housing onto the mount and the crossmember. When everything is properly aligned, tighten all nuts and bolts securely.

28   Remove the jacks supporting the transmission and the engine.

29   On 4WD models, install the transfer case and shift cable (see Chapter 7C).

30   Install the various items removed previously, referring to Chapter 8 for the installation of the driveshaft and clutch release cylinder, Chapter 5 for the starter motor, and Chapter 4 for the exhaust system components.

31   Connect all wiring that was disconnected during removal, and reattach the fuel lines to the transmission brackets.

32   Fill the transmission with the specified lubricant to the proper level (see Chapter 1).

33   Remove the jackstands and lower the vehicle.

34   Connect the negative battery cable.

35   Road test the vehicle for proper operation and check for leakage.

5   Transmission overhaul - general information

Overhauling a manual transmission is a difficult job for the do-it-yourselfer. It involves the disassembly and reassembly of many small parts. Numerous clearances must be precisely measured and, if necessary, changed with select fit spacers and snap-rings. As a result, if transmission problems arise, it can be removed and installed by a competent do-it-yourselfer, but overhaul should be left to a transmission repair shop. Rebuilt transmissions may be available - check with your dealer parts department and auto parts stores. At any rate, the time and money involved in an overhaul is almost sure to exceed the cost of a rebuilt unit.

Nevertheless, it's not impossible for an inexperienced mechanic to rebuild a transmission if the special tools are available and the job is done in a deliberate step-by-step manner so nothing is overlooked.

The tools necessary for an overhaul include internal and external snap-ring pliers, a bearing puller, a slide hammer, a set of pin punches, a dial indicator and possibly a hydraulic press. In addition, a large, sturdy workbench and a vise or transmission stand will be required.

During disassembly of the transmission, make careful notes of how each piece comes off, where it fits in relation to other pieces and what holds it in place. If you note how each part is installed before removing it, getting the transmission back together again will be much easier.

Before taking the transmission apart for repair, it will help if you have some idea what area of the transmission is malfunctioning. Certain problems can be closely tied to specific areas in the transmission, which can make component examination and replacement easier. Refer to the *Troubleshooting* section at the front of this manual for information regarding possible sources of trouble.

Chapter 7 Part B
Automatic transmission

Contents

Specifications

General
Transmission fluid type .... See Chapter 1

Torque specifications
Ft-lbs (unless otherwise indicated)

Note: *One foot-pound (ft-lb) of torque is equivalent to 12 inch-pounds (in-lbs) of torque. Torque values below approximately 15 ft-lbs are expressed in inch-pounds, since most foot-pound torque wrenches are not accurate at these smaller values.*

Manual lever nut	15
Park/Neutral Position switch	
Bolts	20
Screw	27 in-lbs
Transmission fluid pan bolts	84 to 122 in-lbs
Torque converter-to-driveplate bolts	44
Transmission-to-engine block bolts	35
Transmission mount	
Mount-to-transmission bolts	44
Mount-to-transmission crossmember nuts	42

1 General information

All vehicles covered by this manual come equipped with either a five-speed manual transmission or a four-speed automatic transmission. Information on the automatic transmission is included in this Part of Chapter 7.

The models covered by this manual use the 4L60-E electronic four-speed automatic transmission. This transmission is equipped with a torque converter clutch (TCC) that engages in fourth gear, and in third gear when the overdrive switch is turned off. The TCC provides a direct connection between the engine and the drive wheels for improved efficiency and economy. The TCC consists of a solenoid controlled by the Powertrain Control Module (PCM) that locks the converter in

third or fourth when the vehicle is cruising on level ground and the engine is fully warmed up. Some models are also equipped with an auxiliary transmission cooler that is mounted in front of the radiator and air conditioning condenser.

Due to the complexity of the automatic transmission and the need for specialized equipment to perform most service operations, this Chapter contains only general diagnosis, routine maintenance, adjustment and removal and installation procedures.

If the transmission requires major repair work, it should be left to a dealer service department or an automotive or transmission repair shop. Once properly diagnosed you can, however, remove and install the transmission yourself and save the expense, even if the repair work is done by a transmission shop.

2 Diagnosis - general

Note: *Automatic transmission malfunctions may be caused by five general conditions: poor engine performance, improper adjustments, hydraulic malfunctions, mechanical malfunctions or malfunctions in the Powertrain Control Module or its signal network. Diagnosis of these problems should always begin with a check of the easily repaired items: fluid level and condition (see Chapter 1), and shift cable adjustment (see Section 3). Next, perform a road test to determine if the problem has been corrected or if more diagnosis is necessary. Because the transmission relies on many sensors in the engine control system, and since the transmission shift points are controlled by the Powertrain Control Module, you'll also* *want to check to see if any trouble codes have been stored in the PCM (see Chapter 6 for a list of trouble codes and how to extract them). If the problem persists after the preliminary tests and corrections are completed, additional diagnosis should be done by a dealer service department or transmission repair shop. Refer to the Troubleshooting section at the front of this manual for transmission problem diagnosis.*

Preliminary checks

1   Drive the vehicle to warm the transmission to normal operating temperature.
2   Check the fluid level as described in Chapter 1:

a) *If the fluid level is unusually low, add enough fluid to bring the level within the designated area of the dipstick, then check for external leaks.*

b) *If the fluid level is abnormally high, drain off the excess, then check the drained fluid for contamination by coolant. The presence of engine coolant in the automatic transmission fluid indicates that a failure has occurred in the internal radiator walls that separate the coolant from the transmission fluid (see Chapter 3).*

c) *If the fluid is foaming, drain it and refill the transmission, then check for coolant in the fluid or a high fluid level.*

3   Check the engine idle speed. **Note:** *If the engine is malfunctioning, do not proceed with the preliminary checks until it has been repaired and runs normally.*
4   Inspect the shift control cable (see Section 3). Make sure that it's properly adjusted and that it operates smoothly.
5   Check the Park/Neutral Position (PNP) switch adjustment (see Section 5).

Fluid leak diagnosis

6   Most fluid leaks are easy to locate visually. Repair usually consists of replacing a seal or gasket. If a leak is difficult to find, the following procedure may help.
7   Identify the fluid. Make sure it's transmission fluid and not engine oil or brake fluid (automatic transmission fluid is a deep red color).
8   Try to pinpoint the source of the leak. Drive the vehicle several miles, then park it over a large sheet of cardboard. After a minute or two, you should be able to locate the leak by determining the source of the fluid dripping onto the cardboard.
9   Make a careful visual inspection of the suspected component and the area immediately around it. Pay particular attention to gasket mating surfaces. A mirror is often helpful for finding leaks in areas that are hard to see.
10   If the leak still cannot be found, clean the suspected area thoroughly with a degreaser or solvent, then dry it.
11   Drive the vehicle for several miles at normal operating temperature and varying speeds. After driving the vehicle, visually inspect the suspected component again.

12   Once the leak has been located, the cause must be determined before it can be properly repaired. If a gasket is replaced but the sealing flange is bent, the new gasket will not stop the leak. The bent flange must be straightened.
13   Before attempting to repair a leak, check to make sure that the following conditions are corrected or they may cause another leak. **Note:** *Some of the following conditions cannot be fixed without highly specialized tools and expertise. Such problems must be referred to a transmission shop or a dealer service department.*

Gasket leaks

14   Check the pan periodically. Make sure the bolts are tight, no bolts are missing, the gasket is in good condition and the pan is flat (dents in the pan may indicate damage to the valve body inside).
15   If the pan gasket is leaking, the fluid level or the fluid pressure may be too high, the vent may be plugged, the pan bolts may be too tight, the pan sealing flange may be warped, the sealing surface of the transmission housing may be damaged, the gasket may be damaged or the transmission casting may be cracked or porous. If sealant instead of gasket material has been used to form a seal between the pan and the transmission housing, it may be the wrong sealant.

Seal leaks

16   If a transmission seal is leaking, the fluid level or pressure may be too high, the vent may be plugged, the seal bore may be damaged, the seal itself may be damaged or improperly installed, the surface of the shaft protruding through the seal may be damaged or a loose bearing may be causing excessive shaft movement.
17   Make sure the dipstick tube seal is in good condition and the tube is properly seated. Periodically check the area around the speedometer gear or vehicle speed sensor for leakage. If transmission fluid is evident, check the O-ring for damage. Also inspect the driveshaft oil seal for leakage.

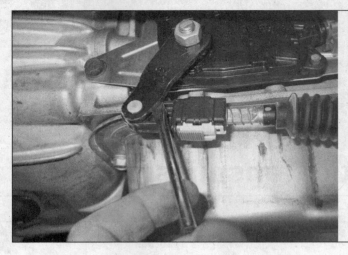

3.4 Pry the shift cable from the ballstud on the shift lever

Case leaks

18   If the case itself appears to be leaking, the casting is porous and will have to be repaired or replaced.
19   Make sure the oil cooler hose fittings are tight and in good condition. The transmission oil cooler lines on these models are equipped with quick connect fittings - always inspect the O-rings if a leak is suspected.

Fluid comes out vent pipe or fill tube

20   If this condition occurs, the transmission is overfilled, there is coolant in the fluid, the case is porous, the dipstick is incorrect, the vent is plugged or the drain back holes are plugged.

---

3   Shift cable - removal, installation and adjustment

Removal

Refer to illustrations 3.4, 3.5, 3.6 and 3.8

1   Disconnect the cable from the negative terminal of the battery.
2   Place the transmission in PARK and apply the parking brake.
3   Block the rear wheels so the vehicle will not accidentally roll in either direction.
4   Carefully pry the shift cable from the ballstud on the transmission shift lever **(see illustration)**.
5   Remove the clip and disengage the shift cable from the cable bracket on the transmission **(see illustration)**. Disengage the cable from the retainer on the underside of the floorboard. If you're working on a 4WD model, disengage the cable from the retainers on the transfer case.
6   Trace the cable to the cable grommet (the point at which it goes through the floorboard). Push the grommet up and out of its hole in the floorpan **(see illustration)**.
7   Remove the trim panel at the driver's side door hinge pillar. Remove the floor mat and pull back the carpet from the driver's side floor.

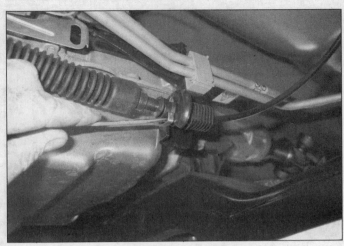

3.5 Remove the retaining clip and detach the shift cable
from the bracket

3.6 Push the shift cable grommet up, out of the floorpan

8   Pry the shift cable ball socket from the shift lever ball pivot (at the base of the steering column) and detach the cable (see illustration).

9   Trace the cable to the cable grommet. Pull the cable through the hole in the floor to remove it.

Installation and adjustment

Refer to illustrations 3.12a and 3.12b

10   Installation of the cable is the reverse of removal with the following exceptions:

11   Make sure the driver's shift lever and the transmission shift lever are in the Park position. If you're in doubt about the position of the transmission shift lever, rotate it fully clockwise.

12   Pull up the locking tab on the secondary lock cover and slide the cover off the primary lock (see illustration). Squeeze the tabs of the primary lock to free it, then pull the primary lock upward (see illustration). When this happens, the cable's spring tension will cause it to lengthen, so the cable end extends past

the ballstud on the transmission shift lever.

13   Push the cable end back just far enough to align with the ballstud, then snap it onto the ballstud. Note: If you accidentally push the cable end too far, let it go so the spring tension can push it past the ballstud again, then push the cable end back to align with the ballstud. The cable end must be pushed back into position in one movement.

14   Once the cable is attached to the lever, push the primary lock down until its tabs lock it, then slide the secondary lock over the primary lock.

15   Make sure the transmission shifts properly into each gear range.

---

4   Park/Lock system - description and component replacement

Description

1   The Park/Lock system prevents the shift lever from being moved out of Park unless the brake pedal is depressed simultaneously.

3.8 Carefully pry the cable eye (A) off the
shift cable end, then pull the clip
to release the cable from the
column bracket (B)

It also prevents the ignition key from being removed from the ignition switch unless the shift lever is in the Park position. When the

3.12a Lift the latch and slide the secondary lock back in the
direction of the arrow . . .

3.12b . . . then squeeze the tabs and pull the primary lock out

4.5 Disconnect the electrical connector (A), then remove the shift-lock solenoid (B) from the steering column

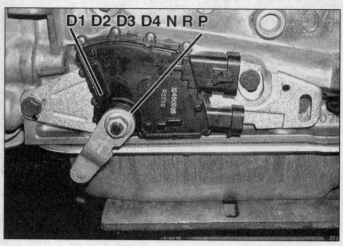

5.1 Transmission manual lever position details

car is started, a solenoid is energized, locking the shift lever in Park; when the brake pedal is depressed, the solenoid is de-energized, unlocking the shift lever so that it can be moved into some other gear.

2   The system has a manual override that allows the transmission to be shifted out of park in the event of an electrical failure. To use the override, remove the shift lever trim boot (see Chapter 11). Locate the override lever, on the upper right side of the shift lever bracket, and move it toward the front of the vehicle.

Shift lock control solenoid replacement

Refer to illustration 4.5
Warning: *These models have airbags. Always disable the airbag system before working in the vicinity of any airbag system component to avoid the possibility of accidental deployment of the airbag, which could cause personal injury (see Chapter 12).*

3   Remove the steering column covers (see Chapter 11).
4   Disconnect the electrical connector from the solenoid, then position the shifter in Neutral.
5   The solenoid can be pried from the column with a flat-bladed screwdriver **(see illustration)**.
6   Installation is the reverse of removal.

---

5   Park/Neutral Position (PNP) switch/back-up light switch - description, adjustment and replacement

---

Description

Refer to illustration 5.1
1   The Park/Neutral Position switch is part of the transmission range switch, which is mounted on the side of the transmission over the transmission manual shaft **(see illustra-**

tion). The switch is an information sensor for the Powertrain Control Module (PCM). Among its functions are those normally handled by a conventional Park/Neutral switch: it prevents the engine from starting in any gear other than park or Neutral, and closes the circuit for the back-up lights when the shift lever is moved to Reverse.

Adjustment

2   Verify that the engine will start only in Park or Neutral. If it starts in any other gear, it will be necessary to readjust the switch.
3   To adjust the switch, loosen the switch mounting bolts and turn it slightly one way or the other until the engine now only starts in Park or Neutral. Then tighten the mounting bolts.

Replacement

Refer to illustrations 5.9 and 5.11
4   Disconnect the cable from the negative terminal of the battery.
5   Apply the parking brake and put the shift lever in Neutral.
6   Locate the Park/Neutral Position (PNP) switch, which is mounted on the transmission

at the manual lever **(see illustration 5.1)**.
7   Disconnect the shift cable from the manual lever.
8   Disconnect the electrical connector from the PNP switch.
9   Remove the manual-lever retaining nut and remove the manual lever **(see illustration)**. **Note:** *Be careful not to move the manual lever from the Neutral position while doing this. If the lever moves, insert the manual lever back on the shift shaft loosely and reposition the lever in the Neutral position before removing the PNP switch* **(see illustration 5.1)**.
10   Remove the switch retaining bolts and detach the switch from the transmission **(see illustration 5.9)**.
11   If you're installing a new switch, align the slots on the switch (where the shaft is inserted) with the notch on the switch body **(see illustration)**. Then install the switch onto the shaft.
12   If you're installing the old switch, simply align the flats of the manual shaft with the flats of the Park/Neutral Position switch and install the switch. If you're installing a new switch, it comes with a plastic alignment tool.
13   Install the switch mounting bolts and tighten them to the torque listed in this Chapter's Specifications.

5.9 Remove the manual lever retaining nut (A), the manual lever (B) and the switch mounting bolts (C)

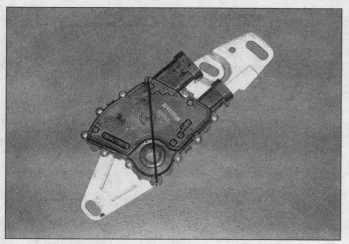

5.11 Before installing the PNP switch, align the tabs on the switch with the notch in the switch body - this is the Neutral position

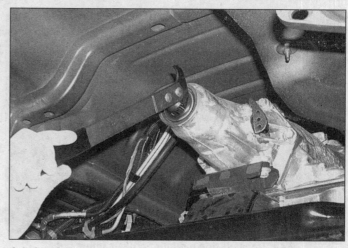

6.4 Carefully pry the old seal out of the extension housing - don't damage the splines on the output shaft

14 Install the manual lever, tightening the nut to the torque listed in this Chapter's Specifications.
15 Attach the shift cable and reconnect the electrical connectors.
16 The remainder of installation is the reverse of removal.

6 Extension housing oil seal (2WD models) - replacement

Refer to illustrations 6.4 and 6.5

1 Oil leaks frequently occur due to wear of the extension housing oil seal. Replacement of this seal is relatively easy, since it can be performed without removing the transmission from the vehicle.
2 The extension housing oil seal is located at the extreme rear of the transmission, where

the driveshaft is attached. If leakage at the seal is suspected, raise the vehicle and support it securely on jackstands. If the seal is leaking, transmission lubricant will be built up on the front of the driveshaft and may be dripping from the rear of the transmission.
3 Remove the driveshaft (see Chapter 8).
4 Using a seal removal tool or a large screwdriver, carefully pry the oil seal out of the rear of the transmission (**see illustration**). Do not damage the splines on the transmission output shaft.
5 Using a seal driver or a very large deep socket as a drift, install the new oil seal (**see illustration**). Drive it into the bore squarely and make sure it's completely seated.
6 Lubricate the splines of the transmission output shaft and the outside of the driveshaft yoke with lightweight grease, then install the driveshaft (see Chapter 8). Be careful not to damage the lip of the new seal.

7 Transmission mount - check and replacement

Check

Refer to illustration 7.2

1 Raise the vehicle and support it securely on jackstands.
2 Insert a large screwdriver or prybar into the space between the transmission extension housing and the crossmember and try to pry the transmission up slightly (**see illustration**).
3 The transmission should not move much at all - if the mount is cracked or torn, replace it.

Replacement

Refer to illustrations 7.4a and 7.4b

4 To replace the mount, remove the bolts or nuts attaching the mount to the crossmember

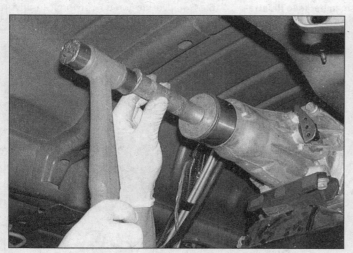

6.5 Drive the new seal into place with a seal driver or a large socket and hammer

7.2 To check the transmission mount, insert a large screwdriver or prybar between the crossmember and the transmission and try to pry the transmission up - it should move very little

7.4a Transmission mount-to-crossmember nuts

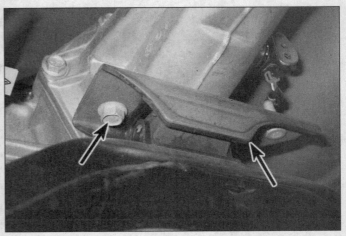

7.4b Transmission mount-to-transmission bolts

and the transmission **(see illustrations)**.

5   Raise the transmission slightly with a jack and remove the mount.

6   Installation is the reverse of the removal procedure. Be sure to tighten all nuts and bolts securely.

8   Automatic transmission - removal and installation

Removal

Refer to illustrations 8.13, 8.15, 8.17a, 8.17b and 8.18

Caution: *The transmission and torque converter must be removed as a single assembly. If you try to leave the torque converter attached to the driveplate, the converter driveplate, pump bushing and oil seal will be damaged. The driveplate is not designed to support the load, so none of the weight of the transmission should be allowed to rest on the plate during removal.*

1   Disconnect the cable from the negative terminal of the battery.

2   Raise the vehicle and support it securely on jackstands. Remove the skid plate and skid plate crossmember, if equipped.

3   Drain the transmission fluid (see Chapter 1).

4   Detach the fluid filler tube from the right side of the engine.

5   Remove all exhaust components that interfere with transmission removal (see Chapter 4).

6   Remove the rear driveshaft (see Chapter 8).

7   Support the engine from above with an engine hoist, or place a jack (with a block of wood as an insulator) under the engine oil pan. The engine must remain supported at all times while the transmission is out of the vehicle.

8   Support the transmission with a jack - preferably a jack made for this purpose (available at most tool rental yards). Safety chains will help steady the transmission on the jack.

9   Remove the nuts securing the transmission mount to the crossmember **(see illustration 7.4a)**. Then raise the transmission slightly

and unbolt the crossmember.

10   Lower the engine and transmission so you can reach the top and sides of the transmission.

11   On 4WD models, remove the transfer case (see Chapter 7C).

12   Disconnect the shift cable from the manual lever and the cable bracket (see Section 3).

13   Remove the transmission heat shield (if equipped) and disconnect the vent hose **(see illustration)**.

14   Working on the left side of the transmission, disconnect the Park/Neutral position switch electrical connector (see Section 5) and main electrical connector. Also free the transmission wiring harness from any retainers. Unbolt the fuel line support bracket from the left side of the transmission.

15   Remove the inspection plug at the bottom of the bellhousing and mark the relationship of the torque converter to the driveplate so they can be installed in the same position **(see illustration)**.

16   Remove the torque converter-to-driveplate bolts. Turn the crankshaft for access to

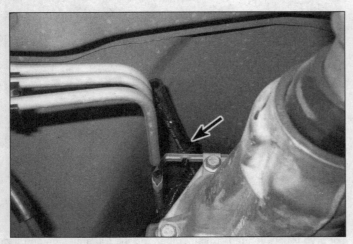

8.13 Disconnect the vent hose from the transmission

8.15 Pry off the inspection plug and mark the relationship between the torque converter and the driveplate

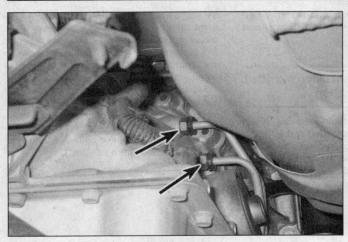

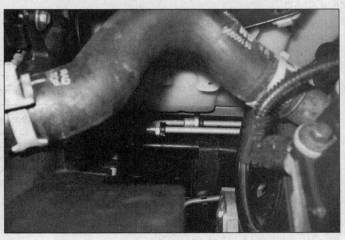

8.17a Disconnect the transmission cooler lines at the transmission . . .

8.17b . . . and at the engine

each bolt. Turn the crankshaft in a clockwise direction (as viewed from the front). **Note:** *Space is limited when accessing converter bolts. Use a short T-50 Torx bit or an 18mm crowfoot wrench.*

17 Disconnect the transmission cooler lines from the right side of the transmission and the engine **(see illustrations)**. To disconnect the lines from the transmission, simply unsnap the plastic collar from the quick-connect fitting, then pry off the quick-connect fitting retaining clip and remove the lines. Plug the ends of the lines to prevent fluid from leaking out after you disconnect them. Always be sure to inspect the O-rings on the cooler lines before reinstallation.

18 Secure the transmission to the jack with a safety chain, then remove the bolts securing the transmission to the engine **(see illustration)**. A long extension and a U-joint socket will greatly simplify this step. **Note:** *The upper bolts are easier to remove after the transmission has been lowered (see the next Step).*

19 Lower the engine and transmission slightly and remove the fill/dipstick tube bracket bolt and pull the tube out of the transmission. Don't lose the tube seal (it can be reused if it's still in good shape).

20 Clamp a pair of locking pliers on the bellhousing case through the lower inspection hole. Clamp the pliers just in front of the torque converter, behind the driveplate. The pliers will prevent the torque converter from falling out while you're removing the transmission. Move the transmission to the rear to disengage it from the engine block dowel pins and make sure the torque converter is detached from the driveplate. Lower the transmission with the jack.

Installation

21 Prior to installation, make sure the torque converter is securely engaged in the pump. If you've removed the converter, apply a small amount of transmission fluid on the torque converter rear hub, where the transmission front seal rides. Install the torque converter

onto the front input shaft of the transmission while rotating the converter back and forth. It should engage into the transmission front pump in stages. To make sure the converter is fully engaged, lay a straightedge across the transmission-to-engine mating surface and make sure the converter lugs are at least 3/4-inch below the straightedge. Reinstall the locking pliers to hold the converter in this position.

22 With the transmission secured to the jack, raise it into position.

23 Turn the torque converter to line up the holes with the holes in the driveplate. The marks on the torque converter and driveplate made in Step 15 must line up.

24 Move the transmission forward carefully until the dowel pins and the torque converter are engaged. Make sure the transmission mates with the engine with no gap. If there's a gap, make sure there are no wires or other objects pinched between the engine and transmission and also make sure the torque converter is completely engaged in the transmission front pump. Try to rotate the converter - if it doesn't rotate easily, it's probably not fully engaged in the pump. If necessary, lower the transmission and install the converter fully.

25 Install the transmission dipstick tube and seal into the transmission housing, then install the transmission-to-engine bolts and tighten them securely. As you're tightening the bolts, make sure that the engine and transmission mate completely at all points. If not, find out why. Never try to force the engine and transmission together with the bolts or you'll break the transmission case!

26 Raise the rear of the transmission and install the transmission crossmember.

27 Remove the jacks supporting the transmission and the engine.

28 Install the torque converter-to-driveplate bolts. Tighten them to the torque listed in this Chapter's Specifications. **Note:** *Install all of the bolts before tightening any of them.*

29 Install new retaining rings onto the quick-connect fittings. **Note:** *Don't push the retaining rings onto the fittings. Instead, hook one of the ends of the clip into a slot in the fitting, then rotate the other end of the ring into the other slot. If the retaining ring isn't installed like this, it may become spread-out and won't be able to retain the cooler lines securely. Connect the transmission fluid cooler lines to the fittings, making sure they click into place, then push the plastic caps onto the fittings.*

8.18 Remove the bellhousing bolts (lower and left side shown)

30　Plug in the transmission electrical connectors and install the heat shield, if equipped.

31　Connect the shift cable (see Section 3).

32　Install the torque converter inspection cover.

33　Install the transfer case, if removed (see Chapter 7C).

34　Install the driveshaft(s) (see Chapter 8).

35　Adjust the shift cable (see Section 3).

36　Install any exhaust system components that were removed or disconnected (see Chapter 4).

37　Remove the jackstands and lower the vehicle.

38　Fill the transmission with the specified fluid (see Chapter 1), run the engine and check for fluid leaks.

9　Automatic transmission overhaul - general information

In the event of a fault occurring, it will be necessary to establish whether the fault is electrical, mechanical or hydraulic in nature, before repair work can be contemplated. Diagnosis requires detailed knowledge of the transmission's operation and construction, as well as access to specialized test equipment, and so is deemed to be beyond the scope of this manual. It is therefore essential that problems with the automatic transmission are referred to a dealer service department or other qualified repair facility for assessment.

Note that a faulty transmission should not be removed before the vehicle has been assessed by a knowledgeable technician equipped with the proper tools, as trouble-shooting must be performed with the transmission installed in the vehicle.

Chapter 7 Part C
Transfer case

Contents

Specifications

Torque specification

Ft-lbs (unless otherwise indicated)

Note: *One foot-pound (ft-lb) of torque is equivalent to 12 inch-pounds (in-lbs) of torque. Torque values below approximately 15 ft-lbs are expressed in inch-pounds, since most foot-pound torque wrenches are not accurate at these smaller values.*

Yoke flange retaining nut	101
Shift motor mounting bolts	16
Transfer case-to-transmission bolts	37
Transfer case speed sensors	156 in-lbs

1 General information

Four-wheel drive (4WD) models are equipped with an Isuzu T150 transfer case mounted on the rear of the transmission. Drive is transmitted from the engine, through the transmission and the transfer case, to the front and rear axles by driveshafts.

The transfer case allows the driver four ranges to choose from: 2WD High, 4WD High, 4WD Low or Neutral. Shifting is accomplished electronically. When any range is selected at a switch on the dash, the transfer case shift control module receives a voltage signal commanding it to energize the transfer case shift motor, thus rotating the sector shaft (clockwise or counterclockwise) and shifting the transfer case into the appropriate range. After the transfer case is positioned in the appropriate range, the transmission control module will send a signal to engage the front axle. The transfer case encoder is mounted to the shift motor and is used to relay sector shaft

position back to the transfer case shift control module.

A handy feature of the transfer case is that it has a Neutral position. In this position, the transmission and transfer case are not forced to rotate when the vehicle is being towed, saving wear and tear on these components.

We don't recommend trying to rebuild the transfer case at home. They're difficult to overhaul without special tools, and rebuilt units are usually available for less than it would cost to rebuild your own.

2 Transfer case control switch - replacement

1 Disconnect the cable from the negative terminal of the battery.
2 Remove the instrument panel center trim panel (see Chapter 11).

3 Pull out the retaining tabs and remove the transfer case control switch from the instrument panel.
4 Disconnect the electrical connector from the rear of the switch and remove the switch from the vehicle.
5 Installation is the reverse of removal.

3 Transfer case shift motor - replacement

1 Make sure the shift motor is in the 2-HI position. Raise the vehicle and place it securely on jackstands.
2 Remove the stone shields (if equipped) from below the transfer case and fuel tank.
3 Disconnect the shift motor electrical connector. Also detach the vent hose from the motor.
4 Detach the retaining bolts and remove the electric shift motor and encoder assembly.

5   Retrieve the O-ring and discard it (a new one should be used upon installation).
6   Install a new O-ring and position the shift motor in place on the transfer case, making sure the actuator shaft is aligned, then install the bolts. Tighten bolts to the torque listed in this Chapter's Specifications.
7   Installation is the reverse of removal.

4   Transfer case speed sensors - check and replacement

The procedure for checking and replacement of the transfer case output-shaft speed sensors is essentially the same as the procedure for the Vehicle Speed Sensor. Refer to the *Vehicle Speed Sensor - replacement* Section in Chapter 6.

5   Transfer case control module - replacement

1   The transfer case control module is located under the driver's seat carpet.
2   Disconnect the cable from the negative terminal of the battery.
3   If the vehicle is equipped with bucket seats, remove the driver's seat. If it's equipped with a bench seat, remove the seat (see Chapter 11).
4   Remove the left sill plate, the left hinge pillar trim and the left center pillar trim, then peel back the carpet.
5   Using a screwdriver, release the control module retaining tabs and detach the control module from the bracket. Disconnect the electrical connectors.
6   Installation is the reverse of removal.

6   Oil seal - replacement

Note: *This procedure applies to both the front and rear output shaft seals.*
1   Raise the vehicle and support it securely on jackstands.
2   If you're replacing the front seal, remove the front driveshaft; if you're replacing the rear seal, remove the rear driveshaft (see Chapter 8).
3   If you're replacing the front seal, then remove the driveshaft yoke flange. **Note:** *Before attempting to loosen the flange nut, be sure to unstake the nut.* Tap around the seal with a screwdriver to loosen it in its bore, then pry it out.

4   To remove the rear output shaft seal, tap it out of its bore with a hammer and chisel.
5   Lubricate the new seal lips with petroleum jelly.
6   Drive the seal into place with a seal driver or a large socket. The outside diameter of the socket should be slightly smaller than the outside diameter of the seal. If you replaced the front seal, install the dust shield back onto the output shaft.
7   The remainder of installation is the reverse of removal. When installing the front driveshaft yoke flange, be sure to use a new O-ring, tighten the nut to the torque listed in this Chapter's Specifications, and stake the flange nut into place.

7   Transfer case - removal and installation

1   Disconnect the cable from the negative terminal of the battery.
2   Raise the vehicle and support it securely on jackstands.
3   Remove the stone shields (if equipped).
4   Drain the transfer case lubricant (see Chapter 1).
5   Remove the front and rear driveshafts (see Chapter 8).
6   Disconnect all electrical connectors and detach the vent hose from the top of the transfer case.
7   Free the wiring harnesses and fuel lines from the retainers on the transfer case. On some models, the post-converter oxygen sensor harness may be clipped to a bracket on the transfer case. Disconnect the harness from the transfer case.
8   Remove any transmission-to-transfer case support braces. Raise the transmission enough to remove the transmission mount (see Chapter 7A), then support the transmission on a jack or jackstands.
9   Support the transfer case with a jack - preferably a special jack made for this purpose. Safety chains will help steady the transfer case on the jack.
10   Remove the transmission-to-transfer case bolts.
11   Make a final check that all wires and hoses have been disconnected from the transfer case, then move the transfer case and jack toward the rear of the vehicle until the transfer case is clear of the transmission. Keep the transfer case level as this is done. Once the input shaft is clear, lower the transfer case and remove it from under the vehicle.

12   Inspect the transfer case gasket. If it's damaged, replace it with a new one. Don't use silicone sealant as a substitute for the gasket.
13   Installation is the reverse of removal. Be sure to tighten the transmission-to-transfer case bolts to the torque listed in this Chapter's Specifications.

8   Transfer case overhaul - general information

Overhauling a transfer case is a difficult job for the do-it-yourselfer. It involves the disassembly and reassembly of many small parts. Numerous clearances must be precisely measured and, if necessary, changed with select-fit spacers and snap-rings. As a result, if transfer case problems arise, it can be removed and installed by a competent do-it-yourselfer, but overhaul should be left to a transmission repair shop. Rebuilt transfer cases may be available - check with your dealer parts department and auto parts stores. At any rate, the time and money involved in an overhaul is almost sure to exceed the cost of a rebuilt unit.

Nevertheless, it's not impossible for an inexperienced mechanic to rebuild a transfer case if the special tools are available and the job is done in a deliberate step-by-step manner so nothing is overlooked.

The tools necessary for an overhaul include internal and external snap-ring pliers, a bearing puller, a slide hammer, a set of pin punches, a dial indicator and possibly a hydraulic press. In addition, a large, sturdy workbench and a vise or transmission stand will be required.

During disassembly of the transfer case, make careful notes of how each piece comes off, where it fits in relation to other pieces and what holds it in place. Note how parts are installed when you remove them; this will make it much easier to get the transfer case back together.

Before taking the transfer case apart for repair, it will help if you have some idea what area of the transfer case is malfunctioning. Certain problems can be closely tied to specific areas in the transfer case, which can make component examination and replacement easier. Refer to the *Troubleshooting* section at the front of this manual for information regarding possible sources of trouble.

Chapter 8
Clutch and driveline

Contents

Specifications

General
Inner CV joint length **(see illustration 13.3r)** .... 11.2 inches

Torque specifications
Ft-lbs (unless otherwise indicated)

Note: *One foot-pound (ft-lb) of torque is equivalent to 12 inch-pounds (in-lbs) of torque. Torque values below approximately 15 ft-lbs are expressed in inch-pounds, since most foot-pound torque wrenches are not accurate at these smaller values.*

Clutch
Pressure plate-to-flywheel bolts	
Step 1	15
Step 2	Tighten an additional 45-degrees (1/8-turn)
Release cylinder mounting bolts	71 in-lbs

Driveshaft
Driveshaft U-joint strap bolts	15
Driveshaft yoke retaining nut	123
Center bearing support bolts (two-piece driveshaft)	59

Driveaxles (4WD models)
Driveaxle/hub nut	191

Rear axle
Backing plate mounting bolts	100
Pinion shaft lock bolt	18
Differential cover bolts	20

Front axle (4WD models)
Intermediate shaft bearing housing bolts	44
Differential carrier-to-bracket bolts	112
Differential carrier bracket-to-frame bolts	112
Differential housing cover bolts	22
Pinion shaft lock bolt	18
Shift actuator bolts	16

1   General information

The information in this Chapter deals with the components from the rear of the engine to the rear wheels, except for the transmission (and transfer case, if equipped), which is dealt with in the previous Chapters. For the purposes of this Chapter, these components are grouped into three categories: clutch, driveshaft(s) and axles. Separate Sections within this Chapter offer general descriptions and checking procedures for components in each of the three groups.

Since nearly all the procedures covered in this Chapter involve working under the vehicle, make sure it's securely supported on sturdy jackstands or on a hoist where the vehicle can be easily raised and lowered.

2   Clutch - description and check

Refer to illustration 2.1

1   All models with a manual transmission use a single dry plate, diaphragm spring type clutch **(see illustration)**. The clutch disc has a splined hub that allows it to slide along the splines of the transmission input shaft. The clutch and pressure plate are held in contact by spring pressure exerted by the diaphragm in the pressure plate.

2   The clutch release system is operated by hydraulic pressure. The hydraulic release system consists of the clutch pedal, a master cylinder and fluid reservoir, the hydraulic line, and a concentric release cylinder/release bearing assembly.

3   When pressure is applied to the clutch pedal to release the clutch, hydraulic pressure is generated in the master cylinder and causes the release cylinder/bearing assembly

to extend. The release bearing then pushes against the fingers of the diaphragm spring of the pressure plate assembly, which in turn releases the clutch plate.

4   Terminology can be a problem when discussing the clutch components because common names are in some cases different from those used by the manufacturer. For example, the driven plate is also called the clutch plate or disc, the clutch release bearing is sometimes called a throwout bearing, the release cylinder is sometimes called the operating or slave cylinder.

5   Other than to replace components with obvious damage, some preliminary checks should be performed to diagnose clutch problems.

a) *The first check should be of the fluid level in the clutch master cylinder. If the fluid level is low, add fluid as necessary and inspect the hydraulic system for leaks.*

b) *To check clutch spin down time, run the engine at normal idle speed with the transmission in Neutral (clutch pedal up - engaged). Disengage the clutch (pedal down), wait several seconds and shift the transmission into Reverse. No grinding noise should be heard. A grinding noise would most likely indicate a problem in the pressure plate or the clutch disc.*

c) *To check for complete clutch release, run the engine (with the parking brake applied to prevent movement) and hold the clutch pedal approximately 1/2-inch from the floor. Shift the transmission between First gear and Reverse several times. If the shift is hard or the transmission grinds, component failure is indicated.*

d) *Visually inspect the pivot bushing at the top of the clutch pedal to make sure there is no binding or excessive play.*

3   Clutch master cylinder - removal and installation

Refer to illustration 3.4

Warning: *Wear eye protection when bleeding the brake system. If the fluid comes in contact with your eyes, immediately rinse them with water and seek medical attention.*

Caution: *Brake fluid will damage paint. Cover all body parts and be careful not to spill fluid during this procedure.*

1   Disconnect the cable from the negative terminal of the battery. **Note:** *Obtain a new plastic master cylinder rod retainer clip before beginning the procedure.*

2   Remove the left-side under-dash panel (see Chapter 11) and the heater/air conditioning duct behind it.

3   Disconnect the electrical connector from the clutch pedal position switch. Detach the pushrod from the pedal by using a flat-bladed tool to pop the plastic retainer off.

4   Raise the front of the vehicle and support it securely on jackstands. Disconnect the hydraulic line from the clutch release cylinder where it enters the transmission **(see illustration)**. A special tool, available at most auto parts stores, is required to separate the line fitting.

5   Open the hood and find the clutch master cylinder - it's located on the firewall, to the left of the brake master cylinder. Grasp the body of the master cylinder and twist it 45-degrees clockwise (when facing the firewall) to unlock it from the firewall.

6   Detach the hydraulic line from any clips which may be securing it, then remove the master cylinder and line from the vehicle.

7   Installation is the reverse of removal. A new plastic retainer should be installed when reconnecting the pushrod to the clutch pedal. Check the fluid level in the reservoir, adding as necessary to bring it to the appropriate level. Bleed the system as described in Section 5.

4   Clutch release cylinder and bearing - removal and installation

1   Detach the hydraulic line from the release cylinder **(see illustration 3.4)**.

2   Remove the transmission (see Chapter 7A).

3   Remove the two release cylinder retaining bolts.

4   Slide the release cylinder off the transmission input shaft. Check the operation of the bearing by turning it while applying pressure; if it is rough or noisy, replace it (it can be removed from the release cylinder).

5   While the transmission is removed, inspect the clutch disc and pressure plate assembly (see Section 6) and replace as necessary.

6   Clean off the transmission input shaft and apply a light film of high-temperature grease to it. Slide the new release cylinder into place,

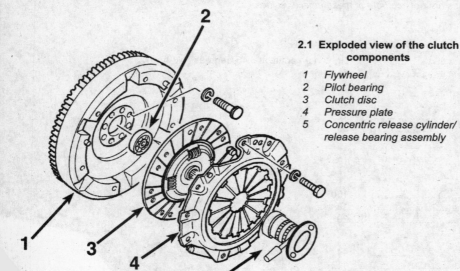

2.1 Exploded view of the clutch components

1   *Flywheel*
2   *Pilot bearing*
3   *Clutch disc*
4   *Pressure plate*
5   *Concentric release cylinder/ release bearing assembly*

24065-8-2.1 HAYNES

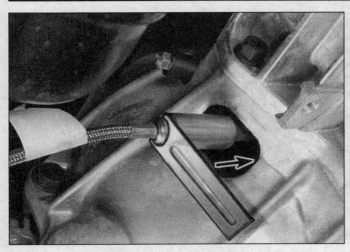

3.4 To disconnect the hydraulic line from the clutch release cylinder, place the special tool against the shoulder of the quick-connect fitting, push in on the fitting and pull the line out

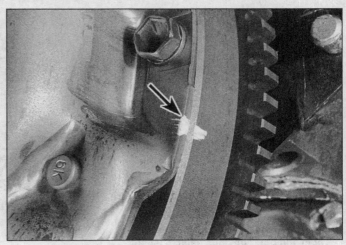

6.5 Be sure to mark the pressure plate and flywheel in order to insure proper alignment during installation (this won't be necessary if a new pressure plate is to be installed)

install the retaining bolts and tighten them to the torque listed in this Chapter's Specifications.

7   Install the transmission (see Chapter 7A).

8   Connect the hydraulic line to the release cylinder.

9   Fill the clutch fluid reservoir with the recommended fluid (see Chapter 1).

10   Bleed the clutch hydraulic system (see Section 5).

5   Clutch hydraulic system - bleeding

1   The hydraulic system should be bled to remove all air whenever any part of the system has been removed or if the fluid level has been allowed to fall so low that air has been drawn into the master cylinder. The procedure is very similar to bleeding a brake system.

2   Fill the master cylinder with new brake fluid conforming to DOT 3 specifications. **Caution:** *Do not re-use any of the fluid coming from the system during the bleeding operation or use fluid which has been inside an open container for an extended period of time.*

3   Raise the vehicle and place it securely on jackstands to gain access to the release cylinder bleeder valve, which is located on the left side of the clutch housing.

4   Remove the dust cap that fits over the bleeder valve and push a length of plastic hose over the valve. Place the other end of the hose into a clear container partially filled with clean brake fluid. The hose end must be submerged in the fluid.

5   Have an assistant depress the clutch pedal and stroke it slowly all the way down and up again 10-15 times, then hold it down. Open the bleeder valve on the release cylinder, allowing fluid to flow through the hose. Close the bleeder valve when the flow of fluid stops. Once closed, have your assistant

release the pedal.

6   Continue this process until all air is evacuated from the system, indicated by a solid stream of fluid being ejected from the bleeder valve each time with no air bubbles in the hose or container. Keep a close watch on the fluid level inside the clutch master cylinder reservoir - if the level drops too low, air will be sucked back into the system and the process will have to be started all over again.

7   Install the dust cap and lower the vehicle. Check carefully for proper operation before placing the vehicle in normal service.

6   Clutch components - removal, inspection and installation

Warning: *Dust produced by clutch wear and deposited on clutch components is hazardous to your health. DO NOT blow it out with compressed air and DO NOT inhale it. DO NOT use gasoline or petroleum-based solvents to remove the dust. Brake system cleaner should be used to flush the dust into a drain pan. After the clutch components are wiped clean with a rag, dispose of the contaminated rags and cleaner in a covered, marked container.*

Removal

Refer to illustration 6.5

1   Access to the clutch components is normally accomplished by removing the transmission, leaving the engine in the vehicle. If, of course, the engine is being removed, then check the clutch for wear and replace worn components as necessary. However, the relatively low cost of the clutch components compared to the time and trouble spent gaining access to them warrants their replacement anytime the engine or transmission is removed, unless they are new or in near perfect condition. The following procedures are based on the assumption the engine will stay

in place.

2   Referring to Chapter 7 Part A, remove the transmission from the vehicle. Support the engine while the transmission is out. Preferably, an engine hoist or support fixture should be used to support it from above. However, if a jack is used underneath the engine, make sure a piece of wood is positioned between the jack and oil pan to spread the load.

3   The clutch release bearing assembly can remain attached to the transmission for the time being.

4   To support the clutch disc during removal, install a clutch alignment tool through the clutch disc hub.

5   Carefully inspect the flywheel and pressure plate for indexing marks. The marks are usually an X, an O or a white letter. If they cannot be found, scribe marks yourself so the pressure plate and the flywheel will be in the same alignment during installation **(see illustration)**.

6   Turning each bolt only 1/4-turn at a time, loosen the pressure plate-to-flywheel bolts. Work in a criss-cross pattern until all spring pressure is relieved. Then hold the pressure plate securely and completely remove the bolts, followed by the pressure plate and clutch disc.

Inspection

Refer to illustrations 6.8, 6.10, 6.12a and 6.12b

7   Ordinarily, when a problem occurs in the clutch, it can be attributed to wear of the clutch driven plate assembly (clutch disc). However, all components should be inspected at this time.

8   Inspect the flywheel for cracks, heat checking, grooves and other ~~~~~~ **(see illustration)**. If the ~~~~~ slight, a machine shop ca~~~~~ face flat and smooth, whi~~~~~ mended regardless of the ~~~~~ ance. Refer to Chapter 2~~~~~

6.8 Check the flywheel for cracks, hot spots and other obvious defects (slight imperfections can be removed by a machine shop)

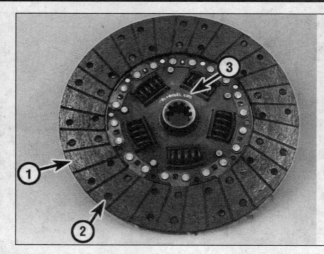

6.10 The clutch plate

1   **Lining** - This will wear down in use
2   **Rivets** - These secure the lining and will damage the flywheel or pressure plate if allowed to contact the surfaces
3   **Markings** - "Flywheel side" or something similar

removal and installation procedure.

9   Inspect the pilot bearing (see Section 7).
10   Inspect the lining on the clutch disc. There should be at least 1/16-inch of lining above the rivet heads. Check for loose rivets, distortion, cracks, broken springs and other obvious damage **(see illustration)**. As mentioned above, ordinarily the clutch disc is routinely replaced, so if in doubt about the condition, replace it with a new one.

11   The release bearing should also be replaced along with the clutch disc (see Section 4).
12   Check the machined surfaces and the diaphragm spring fingers of the pressure plate **(see illustrations)**. If the surface is grooved or otherwise damaged, replace the pressure plate. Also check for obvious damage, distortion, cracking, etc. Light glazing can be removed with sandpaper or emery cloth. If a new pressure plate is required, new and factory-rebuilt units are available.

Installation

Refer to illustration 6.14

13   Before installation, clean the flywheel and pressure plate machined surfaces with brake system cleaner. It's important that no oil or grease is on these surfaces or the lining of the clutch disc. Handle the parts only with clean hands.
14   Position the clutch disc and pressure plate against the flywheel with the clutch held in place with an alignment tool **(see illustration)**. Make sure it's installed properly (most

NORMAL FINGER WEAR

EXCESSIVE WEAR

EXCESSIVE FINGER WEAR

BROKEN OR BENT FINGERS

6.12a Replace the pressure plate if excessive wear is noted

6.12b Examine the pressure plate friction surface for score marks, cracks and evidence of overheating

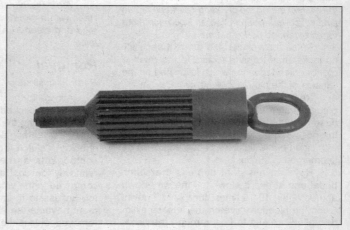

6.14 Center the clutch disc using a clutch alignment tool

7.5 A small slide-hammer puller is handy for removing the pilot bearing (typical)

7.6 When installing a pilot bearing into the crankshaft, a socket can be used (drive it in to the depth listed in the text)

replacement clutch plates will be marked "flywheel side" or something similar - if not marked, install the clutch disc with the damper springs toward the transmission).

15 Tighten the pressure plate-to-flywheel bolts only finger tight, working around the pressure plate.

16 Center the clutch disc by ensuring the alignment tool extends through the splined hub and into the pilot bearing in the crankshaft. Wiggle the tool up, down or side-to-side as needed to bottom the tool in the pilot bearing. Tighten the pressure plate-to-flywheel bolts a little at a time, working in a criss-cross pattern to prevent distorting the cover. After all of the bolts are snug, tighten them to the torque listed in this Chapter's Specifications. Remove the alignment tool.

17 Using a light film of high-temperature grease, lubricate the face of the release bearing.

18 Install the clutch release bearing as described in Section 4.

19 Install the transmission and all components removed previously. Tighten all fasteners to the proper torque specifications.

20 Bleed the clutch hydraulic system (see Section 5).

7   Pilot bearing - replacement

Refer to illustrations 7.5 and 7.6

1   The clutch pilot bearing is pressed into the rear of the crankshaft. It is greased at the factory and does not require additional lubrication. Its primary purpose is to support the front of the transmission input shaft. The pilot bearing should be inspected whenever the clutch components are removed from the engine. Due to its inaccessibility, if you are in doubt as to its condition, replace it with a new one. **Note:** *If the engine has been removed from the vehicle, disregard the following steps that do not apply.*

2   Remove the transmission (refer to Chap-

ter 7 Part A).

3   Remove the clutch components (see Section 6) and the flywheel (see Chapter 2A).

4   Inspect for any excessive wear, scoring, lack of grease, dryness or obvious damage. If any of these conditions are noted, the bearing should be replaced. A flashlight will be helpful to direct light into the recess.

5   Removal can be accomplished with a slide hammer fitted with a puller attachment **(see illustration)**, which are available at most auto parts stores or equipment rental yards.

6   To install the new bearing, lightly lubricate the outside surface with multi-purpose grease, then drive it into the recess **(see illustration)**. A socket with an outside diameter slightly smaller than that of the bearing can be used. Drive it in to a depth of 0.457-inch. **Caution:** *Be careful not to let the bearing become cocked in the bore.*

7   Install the clutch components, transmission and all other components removed previously, tightening all fasteners properly.

8   Clutch start switch - check and replacement

1   Remove the left side under-dash panel.

Check

2   Verify that the engine will not start when the clutch pedal is released. Now, depress the clutch pedal - the engine should start.

3   Locate the switch on the clutch master cylinder pushrod and unplug the electrical connector.

4   Using an ohmmeter, verify that there is continuity between the proper terminals of the clutch start switch when the pedal is depressed (refer to the wiring diagrams at the back of this manual). There should be no continuity when the pedal is released.

5   If the switch does not work as described, replace it.

Replacement

6   Unplug the electrical connector from the switch.

7   Pry up the tabs on the plastic retainer that secures the switch to the pedal assembly, then remove the switch.

8   Installation is the reverse of removal. The switch is self-adjusting, so there's no need for adjustment.

9   Verify that the engine doesn't start when the clutch pedal is released, and does start when the pedal is depressed.

9   Driveshaft and universal joints - general information and inspection

Refer to illustration 9.2

General information

1   A driveshaft is a tube that transmits power between the transmission (or transfer case on 4WD models) and the differential. Universal joints are located at either end of the rear driveshaft and at the front end of the front driveshaft. On some 2WD models, the rear driveshaft is of two-piece design, with a center support bearing assembly

2   The rear driveshaft employs a splined yoke at the front, which slips into the extension housing of the transmission or transfer case. This arrangement allows the driveshaft to slide back-and-forth during vehicle operation to compensate for changes in length due to suspension movement. An oil seal prevents leakage of fluid at this point and keeps dirt from entering the transmission or transfer case. If leakage is evident at the front of the driveshaft, replace the oil seal (see Chapter 7, Part A). Some models have a driveshaft with a center su... (see illustration). On these mo... tion of the driveshaft is equi... yoke.

3   On all models, the dri...

9.2 Rear driveshaft center support bearing

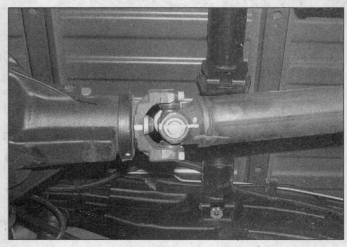

10.2 Mark the relationship of the rear driveshaft to the differential pinion flange

requires very little service. The universal joints are lubricated for life and must be replaced if problems develop. The driveshaft must be removed from the vehicle for this procedure.

4   Since the driveshaft is a balanced unit, it's important that no undercoating, mud, etc. be allowed to stay on it. When the vehicle is raised for service it's a good idea to clean the driveshaft and inspect it for any obvious damage. Also, make sure the small weights used to originally balance the driveshaft are in place and securely attached. Whenever the driveshaft is removed it must be reinstalled in the same relative position to preserve the balance.

5   Problems with the driveshaft are usually indicated by a noise or vibration while driving the vehicle. A road test should verify if the problem is the driveshaft or another vehicle component. Refer to the *Troubleshooting* Section at the front of this manual. If you suspect trouble, inspect the driveline.

Inspection

6   Raise the rear of the vehicle and support it securely on jackstands. Block the front wheels to keep the vehicle from rolling off the stands.

7   Crawl under the vehicle and visually inspect the driveshaft. Look for any dents or cracks in the tubing. If any are found, the driveshaft must be replaced.

8   Check for oil leakage at the front and rear of the driveshaft. Leakage where the driveshaft enters the transmission or transfer case indicates a defective transmission/transfer case seal (see Chapter 7). Leakage where the driveshaft meets the differential indicates a defective pinion seal (see Section 16).

9   While under the vehicle, have an assistant rotate a rear wheel so the driveshaft will rotate. As it does, make sure the universal joints are operating properly without binding, noise or looseness.

0   The universal joint can also be checked the driveshaft motionless, by gripping hands on either side of the joint and

attempting to twist the joint. Any movement at all in the joint is a sign of considerable wear. Lifting up on the shaft will also indicate movement in the universal joints. On models with a two-piece driveshaft, check for movement at the center support bearing assembly.

11   Finally, check the driveshaft mounting bolts at the ends to make sure they're tight.

12   On 4WD models, the above driveshaft checks should be repeated on the front driveshaft, as well. In addition, check for leakage around the sleeve yoke, indicating failure of the yoke seal.

13   Check for leakage where the driveshafts connect to the transfer case and front differential. Leakage indicates worn oil seals.

14   At the same time, check for looseness in the joints of the front driveaxles. Also check for grease or oil leakage from around the driveaxles by inspecting the rubber boots and both ends of each axle. Oil leakage around the axle flanges indicates a defective axleshaft oil seal. Grease leakage at the CV joint boots means a damaged rubber boot. For servicing of these components, see the appropriate Sections.

10   Driveshaft(s) - removal and installation

Rear driveshaft

Refer to illustrations 10.2 and 10.3

Removal

1   Raise the vehicle and support it securely on jackstands. Place the transmission in Neutral with the parking brake off. Block the front wheels to prevent the vehicle from rolling.

2   Make reference marks on the driveshaft and the pinion flange in line with each other **(see illustration)**. This is to make sure the driveshaft is reinstalled in the same position to preserve the balance.

3   Remove the rear universal joint bolts and straps. Turn the driveshaft (or wheels) as nec-

10.3 Insert a screwdriver or prybar through the driveshaft yoke to prevent the shaft from turning when you loosen the bolts

essary to bring the bolts into the most accessible position. To prevent the driveshaft from turning when you loosen the bolts, insert a large screwdriver through the driveshaft yoke **(see illustration)**.

4   Tape the bearing caps to the spider to prevent the caps from coming off during removal. On models with center support bearing, remove the support bearing mounting bolts **(see illustration 9.2)**.

5   Lower the rear of the driveshaft. Slide the front of the driveshaft out of the transmission or transfer case.

6   Wrap a plastic bag over the transmission or transfer case housing and hold it in place with a rubber band. This will prevent loss of fluid and protect against contamination while the driveshaft is out.

Installation

7   Remove the plastic bag from the transmission or transfer case and wipe the area clean. Inspect the oil seal carefully. Procedures for replacement of this seal can be found in Chapter 7.

8   Slide the front of the driveshaft into the

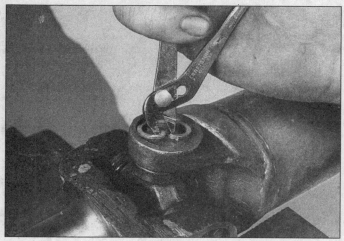

11.3 Use a small pair of pliers to remove the snap-rings from the ends of the universal joint yokes

11.4 To remove the U-joint from the driveshaft, use a vise as a press - the small socket will push the cross bearing cap into the large socket

11.5 Locking pliers can be used to remove the bearing caps from the yoke

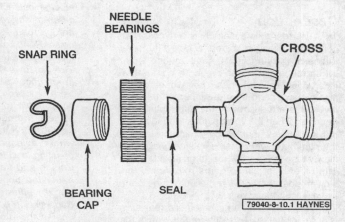

11.6 Exploded view of a universal joint

transmission or transfer case.

9   Raise the rear of the driveshaft into position, checking to be sure the marks are in alignment. If not, turn the rear wheels to match the pinion flange and the driveshaft.

10   Remove the tape securing the bearing caps and install the straps and bolts. Tighten all bolts to the torque listed in this Chapter's Specifications.

Front driveshaft (4WD models)

Removal

11   Raise the front of the vehicle and place it securely on jackstands. Remove the skid plate, if equipped.

12   Mark the relationship of the driveshaft to the front differential companion flange and also to the transfer case flange.

13   Remove the bolts and straps from the differential flange, then remove the bolts securing the driveshaft to the transfer case flange.

14   Push the driveshaft to the rear far enough to separate it from the differential flange, then lower it and pull the shaft out of the transfer case.

Installation

15   Attach the front end of the shaft to the differential companion flange and the rear of the shaft to the transfer case flange (be sure to line up the marks), install the straps and bolts and tighten all of the bolts to the torque listed in this Chapter's Specifications.

16   Install the skid plate (if equipped).

11   Universal joints - replacement

Refer to illustrations 11.3, 11.4, 11.5, 11.6 and 11.16

Note 1: *Always purchase a universal joint service kit for your model vehicle before beginning this procedure. Also, read through the entire procedure before beginning work.*

Note 2: *If inspection reveals looseness or play in the driveshaft center bearing (two-piece driveshafts), bring the driveshaft to a machine shop and have the old bearing pressed off and a new one installed. The yoke flange must be removed to replace the center bearing.*

1   Remove the driveshaft (see Section 3).

2   Place the driveshaft on a bench equipped with a vise.

3   Remove the snap-rings with a small pair of pliers **(see illustration)**.

4   Support the cross (also called a spider) on a short piece of pipe or a large socket and use another socket to press out the cross by closing the vise **(see illustration)**.

5   Press the cross through as far as possible, then grip the bearing cap with pliers and remove it **(see illustration)**.

6   A universal joint repair kit will contain a new cross, seals, bearings, caps and snap-rings **(see illustration)**.

7   Inspect the bearing cap bores in the yokes for wear and damage.

8   If the bearing cap bores in the yoke are so worn that the caps are a loose fit, the driveshaft will have to be replaced with a new one.

9   Make sure the dust seals are properly located on the cross.

10   Using a vise, press one bearing cap into the yoke approximately 1/4-inch.

11   Use chassis grease to hold the needle

rollers in place in the caps.

12   Insert the cross into the partially installed bearing cap, taking care not to dislodge the needle rollers.

13   Hold the cross in correct alignment and press both caps into place by slowly and carefully closing the jaws of the vise.

14   Use a socket slightly smaller in diameter than the caps to press them into the yoke. Press in one side, install the snap-ring, then press the other side to shift the cross assembly tight against the installed snap-ring and install the other snap-ring.

15   Repeat the operations for the remaining two bearing caps.

16   If the joint is stiff after assembly, strike the yoke sharply with a hammer (see illustration). This will spring the yoke ears slightly and free up the joint.

12   Axles - description and check

Description

1   The rear axle assembly is a hypoid (the centerline of the pinion gear is below the centerline of the ring gear), semi-floating type. When the vehicle goes around a corner, the differential allows the outer rear wheel to turn at a higher speed than the inner wheel. The axleshafts are splined to the differential side gears, so when the vehicle goes around a corner, the inner wheel, which turns more slowly than the outer wheel, turns its side gear more slowly than the outer wheel turns its side gear. The differential pinion gears roll around the slower side gear, driving the outer side gear - and wheel - more quickly.

2   An optional locking limited-slip rear axle is also available. This differential allows for normal operation until one wheel loses traction. A limited-slip unit is similar in design to a conventional differential, except for the addition of a pair of multi-disc clutch packs which slow the rotation of the differential case when

one wheel is on a firm surface and the other on a slippery one. The difference in wheel rotational speed produced by this condition applies additional force to the pinion gears and through the cone, which is splined to the axleshafts, equalizing the rotation speed of the axleshaft driving the wheel with traction.

3   On 4WD models, a fully independent front axle assembly is used. This consists of a differential and a pair of driveaxles. Each driveaxle has an inner and outer constant velocity (CV) joint.

Check

4   Often, a suspected axle problem lies elsewhere. Do a thorough check of other possible causes before assuming the axle is the problem.

5   The following noises are those commonly associated with axle diagnosis procedures:

a) *Road noise is often mistaken for mechanical faults. Driving the vehicle on different surfaces will show whether or not the road surface is the cause of the noise. Road noise will remain the same if the vehicle is under power or coasting.*

b) *Tire noise is sometimes mistaken for mechanical problems. Tires that are worn or low on pressure are particularly susceptible to emitting vibrations and noises. Tire noise will remain about the same during varying driving situations, where axle noise will change during coasting, acceleration, etc.*

c) *Engine and transmission noise can be deceiving because it will travel along the driveline. To isolate engine and transmission noises, make a note of the engine speed at which the noise is most pronounced. Stop the vehicle and place the transmission in Neutral and run the engine to the same speed. If the noise is the same, the axle is not at fault.*

6   Because of the special tools needed,

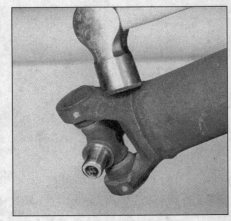

11.16 Strike the yoke sharply with a hammer to spring the yoke ears, which will free-up the joint

overhauling the differential isn't cost effective for a do-it-yourselfer. The procedures included in this Chapter describe axleshaft removal and installation, axleshaft oil seal replacement, axleshaft bearing replacement and removal of the entire unit for repair or replacement. Any further work should be left to a qualified repair shop.

13   Axleshaft (rear) - removal and installation

Refer to illustrations 13.3, 13.4, 13.5a and 13.5b

Removal

1   Loosen the rear wheel lug nuts. Raise the rear of the vehicle, support it securely on jackstands and block the front wheels. Remove the wheel and brake drum (see Chapter 9).

2   Remove the differential cover and allow the lubricant to drain into a container.

13.3 Remove the pinion shaft lock bolt

13.4 Withdraw the pinion shaft for access to the C-locks (don't turn the axleshafts after the shaft has been pulled out, or the spider gears may become mispositioned)

13.5a Push the axle flange in, then remove the C-lock from the inner end of the axleshaft

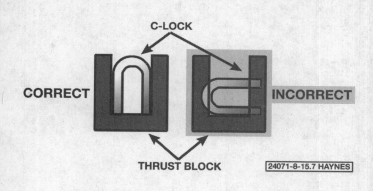

13.5b On models with a locking differential, the C-lock must be positioned as shown before it can be removed

3   Remove the lock bolt **(see illustration)**.
4   On models with a conventional differential (non-locking), remove the pinion shaft **(see illustration)**. On models with a locking differential, withdraw the pinion shaft part way, then rotate the differential until the shaft touches the case, providing enough clearance for access to the C-locks.
5   Have an assistant push in on the outer flanged end of the axleshaft while you remove the C-lock from the groove in the inner end of the shaft **(see illustration)**. **Note:** *On models with a locking differential, use a screwdriver to rotate the C-lock until the open end points in* **(see illustration)**.
6   With the C-lock removed, withdraw the axleshaft, taking care not to damage the oil seal (but note that it is a good idea to replace the seal whenever the axleshaft is removed - see Section 14). Some models have a thrust washer in the differential; make sure it doesn't fall out when the axleshaft is removed.

Installation

7   To install, carefully insert the axleshaft into the housing and seat it securely in the differential.
8   Install the C-lock in the axleshaft groove and pull out on the flange to lock it.
9   Insert the pinion shaft, align the hole in the shaft with the lock bolt hole and install the lock bolt. **Note:** *Apply a non-hardening, thread-locking compound to the threads of the lock bolt before installing it. Tighten the lock bolt to the torque listed in this Chapter's Specifications.*
10   Check the cover gasket. If it's in good condition it can be re-used. If it isn't, replace it. Install the cover and tighten the bolts to the torque listed in this Chapter's Specifications, then fill the differential with the lubricant specified in Chapter 1.
11   Install the brake drum. Install the wheel and lug nuts, then lower the vehicle. Tighten the lug nuts to the torque listed in the Chapter 1 Specifications.

14   Axleshaft oil seal (rear) - replacement

Refer to illustrations 14.2 and 14.3

1   Remove the axleshaft (see Section 13).
2   Pry the oil seal out of the end of the axle housing **(see illustration)**.
3   Apply a film of multi-purpose grease to the oil seal recess and tap the new seal evenly into place with a hammer and seal installation tool **(see illustration)**, large socket or piece of pipe so the lips are facing in and the metal face is visible from the end of the axle housing. When correctly installed, the face of the oil seal should be flush with the end of the axle housing.
4   Install the axleshaft (see Section 13).

14.2 Prying out the axleshaft oil seal with a seal removal tool

14.3 Using a seal driver to install the axleshaft oil seal - drive the seal in until it's flush with the bore

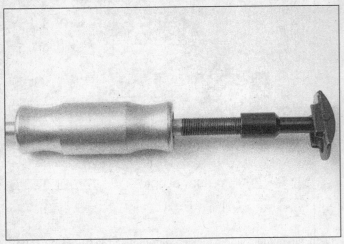

15.2 A typical slide hammer and axleshaft bearing remover attachment

15.3 Removing the axleshaft bearing with a slide hammer

15.4 Use a bearing driver or a large socket to tap the bearing evenly into the axle housing

16.3 Use an inch-pound torque wrench to check the torque required to rotate the pinion shaft

15 Axleshaft bearing (rear) - replacement

Refer to illustrations 15.2, 15.3 and 15.4

1   Remove the axleshaft (see Section 13) and the oil seal (see Section 14).

2   A bearing puller which grips the bearing from behind will be required for this job **(see illustration)**.

3   Attach a slide hammer to the puller and extract the bearing from the axle housing **(see illustration)**.

4   Clean out the bearing recess and drive in the new bearing with a bearing installer or a piece of pipe positioned against the outer bearing race **(see illustration)**. Make sure the bearing is tapped in to the full depth of the recess.

5   Install a new oil seal (see Section 14), then install the axleshaft (see Section 13).

16 Pinion oil seal - replacement

Refer to illustrations 16.3, 16.4, 16.5, 16.8 and 16.9

Note: *This procedure applies to the front and rear pinion oil seals.*

1   Loosen the wheel lug nuts. Raise the front (for front differential) or rear (for rear differential) of the vehicle and support it securely on jackstands. Block the opposite set of wheels to keep the vehicle from rolling off the stands. Remove the wheels.

2   Disconnect the driveshaft from the differential pinion flange and fasten it out of the way (see Section 3).

3   Rotate the pinion a few times by hand. Use a beam-type or dial-type inch-pound torque wrench to check the torque required to rotate the pinion **(see illustration)**. Record it for use later.

16.4 Before removing the nut, mark the position of the flange to the shaft and count the number of exposed threads

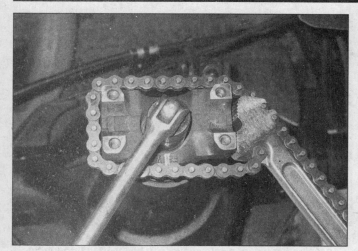

16:5 A chain wrench can be used to hold the pinion flange while removing the nut

16.8 Use a seal removal tool or a large screwdriver to remove the pinion seal (be careful not to disturb the pinion while doing this)

4   Mark the relationship of the pinion flange to the shaft (see illustration), then count and write down the number of exposed threads on the shaft.

5   A special tool, available at most auto parts stores, can be used to keep the companion flange from moving while the self-locking pinion nut is loosened. A chain wrench can also be used to immobilize the flange (see illustration).

6   Remove the pinion nut.

7   Withdraw the flange. It may be necessary to use a two-jaw puller engaged behind the flange to draw it off. Do not attempt to pry or hammer behind the flange or hammer on the end of the pinion shaft.

8   Pry out the old seal and discard it (see illustration).

9   Lubricate the lips of the new seal and fill the space between the seal lips with wheel bearing grease, then tap it evenly into position with a seal installation tool or a large socket (see illustration). Make sure it enters the housing squarely and is tapped in to its full depth.

10   Install the pinion flange, lining up the marks made in Step 4. If necessary, tighten the pinion nut to draw the flange into place. Do not try to hammer the flange into position.

11   Apply a bead of RTV sealant to the ends of the splines visible in the center of the flange so oil will be sealed in.

12   Install the washer and a new pinion nut. Tighten the nut until the number of threads recorded in Step 4 are exposed.

13   Measure the torque required to rotate the pinion and tighten the nut in small increments (no more than 5 ft-lbs) until it matches the figure recorded in Step 3. To compensate for the drag of the new oil seal, the nut should be tightened a little more until the rotational torque of the pinion exceeds the earlier recording by 5 in-lbs.

14   Reinstall all components removed previously by reversing the removal Steps, tightening all fasteners to their specified torque values.

17   Axle assembly (rear) - removal and installation

Removal

1   Loosen the rear wheel lug nuts, raise the rear of the vehicle and support it securely on jackstands placed under the frame rails. Block the front wheels to keep the vehicle from rolling off the stands. Remove the rear wheels.

2   Drain the rear axle lubricant.

3   Disconnect the driveshaft from the rear axle pinion flange (see Section 3). Fasten the driveshaft out of the way with a piece of wire from the underbody.

4   Position a jack under the rear axle differential housing, then raise it slightly.

5   Disconnect the shock absorbers at their lower mounts, then lower the jack far enough so the leaf springs aren't compressed at all.

6   Disconnect the vent hose from the fitting on the axle housing and fasten it out of the way.

7   Disconnect the flexible brake hose from the junction block on the axle housing, then plug the hose to prevent fluid leakage.

8   Remove the brake drums (see Chapter 9).

9   Remove the bolts securing the parking brake cables to the rear leaf springs, then disconnect the parking brake cables from the parking brake mechanism at the brake shoes (see Chapter 9).

10   With a jack under the differential for support, remove the leaf spring U-bolts (see Chapter 10).

11   With the help of an assistant, maneuver the rear axle over the leaf springs, rotate it to clear the springs, then remove the rear axle assembly from under the vehicle.

Installation

12   Installation is the reverse of removal. Tighten the U-joint strap bolts to the torque listed in this Chapter's Specifications. Tighten all suspension fasteners to the torque values listed in the Chapter 10 Specifications. Tighten the brake fasteners to the torque values listed in the Chapter 9 Specifications.

13   Bleed the brakes (see Chapter 9).

14   Install the wheels and tighten the lug nuts to the torque listed in the Chapter 1 Specifications.

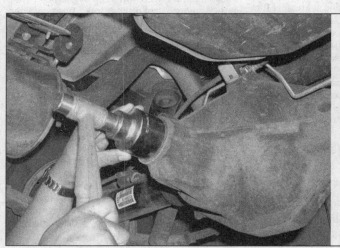

16.9 A large socket with a diameter the same as that of the new pinion seal can be used to drive the seal into the differential housing

19.3 A hammer and chisel can be used to knock the cover off the hub

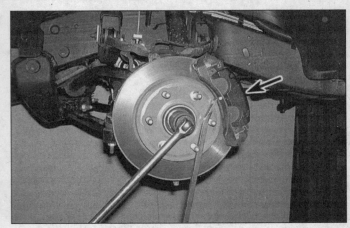

19.4 A large prybar can be used to immobilize the hub while loosening the nut, or a screwdriver can be inserted through the window in the brake caliper (arrow) and into the disc cooling vanes

18 Driveaxles (4WD models) - general information and inspection

1   Power is transmitted from the front differential/axle to the front wheels through a pair of driveaxles. The inner end of the driveaxles are splined to the differential side gears. The outer end of each driveaxle has a stub shaft that is splined to the front hub and bearing assembly and locked in place with a large nut.

2   The inner ends of the driveaxles are equipped with sliding constant velocity (CV) joints, which are capable of both angular and axial motion. Each inner CV joint assembly consists of a ball-and-cage type bearing and a housing in which the joint is free to slide in-and-out as the driveaxle moves up-and-down with the wheel.

3   The outer ends of the driveaxles are also equipped with ball-and-cage type CV joints, which are capable of angular but not axial movement. Each outer CV joint consists of six caged ball bearings running between an inner race and the housing.

4   The boots should be inspected periodically for damage and leaking lubricant. Torn CV joint boots must be replaced immediately or the joints will be damaged. If either boot of a driveaxle is damaged, that driveaxle must be removed in order to replace the boot (see Section 19).

5   Should a boot be damaged, the CV joint can be disassembled and cleaned (see Section 20), but if any parts are damaged, the entire driveaxle assembly must be replaced as a unit.

6   The most common symptom of worn or damaged CV joints, besides lubricant leaks, is a clicking noise in turns, a clunk when accelerating after coasting and vibration at highway speeds. To check for wear in the CV joints and driveaxle shafts, grasp each axle (one at a time) and rotate it in both directions while holding the CV joint housings, feeling for play indicating worn splines or sloppy CV joints. Also check the driveaxle shafts for cracks, dents and distortion.

19 Driveaxle (4WD models) - removal and installation

Refer to illustrations 19.3 and 19.4

Removal

1   Loosen the wheel lug nuts, raise the front of the vehicle and support it securely on jackstands. Remove the wheel.

2   Remove the splash shield from under the vehicle (see Chapter 11).

3   Pry off the hub cover (**see illustration**).

4   Remove and discard the driveaxle/hub nut. To prevent the hub from rotating, brace a large prybar across two of the wheel studs (**see illustration**), or insert a long punch or screwdriver through the window in the brake caliper and into the disc cooling vanes. **Warning**: *The hub nut should not be reused. Install a new hub nut when installing the shaft.*

5   Disconnect the wheel speed sensor electrical connector and free the harness from its retainers. Unbolt the brake hose retainer where it joins the metal brake line at the frame (see Chapter 9).

6   Remove the steering knuckle (see Chapter 10) and simultaneously pull the driveaxle stub shaft out of the hub. **Note**: *If the stub shaft sticks in the hub splines, tap on the end of the shaft with a brass punch and a hammer. If that doesn't free the splines, push the driveaxle from the hub with a puller.*

7   Drive the inner end of the driveaxle away from the differential or intermediate shaft with a hammer and brass drift. Place the end of the brass drift against the inner driveaxle joint housing. Apply enough force to disengage the retaining ring on the inner end of the driveaxle from the differential or intermediate shaft. Remove the driveaxle from the differential.

Installation

8   Installation is the reverse of removal, with the following additions.

9   Before installing the driveaxle, lubricate the splines on the stub shaft with multi-purpose grease.

10   Install a new driveaxle/hub nut and tighten it to the torque value listed in this Chapter's Specifications.

11   Tighten the suspension fasteners to the torque listed in the Chapter 10 Specifications.

12   Tighten the wheel lug nuts to the torque listed in the Chapter 1 Specifications.

20 Driveaxle boot (4WD models) - replacement

Note: *If the CV joint boots must be replaced, explore all options before beginning the job. Complete rebuilt driveaxles are available on an exchange basis, which eliminates much time and work. Whichever route you choose to take, check on the cost and availability of parts before disassembling the vehicle.*

1   Remove the driveaxle (see Section 19).

2   Place the driveaxle in a vise lined with rags to avoid damage to the axleshaft. Check the CV joint for excessive play in the radial direction, which indicates worn parts. Check for smooth operation throughout the full range of motion for each CV joint. If a boot is torn, disassemble the joint, clean the components and inspect for damage due to loss of lubrication and possible contamination by foreign matter. **Note:** *Some models are equipped with a protective cover that clamps around the larger diameter of each boot. Use diagonal cutting pliers to remove the clamps, then slide the cover off for access to the boots.*

Inner CV joint

Refer to illustrations 20.3a through 20.3p

3   To replace the inner boot, refer to the accompanying illustrations (**see illustrations 20.3a through 20.3p**).

20.3a Cut off the old boot clamps with a pair of diagonal cutting pliers (the smaller diameter clamp is actually a swage ring; you may have to use a hand-held grinder to cut through it. When reassembling the joint, use a conventional boot clamp, since special tools are required to swage the ring in place)

20.3b Pry the wire retainer ring from the CV joint housing with a small screwdriver

20.3c With the retainer removed, the outer race can be pulled off the bearing assembly

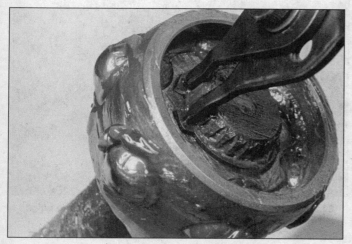

20.3d Remove the snap-ring from the end of the axleshaft

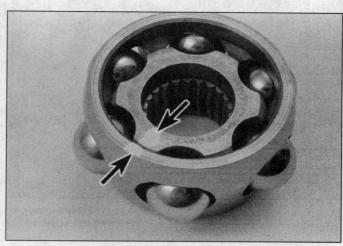

20.3e Make index marks on the inner race and cage so they'll both be facing the same direction when reassembled

20.3f Pry the balls from the cage with a screwdriver (be careful not to nick or scratch them)

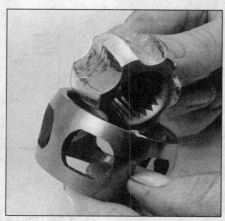

20.3g Tilt the inner race 90-degrees and rotate it out of the cage

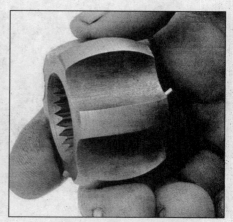

20.3h Inspect the inner race lands and grooves for pitting and score marks

20.3i Inspect the cage for cracks, pitting and score marks (shiny spots are normal and don't affect operation)

20.3j Press the balls into the cage through the windows

20.3k Wrap the axleshaft splines with tape to avoid damaging the boot, then slide the small clamp and boot onto the axleshaft

20.3l Install the inner race and cage assembly with the bulge facing the end of the axleshaft

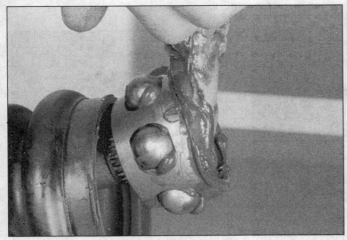

20.3m Pack CV joint grease into the bearing until it's completely full, then assemble the outer race onto the inner race and install the retaining ring. Caution: *Don't use any other kind of grease*

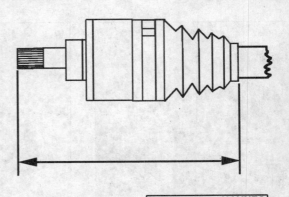

24072-8-13.3r HAYNES

20.3n Seat the boot in the housing and axle seal grooves, then adjust the length of the joint to the dimension listed in this Chapter's Specifications

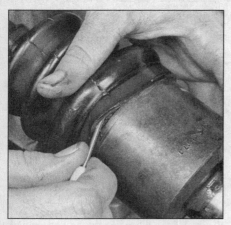

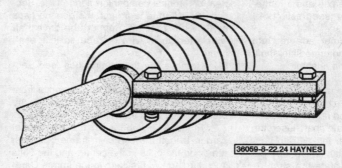

20.3p . . . then secure the boot clamps with a clamp-crimping tool (available at auto parts stores)

36059-8-22.24 HAYNES

20.3o With the joint set to the proper length, equalize the pressure in the boot by inserting a small screwdriver between the boot and the housing (make sure the boot isn't dimpled, stretched or out of shape) . . .

Outer CV joint

Refer to illustration 20.6

Caution: *Don't remove the outer CV joint from the axle shaft.*

4   Remove the inner CV joint and boot.
5   Cut off the clamps and remove the outer boot from the axle shaft.
6   Wash the outer CV joint assembly in solvent and inspect it for wear and damage **(see illustration)**. Replace the axle assembly if any CV joint components are excessively worn.
7   Wrap the splines of the shaft with tape, then slide the new boot and clamps onto the shaft **(see illustration 20.3k)**.
8   Repack the outer CV joint with CV joint grease and spread grease inside the new boot as well.

20.6 After the old grease has been rinsed away and the cleaning solvent has been blown out with compressed air, rotate the outer joint housing through its full range of motion and inspect the bearing surfaces for wear or damage - if any of the balls, the race or cage look damaged, replace the driveaxle and outer joint

9   Position the outer boot on the CV joint and install new boot clamps **(see illustration 20.3p)**.
10   Reassemble the inner CV joint and boot.
11   Install the driveaxle (see Section 13).

21   Front axle actuator (4WD models) - replacement

1   Raise the front of the vehicle and support it securely on jackstands. Remove the splash shield.
2   Disconnect the electrical connector from the actuator.
3   Remove the actuator mounting bolts and detach the actuator from the intermediate shaft housing.
4   To install the actuator, reverse the removal procedure. Tighten the bolts to the torque listed in this Chapter's Specifications.

22   Intermediate shaft bearing housing oil seals (4WD models) - replacement

1   Loosen the left front wheel lug nuts, raise the vehicle, place it securely on jackstands and remove the left front wheel.
2   Remove the splash shield.
3   Remove the driveaxle from the left side of the vehicle (see Section 19).
4   The outer seal can be replaced with the bearing housing installed on the vehicle. Pry the seal out with a seal removal tool, or use a slide hammer and seal remover adapter to pull the seal. Drive the new seal into its bore with a seal driver or a socket slightly smaller in diameter than the seal. **Caution:** *The seal must be driven in to a depth of 0.35 to 0.43-inch below the bore, or it will be damaged by the intermediate shaft.*
5   To replace the seal on the inner side, remove the housing (see Section 23). Place the intermediate shaft housing in a vise with padded jaws, then remove the seal from the bore with a seal removal tool, or use a slide hammer and seal remover adapter to pull the seal. Drive the new seal into its bore with a

seal driver or a socket slightly smaller in diameter than the seal.
6   Install the bearing housing (if removed).
7   The remainder of installation is the reverse of the removal steps.

23   Intermediate shaft bearing housing (4WD models) - removal and installation

1   The intermediate shaft bearing housing contains the bearing that supports the left end of the intermediate shaft. It also contains the shifting fork and sleeve that engage and disengage the left front driveaxle.
2   Loosen the wheel lug nuts, raise the vehicle, place it securely on jackstands and remove the left front wheel.
3   Remove the splash shield.
4   Remove the driveaxle from the left side of the vehicle (see Section 19).
5   Disconnect the electrical connector and free the harness from its retainer. Disconnect the stabilizer bar link from the lower control arm.
6   Support the bottom of the front differential with a floorjack and remove the bolts securing the left-side carrier mounting bracket.
7   Remove the bolts and the housing. If the bearing housing is removed, the bearing should be replaced. Clamp the housing in a vise with soft-jaws, and use a slide-hammer with a bearing puller on the end to remove the bearing. Press the new bearing in to the same depth as the old one.
8   Use a new gasket between the housing and the differential during installation and use thread-locking material on the bolts. Tighten the bolts to the torque listed in this Chapter's Specifications. The remainder of installation is the reverse of removal.

24   Intermediate shaft (4WD models) - removal and installation

1   Loosen the left front wheel lug nuts, raise the vehicle, place it securely on jackstands and remove the left front wheel.

2   Remove the splash shield.

3   Remove the left driveaxle and intermediate shaft bearing housing (see Sections 19 and 23).

4   Thread a slide hammer adapter into the hole in the end of the intermediate shaft. Attach a slide hammer to the adapter.

5   Pull the intermediate shaft out of the differential, taking care not to damage the seal on the opposite side of the oil pan.

6   Make sure the retaining ring is in position on the end of the intermediate shaft. Insert the intermediate shaft through the oil pan passage and into the differential, taking care not to damage the oil seal. Rotate the shaft as necessary to align its splines with the differential.

7   Install the slide hammer on the shaft, then use the slide hammer to drive the shaft in until its retaining ring locks into place in the differential.

8   The remainder of installation is the reverse of the removal steps.

25   Front differential carrier - removal and installation

1   Disconnect the cable from the negative terminal of the battery.

2   Loosen the front wheel lug nuts, raise the front of the vehicle and support it securely on jackstands.

3   Remove the under-vehicle splash shield. Drain the front differential lubricant (see Chapter 1).

4   Disconnect the front driveshaft from the front differential companion flange (see Section 10). Wrap tape around the bearing caps so they don't fall off. Support the driveshaft with a length of wire or rope so it doesn't hang.

5   Remove the front driveaxles (see Section 19).

6   Disconnect the electrical connector from the front axle actuator motor. Disconnect the breather tube from the differential housing.

7   Place a jack beneath the differential carrier. Unbolt the carrier-to-frame brackets, removing the bolts to the carrier and the bolts securing the two brackets to the frame. Carefully lower the differential, using a chain or straps to secure the differential to the jack.

8   Installation is the reverse of the removal procedure. Tighten all fasteners to the proper torque values (see the Specifications at the beginning of this Chapter, Chapter 2A and Chapter 10). Tighten the wheel lug nuts to the torque listed in the Chapter 1 Specifications.

9   Refill the front differential with the proper lubricant (see Chapter 1).

26   Differential oil seals (front, 4WD models) - replacement

Right side seal

1   Loosen the wheel lug nuts, raise the vehicle, place it securely on jackstands and remove the wheel. Remove the splash shield from under the front axle.

2   Remove the left driveaxle (see Section 19).

3   Drain the lubricant from the front differential (see Chapter 1).

4   Disconnect the lower stabilizer bar link from the lower control arm.

5   Pry the seal out with a seal remover or pull it out with a slide hammer and adapter.

6   Drive in a new seal, using a seal driver or a socket slightly smaller in diameter than the seal. Lubricate the lips of the seal with multi-purpose grease.

7   Fill the differential with the proper lubricant (see Chapter 1).

8   Install the driveaxle (see Section 19). Reconnect the lower stabilizer bar link.

9   Install the splash shield, if equipped.

10   Install the wheel, lower the vehicle and check for proper operation.

Left side seal

11   Remove the driveaxle (see Section 19).

12   Drain the lubricant from the front differential (see Chapter 1).

13   Pry the seal out of the end of the axle-shaft tube with a seal remover or pull it out with a slide hammer and adapter.

14   Drive in a new seal, using a seal driver or a socket slightly smaller in diameter than the seal. Lubricate the lips of the seal with multi-purpose grease.

15   Reinstall the driveaxle (see Section 19).

Chapter 9
Brakes

Contents

Specifications

General
Brake fluid type	See Chapter 1
Brake pedal travel (maximum)	2.4 inches

Disc brakes
Minimum pad thickness	See Chapter 1
Brake disc minimum thickness	Cast into disc
Maximum disc runout	0.002 inch
Maximum disc thickness variation	0.002 inch

Rear drum brakes
Brake drum inner diameter, maximum	11.673 inches
Brake lining thickness minimum	See Chapter 1

Torque specifications
Ft-lbs (unless otherwise indicated)

Note: *One foot-pound (ft-lb) of torque is equivalent to 12 inch-pounds (in-lbs) of torque. Torque values below approximately 15 ft-lbs are expressed in inch-pounds, since most foot-pound torque wrenches are not accurate at these smaller values.*

Brake booster mounting nuts	15
Brake caliper mounting (guide pin) bolts	29
Caliper mounting bracket bolts	129
Brake hose-to-caliper inlet fitting bolt	29
Master cylinder-to-brake booster retaining nuts	22
Wheel cylinder mounting bolts	156 in-lbs
Rear drum brake backing plate bolts	100
Parking brake cable mounting nuts	
2004 through 2007 models	151 inch-lbs
2008 and later models	80 in-lbs
Wheel hub-to-brake disc bolts	
2004 and 2005 models	88
2006 and later models	
Initial torque	15
Final torque	81
Wheel lug nuts	See Chapter 1

1   General information

General

The vehicles covered by this manual are equipped with hydraulically operated front disc brakes and rear drum brakes. Both the front and rear brakes are self adjusting.

Hydraulic system

The hydraulic system consists of two separate circuits. The master cylinder has separate reservoirs for the two circuits, and, in the event of a leak or failure in one hydraulic circuit, the other circuit will remain operative and a warning indicator will light up on the instrument panel when a substantial amount of brake fluid is lost, showing that a failure has occurred.

Power brake booster

The power brake booster uses engine manifold vacuum to provide assistance to the brakes. It is mounted on the firewall in the engine compartment, directly behind the master cylinder.

Parking brake

The parking brake operates the rear brakes only, through cable actuation. It's activated by a foot pedal located at the driver's side kick panel.

Service

After completing any operation involving disassembly of any part of the brake system, always test drive the vehicle to check for proper braking performance before resuming normal driving. When testing the brakes, perform the tests on a clean, dry, flat surface. Conditions other than these can lead to inaccurate test results.

Test the brakes at various speeds with both light and heavy pedal pressure. The vehicle should stop evenly without pulling to one side or the other.

Tires, vehicle load and wheel alignment are factors which also affect braking performance. **Warning:** *Never, under any circumstances, rely on a jack to support the vehicle while working on it. Whenever any of the suspension or steering fasteners are loosened or removed they must be inspected and, if necessary, replaced with new ones of the same part number or of original equipment quality and design. Torque specifications must be followed for proper reassembly and component retention. Never attempt to heat or straighten any suspension or steering components. Instead, replace any bent or damaged part with a new one.*

2   Anti-lock Brake System (ABS) - general information

Refer to illustration 2.2

Anti-lock Brake Systems (ABS) maintain vehicle maneuverability, directional stability, and optimum deceleration under severe braking conditions on most road surfaces. They do so by monitoring the rotational speed of the wheels and controlling the brake line pressure to the wheels during braking. This prevents the wheels from locking up on slippery roads or during hard braking.

The ABS system on these vehicles is a three-sensor system; each front wheel is equipped with its own sensor, and the rear wheels share a sensor (mounted in the extension housing of the transmission on 2WD models and in the transfer case on 4WD models). This means that the brake line pressure to the front wheels can be controlled individually, but the two rear brakes are controlled together.

Electro-Hydraulic Control Unit (EHCU)

The Electro-Hydraulic Control Unit (EHCU), mounted in the left-rear corner of the engine compartment, controls hydraulic pressure to the brake calipers by modulating hydraulic pressure to prevent wheel lock-up **(see illustration)**. It is made up of the Brake Pressure Modulator Valve (BPMV) and the Electronic Brake Control Module (EBCM).

Basically, the BPMV bleeds off pressure in a brake line when the Electronic Brake Control Module (EBCM) detects an abnormal deceleration in the speed of a wheel (via a wheel speed sensor signal). When the speed of the wheel is restored to normal, the modulator once again allows full pressure to the brake. This cycle is repeated as many times as necessary, which results in a pulsing of the brake pedal. **Note:** *The EHCU can't increase brake line pressure above that which is generated by the master cylinder, and it can't apply the brakes by itself.*

In addition to sensing and processing information received from the brake switch and wheel speed sensors to control the hydraulic line pressure and avoid wheel lock up, the EBCM also continually monitors the system and stores fault codes which indicate specific problems.

Wheel speed sensors

Each front wheel is equipped with a speed sensor, which is integral with each front hub and wheel bearing assembly. If it becomes damaged, the entire hub/wheel bearing assembly must be replaced. The sensors are neither adjustable nor rebuildable.

Rear wheel speed is monitored by the Vehicle Speed Sensor (VSS), which is located in the extension housing on 2WD models and the transfer case on 4WD models. For more information on the VSS, see Chapter 6.

A wheel speed sensor measures wheel speed by monitoring the rotation of a toothed ring. As the teeth of the ring move through the magnetic field of the sensor, an AC voltage signal is generated. This signal frequency increases or decreases in proportion to the speed of the wheel. The EBCM monitors these signals for changes in wheel speed; if it detects the sudden deceleration of a wheel, i.e. wheel lockup, the EBCM activates the ABS system.

Warning lights

The ABS system has self-diagnostic capabilities. Each time the vehicle is started, the EBCM runs a self-test. There are two warning lights on the instrument panel, a red BRAKE light and an amber ABS light, each with their own functions. During starting, these lights should come on briefly then go out. If the red BRAKE light stays on, it indicates a problem with the main braking system, such as low fluid level detected or the parking brake is still on. If the light stays on after the parking brake is released, check the brake fluid level in the master cylinder reservoir (see Chapter 1).

The amber ABS light indicates a problem with the ABS system, not the main or basic brake system. If the light stays on, it indicates that there is a problem with the ABS system, but the main system is still working. Take the vehicle to a dealer service department or other qualified repair shop for diagnosis and repair.

2.2 The ABS Electro-Hydraulic Control Unit (EHCU) is located at the left-rear corner of the engine compartment, next to the brake master cylinder and booster

3.5a Before disassembling the brake, wash it thoroughly with brake system cleaner and allow it to dry - position a drain pan under the brake to catch the residue - DO NOT use compressed air to blow off brake dust!

3.5b To make room for the new pads, use a C-clamp to depress the piston into the caliper before removing the caliper and pads - do this a little at a time, keeping an eye on the fluid level in the master cylinder to make sure it doesn't overflow

Checks

Although a special electronic tester is necessary to properly diagnose the system, the home mechanic can perform a few preliminary checks before taking the vehicle to a dealer service department or other repair shop that is equipped with this tester:

a) *Check the fuses.*
b) *Check the electrical connectors at the EBCM and the hydraulic modulator/ motor pack.*
c) *Follow the wiring harness to the speed sensors and brake light switch and make sure all connections are secure and the wiring isn't damaged.*
d) *Make sure the brake lines, calipers and wheel cylinders are in good condition.*

If the above preliminary checks don't rectify the problem, the vehicle should be diagnosed by a dealer service department or other qualified repair shop.

Traction control

An added feature of some models is an optional traction control system that uses the functions of the EBCM to provide for safer driving. If the wheel speed sensors indicate wheel slip, the EBCM signals the PCM to retard engine timing and reduce the throttle opening, slowing the drive wheels.

3 Disc brake pads - replacement

Refer to illustrations 3.5a through 3.5l

Warning: *Disc brake pads must be replaced on both front wheels at the same time - never replace the pads on only one wheel. Also, the dust created by the brake system is harmful to your health. Never blow it out with compressed air and don't inhale any of it. An approved filtering mask should be worn when working on the brakes. Do not, under any circumstances,*

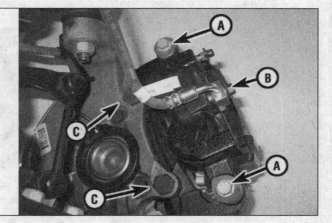

3.5c Front caliper mounting details

A Caliper mounting bolts
B Brake hose inlet fitting bolt
C Caliper mounting bracket bolts

use petroleum-based solvents to clean brake parts. Use brake system cleaner only!
Note: *New Chevrolet brake pad sets come with new pad retainer clips, and the manufacturer recommends using new clips whenever pads are replaced. When buying aftermarket pads, check to see if they come with new clips. If not, order the clips separately.*

1   Remove the cap from the brake fluid reservoir. Remove about two-thirds of the fluid from the reservoir, then reinstall the cap. **Caution:** *Brake fluid will damage paint. If any fluid is spilled, wash it off immediately with plenty of clean, cold water.*

2   Loosen the front wheel lug nuts, raise the front of the vehicle and support it securely on jackstands. Block the wheels at the opposite end.

3   Remove the wheels. Work on one brake assembly at a time, using the assembled brake for reference if necessary.

4   Inspect the brake disc carefully as outlined in Section 5. If machining is necessary, follow the information in that Section to remove the disc.

5   Follow the accompanying photo sequence for the actual pad replacement pro-

3.5d Remove the lower mounting bolt and pivot the caliper up, supporting it in this position

cedure **(see illustrations)**. Be sure to stay in order and read the caption under each illustration.

3.5e Remove the inner brake pad

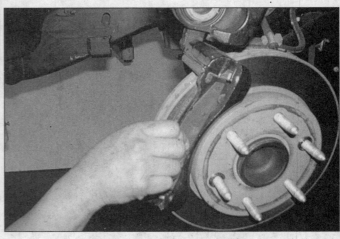

3.5f Remove the outer brake pad

6   When reinstalling the caliper, be sure to tighten the mounting bolts to the torque listed in this Chapter's Specifications. Tighten the wheel lug nuts to the torque listed in the Chapter 1 Specifications.

7   After the job has been completed, firmly depress the brake pedal a few times to bring the pads into contact with the disc. Check the level of the brake fluid, adding some if necessary (see Chapter 1). Check the operation of the brakes carefully before placing the vehicle into normal service.

3.5g Remove the upper and lower pad retainers from the caliper mounting bracket; if they are cracked or distorted, replace them

3.5h Apply anti-squeal compound to the back of both pads (let the compound set up a few minutes before installing them)

3.5i Install the upper and lower pad retainers on the caliper mounting bracket

3.5j Install the inner brake pad . . .

3.5k . . . and the outer brake pad

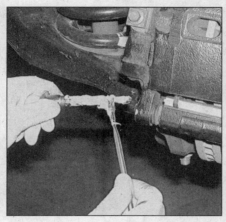

3.5l Inspect the caliper mounting bolt for scoring and corrosion, then lubricate it with high-temperature brake grease (if it was dry, pivot the caliper up again, slide the upper mounting bolt out of the bracket and lubricate it, too)

4.2 There is a sealing washer on either side of the brake hose inlet fitting; be sure to replace these with new ones when reconnecting the hose

4   Brake caliper - removal and installation

Refer to illustration 4.2
Warning: *The dust created by the brake system is harmful to your health. Never blow it out with compressed air and don't inhale any of it. An approved filtering mask should be worn when working on the brakes. Do not, under any circumstances, use petroleum-based solvents to clean brake parts. Use brake system cleaner only!*

Removal

1   Loosen the front wheel lug nuts, raise the front of the vehicle and place it securely on jackstands. Block the wheels at the opposite end. Remove the front wheel.
2   Remove the inlet fitting bolt and disconnect the brake hose from the caliper. Discard the old sealing washers **(see illustration)**. Plug the brake hose immediately to keep contaminants and air out of the brake system and to prevent losing any more brake fluid than is necessary. **Note:** *If you are simply removing the caliper for access to other components, leave the brake hose connected and suspend the caliper with a length of wire - don't let it hang by the hose* **(see illustration 5.2)**.
3   Remove the caliper mounting bolts and detach the caliper from the mounting bracket.

Installation

4   Installation is the reverse of removal. Don't forget to use new sealing washers on each side of the brake hose inlet fitting and be sure to tighten the fitting bolt and the caliper mounting bolts to the torque listed in this Chapter's Specifications. Tighten the wheel lug nuts to the torque listed in the Chapter 1 Specifications.
5   Bleed the brake system (see Section 8).
Note: *If the brake hose was not disconnected, bleeding won't be required. Make sure there are no leaks from the hose connections. Test the brakes carefully before returning the vehicle to normal service.*

5   Brake disc - inspection, removal and installation

Inspection

Refer to illustrations 5.2, 5.3, 5.4a, 5.4b, 5.5a and 5.5b
1   Loosen the wheel lug nuts, raise the vehicle and support it securely on jackstands.
2   Remove the brake caliper. It isn't necessary to disconnect the brake hose. After removing the caliper bolts, suspend the caliper out of the way with a piece of wire **(see illustration)**.
3   Visually inspect the disc surface for score marks and other damage. Light scratches and shallow grooves are normal after use and may not always be detrimental to brake operation, but deep scoring requires disc removal and refinishing by an automotive machine shop. Be sure to check both sides of the disc **(see illustration)**. If pulsating has been noticed during application of the brakes, suspect disc runout.

5.2 Hang the caliper out of the way with a piece of wire - don't let it hang by the brake hose!

5.3 The brake pads on this vehicle were obviously neglected, as they wore down completely and cut deep grooves into the disc - wear this severe means the disc must be replaced

5.4a To check disc runout, mount a dial indicator as shown and rotate the disc

5.4b Using a swirling motion, remove the glaze from the disc with sandpaper or emery cloth

4   To check disc runout, place a dial indicator at a point about 1/2-inch from the outer edge of the disc **(see illustration)**. Set the indicator to zero and turn the disc. The indicator reading should not exceed the specified allowable runout limit. If it does, the disc should be refinished by an automotive machine shop. **Note:** *When replacing the brake pads, it's a good idea to resurface the discs regardless of the dial indicator reading, as this will impart a smooth finish and ensure a perfectly flat surface, eliminating any brake pedal pulsation or other undesirable symptoms related to questionable discs. At the very least, if you elect not to have the discs resurfaced, remove the glaze from the surface with emery cloth or sandpaper, using a swirling motion* **(see illustration).**

5   It's absolutely critical that the disc not be machined to a thickness under the specified minimum thickness. The minimum wear (or discard) thickness is cast into the underside of the front discs **(see illustration)**. The disc thickness can be checked with a micrometer **(see illustration)**.

Removal

6   Remove the two caliper mounting bracket bolts and detach the mounting bracket **(see illustration 3.5c)**.

7   If you're working on a 4WD model, remove the steering knuckle (see Chapter 10).

8   On all models, remove the hub and bearing assembly-to-steering knuckle bolts (see Chapter 10), then separate the brake disc and hub and bearing assembly from the knuckle.

9   Remove the bolts and separate the brake disc from the hub and bearing assembly.

Installation

10   Assemble the disc and hub and bearing assembly. Install the bolts and tighten them to the torque listed in this Chapter's Specifications.

11   The remainder of installation is the reverse of removal. Tighten the hub and bearing-to-steering knuckle bolts to the torque listed in the Chapter 10 Specifications. Tighten all brake fasteners to the torque listed in this Chapter's Specifications.

12   Install the wheel and lug nuts. Lower the vehicle and tighten the lug nuts to the torque listed in the Chapter 1 Specifications. Depress the brake pedal a few times to bring the brake pads into contact with the disc. Bleeding won't be necessary unless the brake hose was disconnected from the caliper. Check the operation of the brakes carefully before driving the vehicle.

6   Drum brake shoes - replacement

Refer to illustrations 6.4a through 6.4n

Warning: *Drum brake shoes must be replaced on both wheels at the same time - never replace the shoes on only one wheel. Also, the dust created by the brake system is harmful to your health. Never blow it out with compressed air and don't inhale any of it. An approved filtering mask should be worn when working on the brakes. Do not, under any circumstances, use petroleum-based solvents to clean brake parts. Use brake system cleaner only!*

5.5a The minimum thickness is cast into the disc (typical)

5.5b Use a micrometer to measure disc thickness

6.4a Rear drum brake assembly

1 Shoe retractor spring
2 Trailing brake shoe (parking brake lever behind)
3 Adjuster lever
4 Wheel cylinder
5 Adjuster lever spring
6 Adjuster screw assembly
7 Leading brake shoe

6.4b Remove the adjuster lever spring

1 Loosen the wheel lug nuts, raise the rear of the vehicle and support it securely on jackstands. Block the front wheels to keep the vehicle from rolling.
2 Release the parking brake.
3 Remove the wheel. **Note:** *All four rear*

brake shoes must be replaced at the same time, but to avoid mixing up parts, work on only one brake assembly at a time.
4 Follow the accompanying illustrations for the brake shoe replacement procedure **(see illustrations 6.4a through 6.4n)**. Be sure to

stay in order and read the caption under each illustration. **Note 1:** *The parking brake lever is connected to the trailing shoe but cannot be disassembled from it. The shoe and lever are replaced as a unit.* **Note 2:** *If the brake drum cannot be easily removed, make sure*

6.4c Remove the brake adjuster lever (A) and the adjuster screw assembly (B)

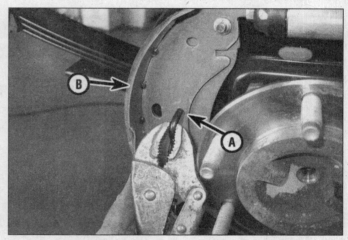

6.4d With locking pliers, lift the end of the shoe hold-down spring (A) away from the shoe (B), and remove the trailing shoe

6.4e The trailing shoe is connected to the parking brake lever; lower the shoe and lever away from the backing plate

6.4f Lift the hold-down spring and remove the leading shoe from the backing plate

6.4g Remove the shoe retractor spring from the backing plate

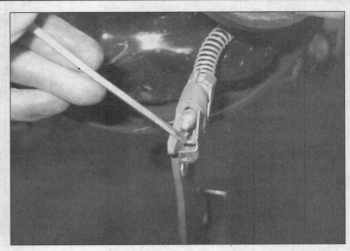

6.4h To remove the trailing shoe/parking brake lever, depress the tab at the park cable end and twist the lever off the cable end

the parking brake is completely released. If the drum still cannot be pulled off, the brake shoes will have to be retracted. This is done by first removing the plug from the backing plate. With the plug removed, push the lever off the adjuster star wheel with a narrow screwdriver while turning the adjuster wheel with another screwdriver, moving the shoes away from the drum **(see illustration 6.4n)**. *The drum should now come off.*

5   Before reinstalling the drum, it should be checked for cracks, score marks, deep

6.4i Clean the backing plate with brake cleaner and lightly lube the shoe contact points with brake grease

6.4j Use a socket extension and a hammer to secure the center of the hairpin spring in its clip on the backing plate

6.4k Install the new leading brake shoe

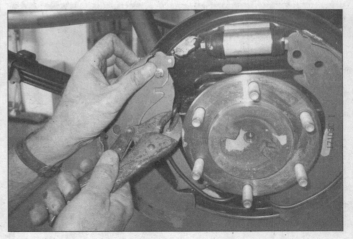

6.4l Reconnect the parking brake cable end to the lever and install the new trailing shoe/lever

6.4m Clean and lube the threads of the adjuster and reinstall it between the shoes

6.4n Install the adjuster lever and spring, then adjust the shoes by holding the lever up while turning the star wheel (the drum should just be able to slide over the shoes)

scratches and hard spots, which will appear as small discolored areas. If the hard spots cannot be removed with fine emery cloth or if any of the other conditions listed above exist, the drum must be taken to an automotive machine shop to have it resurfaced. **Note:** *Professionals recommend resurfacing the drums each time a brake job is done. Resurfacing will eliminate the possibility of out-of-round drums. If the drums are worn so much that they can't be resurfaced without exceeding the maximum allowable diameter (stamped into the drum), then new drums will be required. At the very least, if you elect not to have the drums resurfaced, remove the glaze from the surface with emery cloth using a swirling motion.*

6   Install the brake drum on the axle flange. Pump the brake pedal a couple of times, then turn the drum and listen for the sound of the shoes rubbing. If they are, turn the adjuster star wheel until the shoes stop rubbing.

7   Install the wheel and lug nuts, then lower the vehicle. Tighten the lug nuts to the torque listed in this Chapter's Specifications.

8   Make a number of forward and reverse

stops and operate the parking brake to adjust the brakes until satisfactory pedal action is obtained.

9   Check the operation of the brakes carefully before driving the vehicle.

7   Wheel cylinder - removal and installation

Removal

Refer to illustration 7.5

1   Raise the rear of the vehicle and support it securely on jackstands. Block the front wheels to keep the vehicle from rolling.

2   Remove the brake shoe assembly (see Section 6).

3   Remove all dirt and foreign material from around the wheel cylinder.

4   Disconnect the brake line with a flare-nut wrench, if available. Don't pull the brake line away from the wheel cylinder.

5   Remove the wheel cylinder mounting bolts **(see illustration)**.

6   Detach the wheel cylinder from the brake backing plate. Immediately plug the brake line to prevent fluid loss and contamination.

Installation

7   Place the wheel cylinder in position and install the bolts finger tight. Connect the brake line to the cylinder, being careful not to cross-thread the fitting. Tighten the wheel cylinder bolts to the torque listed in this Chapter's Specifications.

8   Tighten the brake line fitting and install the brake shoes and drum.

9   Bleed the brakes (see Section 10). Install the wheel and lug nuts. Lower the vehicle to the ground and tighten the lug nuts to the torque listed in this Chapter's Specifications.

10   Check the operation of the brakes carefully before driving the vehicle.

8   Master cylinder - removal, installation and reservoir/O-ring replacement

Removal

Refer to illustration 8.2

1   Disconnect the cable from the negative terminal of the battery.

2   Unplug the electrical connector for the fluid level warning switch **(see illustration)**.

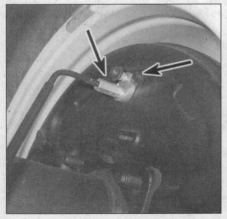

7.5 Use a flare-nut wrench to disconnect the brake line at the wheel cylinder, then remove the two mounting bolts

8.2 Master cylinder mounting details

1   *Electrical connector for fluid level sensor*
2   *Brake line fittings*
3   *Mounting nuts*

8.8 The best way to bleed air from the master cylinder before installing it on the vehicle is with a pair of bleeder tubes that direct brake fluid into the reservoir during bleeding

8.16 Have an assistant depress the brake pedal and hold it down, then loosen the fitting nut, allowing air and fluid to escape; repeat this procedure on both fittings until the fluid is clear of air bubbles

3   Remove as much fluid as possible from the reservoir with a suction gun, large syringe or a poultry baster. **Warning:** *If a poultry baster is used, never again use it for the preparation of food.*

4   Place rags under the fittings and prepare caps or plastic bags to cover the ends of the lines once they're disconnected. **Caution:** *Brake fluid will damage paint. Cover all body parts and be careful not to spill fluid during this procedure. Loosen the fittings at the ends of the brake lines where they enter the master cylinder. To prevent rounding off the flats, use a flare-nut wrench, which wraps around the fitting hex.*

5   Pull the brake lines away from the master cylinder and plug the ends to prevent contamination.

6   Remove the nuts attaching the master cylinder to the power booster **(see illustration 8.2).** Pull the master cylinder off the studs to remove it. Again, be careful not to spill the fluid as this is done.

Installation

Refer to illustrations 8.8 and 8.16

7   Bench bleed the new master cylinder before installing it. Mount the master cylinder in a vise, with the jaws of the vise clamping on the mounting flange.

8   Attach a pair of master cylinder bleeder tubes to the outlet ports of the master cylinder **(see illustration).**

9   Fill the reservoir with brake fluid of the recommended type (see Chapter 1).

10   Slowly push the pistons into the master cylinder (a large Phillips screwdriver can be used for this) - air will be expelled from the pressure chambers and into the reservoir. Because the tubes are submerged in fluid, air can't be drawn back into the master cylinder when you release the pistons.

11   Repeat the procedure until no more air bubbles are present.

12   Remove the bleed tubes, one at a time, and install plugs in the open ports to prevent fluid leakage and air from entering. Install the

reservoir cap.

13   Install the master cylinder over the studs on the power brake booster and tighten the attaching nuts only finger tight at this time. Don't forget to use a new gasket.

14   Thread the brake line fittings into the master cylinder. Since the master cylinder is still a bit loose, it can be moved slightly so the fittings thread in easily. Don't strip the threads as the fittings are tightened.

15   Tighten the mounting nuts to the torque listed in this Chapter's Specifications. Tighten the brake line fittings securely.

16   Fill the master cylinder reservoir with fluid, then bleed the lines at the master cylinder, followed by bleeding the remainder of the brake system (see Section 10). To bleed the lines at the master cylinder, have an assistant depress the brake pedal and hold it down. Loosen the fitting to allow air and fluid to escape **(see illustration).** Tighten the fitting, then allow your assistant to return the pedal to its rest position. Repeat this procedure on both fittings until the fluid is free of air bubbles, then bleed the rest of the system. **Note:** *When bleeding the lines at the master cylinder, bleed the front line first, followed by the rear line.* Check the operation of the brake system carefully before driving the vehicle.

Warning: *If you do not have a firm brake pedal at the end of the bleeding procedure, or have any doubts as to the effectiveness of the brake system, DO NOT drive the vehicle. Have it towed to a dealer service department or other qualified repair shop for diagnosis.*

Reservoir/O-ring replacement

Refer to illustrations 8.19 and 8.21

Note: *The brake fluid reservoir can be replaced separately from the master cylinder body if it becomes damaged. If there is leakage between the reservoir and the master cylinder body, the O-rings on the reservoir can be replaced.*

17   Remove as much fluid as possible from the reservoir with a suction gun, large syringe or a poultry baster. **Warning:** *If a poultry baster is used, never again use it for the preparation of food.*

18   Place rags under the master cylinder to absorb any fluid that may spill out once the reservoir is detached from the master cylinder. **Caution:** *Brake fluid will damage paint. Cover all body parts and be careful not to spill fluid during this procedure.*

19   Using a hammer and a small punch, drive out the roll pins that retain the reservoir to the master cylinder **(see illustration).**

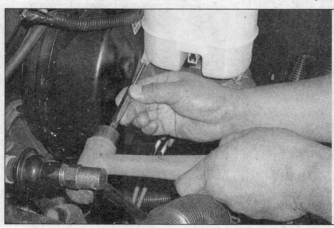

8.19 Driving out the roll pins that retain the master cylinder fluid reservoir

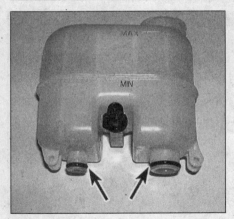

8.21 The reservoir O-rings can be replaced if they are leaking

20 Pull the reservoir out of the master cylinder body.
21 If you are simply replacing the O-rings, carefully pry the old O-rings off and install new ones **(see illustration)**.
22 Lubricate the reservoir O-rings with clean brake fluid, then press the reservoir into place on the master cylinder body and secure it with new roll pins.
23 Refill the reservoir with the recommended brake fluid (see Chapter 1) and check for leaks.
24 Bleed the master cylinder **(see illustration 8.16)**.

9 Brake hoses and lines - inspection and replacement

Inspection

1 About every six months, with the vehicle raised and supported securely on jackstands, the rubber hoses which connect the steel brake lines with the front and rear brake assemblies should be inspected for cracks, chafing of the outer cover, leaks, blisters and other damage. These are important and vulnerable parts of the brake system and inspection should be complete. A light and mirror will be helpful for a thorough check. If a hose exhibits any of the above conditions, replace it with a new one.

Replacement
Front flexible brake hoses

Refer to illustration 9.3

2 Loosen the wheel lug nuts, raise the vehicle and support it securely on jackstands. Remove the wheel.
3 At the bracket, unscrew the brake line fitting from the hose **(see illustration)**. Use a flare-nut wrench to prevent rounding off the corners of the fitting nut, and hold the hose end with a wrench to prevent twisting the frame bracket.
4 Remove the clip from the bracket, then detach the hose from the bracket.
5 At the caliper end of the hose, remove the inlet fitting bolt, then separate the hose from the caliper. Note that there are two copper sealing washers on either side of the inlet fitting **(see illustration 4.2)** - they should be replaced with new ones during installation.
6 To install the hose, connect the fitting to the caliper with the inlet fitting bolt and new sealing washers. Tighten the inlet fitting bolt to the torque listed in this Chapter's Specifications.
7 Route the hose into its original location, making sure it isn't twisted. Tighten the hose bracket bolt securely. Connect the brake line fitting, starting the threads by hand. Tighten the fitting securely.
8 Bleed the caliper (see Section 10).
9 Install the wheel and lug nuts, lower the vehicle and tighten the lug nuts to the torque listed in the Chapter 1 Specifications.

Rear flexible brake hose

Refer to illustration 9.13

10 Raise the rear of the vehicle and support it securely on jackstands. Block the front wheels to prevent the vehicle from rolling.
11 At the chassis end of the flexible hose, unscrew the brake line fitting from the hose. Use a flare-nut wrench to prevent rounding off the corners of the fitting nut, and hold the hose end with a wrench to prevent twisting the frame bracket.
12 Remove the clip from the bracket, then detach the hose from the bracket.
13 At the brake fitting junction block on top of the left side of the rear axle housing, remove the hose from the junction block **(see illustration)**.
14 To install the hose, connect the fitting to the junction block with a new sealing washer.
15 Route the hose into its original location, making sure it isn't twisted, into the bracket on the frame. Connect the brake line fitting, starting the threads by hand. Tighten the fitting securely and secure the hose with its clip.
16 Bleed the rear brakes (see Section 10).
17 Install the wheel and lug nuts, lower the vehicle and tighten the lug nuts to the torque listed in the Chapter 1 Specifications.

Metal brake lines

18 When replacing brake lines, be sure to use the correct parts. Don't use copper tubing for any brake system components. Purchase steel brake lines from a dealer or auto parts store.
19 Prefabricated brake line, with the tube ends already flared and fittings installed, is available at auto parts stores and dealer parts departments. These lines must be bent to the proper shapes using a tubing bender.
20 When installing the new line, make sure it's securely supported in the brackets and has plenty of clearance between moving or hot components. Make sure there's at least 1/4-inch of clearance between parallel brake lines.
21 After installation, check the master cylinder fluid level and add fluid as necessary. Bleed the brake system (see Section 10) and test the brakes carefully before driving the vehicle in traffic.

9.3 Using a flare-nut wrench, unscrew the threaded fitting (A) on the brake line, then remove the clip (B) and detach the hose from the bracket

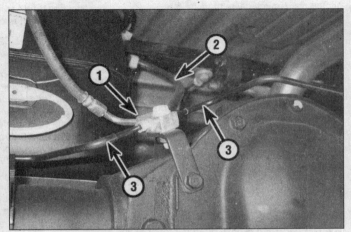

9.13 Disconnect the rear flexible hose from the chassis and the junction block at the rear axle (1), 2 is the rear axle vent hose, 3 are the steel brake lines to each wheel cylinder

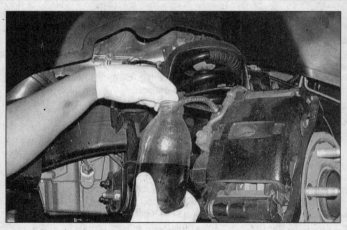

10.8 When bleeding the brakes, a hose is connected to the bleed screw at the caliper and then submerged in brake fluid - air will be seen as bubbles in the tube and container (all air must be expelled before moving to the next wheel)

11.6 Pull the vacuum hose fitting straight out of the grommet in the booster

10   Brake hydraulic system - bleeding

Refer to illustration 10.8

Warning: *Wear eye protection when bleeding the brake system. If the fluid comes in contact with your eyes, immediately rinse them with water and seek medical attention.*

Note: *Bleeding the hydraulic system is necessary to remove any air that manages to find its way into the system when it's been opened during removal and installation of a hose, line, caliper or master cylinder.*

1   You'll probably have to bleed the system at all four brakes if air has entered it due to low fluid level, or if the brake lines have been disconnected at the master cylinder.

2   If a brake line was disconnected only at a wheel, then only that caliper or wheel cylinder (rear) must be bled.

3   If a brake line is disconnected at a fitting located between the master cylinder and any of the brakes, that part of the system served by the disconnected line must be bled.

4   Remove any residual vacuum from the power brake booster by applying the brake several times with the engine off.

5   Remove the master cylinder reservoir cap and fill the reservoir with brake fluid. Reinstall the cap. **Note:** *Check the fluid level often during the bleeding operation and add fluid as necessary to prevent the fluid level from falling low enough to allow air bubbles into the master cylinder.*

6   Have an assistant on hand, as well as a supply of new brake fluid, a clear container partially filled with clean brake fluid, a length of clear tubing to fit over the bleeder valve and a wrench to open and close the bleeder valve.

7   Beginning at the right rear wheel, loosen the bleeder valve slightly, then tighten it to a point where it's snug but can still be loosened quickly and easily.

8   Place one end of the tubing over the bleeder valve and submerge the other end in brake fluid in the container **(see illustration)**.

9   Have the assistant depress the brake pedal slowly and hold it in the depressed position.

10   While the pedal is held down, open the bleeder valve just enough to allow a flow of fluid to leave the valve. Watch for air bubbles to exit the submerged end of the tube. When the fluid flow slows after a couple of seconds, close the valve and have your assistant release the pedal.

11   Repeat Steps 9 and 10 until no more air is seen leaving the tube, then tighten the bleeder valve and proceed to the left rear wheel, the right front wheel and the left front wheel, in that order, and perform the same procedure. Be sure to check the fluid in the master cylinder reservoir frequently.

12   Never use old brake fluid. It contains moisture which can cause the fluid to boil, rendering the brake system inoperative.

13   Refill the master cylinder with fluid at the end of the operation.

14   Check the operation of the brakes. The pedal should feel solid when depressed, with no sponginess. If necessary, repeat the entire process.

15   Before driving the vehicle, sit in the driver's seat and:

a)   *Take your foot off the brake pedal.*
b)   *Start the engine and let it run for a minimum of 10 seconds. Watch the amber ABS light on the dash.*
c)   *If the light comes on and does not turn off after 10 seconds, have the vehicle towed to a dealer service department or other qualified repair shop. A scan tool will have to be used to diagnose the ABS system.*
d)   *If the ABS light goes off after three seconds or so, turn off the ignition.*
e)   *Repeat paragraphs a) through d) one more time. If the amber ABS light turns off, test drive the vehicle in an isolated area before returning the vehicle to normal service.*

Warning: *Do not operate the vehicle if you're in doubt about the effectiveness of the brake system.*

11   Power brake booster - check, removal and installation

Refer to illustrations 11.6, 11.9 and 11.10

Warning: *These models have airbags. Always disable the airbag system before working in the vicinity of any airbag system component to avoid the possibility of accidental deployment of the airbag(s), which could cause personal injury (see Chapter 12).*

Check

Operating check

1   Depress the pedal and start the engine. If the pedal goes down slightly, operation is normal.

2   Depress the brake pedal several times with the engine running and make sure that there is no change in the pedal reserve distance.

Airtightness check

3   Start the engine and turn it off after one or two minutes. Depress the brake pedal several times slowly. If the pedal goes down farther the first time but gradually rises after the second or third depression, the booster is airtight.

4   Depress the brake pedal while the engine is running, then stop the engine with the pedal depressed. If there is no change in the pedal reserve travel after holding the pedal for 30 seconds, the booster is airtight.

Removal

5   Disable the airbag system (see Chapter 12). Disconnect the cable from the negative terminal of the battery.

6   Detach the vacuum hose from the booster **(see illustration)**.

11.9 Remove the retaining clip and pull out the clevis pin securing the booster rod to the brake pedal

11.10 Unscrew the booster mounting nuts (three indicated here)

7   Remove the master cylinder (see Section 8).
8   Remove the left side under-dash panel.
9   Remove the retaining clip and slip out the pin securing the booster rod to the pedal (see illustration).
10   Remove the four nuts holding the brake booster to the firewall (see illustration).
11   Slide the booster straight out from the firewall until the studs clear the holes and pull the booster and gasket from the engine compartment.

Installation

12   Installation is the reverse of removal. Be sure to use a new gasket, and tighten the booster mounting nuts and the master cylinder mounting nuts to the torque values listed in this Chapter's Specifications.

12 Brake pedal travel - check

1   The brake pedal is not adjustable, but the travel should be checked if the pedal seems low. You'll need a tape measure, yardstick or ruler for this procedure.
2   Depress the pedal a few times to deplete the reserve in the power brake booster.
3   Measure the position of the pedal at rest. You can either measure from the floor to the pedal or from the pedal to the steering wheel. Record your reading.
4   Now, depress the pedal (exerting approximately 100 lbs. of force) and measure how far the pedal has traveled. Compare your findings with the measurement listed in this Chapter's Specifications.
5   If the pedal travel is excessive, check for air in the system (bleed the brakes - see Section 10). A failed seal in the master cylinder could also cause excessive pedal travel.

13 Parking brake - adjustment

Refer to illustration 13.2

1   Pull the release for the parking brake pedal. Raise the vehicle at the rear and support it on secure jackstands or a lift.

2   Tighten the adjuster nut securing the front cable to the equalizer until the right rear wheel won't turn anymore (see illustration).
3   Step on the parking brake pedal, then release it. Repeat this four more times.
4   Release the parking brake pedal, then back off the cable adjuster nut until the right rear brake just begins to exhibit drag, then back off the nut two further turns.

14 Brake light switch - check and replacement

Refer to illustration 14.1

Check

Note: The brake light switch on 2004 through 2006 models is not adjustable. If it doesn't work as described below, replace it.
1   The brake light switch (see illustration) is located on a bracket that also holds the Traction Control/Cruise Control switch. The switch activates the brake lights at the rear of the vehicle when the pedal is depressed.

13.2 Adjuster nut at the brake cable equalizer assembly

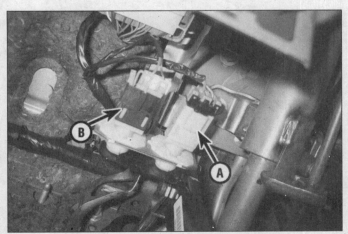

14.1 The brake light switch (A) is mounted on a bracket at the brake pedal assembly - the other switch is for the Traction Control/Cruise Control (B)

To gain access to the switch, remove the left-side under-dash panel and the heater/air conditioning duct.

2   If the brake lights are inoperative, check the fuse first (see Chapter 12).

3   If the fuse is good, check for voltage to the switch on the feed wire (refer to the wiring diagrams at the end of this manual for the proper color wire to check). If no voltage is present, repair the wire between the switch and the fuse box.

4   If voltage is present, depress the brake pedal and check for voltage at the output wire terminal (again, refer to the wiring diagrams). If no voltage is present, replace the switch.

5   If voltage is present, check for power on the brake light wires at the tail light housings (with the brake pedal depressed). If voltage is not present, repair the circuit between the switch and the brake lights.

6   If voltage is present, check for a bad ground; using a jumper wire connected to a good ground, probe the ground wire terminal at the tail light connector. If the brake lights go on, repair the ground circuit (follow the ground wire from the tail light housing).

7   Keep in mind that the brake light bulbs could be burned out, but the likelihood of all the bulbs being burned out is very slim.

Removal

8   Remove left-side under-dash panel and the heater/air conditioning duct, if not already done.

9   Unplug the electrical connector from the switch.

10   Rotate the switch counterclockwise to remove it from the bracket **(see illustration 14.1)**.

Installation and adjustment

11   Installing the new switch is the reverse of the removal procedure, but 2007 and later models require adjustment, as follows.

12   Rotate the switch counterclockwise until it releases, then pull the brake pedal firmly rearward (away from the firewall) and keep it there.

13   Push the switch toward the pedal until the plunger of the switch contacts the pedal, and continue until the switch body just touches the pedal.

14   Rotate the switch clockwise until a click is heard. Adjustment is correct when there is about 0.028-inch between the end of the switch and the contact point on the pedal, with no pressure on the pedal.

Chapter 10
Suspension and steering systems

Contents

Specifications

Torque specifications   Ft-lbs

Front suspension

	Ft-lbs
Shock absorber	
Upper mounting nuts	20
Lower mounting bolts	
2WD	81
4WD	52
Shock absorber damper shaft nut	
2WD	15
4WD	18
Upper control arm pivot bolts	
2WD	118
4WD	114
Lower control arm-to-frame nuts, 2WD	114
Lower control arm-to-frame bolts, 4WD	
Front	122
Rear	133
Balljoint-to-lower-control-arm nuts	
2WD	44
4WD and Z71 suspension	47
Balljoint-to-upper-control-arm nuts	
2WD	12
4WD and Z71 suspension	35
Stabilizer bar (front)	
Link nuts	32
Clamp bolts	37
Hub/bearing assembly-to-steering knuckle bolts	
2004 through 2006 models	133
2007 and later models	81

Rear suspension

Leaf spring U-bolt nuts	56
Shock absorber	
Upper bolts...	26
Lower bolt...	70
Spring shackle-to-frame nut	63
Spring shackle-to-spring nut...	63
Spring to front frame bracket nut	
2004 and 2005 models	
Step 1	59
Step 2	Rotate an additional 80 degrees
2006 and later models..	92
Stabilizer bar link nuts	32
Stabilizer bar clamp bolts	37

Steering

Steering gear-to-frame bolts/nuts	
Horizontal bolts	96
Vertical (isolator) bolts...	74
Intermediate shaft pinch bolts	
Upper-shaft-to-column	17
Lower shaft to power steering gear..	33
Tie-rod end-to-steering knuckle ballstud nut	
Step 1	33
Step 2	Rotate an additional 95 degrees
Steering wheel nut...	26
Steering column mounting nuts...	20
Power steering pump	
Mounting bolts...	18
Power steering pump bracket bolts...	37

Wheel lug nuts

Wheel lug nuts...	See Chapter 1

1.1 Front suspension and steering components (2WD model)

1	Upper control arm	5	Lower balljoint	9	Shock absorber/coil spring module
2	Stabilizer bar clamp	6	Tie-rod end	10	Lower control arm
3	Stabilizer bar	7	Steering gear	11	Steering knuckle
4	Stabilizer bar link	8	Steering gear boot		

1 General information

Refer to illustrations 1.1 and 1.2

Front suspension

The front suspension **(see illustration)** is fully independent. Each wheel is connected to the frame by a steering knuckle, upper and lower balljoints and upper and lower control arms. Shock absorber/coil spring assemblies are used on 2WD models, while 4WD models have shock absorbers with torsion bars instead of coil springs. A stabilizer bar connected to the frame and to the two lower control arms reduces body roll during cornering.

Rear suspension

The rear suspension consists of a pair of parallel leaf springs mounted under the rear axle, with shock absorbers and a stabilizer bar **(see illustration)**.

Steering system

The steering system consists of a rack-and-pinion steering gear and two adjustable tie-rods. Power assist is standard. The steering damper, if equipped, is attached to a bracket on the frame and to the relay rod.

Precautions

Frequently, when working on the suspension or steering system components, you may come across fasteners that seem impossible to loosen. These fasteners on the underside of the vehicle are continually subjected to water, road grime, mud, etc., and can become rusted or "frozen," making them extremely difficult to remove. In order to unscrew these stubborn fasteners without damaging them (or other components), be sure to use lots of penetrating oil and allow it to soak in for a while. Using a wire brush to clean exposed threads will also ease removal of the nut or bolt and prevent damage to the threads. Sometimes a sharp blow with a hammer and punch is effective in breaking the bond between a nut and bolt threads, but care must be taken to prevent the punch from slipping off the fastener and ruining the threads. Heating the stuck fastener and surrounding area with a torch sometimes helps too, but isn't recommended because of the obvious dangers associated with fire. Long breaker bars and extension, or "cheater," pipes will increase leverage, but never use an extension pipe on a ratchet - the ratcheting mechanism could be damaged. Sometimes, turning the nut or bolt in the tightening (clockwise) direction first will help to break it loose. Fasteners that require drastic measures to unscrew should always be replaced with new ones.

Since most of the procedures that are dealt with in this Chapter involve jacking up the vehicle and working underneath it, a good pair of jackstands will be needed. A hydraulic floor jack is the preferred type of jack to lift the vehicle, and it can also be used to support certain components during various operations.

1.2 Rear suspension/underside components

1 Spring shackles	3 Leaf spring	5 Leaf spring front mounting bolt
2 Shock absorber	4 Spring plate/U-bolt nuts	6 Rear axle

Warning: *Never, under any circumstances, rely on a jack to support the vehicle while working on it. Also, whenever any of the suspension or steering fasteners are loosened or removed they must be inspected and, if necessary, replaced with new ones of the same part number or original equipment quality and design. Torque specifications must be followed for proper reassembly and component retention. Never attempt to heat or straighten suspension or steering components. Instead, replace bent or damaged parts with new ones.*

2   Shock absorber module (front, 2WD models) - removal, overhaul and installation

Removal and installation

Refer to illustrations 2.1 and 2.5

1   Open the hood and remove the shock module upper nuts **(see illustration)**.

2   Loosen the front wheel lug nuts. Raise the front of the vehicle and support it securely on jackstands, then remove the wheel.

3   Support the outer end of the lower control arm with a floor jack (the shock absorber module serves as the down-stop for the suspension). The jack must remain in this position throughout the entire procedure.

4   Remove the stabilizer bar link (see Section 4).

5   Remove the bolt that secures the shock absorber to the control arm **(see illustration)**.

6   Lower the shock module clear of the vehicle and take it out.

7   Install the shock module in the vehicle with its upper studs in the upper mounting holes and install the nuts to hold it in place. Slip the bottom of the shock into its mounting bracket on the control arm and install the bolt and nut.

8   Tighten the upper mounting nuts and the stabilizer bar link nut to the torque values listed in this Chapter's Specifications. Raise

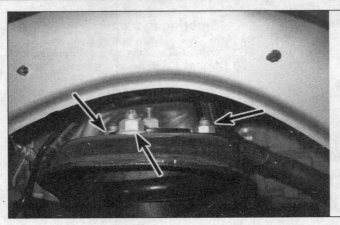

2.1 Loosen the nuts that secure the upper end of the shock module to the body (viewed through wheel opening, fender liner removed)

the control arm with the floor jack to simulate normal ride height, then tighten the lower mounting bolt/nut to the torque listed in this Chapter's Specifications.

9   Install the wheels and lug nuts, then lower the vehicle and tighten the lug nuts to the torque listed in the Chapter 1 Specifications.

Overhaul

Refer to illustrations 2.12, 2.13, 2.14a and 2.14b

Note: *Overhaul, in this case, is the replacement of either the shock absorber unit or the coil spring. This procedure requires the use of a heavy-duty spring compressor. If you don't have one of these tools, it may be more economical to have the procedure performed by a qualified automotive repair facility.*

10   Remove the shock module from the vehicle.

11   Check the shock absorber for leaking fluid, dents, cracks or other obvious damage. Check the coil spring for chips, cracks, or damage to the coating, which could cause premature failure. Inspect the spring seats for hardness or general deterioration. Before disassembling your shock module to replace individual components, check on the availability of

parts and the price of a complete rebuilt unit.

Warning: *Disassembling a shock absorber/coil spring assembly is potentially dangerous and utmost attention must be directed to the job, or serious injury may result. Use only a high-quality spring compressor and carefully follow the manufacturer's instructions furnished with the tool. After compressing the coil spring, set it aside in a safe, isolated area.*

12   Following the tool manufacturer's instructions, install the spring compressor (which can be obtained at most auto parts stores or equipment rental yards on a daily rental basis) on the spring and compress it sufficiently to relieve all pressure from the shock absorber **(see illustration)**. **Caution:** *Don't damage the anti-corrosion coating on the spring when tightening the compressor.*

13   Unscrew the nut from the top of the shock absorber **(see illustration)**.

14   Remove the upper mounting plate, spring and lower mounting plate **(see illustrations)**.

15   Reassemble the shock module by reversing the disassembly procedure. Thread the nut onto the upper end of the shock absorber and tighten it to the torque listed in this Chapter's Specifications.

16   Release the spring compressor tension and remove it from the spring.

17   Install the shock module.

2.5 Remove the lower shock bolt at the lower control arm

2.12 Install a spring compressor on the shock module

2.13 With the spring compressed, unscrew the nut from the top of the shock module (prevent the shaft from turning by inserting a hex bit into the end of the shaft)

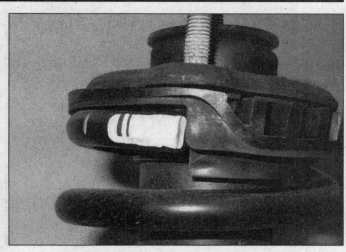

2.14a Remove the upper mounting plate, noting how it fits in the spring end . . .

3 Shock absorber (front, 4WD models) - removal and installation

1   Loosen the front wheel lug nuts. Raise the front of the vehicle and support it securely on jackstands, then remove the wheel.
2   Support the outer end of the lower control arm with a floor jack (the shock absorber module serves as the down-stop for the suspension). The jack must remain in this position throughout the entire procedure.
3   Remove the bolt that secures the shock absorber to the control arm (see illustration 2.5).
4   Remove the shock absorber damper shaft nut. Hold the shaft with a wrench to prevent it from turning.
5   Remove the upper insulator, then pull the shock absorber out of the frame mount and remove it.
6   Installation is the reverse of the removal procedure, noting the following points:

a) Assemble the insulators and the plastic pilot ring in the same orientation as they were during removal.
b) Tighten the damper shaft nut to the torque listed in this Chapter's Specifications.
c) Raise the control arm with the floor jack to simulate normal ride height, then tighten the lower mounting bolt/nut to the torque listed in this Chapter's Specifications.
d) Install the wheels and lug nuts, then lower the vehicle and tighten the lug nuts to the torque listed in the Chapter 1 Specifications.

4 Stabilizer bar and bushings (front) - removal and installation

Refer to illustrations 4.2 and 4.3
1   Raise the vehicle and support it securely on jackstands.

2   Remove the nuts from the links and remove the links (see illustration). Note: Be sure to keep the parts for the left and right sides separate.
3   Remove the stabilizer bar clamp bolts (see illustration).
4   Remove the stabilizer bar.
5   Remove the rubber bushings, noting which way the slits are facing.
6   Inspect all parts for wear and damage.
7   Installation is otherwise the reverse of removal. Be sure to tighten all fasteners to the torque values listed in this Chapter's Specifications.

5 Torsion bar (4WD models) - removal and installation

Note: Torsion bars must be replaced as a pair only, and are specific to the left or right side. When working around the torsion bars, take care not to chip the exterior coating, or the bar could be damaged by rust.

2.14b . . . then remove the spring from the lower mounting plate, again noting how the spring end fits in the plate

4.2 Unscrew the stabilizer link nuts and separate the links from the stabilizer bar

4.3 Remove the clamp bolts and take the stabilizer bar off the vehicle

6.2 Detach the wheel speed sensor harness from the clips on the control arm

6.5 Unscrew the control arm pivot bolts

1   Raise the front of the vehicle and support it securely on jackstands. Block the rear wheels, and allow the front wheels to hang down fully.

2   Work on one side at a time. Begin by marking the relationship of the adjuster arm to the rear end of the bar, and count the number of exposed threads on the adjuster bolt.

3   Remove the adjuster bolt, the spacer and the nut.

4   Move the torsion bar rearward with the adjustment arm still in position until the front end of the bar clears the lower control arm anchor. Remove the torsion bar and arm.

5   For installation, slide the adjustment arm onto the torsion bar, using the marks made previously to align their splines.

6   Slip the front end of the bar into the splined anchor in the lower control arm and reinstall the adjuster bolt, spacer and nut.

7   Tighten the adjuster nut the same number of turns you have recorded before disassembly.

8   Drive the vehicle so the suspension will settle, then compare the left and right side ride-heights and adjust the torsion bars, if necessary, by turning the adjuster nuts a little at a time in the desired direction. Be sure to roll the vehicle back-and-forth a few feet between adjustments, and keep in mind that the final adjustment should be made as the adjuster nut is tightened, not loosened.

6   Upper control arm - removal and installation

Refer to illustrations 6.2 and 6.5

Removal

1   Loosen the wheel lug nuts, raise the front of the vehicle and support it securely on jackstands. Remove the wheel. Position a floor jack under the lower control arm in the area underneath the balljoint. Raise the jack slightly to simulate normal ride height.

2   Remove the ABS sensor harness from the control arm **(see illustration)**. Note how the harness is oriented before removal.

3   Disconnect the front brake hose from the control arm, if attached.

4   To free the upper control arm balljoint stud from the steering knuckle, loosen the balljoint nut a few turns (don't remove it), install a balljoint remover and break the balljoint loose from the knuckle **(see illustration 7.4)**. Now remove the nut. **Note:** *If you don't have the proper balljoint removal tool, a "picklefork" type balljoint separator can be used, but keep in mind that this type of tool will probably destroy the balljoint boot.*

5   If you're working on a 4WD model, mark the positions of the adjustment cams to the frame.

6   Unscrew the upper control arm pivot bolts and remove the control arm **(see illustration)**.

Installation

7   Installation is the reverse of the removal steps. If you're working on a 4WD model, align the marks you made on the adjustment cams and the frame. Tighten the control arm pivot bolts and balljoint nut to the torque listed in this Chapter's Specifications. Tighten the wheel lug nuts to the torque listed in the Chapter 1 Specifications.

8   Have the front end alignment checked and, if necessary, adjusted.

7   Lower control arm - removal and installation

Refer to illustrations 7.4 and 7.6

Removal

1   Loosen the wheel lug nuts, raise the vehicle and support it securely on jackstands placed under the frame rails. Remove the wheel.

7.4 Use a two-jaw puller or a balljoint tool to separate the balljoint from the control arm

2   Disconnect the stabilizer bar link from the lower control arm (see Section 4). On 4WD models, remove the torsion bar (see Section 5).

3   Detach the shock absorber from the lower control arm (see Section 3). If you're working on a 4WD model, remove the steering knuckle (see Section 11).

4   To free the lower control arm balljoint stud from the steering knuckle, loosen the balljoint nut a few turns (don't remove it), install a balljoint remover and break the balljoint loose from the knuckle **(see illustration)**. Now remove the nut. **Note:** *If you don't have the proper balljoint removal tool, a "picklefork" type balljoint separator can be used, but keep in mind that this type of tool will probably destroy the balljoint boot.*

5   If you're working on a 2WD model, mark the positions of the adjustment cams to the frame.

6   Remove the lower control arm pivot bolts and nuts, noting which way the bolts

are installed **(see illustration)**. Pull the lower control arm from its frame brackets. Slip the balljoint stud out of the steering knuckle and remove the lower control arm from the vehicle.

Installation

7   Installation is the reverse of removal. If you're working on a 2WD model, align the marks you made on the adjustment cams and the frame. Be sure to tighten all fasteners to the torque values listed in this Chapter's Specifications.

8   Install the wheel and lug nuts. Lower the vehicle and tighten the lug nuts to the torque listed in the Chapter 1 Specifications.

9   Have the front end alignment checked and, if necessary, adjusted.

7.6 Lower control arm pivot bolts. Note the marks on the adjustment cams and the frame (2WD models only; on 4WD models, the adjustment cams are on the upper control arm pivot bolts)

8   Balljoints - check and replacement

Check

1   Inspect the control arm balljoints for looseness anytime either of them is separated. See if you can turn the ballstud in its socket with your fingers. If the balljoint is loose, or if the ballstud can be turned, replace the balljoint. You can also check the lower balljoints with the suspension assembled as follows.

2   Loosen the wheel lug nuts. Raise the vehicle and support it securely on jackstands placed under the frame rails. Remove the wheels.

3   Wipe the balljoints clean and inspect the seals for cuts and tears. If a balljoint seal is damaged, replace the balljoint.

4   Check the balljoints for wear by trying to move each control arm up and down, in relation to the steering knuckle, with a prybar to ensure that the balljoint has no play. If any balljoint does have any significant play, replace it.

Replacement

Refer to illustrations 8.7a and 8.7b

5   Both upper and lower balljoints are replaceable. The control arm does not have to be removed. Follow the procedure for the upper or lower control arm removal (Sections 6 or 7) but do not remove the control arm mounting bolts.

6   Separate the balljoint from the steering knuckle (Section 6 or 7).

7   Remove the bolts securing the balljoint to the control arm **(see illustrations)**.

8   Install the new balljoint, tightening the bolts to the torque listed in this Chapter's Specifications. Be sure to use new bolts and nuts. The remainder of installation is the reverse of the removal procedure.

9   Have the front end alignment checked and, if necessary, adjusted.

9   Hub and bearing assembly (front) - removal and installation

Refer to illustration 9.5

Warning: *The dust created by the brake system is harmful to your health. Never blow it*

out with compressed air and don't inhale any of it. Do not, under any circumstances, use petroleum-based solvents to clean brake parts. Use brake system cleaner only.
Note 1: *The hub and bearing assembly is sealed-for-life. If worn or damaged, it must be replaced as a unit.*
Note 2: *The ABS wheel sensor is an integral part of the hub/bearing assembly, which is replaced as a unit.*

Removal

1   Loosen the front wheel lug nuts, raise the vehicle and support it securely on jackstands. Remove the wheel.

2   If you're working on a 4WD model, remove the hub cover, then unscrew the driveaxle/hub nut with a socket and large breaker bar (see Chapter 8). Brace a large prybar across two of the wheel studs or insert a large screwdriver through the center of the brake caliper and into the disc cooling vanes to prevent the hub from turning as the nut is loosened. **Note:** *Discard the nut. A new one should be used during installation.*

3   Remove the brake caliper and hang it out of the way with a piece of wire, then remove the caliper mounting bracket (see Chapter 9).

8.7a Upper balljoint mounting bolts

8.7b Lower balljoint mounting bolts

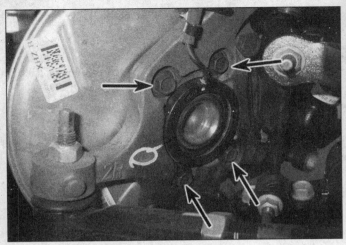

9.5 Remove the bolts that secure the hub and bearing assembly to the steering knuckle

10.3 Use a small press tool such as this to push the stud out of the flange

4   Disconnect the ABS sensor electrical connector and mark the position of the bolts securing the ABS bracket. Remove the bolts and tie the harness and bracket aside. On 4WD models, the steering knuckle must be removed for access to the hub/bearing assembly mounting bolts (see Section 11).

5   Remove the hub and brake disc from the spindle as an assembly **(see illustration)**. The splash shield will come off as the components are separated.

6   With the disc/hub assembly on the floor or a workbench, remove the bolts securing the disc to the hub.

Installation

7   Clean the mating surfaces on the hub and brake disc.

8   Assemble the disc and hub on a flat surface. Install the bolts, tightening them to the torque listed in the Chapter 9 Specifications.

9   Install the hub and bearing/brake disc assembly and disc splash shield to the steering knuckle, tightening the bolts to the torque listed in this Chapter's Specifications.

10   The remainder of installation is the reverse of the removal procedure.

11   Install the wheel, lower the vehicle and tighten the lug nuts to the torque listed in the Chapter 1 Specifications.

10 Wheel studs - replacement

Refer to illustration 10.3

Note: *This procedure applies to both the front and rear wheel studs.*

1   Loosen the wheel lug nuts, raise the vehicle and support it securely on jackstands. Remove the wheel.

2   Remove the brake disc (see Chapter 9).

3   Push the stud out of the hub flange with a press tool **(see illustration)**.

4   Insert the new stud into the hub flange from the back side and install some flat washers and a lug nut on the stud.

5   Tighten the lug nut until the stud is seated in the flange.

6   Reinstall the disc and caliper (see Chapter 9). Install the wheel and lug nuts. Lower the vehicle and tighten the lug nuts to the torque listed in the Chapter 1 Specifications.

11 Steering khuckle - removal and installation

1   Loosen the wheel lug nuts, raise the vehicle and support it securely on jackstands. Remove the wheel.

2   If you're working on a 4WD model, remove the hub cover, then unscrew the driveaxle/hub nut with a socket and large breaker bar (see Chapter 8). Brace a large prybar across two of the wheel studs or insert a large screwdriver through the center of the brake caliper and into the disc cooling vanes to prevent the hub from turning as the nut is loosened.

3   Remove the brake caliper and brake disc (see Chapter 9). Hang the caliper out of the way on a piece of wire (don't disconnect the brake hose). **Note:** *Only the caliper mounting bracket-to-knuckle bolts need to be removed. The caliper and bracket can be removed and wired out of the way as an assembly.*

4   Remove the hub and bearing assembly (see Section 9). On 4WD models, remove the driveaxle.

5   Remove the disc splash shield from the steering knuckle.

6   Unbolt the brake hose bracket from the top of the steering knuckle, if attached.

7   Disconnect the tie-rod end from the steering knuckle (see Section 18).

8   Disconnect the balljoints from the steering knuckle (see Sections 6 and 7).

9   Remove the steering knuckle.

10   Installation is the reverse of removal. Be sure to tighten the balljoint, tie-rod end and hub and bearing assembly fasteners to the torque values listed in this Chapter's Specifications. Tighten the caliper mounting bolts to the torque values listed in the Chapter 9

Specifications. Tighten the driveaxle/hub nut to the torque listed in the Chapter 8 Specifications (4WD models). Tighten the wheel lug nuts to the torque listed in the Chapter 1 Specifications.

12 Shock absorber (rear) - removal and installation

Refer to illustrations 12.3a and 12.3b

1   Raise the rear of the vehicle and support it securely on jackstands placed underneath the frame rails. Block the front wheels so the vehicle doesn't roll off the stands. **Note:** *It isn't necessary to remove the rear wheels, but doing so will improve access to the shock absorbers.*

2   Support the rear axle with a floor jack placed under the axle tube closest to the shock absorber being removed.

3   Remove the shock absorber upper and lower mounting fasteners **(see illustrations)**.

4   Remove the shock absorber.

5   Installation is the reverse of removal. Tighten all fasteners to the torque values listed in this Chapter's Specifications.

12.3a Rear shock absorber upper mounting bolts (one not visible)

12.3b Rear shock absorber lower mounting bolt/nut

14.2 Detach the parking brake cable from the leaf spring

13 Stabilizer bar and bushings (rear) - removal and installation

1   Loosen the rear wheel lug nuts, raise the rear of the vehicle and support it securely on jackstands. Block the front wheels to keep the vehicle from rolling off the stands. Remove the rear wheels.

14.4 Remove the four U-bolt nuts and the lower leaf spring plate

2   Remove the stabilizer bar link-to-frame nuts/bolts.
3   Remove the nuts from the lower ends of the links, then separate the links from the bar.
4   Remove the stabilizer bar clamp nuts and remove the stabilizer bar.
5   Inspect the stabilizer bar bushings and link bushings for cracks, tears and other signs of deterioration. Replace as necessary.
6   Installation is the reverse of removal. Be sure to tighten all fasteners to the torque listed in this Chapter's Specifications.

14 Leaf spring (rear) - removal and installation

Removal

Refer to illustrations 14.2, 14.4, 14.5 and 14.6

1   Loosen the rear wheel lug nuts. Raise the rear of the vehicle and support it securely on jackstands placed underneath the frame rails. Block the front wheels to prevent the vehicle from rolling. Remove the rear wheels.
2   Support the rear axle housing with a floor jack placed underneath the differential. Detach the parking brake cable from its bracket on the leaf spring **(see illustration)**.

3   Disconnect the lower ends of the shock absorbers from the axle housing (see Section 12).
4   Spray the nuts on the U-bolts with penetrating oil and allow it to sit a few minutes. Remove the U-bolt nuts and the anchor plate from below the spring **(see illustration)**. Work on only one leaf spring at a time; the other spring will keep the axle assembly located under the vehicle.
5   Remove the nuts and bolts and detach the rear spring shackle, then carefully lower the spring down **(see illustration)**. The spring is heavy.
6   Remove the bolt and nut from the front spring mount and remove the leaf spring **(see illustration)**.

Installation

7   Mount the spring at the front bracket, but do not fully tighten the bolt.
8   Using an assistant or another jack, raise the spring until it sits between the U-bolts and the anchor plate can be installed and the U-bolt nuts tightened hand-tight. **Note:** *The manufacturer recommends using new U-bolts and nuts when reinstalling the springs.*
9   Reassemble the rear shackle to the rear spring eye.
10   Before tightening the bolts/nuts, raise the rear axle with a floor jack to simulate normal ride height, then tighten the fasteners to the torque listed in this Chapter's Specifications.
11   Install the wheels and lug nuts. Lower the vehicle and tighten the lug nuts to the torque listed in the Chapter 1 Specifications.

15 Steering wheel - removal and installation

Warning: *These models are equipped with airbags. Always disable the airbag system (see Chapter 12) before working in the vicinity of any airbag system component to avoid the possibility of accidental deployment of the airbag, which could cause personal injury.*

14.5 Remove the bolts and separate the shackle from the leaf spring and frame

14.6 Front leaf spring mounting bolt

15.3a To release the pins that secure the airbag module to the steering wheel, insert a screwdriver into the holes in the back side of the steering wheel . . .

Removal

Refer to illustrations 15.3a, 15.3b, 15.4 and 15.6

1   Park the vehicle with the wheels pointing straight ahead. Disconnect the cable from the negative terminal of the battery.
2   Refer to Chapter 12 and disable the airbag system.
3   Insert a screwdriver into the hole for the spring clip that retains the airbag module **(see illustrations)** and push the spring aside to release the pin. Now do the same thing to release the pin on the other side of the steering wheel.
4   Pry up the connector lock and disconnect the yellow electrical connector from the module **(see illustration)**. Set the module aside in a safe, isolated area, with the airbag side of the module facing UP. **Warning:** *When carrying the airbag module, keep the driver's (trim) side of it away from your body, and when you set it down, make sure the driver's side is facing up.*
5   Center the steering wheel.

15.3b . . . and pry each spring clip aside to clear the pin (there are two pins; one on each side of the steering wheel) - steering wheel removed for clarity

6   Remove the steering wheel retaining nut and mark the position of the steering wheel to the shaft, if marks don't already exist or don't line up **(see illustration)**.
7   Loosen the steering wheel retaining nut two full turns, then pull on and rock the steering wheel to remove it by hand. If the wheel doesn't come off by hand, use a steering wheel puller to remove it. **Warning:** *Do not hammer on the shaft of the puller in an attempt to loosen the wheel from the shaft.*
8   Lift the steering wheel from the shaft. **Warning:** *Don't allow the steering shaft to turn with the steering wheel removed. If the shaft turns, the airbag clockspring will become uncentered, which may cause the wire inside to break when the vehicle is returned to service.*

Installation

Refer to illustrations 15.9a, 15.9b and 15.12
Warning: *The airbag clockspring assembly is a ribbon-like mechanism that allows electrical current to flow to the airbag module regardless*

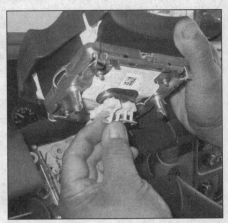

15.4 Pry up the connector lock, then pull the connector out of the airbag module

of steering wheel position. If the clockspring becomes uncentered, it may break when the vehicle is returned to service.
Note: *It is not necessary to remove the clockspring unless repairs to the steering column are required. The clockspring does not have to be centered unless the center hub of the clockspring was moved while the steering wheel was off or the clockspring was removed from the steering column. Follow the centering procedure if the clockspring was removed and the alignment was changed.*
9   Before installing the steering wheel, make sure the airbag clockspring is centered. **Note:** *On the models covered by this manual, two style clocksprings are used; one type has a window on the front face and no spring lock tab on the back. The other type does not have a window but does have a spring lock tab* **(see illustrations)**.
10   If the airbag system clockspring is not centered, remove the steering column covers (see Chapter 11). Remove the three screws and lift the clockspring off the steering column. You may have to cut a plastic wire-tie securing the clockspring harness to the steering column.

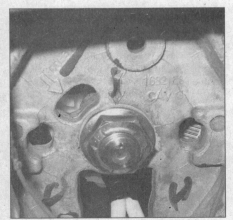

15.6 Check to see if there are alignment marks on the steering wheel and the steering shaft; if there are none, make your own

15.9a When the clockspring is centered on models with a spring lock tab, the arrow on the housing will be aligned with the arrow on the hub

15.9b On clocksprings with a centering window, the clockspring is centered when the window (A) appears yellow and the two arrows (B) are aligned

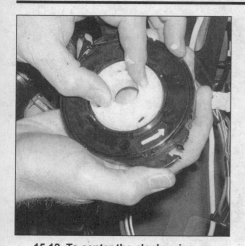

15.12 To center the clockspring on models with a spring lock tab, hold it with its underside facing up, depress the spring lock and rotate the hub in the direction of the arrow until it stops, then turn it in the opposite direction 2-1/2 turns

11   If your clockspring has a window on the front and no spring lock tab on the back, hold it face up and turn the hub clockwise until it stops (don't apply excessive force). Now slowly turn the hub counterclockwise at least two turns until the window turns yellow and the arrows on the hub and the housing are in alignment **(see illustration 15.9b)**. Proceed to Step 13.

12   If your clockspring does not have a window on the front, turn it over and depress the spring lock on the back, then rotate the hub in the direction of the arrow on the housing until it stops (don't apply too much force). Now turn the hub 2-1/2 turns in the opposite direction and release the spring lock tab **(see illustration)**. Proceed to the next Step.

13   Install the clockspring with its screws. Secure the wiring harness with a new wire-tie, making sure the harness isn't kinked. Also install the steering column covers.

14   Install the wheel on the steering shaft, aligning the marks.

15   Install the steering wheel nut and tighten it to the torque listed in this Chapter's Specifications.

16   Connect the airbag connector to the back of the airbag module. Make sure the connector lock is securely engaged.

17   Position the airbag module on the steering wheel and push it in until the pins on the module engage with the spring clips.

18   Refer to Chapter 12 for the procedure to enable the airbag system.

16 Steering column - removal and installation

Refer to illustrations 16.7 and 16.8

Warning: *The models covered by this manual are equipped with airbags. Always disable the airbag system when working in the vicinity of airbag system components (see Chapter 12).*

Removal

1   Park the vehicle with the wheels pointing straight ahead. Disconnect the cable from the negative terminal of the battery. Disable the airbag system (see Chapter 12).

2   Remove the steering wheel (see Section 15), then turn the ignition key to the LOCK position to prevent the steering shaft from turning. **Caution:** *If this is not done, the airbag clockspring could be damaged.*

3   Remove the knee bolster and the reinforcement behind it (see Chapter 11).

4   If the vehicle is equipped with a tilt column, pull the tilt lever out of the steering column.

5   Remove the steering column covers (see Chapter 11). Disconnect the shift cable at the column (see Chapter 7B).

6   Disconnect the electrical connectors for the steering column harness, body harness and the electrical connector at the shift-lock solenoid.

7   Remove the pinch bolt securing the steering shaft to the upper intermediate shaft **(see illustration)**. **Note:** *Mark the relationship of the intermediate shaft to the steering column shaft.*

8   Remove the steering column mounting bolts **(see illustration 16.7 and the accompanying illustration)**, lower the column and pull it to the rear, making sure nothing is still connected. Separate the intermediate shaft from the steering shaft and remove the column.

Installation

Note: *If a new column is being installed, check to see if a shipping lock pin is present. If so, remove it.*

9   Guide the steering column into position, connect the intermediate shaft, then install the mounting nuts, but don't tighten them yet.

10   Install the coupler pinch bolt, then tighten the bolt to the torque listed in this Chapter's Specifications.

11   Tighten the column mounting nuts to the torque listed in this Chapter's Specifications. **Note:** *Clean the old adhesive from the bolt threads, then apply new threadlocker adhesive before installation.*

12   The remainder of installation is the reverse of removal.

17 Intermediate shaft - removal and installation

Refer to illustration 17.3

1   Park the vehicle with the wheels pointing straight ahead. Disconnect the cable from the negative terminal of the battery. Disable the airbag system (see Chapter 12).

2   Turn the ignition key to the LOCK position to prevent the steering shaft from turning. **Caution:** *If this is not done, the airbag clockspring could be damaged.*

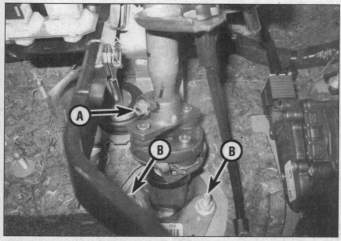

16.7 Upper intermediate shaft-to-steering column shaft pinch bolt (A). B are the nuts securing the intermediate shaft to the firewall

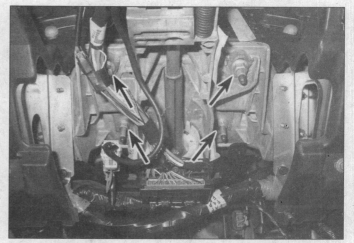

16.8 Remove the steering column mounting nuts

17.3 Mark the relationship of the upper and lower halves of the intermediate shaft, then remove the coupler bolt

18.2 Hold the hex with a wrench while loosening the jam nut

3   Working under the hood, mark the relationship of the upper intermediate shaft to the lower intermediate shaft **(see illustration)**. Remove the shaft coupler nut and remove the bolt securing the lower intermediate shaft to the upper intermediate shaft. Note the direction that the bolt is inserted (it must be reinstalled in the same direction).

4   Mark the relationship of the lower intermediate shaft to the steering gear input shaft, then remove the intermediate shaft-to-steering gear pinch bolt.

5   Slide the lower portion of the intermediate shaft downwards and off the upper intermediate shaft, then remove the lower shaft from the steering gear.

6   If it is necessary to remove the upper portion of the intermediate shaft, refer to Section 16, Step 7.

7   Installation is the reverse of removal. Be sure to align the matchmarks and tighten the coupler bolt and the shaft-to-steering gear pinch bolt to the torque listed in this Chapter's Specifications.

18 Tie-rod ends - removal and installation

Refer to illustrations 18.2 and 18.3

Removal

1   Loosen the wheel lug nuts, raise the front of the vehicle and support it securely on jackstands. Apply the parking brake and block the rear wheels to keep the vehicle from rolling off the jackstands. Remove the wheel.

2   Measure the length of exposed threads on the tie-rod end and write this figure down, then break loose the tie-rod end jam nut **(see illustration). Warning:** *The manufacturer recommends replacing the jam nut with a new one whenever it has been removed.*

3   Loosen (but don't remove) the nut on the tie-rod end ballstud and break loose the tie-rod end from the steering knuckle arm with a puller **(see illustration)**. Now remove the nut and detach the tie-rod end from the steering knuckle.

4   Unscrew the tie-rod end from the tie-rod.

Installation

5   Thread the new jam nut on the new tie-rod end so that the same length of threads are exposed as in Step 2.

6   Connect the tie-rod end to the steering knuckle arm. Install the nut on the ballstud and tighten it to the torque listed in this Chapter's Specifications.

7   Tighten the jam nut securely and install the wheel. Lower the vehicle and tighten the lug nuts to the torque listed in the Chapter 1 Specifications.

8   Have the front end alignment checked and, if necessary, adjusted.

19 Steering gear boots - replacement

Refer to illustration 19.3

1   Loosen the wheel lug nuts, raise the front of the vehicle and support it securely on jackstands. Remove the wheels.

18.3 Use a puller to remove the tie-rod end without damage to its boot

19.3 Cut the steering gear boot clamps off with a pair of side cutters

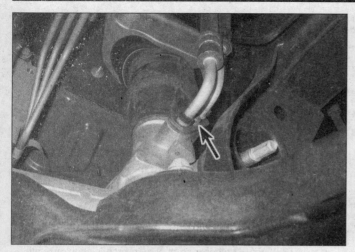

20.5 Unscrew the bolt and remove the pressure and return line fitting from the power steering gear

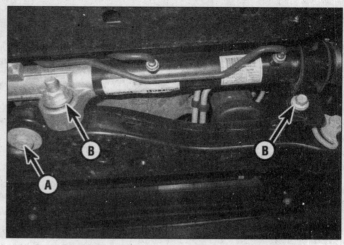

20.6 Rack-and-pinion steering gear mounting bolts: A, vertical; B, horizontal

2   Remove the tie-rod ends from the tie-rods (see Section 17).
3   Cut off the boot clamps and discard them **(see illustration)**.
4   Note the location of the alignment marks on the boots and steering gear (one arrow-head mark on the rear side of each boot and two on the gear next to it). Remove the boots.
5   Install a new clamp on the inner end of the boot.
6   Apply multi-purpose grease to the groove on the tie-rod (where the outer end of the boot will ride) and the mounting grooves on the steering gear (where the inner boot end will be clamped).
7   Line up the marks on the boot and steering gear and slide the new boot onto the steering gear housing.
8   Make sure the boot isn't twisted, then tighten the new inner clamp with a clamp-crimping tool (available at most auto parts stores).
9   Install and tighten the outer clamps.
10   Install the tie-rod ends (see Section 18).
11   Have the front end alignment checked and, if necessary, adjusted.

20 Steering gear - removal and installation

Refer to illustrations 20.5 and 20.6

Warning: *DO NOT allow the steering column shaft to rotate with the steering gear removed or damage to the airbag system could occur. As a method of preventing the shaft from turning, wrap the seat belt around the rim of the steering wheel and buckle the belt in place.*
1   Loosen the front wheel lug nuts, raise the front of the vehicle and support it securely on jackstands. Apply the parking brake. Remove the wheels.
2   Remove the under-vehicle splash shield. Also remove the skid plate bolts and the skid plate, if equipped. Remove the steering gear crossmember (see Chapter 11). On 4WD models, remove the front differential housing (see Chapter 8).
3   Mark the relationship of the intermediate shaft coupler to the steering gear input shaft and remove the pinch bolt **(see illustration 17.3)**.
4   Detach the tie-rod ends from the steer-

ing knuckles (see Section 18).
5   Position a drain pan under the steering gear. Remove the bolt and detach the pressure and return lines from the steering gear **(see illustration)**. Cap the lines to prevent leakage.
6   Unscrew the mounting nuts, remove the washers and slide the bolts out. Lower the steering gear from the vehicle **(see illustration)**. There are two vertical bolts and two horizontal bolts securing the steering gear.
7   Installation is the reverse of removal. Be sure to tighten all fasteners to the torque values listed in this Chapter's Specifications and the Chapter 11 Specifications. Tighten the wheel lug nuts to the torque listed in the Chapter 1 Specifications. Check the power steering fluid level and add some, if necessary (see Chapter 1), then bleed the system as described in Section 22.

21 Power steering pump - removal and installation

Removal

Refer to illustrations 21.3 and 21.4

1   Disconnect the cable from the negative terminal of the battery, and remove the air filter assembly (see Chapter 4).
2   Remove the serpentine drivebelt (see Chapter 1).
3   Position a drain pan under the power steering pump. Unscrew the pressure hose fitting from the pump with a flare nut wrench **(see illustration)**. Plug the hoses to prevent contaminants from entering.
4   Remove the pulley from the pump with a special power steering pump pulley remover **(see illustration)**.
5   Free the wiring harness from the retainer on the power steering pump.
6   Remove the pump mounting fasteners and lift the pump from the vehicle, taking care not to spill fluid on the painted surfaces.

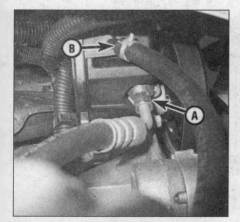

21.3 Detach the power steering pressure line (A) and return hose (B) from the pump

21.4 Remove the pulley from the power steering pump with a pulley removal tool

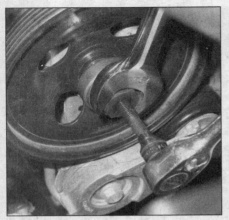

21.7 Press the pulley onto the shaft using a pulley installation tool - don't attempt to drive it on with a hammer or push it on with a traditional press!

Installation

Refer to illustration 21.7

7   Press the pulley onto the shaft using a special pulley installer tool **(see illustration)**. An alternative tool can be fabricated from a long bolt, nut, washer and a socket of the same diameter as the pulley hub. Push the pulley onto the shaft until the front of the hub is flush with the shaft, but no further.

8   Position the pump in the mounting bracket and install the mounting bolts or nuts. Tighten the fasteners to the torque listed in this Chapter's Specifications.

9   Connect the hoses to the pump. Tighten the fittings securely.

10   Install the drivebelt and fan shroud.

11   Fill the power steering reservoir with the recommended fluid (see Chapter 1) and bleed the system following the procedure described in the next Section.

22 Power steering system - bleeding

1   Following any operation in which the power steering fluid lines have been disconnected, the power steering system must be bled to remove all air and obtain proper steering performance.

2   With the front wheels in the straight ahead position, check the power steering fluid level and, if low, add fluid until it reaches the Cold mark on the dipstick.

3   Start the engine and allow it to run at fast idle. Recheck the fluid level and add more if necessary to reach the Cold mark on the dipstick.

4   Bleed the system by turning the wheels from side-to-side, without hitting the stops. This will work the air out of the system. Keep the reservoir full of fluid as this is done.

5   When the air is worked out of the system, return the wheels to the straight-ahead position and leave the vehicle running for several more minutes before shutting it off. Recheck the fluid level.

6   Road test the vehicle to be sure the steering system is functioning normally and noise free.

7   Recheck the fluid level to be sure it's up to the Hot mark on the dipstick while the engine is at normal operating temperature. Add fluid if necessary (see Chapter 1).

23 Wheels and tires - general information

Refer to illustration 23.1

Most of the vehicles covered by this manual are equipped with metric-size fiberglass or steel belted radial tires **(see illustration)**. Use of other size or type of tires may affect the ride and handling of the vehicle. Don't mix different types of tires, such as radials and bias belted, on the same vehicle as handling may be seriously affected. It's recommended that tires be replaced in pairs on the same axle, but if only one tire is being replaced, be sure it's the same size, structure and tread design as the other.

Because tire pressure has a substantial effect on handling and wear, the pressure on all tires should be checked at least once a month or before any extended trips (see Chapter 1).

Wheels must be replaced if they're bent, dented, leak air, have elongated bolt holes, are heavily rusted, out of vertical symmetry or if the lug nuts won't stay tight. Wheel repairs that use welding or peening are not recommended.

Tire and wheel balance is important to the overall handling, braking and performance of the vehicle. Unbalanced wheels can adversely affect handling and ride characteristics as well as tire life. Whenever a tire is installed on a wheel, the tire and wheel should be balanced by a shop with the proper equipment.

24 Front end alignment - general information

Refer to illustration 24.1

A front-end alignment **(see illustration)** refers to the adjustments made to the front wheels so they're in proper angular relationship to the suspension and the ground. Front wheels that are out of proper alignment not only affect steering control, but also increase tire wear.

Getting the proper front wheel alignment is a very exacting process, one in which complicated and expensive machines are necessary to perform the job properly. Because of this, you should have a technician with the proper equipment perform these tasks. We will, however, use this space to give you a basic idea of what is involved with front-end alignment so you can better understand the process and deal intelligently with the shop that does the work.

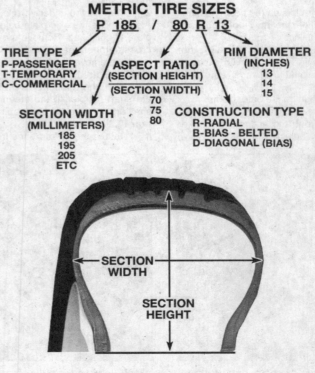

23.1 Metric tire size code

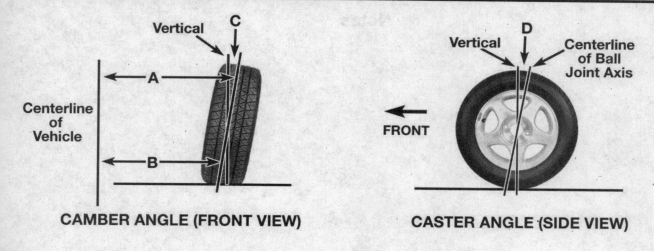

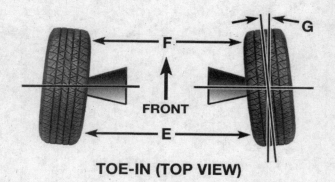

24.1 Front end alignment details

A minus B = C (degrees camber)
D = degrees caster
E minus F = toe-in (measured in inches)
G = toe-in (expressed in degrees)

Toe-in is the turning in of the front wheels. The purpose of a toe specification is to ensure parallel rolling of the front wheels. In a vehicle with zero toe-in, the distance between the front edges of the wheels will be the same as the distance between the rear edges of the wheels. The actual amount of toe-in is normally only a fraction of an inch. Toe-in is adjusted by turning the tie-rod in the tie-rod end to lengthen or shorten the tie-rod. Incorrect toe-in will cause the tires to wear improperly by making them scrub against the road surface.

Camber is the tilting of the front wheels from vertical when viewed from the front of the vehicle. When the wheels tilt out at the top, the camber is said to be positive (+). When the wheels tilt in at the top the camber is negative (-). The amount of tilt is measured in degrees from the vertical and this measurement is called the camber angle. This angle affects the amount of tire tread which contacts the road and compensates for changes in the suspension geometry when the vehicle is cornering or traveling over an undulating surface. Camber is adjusted by loosening the lower control arm adjustment bolts and repositioning the arm on the frame.

Caster is the tilting of the top of the front steering axis from vertical. A tilt toward the rear is positive caster and a tilt toward the front is negative caster. Caster is also adjusted by loosening the lower control arm adjustment bolts and repositioning the arm on the frame.

When making adjustments to the front-end alignment, the caster is set first, then the camber, and then the toe-in.

Notes

Chapter 11
Body

Contents

Specifications

Torque specifications

	Ft-lbs
Front bumper bracket-to-frame bolts	30
Front bumper-to-bracket bolts	30
Rear bumper bracket-to-frame bolts	118
Rear bumper-to-bracket bolts	118
Steering gear crossmember bolts	44

1 General information

Warning: *The models covered by this manual are equipped with Supplemental Restraint Systems (SRS), more commonly known as airbags. Always disable the airbag system before working in the vicinity of any airbag system components to avoid the possibility of accidental deployment of the airbags, which could cause personal injury (see Chapter 12).*

The vehicles covered by this manual are built with body-on-frame construction. The frame is a hydroformed, ladder-type, consisting of C-shaped center rails welded to boxed front and rear sections, with both welded-in and bolt-in crossmembers.

Certain components are particularly vulnerable to accident damage and can be unbolted and repaired or replaced. Among these parts are the hood, doors, seats, tailgate, bumpers, front fenders, grille and the pickup bed.

Only general body maintenance practices and body panel repair procedures within the scope of the do-it-yourselfer are included in this Chapter.

2 Body - maintenance

1 The condition of your vehicle's body is very important, because the resale value depends a great deal on it. It's much more difficult to repair a neglected or damaged body than it is to repair mechanical components. The hidden areas of the body, such as the wheel wells, the frame and the engine compartment, are equally important, although they don't require as frequent attention as the rest of the body.

2 Once a year, or every 12,000 miles, it's

a good idea to have the underside of the body steam cleaned. All traces of dirt and oil will be removed and the area can then be inspected carefully for rust, damaged brake lines, frayed electrical wires, damaged cables and other problems. The front suspension components should be greased after completion of this job.

3   At the same time, clean the engine and the engine compartment with a steam cleaner or water-soluble degreaser.

4   The wheel wells should be given close attention, since undercoating can peel away and stones and dirt thrown up by the tires can cause the paint to chip and flake, allowing rust to set in. If rust is found, clean down to the bare metal and apply an anti-rust paint.

5   The body should be washed about once a week. Wet the vehicle thoroughly to soften the dirt, then wash it down with a soft sponge and plenty of clean, soapy water. If the surplus dirt is not washed off very carefully, it can wear down the paint.

6   Spots of tar or asphalt thrown up from the road should be removed with a cloth soaked in tar remover or kerosene lamp oil.

7   Once every six months, wax the body and chrome trim. If a chrome cleaner is used to remove rust from any of the vehicle's plated parts, remember that the cleaner also removes part of the chrome, so use it sparingly.

3   Vinyl trim - maintenance

Don't clean vinyl trim with detergents, caustic soap or petroleum-based cleaners. Plain soap and water works just fine, with a soft brush to clean dirt that may be ingrained. Wash the vinyl as frequently as the rest of the vehicle. After cleaning, application of a high-quality rubber and vinyl protectant will help prevent oxidation and cracks. The protectant can also be applied to weatherstripping, vacuum lines and rubber hoses, which often fail as a result of chemical degradation, and to the tires.

4   Upholstery and carpets - maintenance

1   Every three months remove the floormats and clean the interior of the vehicle (more frequently if necessary). Use a stiff whiskbroom to brush the carpeting and loosen dirt and dust, then vacuum the upholstery and carpets thoroughly, especially along seams and crevices.

2   Dirt and stains can be removed from carpeting with basic household or automotive carpet shampoos available in spray cans. Follow the directions and vacuum again, then use a stiff brush to bring back the "nap" of the carpet.

3   Most interiors have cloth or vinyl upholstery, either of which can be cleaned and maintained with a number of material-specific

cleaners or shampoos available in auto supply stores. Follow the directions on the product for usage, and always spot-test any upholstery cleaner on an inconspicuous area (bottom edge of a backseat cushion) to ensure that it doesn't cause a color shift in the material.

4   After cleaning, vinyl upholstery should be treated with a protectant. **Note:** *Make sure the protectant container indicates the product can be used on seats - some products may make a seat too slippery.* **Caution:** *Do not use protectant on vinyl-covered steering wheels.*

5   Leather upholstery requires special care. It should be cleaned regularly with saddle-soap or leather cleaner. Never use alcohol, gasoline, nail polish remover or thinner to clean leather upholstery.

6   After cleaning, regularly treat leather upholstery with a leather conditioner, rubbed in with a soft cotton cloth. Never use car wax on leather upholstery.

7   In areas where the interior of the vehicle is subject to bright sunlight, cover leather seating areas of the seats with a sheet if the vehicle is to be left out for any length of time.

5   Body repair - minor damage

Plastic body panels

The following repair procedures are for minor scratches and gouges. Repair of more serious damage should be left to a dealer service department or qualified auto body shop. Below is a list of the equipment and materials necessary to perform the following repair procedures on plastic body panels.

Wax, grease and silicone-removing solvent
Cloth-backed body tape
Sanding discs
Drill motor with three-inch disc holder
Hand sanding block
Rubber squeegees
Sandpaper
Non-porous mixing palette
Wood paddle or putty knife
Curved-tooth body file
Flexible parts repair material

Flexible panels (front and rear bumper trim)

1   Remove the damaged panel, if necessary or desirable. In most cases, repairs can be carried out with the panel installed.

2   Clean the area(s) to be repaired with a wax, grease and silicone removing solvent applied with a water-dampened cloth.

3   If the damage is structural, that is, if it extends through the panel, clean the backside of the panel area to be repaired as well. Wipe dry.

4   Sand the rear surface about 1-1/2 inches beyond the break.

5   Cut two pieces of fiberglass cloth large enough to overlap the break by about 1-1/2 inches. Cut only to the required length.

6   Mix the adhesive from the repair kit according to the instructions included with the

kit, and apply a layer of the mixture approximately 1/8-inch thick on the backside of the panel. Overlap the break by at least 1-1/2 inches.

7   Apply one piece of fiberglass cloth to the adhesive and cover the cloth with additional adhesive. Apply a second piece of fiberglass cloth to the adhesive and immediately cover the cloth with additional adhesive in sufficient quantity to fill the weave.

8   Allow the repair to cure for 20 to 30 minutes at 60-degrees to 80-degrees F.

9   If necessary, trim the excess repair material at the edge.

10   Remove all of the paint film over and around the area(s) to be repaired. The repair material should not overlap the painted surface.

11   With a drill motor and a sanding disc (or a rotary file), cut a "V" along the break line approximately 1/2-inch wide. Remove all dust and loose particles from the repair area.

12   Mix and apply the repair material. Apply a light coat first over the damaged area; then continue applying material until it reaches a level slightly higher than the surrounding finish.

13   Cure the mixture for 20 to 30 minutes at 60-degrees to 80-degrees F.

14   Roughly establish the contour of the area being repaired with a body file. If low areas or pits remain, mix and apply additional adhesive.

15   Block sand the damaged area with sandpaper to establish the actual contour of the surrounding surface.

16   If desired, the repaired area can be temporarily protected with several light coats of primer. Because of the special paints and techniques required for flexible body panels, it is recommended that the vehicle be taken to a paint shop for completion of the body repair.

Steel body panels

See photo sequence

Repair of minor scratches

17   If the scratch is superficial and does not penetrate to the metal of the body, repair is very simple. Lightly rub the scratched area with a fine rubbing compound to remove loose paint, then use a wax-and-grease remover (available at auto parts stores) to clean the area. Rinse the area with clean water.

18   Apply touch-up paint to the scratch, using a small brush. Continue to apply thin layers of paint until the surface of the paint in the scratch is level with the surrounding paint. Allow the new paint at least two weeks to harden, then blend it into the surrounding paint by rubbing with a very fine rubbing compound. Finally, apply a coat of wax to the scratch area.

19   If the scratch has penetrated the paint and exposed the metal of the body, causing the metal to rust, a different repair technique is required. Remove all loose rust from the bottom of the scratch with a pocketknife, then apply rust inhibiting paint to prevent the formation of rust in the future. Using a rubber

or nylon applicator, coat the scratched area with glaze-type filler. If required, the filler can be mixed with thinner to provide a very thin paste, which is ideal for filling narrow scratches. Before the glaze filler in the scratch hardens, wrap a piece of smooth cotton cloth around the tip of a finger. Dip the cloth in thinner and then quickly wipe it along the surface of the scratch. This will ensure that the surface of the filler is slightly hollow. The scratch can now be painted over as described earlier in this Section.

Repair of dents

20   When repairing dents, the first job is to pull the dent out until the affected area is as close as possible to its original shape. There is no point in trying to restore the original shape completely as the metal in the damaged area will have stretched on impact and cannot be restored to its original contours. It is better to bring the level of the dent up to a point that is about 1/8-inch below the level of the surrounding metal. In cases where the dent is very shallow, it is not worth trying to pull it out at all.

21   If the backside of the dent is accessible, it can be hammered out gently from behind using a soft-face hammer. While doing this, hold a block of wood firmly against the opposite side of the metal to absorb the hammer blows and prevent the metal from being stretched.

22   If the dent is in a section of the body which has double layers, or some other factor makes it inaccessible from behind, a different technique is required. Drill several small holes through the metal inside the damaged area, particularly in the deeper sections. Screw long, self-tapping screws into the holes just enough for them to get a good grip in the metal. Now pulling on the protruding heads of the screws with locking pliers can pull out the dent.

23   The next stage of repair is the removal of paint from the damaged area and from an inch or so of the surrounding metal. This is easily done with a wire brush or sanding disk in a drill motor, although it can be done just as effectively by hand with sandpaper. To complete the preparation for filling, score the surface of the bare metal with a screwdriver or the tang of a file or drill small holes in the affected area. This will provide a good grip for the filler material. To complete the repair, see the Section on filling and painting.

Repair of rust holes or gashes

24   Remove all paint from the affected area and from an inch or so of the surrounding metal using a sanding disk or wire brush mounted in a drill motor. If these are not available, a few sheets of sandpaper will do the job just as effectively.

25   With the paint removed, you will be able to determine the severity of the corrosion and decide whether to replace the whole panel, if possible, or repair the affected area. New body panels are not as expensive as most people think and it is often quicker to install a new panel than to repair large areas of rust.

26   Remove all trim pieces from the affected area except those which will act as a guide to the original shape of the damaged body, such as headlight shells, etc. Using metal snips or a hacksaw blade, remove all loose metal and any other metal that is badly affected by rust. Hammer the edges of the hole in to create a slight depression for the filler material.

27   Wire-brush the affected area to remove the powdery rust from the surface of the metal. If the back of the rusted area is accessible, treat it with rust inhibiting paint.

28   Before filling is done, block the hole in some way. This can be done with sheet metal riveted or screwed into place, or by stuffing the hole with wire mesh.

29   Once the hole is blocked off, the affected area can be filled and painted. See the following subsection on filling and painting.

Filling and painting

30   Many types of body fillers are available, but generally speaking, body repair kits which contain filler paste and a tube of resin hardener are best for this type of repair work. A wide, flexible plastic or nylon applicator will be necessary for imparting a smooth and contoured finish to the surface of the filler material. Mix up a small amount of filler on a clean piece of wood or cardboard (use the hardener sparingly). Follow the manufacturer's instructions on the package, otherwise the filler will set incorrectly.

31   Using the applicator, apply the filler paste to the prepared area. Draw the applicator across the surface of the filler to achieve the desired contour and to level the filler surface. As soon as a contour that approximates the original one is achieved, stop working the paste. If you continue, the paste will begin to stick to the applicator. Continue to add thin layers of paste at 20-minute intervals until the level of the filler is just above the surrounding metal.

32   Once the filler has hardened, the excess can be removed with a body file. From then on, progressively finer grades of sandpaper should be used, starting with a 180-grit paper and finishing with 600-grit wet-or-dry paper. Always wrap the sandpaper around a flat rubber or wooden block, otherwise the surface of the filler will not be completely flat. During the sanding of the filler surface, the wet-or-dry paper should be periodically rinsed in water. This will ensure that a very smooth finish is produced in the final stage.

33   At this point, the repair area should be surrounded by a ring of bare metal, which in turn should be encircled by the finely feathered edge of good paint. Rinse the repair area with clean water until all of the dust produced by the sanding operation is gone.

34   Spray the entire area with a light coat of primer. This will reveal any imperfections in the surface of the filler. Repair the imperfections with fresh filler paste or glaze filler and once more smooth the surface with sandpaper. Repeat this spray-and-repair procedure until you are satisfied that the surface of the filler and the feathered edge of the paint are perfect. Rinse the area with clean water and allow it to dry completely.

35   The repair area is now ready for painting. Spray painting must be carried out in a warm, dry, windless and dust free atmosphere. These conditions can be created if you have access to a large indoor work area, but if you are forced to work in the open, you will have to pick the day very carefully. If you are working indoors, dousing the floor in the work area with water will help settle the dust that would otherwise be in the air. If the repair area is confined to one body panel, mask off the surrounding panels. This will help minimize the effects of a slight mismatch in paint color. Trim pieces such as chrome strips, door handles, etc., will also need to be masked off or removed. Use masking tape and several thickness of newspaper for the masking operations.

36   Before spraying, shake the paint can thoroughly, then spray a test area until the spray painting technique is mastered. Cover the repair area with a thick coat of primer. The thickness should be built up using several thin layers of primer rather than one thick one. Using 600-grit wet-or-dry sandpaper, rub down the surface of the primer until it is very smooth. While doing this, the work area should be thoroughly rinsed with water and the wet-or-dry sandpaper periodically rinsed as well. Allow the primer to dry before spraying additional coats.

37   Spray on the top coat, again building up the thickness by using several thin layers of paint. Begin spraying in the center of the repair area and then, using a circular motion, work out until the whole repair area and about two inches of the surrounding original paint is covered. Remove all masking material 10 to 15 minutes after spraying on the final coat of paint. Allow the new paint at least two weeks to harden, then use a very fine rubbing compound to blend the edges of the new paint into the existing paint. Finally, apply a coat of wax.

6   Body repair - major damage

1   Major damage must be repaired by an auto body shop specifically equipped to perform body and frame repairs. These shops have the specialized equipment required to do the job properly.

2   If the damage is extensive, the body must be checked for proper alignment or the vehicle's handling characteristics may be adversely affected and other components may wear at an accelerated rate.

3   Due to the fact that all of the major body components (hood, fenders, etc.) are separate and replaceable units, any seriously damaged components should be replaced rather than repaired. Sometimes the components can be found in a wrecking yard that specializes in used vehicle components, often at considerable savings over the cost of new parts.

These photos illustrate a method of repairing simple dents. They are intended to supplement *Body repair - minor damage* in this Chapter and should not be used as the sole instructions for body repair on these vehicles.

1 If you can't access the backside of the body panel to hammer out the dent, pull it out with a slide-hammer-type dent puller. In the deepest portion of the dent or along the crease line, drill or punch hole(s) at least one inch apart . . .

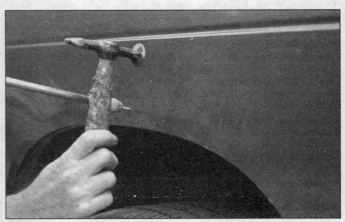

2 . . . then screw the slide-hammer into the hole and operate it. Tap with a hammer near the edge of the dent to help 'pop' the metal back to its original shape. When you're finished, the dent area should be close to its original contour and about 1/8-inch below the surface of the surrounding metal

3 Using coarse-grit sandpaper, remove the paint down to the bare metal. Hand sanding works fine, but the disc sander shown here makes the job faster. Use finer (about 320-grit) sandpaper to feather-edge the paint at least one inch around the dent area

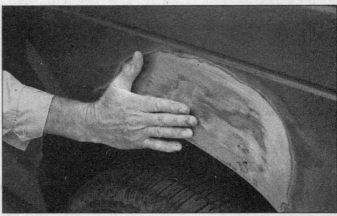

4 When the paint is removed, touch will probably be more helpful than sight for telling if the metal is straight. Hammer down the high spots or raise the low spots as necessary. Clean the repair area with wax/silicone remover

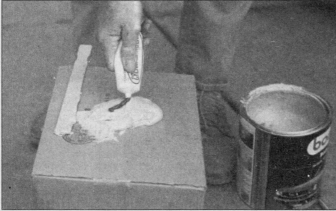

5 Following label instructions, mix up a batch of plastic filler and hardener. The ratio of filler to hardener is critical, and, if you mix it incorrectly, it will either not cure properly or cure too quickly (you won't have time to file and sand it into shape)

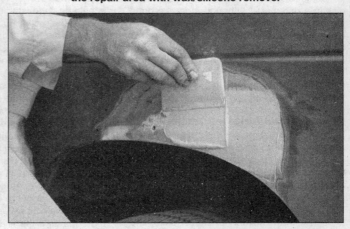

6 Working quickly so the filler doesn't harden, use a plastic applicator to press the body filler firmly into the metal, assuring it bonds completely. Work the filler until it matches the original contour and is slightly above the surrounding metal

7 Let the filler harden until you can just dent it with your fingernail. Use a body file or Surform tool (shown here) to rough-shape the filler

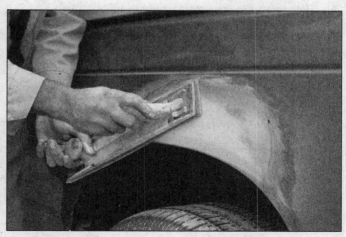

8 Use coarse-grit sandpaper and a sanding board or block to work the filler down until it's smooth and even. Work down to finer grits of sandpaper - always using a board or block - ending up with 360 or 400 grit

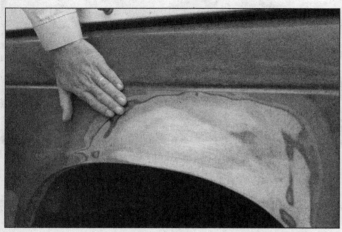

9 You shouldn't be able to feel any ridge at the transition from the filler to the bare metal or from the bare metal to the old paint. As soon as the repair is flat and uniform, remove the dust and mask off the adjacent panels or trim pieces

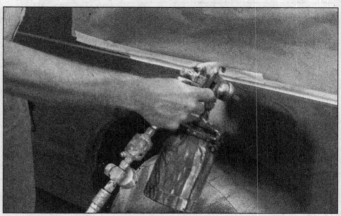

10 Apply several layers of primer to the area. Don't spray the primer on too heavy, so it sags or runs, and make sure each coat is dry before you spray on the next one. A professional-type spray gun is being used here, but aerosol spray primer is available inexpensively from auto parts stores

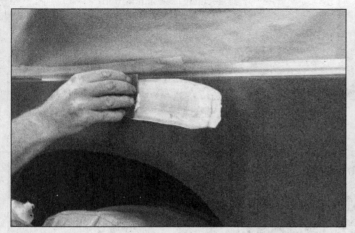

11 The primer will help reveal imperfections or scratches. Fill these with glazing compound. Follow the label instructions and sand it with 360 or 400-grit sandpaper until it's smooth. Repeat the glazing, sanding and respraying until the primer reveals a perfectly smooth surface

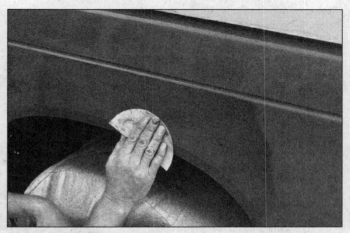

12 Finish sand the primer with very fine sandpaper (400 or 600-grit) to remove the primer overspray. Clean the area with water and allow it to dry. Use a tack rag to remove any dust, then apply the finish coat. Don't attempt to rub out or wax the repair area until the paint has dried completely (at least two weeks)

7 Hinges and locks - maintenance

Once every 3000 miles, or every three months, the hinges and latch assemblies on the doors, hood and trunk should be given a few drops of light oil or lock lubricant. The door latch strikers should also be lubricated with a thin coat of grease to reduce wear and ensure free movement. Lubricate the door and trunk locks with spray-on graphite lubricant.

8 Windshield and fixed glass - replacement

Replacement of the windshield and fixed glass requires the use of special fast-setting adhesive/caulk materials and some specialized tools and techniques. These operations should be left to a dealer service department or a shop specializing in glasswork.

9 Radiator grille - removal and installation

Refer to illustrations 9.2a and 9.2b

1   Open the hood and remove the headlamp/park light housings (see Chapter 12).
2   Locate the clips that secure the grille/headlight bezels to the body, then release the clips with a flat-bladed screwdriver and pull the grille off the vehicle **(see illustrations)**.
3   The clips will stay in the body. Before installation, depress the tabs and remove the clips from the body, then snap them into their holes in the grille. Now install the grille to the body, pushing in to secure the clips to the body.

10 Hood - removal, installation and adjustment

Refer to illustrations 10.2, 10.10 and 10.11
Note: *The hood is heavy and somewhat awkward to remove and install - at least two people should perform this procedure.*

Removal and installation

1   Use blankets or pads to cover the cowl area of the body and the fenders. This will protect the body and paint as the hood is lifted off.
2   Scribe alignment marks around the hinge flanges to insure proper alignment during installation (paint or a permanent-type felt-tip marker also will work for this) **(see illustration)**.
3   Disconnect the electrical connector at the underhood light, if equipped, and the ground wire lug attached to the rear of the hood.
4   Have an assistant support one side of the hood while you support the other. Take turns removing the hinge-to-hood bolts, then lift off the hood.
5   Installation is the reverse of removal.

9.2a Release the grille clips (two indicated here) with a screwdriver

9.2b Depress the tab to release the clips from the grille

Adjustment

6   Fore-and-aft and side-to-side adjustment of the hood is done by moving the hood in relation to the hinge flanges after loosening the bolts.
7   Scribe or trace a line around the entire hinge plate so you can judge the amount of movement.
8   Loosen the nuts and move the hood into

10.10 Mark the position of the latch for reference, then loosen the latch bolts and move the latch as necessary to adjust the hood-closed position

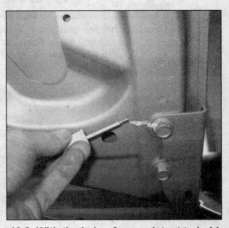

10.2 With the help of an assistant to hold the hood, mark the relationship of the hinges to the hood, remove the bolts and lift the hood off

correct alignment. Move it only a little at a time.
9   Tighten the hinge nuts and carefully lower the hood to check the alignment.
10   Adjust the hood latch so the hood closes securely **(see illustration)**.
11   Adjust the hood bumpers on the radiator support so the hood is flush with the fenders

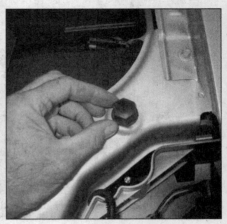

10.11 Twist the rubber bumpers in or out to make fine adjustments to the hood closed height

when closed **(see illustration)**.

12   The safety catch assembly on the hood itself can also be adjusted fore-and-aft and side-to-side after loosening the bolts.

13   The hood latch assembly, as well as the hinges, should be periodically lubricated with white lithium-base grease to prevent sticking and wear.

11.1 To disconnect the cable from the hood latch mechanism, detach the cable casing from the bracket, then unhook the cable end from the latch lever

---

11   Hood latch and release cable - removal and installation

Warning: *The models covered by this manual are equipped with Supplemental Restraint Systems (SRS), more commonly known as airbags. Always disable the airbag system before working in the vicinity of any airbag system components to avoid the possibility of accidental deployment of the airbags, which could cause personal injury (see Chapter 12).*

Latch

Refer to illustration 11.1

1   Remove the grille (see Section 9). Remove the bolts and detach the latch assembly **(see illustration 10.10)**. Detach the cable end from the latch **(see illustration)**.

2   Installation is the reverse of removal. Adjust the latch so the hood engages securely when closed and the hood bumpers are slightly compressed (see Section 10).

Release cable

Refer to illustration 11.6

3   Disconnect the release cable from the hood latch as described in Step 1.

4   Unclip the release cable from the engine wiring harness. Attach a length of wire to the cable to assist with the installation of the new cable.

5   Release the cable from its clips along the inner fender panel.

6   Inside the vehicle, remove the screws and separate the hood release handle from the driver's knee bolster panel **(see illustra-**

tion)**. With the handle off, twist the cable eye out of the handle assembly.

7   Trace the cable forward to the grommet where the cable goes through the firewall and pry the grommet through to the interior. Pull the handle and cable rearward into the passenger compartment.

8   Disconnect the guide wire from the old cable and fasten it to the new cable.

9   With the new cable attached to the wire, pull the wire back through the firewall until the new cable reaches the latch assembly. Make sure that the grommet is properly seated on both sides of the hole in the firewall. Push on the grommet with your fingers from the passenger compartment side to seat the grommet in the firewall correctly.

10   The remainder of installation is the reverse of removal.

---

12   Bumpers - removal and installation

Warning: *The models covered by this manual are equipped with Supplemental Restraint Systems (SRS), more commonly known as airbags. Always disable the airbag system before working in the vicinity of any airbag system component to avoid the possibility of*

accidental deployment of the airbags, which could cause personal injury (see Chapter 12).*

1   Front and rear bumpers on all models use a plastic fascia panel over a metal impact bar.

Front bumper

Refer to illustrations 12.5a and 12.5b

2   Disconnect the electrical connectors at the fog lights, if equipped. Remove the grille (see Section 9).

3   If the fascia is being replaced, remove the pushpins to detach the fascia from the bumper. If both the fascia and bumper are being removed for other repair procedures, it is easier to remove them as an assembly (see Step 5).

4   Pull the fascia forward off the body. **Note:** *In addition to the pushpins, on XTREME models the upper center of the fascia is secured with adhesive tape. Use a heat gun to soften the adhesive until you can separate the fascia with a large putty knife.*

5   With an assistant supporting the impact bar (bumper), unbolt the impact bar from the frame and take it off **(see illustrations)**.

6   Disconnect any wiring harnesses or any other components that would interfere with bumper removal and detach the bumper.

7   Installation is the reverse of removal.

11.6 Remove the hood release handle screws at the driver's knee bolster

12.5a Remove the bolts on each side and take the impact bar off the vehicle

12.5b On models with steel front bumpers, remove the grille to access the upper bumper bolts (right side shown)

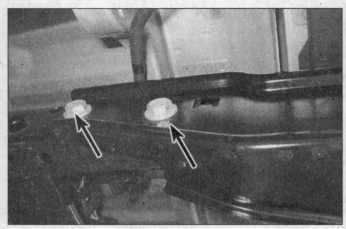

12.11 Remove the rear impact bar retaining bolts

13.2a Remove the pushpins securing the lower fenderwell liner

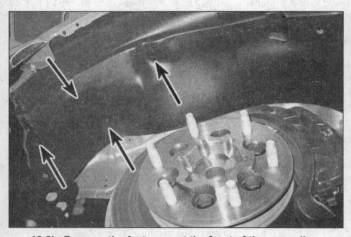

13.2b Remove the fasteners at the front of the upper liner

13.2c Remove the fasteners at the rear of the upper liner

Tighten the retaining bolts to the torque listed in this Chapter's Specifications. When reinstalling the fascia on XTREME models, clean off any adhesive with alcohol and use double-sided tape to secure the upper edge.

Rear bumper

Refer to illustration 12.11

8   Disconnect the license plate light connector. On Canyon and XTREME models, remove the license plate and holder.
9   On Canyon and XTREME models, first remove the step pads using a flat-bladed plastic tool to separate the pads from the bumper, then remove the pushpins from the top-left and top-right sides of the fascia panel.
10   On Canyon and XTREME models, remove the screws that secure each end of the fascia panel under the bumper. On some XTREME models, the fascia is fastened to the bumper with adhesive strips. After the fasteners are removed, pull the fascia until the adhesive strips release from the bumper.
11   Remove two of the impact bar retaining bolts from each side of the vehicle **(see illustration)**.
12   With an assistant supporting the impact bar, remove the remaining bolt from each side. Take the impact bar off the vehicle.
13   Installation is the reverse of removal. Tighten the bolts to the torque listed in this Chapter's Specifications. On models where the fascia was retained by adhesive strips, scrape the old strips off, clean the mounting areas with alcohol and, when dry, apply new adhesive strips before installing the fascia to the bumper.

13   Front fenders - removal and installation

Refer to illustrations 13.2a, 13.2b, 13.2c, 13.3a, 13.3b, 13.3c and 13.4

Warning: *The models covered by this manual are equipped with Supplemental Restraint Systems (SRS), more commonly known as airbags. Always disable the airbag system before working in the vicinity of any airbag system components to avoid the possibility of accidental deployment of the airbags, which could cause personal injury (see Chapter 12).*
1   Disconnect the negative cable from the battery. Loosen the wheel lug nuts, raise the vehicle, support it securely on jackstands and remove the front wheel. Apply masking tape to the panels next to the fender to protect them from scratches during fender removal.
2   Pry out the plastic pushpins and remove the inner fenderwell liner **(see illustrations)**.

13.3a Remove the bolt at the front of the fender opening (on some models it's behind the fender liner)

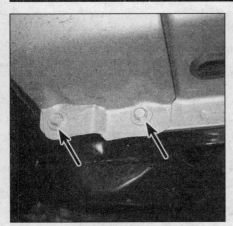

13.3b Remove the bolts at the front of the
rocker panel area

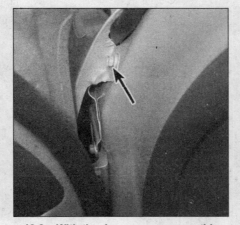

13.3c With the door open, remove this
bolt at the top-rear of the fender

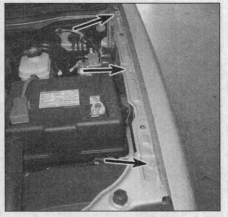

13.4 Remove the bolts along the top edge
of the fender

3   From below, remove the fender bolt at
the front of the fender opening, the bolts at
the lower rear and the bolt securing the fender
to the doorjamb **(see illustrations)**.
4   Remove the upper fender mounting bolts
(see illustration). On 2008 models, remove
the upper fender reinforcement and its mounting bolt.
5   Detach the fender. It's a good idea to have
an assistant support the fender while it's being
moved away from the vehicle to prevent damage to the surrounding body panels.
6   Installation is the reverse of the removal
procedure. Check for alignment with the door
and hood, then tighten all nuts, bolts and
screws securely.

14   Cowl cover - removal and installation

Refer to illustration 14.3

1   Mark the position of the windshield wiper
blades on the windshield with a wax marking

pencil or pieces of tape.
2   Remove the wiper arms (see Chapter 12).
3   Remove the six cowl cover pushpins
and disconnect the windshield washer hose.
Carefully lift the cowl cover to free the retaining clips and take it off the vehicle **(see illustration)**.
4   Installation is the reverse of removal.
Make sure to align the wiper blades with the
marks made during removal.

15   Door trim panel - removal and installation

*Refer to illustrations 15.2a, 15.2b, 15.3
and 15.6*

1   Disconnect the cable from the negative
terminal of the battery (see Chapter 1).
2   If you're working on a front door, remove
the two screws and pry the power switch
assembly out of the door panel with a flat-
bladed trim tool **(see illustrations)**. If you're

14.3 Remove the cowl cover pushpins

working on a rear door, remove the power
window switch (see Chapter 12).
3   Remove the door trim panel retaining
screws; one secures the inside handle bezel

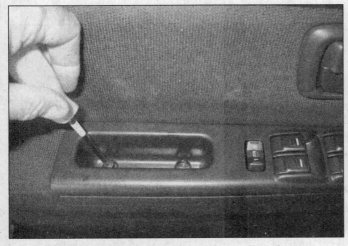

15.2a Remove the screws in the door pull pocket . . .

15.2b . . . then pry up the power window switch assembly and
disconnect the electrical connectors

15.3 Remove the screw and slide the door handle bezel off

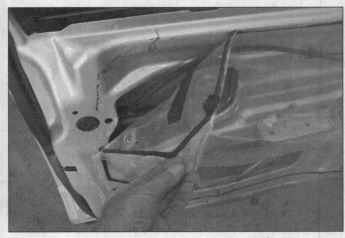

15.6 Peel the water deflector carefully away from the door, taking care not to tear it

(see illustration), others are at the bottom of the door and midway up the door panel. Remove the upper trim panel over the door panel.

4   Pry the panel outward with a flat-bladed trim tool to release the door panel clips from the door.

5   Once all of the clips are disengaged, raise the trim panel up and off the door. Remove the trim panel from the vehicle.

6   For access to the inner door, carefully peel back the plastic watershield (see illustration).

7   Prior to installation of the door panel, be sure to reinstall any clips in the panel which may have come out during the removal procedure and remain in the door itself. Any panel retaining screws should be reinserted into the panel before installation.

8   Place the panel in position on the door and hook its upper edge into the window slot.

9   If you're working on a front door, install the upper rear retaining clip in its hole, then the upper front retaining clip, then the remaining retaining clips.

10   The procedure for the rear doors is similar to the front door procedure.

11   Install the switch panel (front door) or power window switch (rear door). Connect the negative battery cable.

16   Doors - removal and installation

Refer to illustration 16.4

1   Remove the door trim panel (see Section 15). Disconnect any electrical connectors and push them through the door opening so they won't interfere with door removal. Leave the wiring harness boot attached to the door but disconnected from the body.

2   Place a jack under the door or have an assistant on hand to support it when the hinge bolts are removed. **Note**: *If a jack is used, place a folded towel between it and the door to protect the door's painted surfaces.*

3   Unbolt the check strap from the door pillar.

4   Remove the two hinge-keeper bolts (one per hinge) and carefully lift the door from the hinge pins (see illustration).

5   Installation is the reverse of removal. Alignment of the door is made by loosening

the hinge-to-body bolts, adjusting the gaps with other panels, then tightening the bolts.

17   Door latch, lock cylinder and handles - removal and installation

Latch

Refer to illustrations 17.2 and 17.3

1   Raise the window completely and remove the door trim panel and the rear section of the watershield (see Section 15).

2   Detach the latch rods from the lock cylinder, outside handle and inside handle (see illustration).

3   Remove the three Torx-head mounting screws (it may be necessary to use an impact-type driver to loosen them), then remove the latch from the door (see illustration). If possible, disconnect the rods while the latch is in the door. If not, pull the latch out with the rods attached, then disconnect the rods and electrical connectors.

4   Installation is the reverse of the removal procedure. Check the door to make sure it latches and unlatches properly.

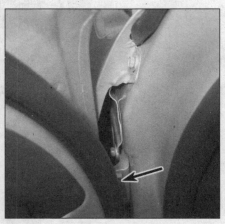

16.4 Remove the door hinge keeper bolts (upper bolt indicated)

17.2 Detach the cables at the latch, working through the opening in the door

17.3 The door latch is retained by three Torx-head screws

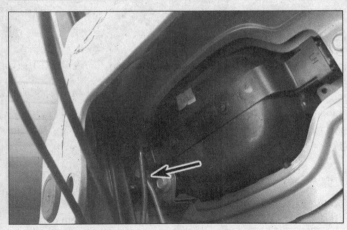

17.5 Disconnect the link and pry off the C-clip, then remove the lock cylinder

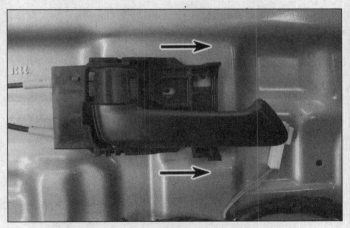

17.10 Slide the handle forward until the clips are released from the door

Lock cylinder

Refer to illustration 17.5

5   Remove the outside door handle (see below). Disconnect the link, use a screwdriver to push the key lock cylinder retainer off and withdraw the lock cylinder from the door handle **(see illustration)**.
6   Installation is the reverse of removal.

Outside handle

7   Disconnect the outside handle links from the handle and the lock cylinder rod, remove the mounting bolts and detach the handle from the door.
8   Place the handle in position, attach the link and install the nut(s). Tighten the nut(s) securely.

Inside handle

Refer to illustration 17.10

9   Follow the Steps in Section 15 to remove the door trim panel.
10   Slide the handle forward to detach it from the location holes, then remove it from the door **(see illustration)**. The two cables can now be disconnected.

Latch striker

Refer to illustration 17.11

11   To make minor door adjustments for latch alignment, the bolts on the latch striker (which is mounted opposite the latch) can be loosened and the striker moved slightly **(see illustration)**. Retighten the striker mounting bolts and check for proper latch operation. **Note:** *The striker can be moved up-and-down, or left-and-right to make adjustments.*

---

18   Door window glass - removal and installation

Refer to illustration 18.3

Warning: *Disconnect the power window switch connector when working inside the driver's door to prevent the window from lowering suddenly and causing injury.*

1   Remove the door trim panel and watershield (see Section 15). Remove the radio speaker from the door (see Chapter 12).
2   Remove the beltline weatherstripping from the door.

3   With the door switch panel temporarily reconnected, lower the glass about halfway down until the glass channel bolts are visible in the door openings. Remove two glass channel bolts **(see illustration)**.
4   Refer to Section 20 and remove the outside mirror. Pry up the exterior beltline weatherstrip.
5   Lift the glass out of the door through the glass opening (to the outside of the door), by tilting the rear of the glass up and out first.
6   To install, lower the glass into the door, slide it into position and install the two bolts.
7   The remainder of installation is the reverse of removal.

---

19   Door window glass regulator - removal and installation

Refer to illustration 19.4

1   Remove the door trim panel, watershield and radio speaker (see Section 15 and Chapter 12).
2   Remove the door window glass (see Section 18).

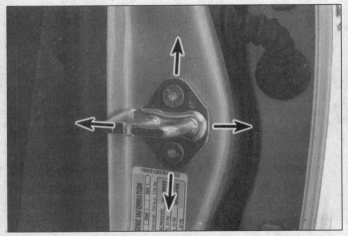

17.11 The latch striker on the door jamb can be adjusted slightly up/down or in/out

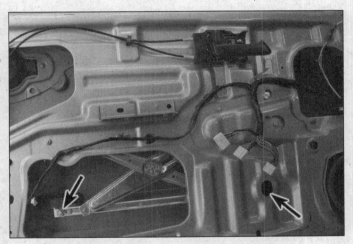

18.3 Remove the glass channel bolts

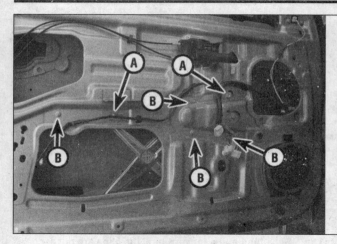

19.4 Door window regulator mounting bolt locations:

A   Loosen these bolts
B   Remove these bolts

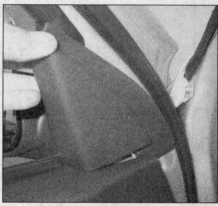

20.1 Carefully pry off this trim panel for access to the mirror mounting bolts

3   Disconnect the window motor's electrical connector.
4   The regulator bolts fit into slots in the door. Loosen the two regulator bolts at the slotted holes, but don't remove them **(see illustration)**. Remove the remaining regulator mounting fasteners, then slide the regulator until the loosened bolts clear the slots. Tilt the regulator toward the front of the door and lift it out.
5   Installation is the reverse of removal. Removal and installation of rear door regulators is similar to the front doors, except for the location and number of mounting bolts.

---

20   Mirrors - removal and installation

Refer to illustrations 20.1, 20.3 and 20.6

Outside mirrors

1   Remove the upper interior door trim panel to access the mirror fasteners **(see illustration)**.
2   Detach the mirror wiring harness from the door and disconnect the connector.
3   Remove the bolts and detach the mirror from the door **(see illustration)**.
4   Installation is the reverse of removal.

Inside mirror

5   If the mirror is equipped with an electrical connector, use a flat-bladed tool to pry the cover off and disconnect the connector.
6   Loosen the Torx setscrew, then slide the mirror up off the support base on the windshield **(see illustration)**.
7   Installation is the reverse of removal.
8   If the support base for the mirror has come off the windshield, it can be reattached with a special mirror adhesive kit available at auto parts stores. Clean the glass and support base thoroughly and follow the directions on the adhesive package, allowing the base to bond overnight before attaching the mirror.

---

21   Tailgate - removal and installation

Refer to illustration 21.2

Note: *The tailgate is heavy and awkward to handle, have an assistant help you.*
1   Open the tailgate and hold it at a 45-degree angle away from the vehicle (halfway down).
2   Detach the cables by sliding the keyhole slots in the cable ends apart at each side **(see illustration)**.
3   With a person supporting each side of

the tailgate, lift up the right side until the tailgate hinge-pin comes out of its slot.
4   Move the tailgate to the right until the left hinge-pin comes out of its hole. Remove the tailgate.
5   Installation is the reverse of the removal procedure.

---

22   Console - removal and installation

Warning: *The models covered by this manual are equipped with Supplemental Restraint Systems (SRS), more commonly known as airbags. Always disable the airbag system before working in the vicinity of any airbag system component to avoid the possibility of accidental deployment of the airbags, which could cause personal injury (see Chapter 12).*
1   On models with manual transmission and a small console, the console is basically the shift lever bezel. Lift up on the console to release the retainers holding it to the floor. On 2008 models, remove the two inner rear seat track bolts from both seats.
2   On models with a large console, open the console lid and remove the screws securing the storage bin to the console. Lift the bin off.

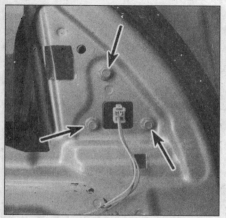

20.3 Remove the three outside mirror mounting bolts; on power models (shown), also disconnect the electrical connector

20.6 Using a Torx screwdriver, loosen the setscrew and slide the inside mirror off the support base

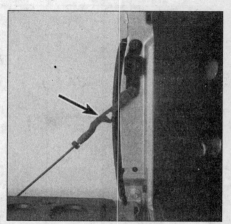

21.2 Lift the tailgate enough to twist and separate the two halves of the support cable

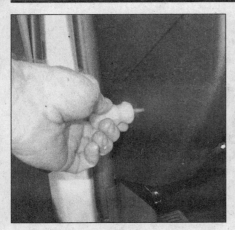

23.1 Remove the screw that secures the knee bolster trim panel

23.4 Mounting bolt locations for the knee bolster reinforcement plate

23.6 Pry off the center trim panel with a trim tool

Also remove the console tray by carefully prying it up. Remove the passenger front bucket seat (regular-cab models). On other models, remove the two front bucket seat track bolts.

3   Remove the console mounting screws. In addition to the screws under the storage bin, there are two floor bolts at the rear of the console.

4   Installation is the reverse of removal.

23   Dashboard trim panels - removal and installation

Warning: *The models covered by this manual are equipped with Supplemental Restraint Systems (SRS), more commonly known as airbags. Always disable the airbag system before working in the vicinity of any airbag system component to avoid the possibility of accidental deployment of the airbags, which could cause personal injury (see Chapter 12).*

Knee bolster trim panel

Refer to illustration 23.1

1   Remove the screws and detach the hood release handle for the knee bolster panel.

Remove the diagnostic connector from the knee bolster by releasing the clip at the bottom of the connector.

2   Remove the one screw at the far left of the instrument panel and pull the panel back to release the clips **(see illustration)**. Pry the parking brake release handle from the cable, then remove the cable from the panel by twisting the cable casing clockwise. Installation is the reverse of removal.

Knee bolster reinforcement plate

Refer to illustration 23.4

3   Remove the knee bolster trim panel (see Step 1).

4   Remove the upper and lower fasteners and take down the reinforcement plate **(see illustration)**.

5   Installation is the reverse of removal.

Center accessory trim panel

Refer to illustration 23.6

6   Use a flat-bladed plastic trim tool to pry up the edges of the accessory trim panel **(see illustration)**.

7   Disconnect the panel electrical connectors and remove it from the vehicle.

8   Installation is the reverse of the removal steps.

Instrument cluster bezel

Refer to illustration 23.10

9   On models equipped with tilt steering columns, tilt the steering wheel down as far as possible. On models with a column-mounted shift lever, apply the parking brake, block the wheels and position the shifter in First gear.

10   Release the clips around the edges of the bezel with a flat-bladed plastic trim tool **(see illustration)**.

11   Installation is the reverse of the removal steps.

Glove box

Refer to illustration 23.12

12   Remove three screws along the bottom of the glove box door **(see illustration)**, then open the glove box door and take out the glove box assembly.

13   Installation is the reverse of the removal steps.

23.10 Pry up the instrument cluster bezel with a trim tool

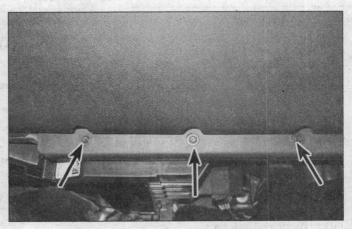

23.12 Glove box door retaining screws

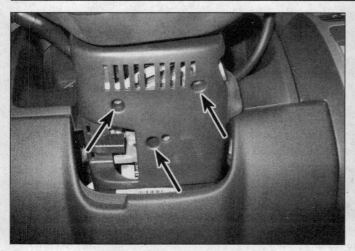

24.2 Lower steering column cover mounting screws

25.4 Detach the covers from the instrument panel, near the windshield, then remove the nuts underneath

24 Steering column covers - removal and installation

Refer to illustration 24.2

Warning: *The models covered by this manual are equipped with Supplemental Restraint Systems (SRS), more commonly known as airbags. Always disable the airbag system before working in the vicinity of any airbag system component to avoid the possibility of accidental deployment of the airbags, which could cause personal injury (see Chapter 12).*

1   Remove the steering wheel (see Chapter 10). If equipped with a tilt column, tilt the column all the way down.
2   Remove the screws from the lower cover **(see illustration)**.
3   Unsnap the lower cover from the upper cover. **Note:** *On some models there may be a screw from below that secures the upper trim cover.*
4   Installation is the reverse of removal.

25 Instrument panel - removal and installation

Refer to illustration 25.4

Warning: *The models covered by this manual are equipped with Supplemental Restraint Systems (SRS), more commonly known as airbags. Always disable the airbag system before working in the vicinity of any airbag system component to avoid the possibility of accidental deployment of the airbags, which could cause personal injury (see Chapter 12).* **Note:** *This procedure is lengthy and difficult, even for an experienced mechanic. Due to the number of electrical connections, fasteners used, and the various safety systems involved, we don't recommend instrument panel removal for the home mechanic.*

1   Turn the front wheels to the straight-ahead position and lock the steering column, then disconnect the negative battery cable

(see Chapter 1).
2   Disable the airbag system (see Chapter 12).
3   Use a trim tool to remove the windshield post interior trim strips.
4   Carefully pull up the three trim covers along the length of the upper trim pad, then remove the nuts **(see illustration)**.
5   Locate the ambient light sensor in the center of the trim pad. Pry it from the pad with a small screwdriver, then disconnect the electrical connector.
6   Remove the center console (see Section 22).
7   Remove all of the panels described in Section 23. Also remove the instrument cluster (see Chapter 12).
8   Detach the steering column from the dash and lower it (see Chapter 10). If you're planning to remove the instrument panel support structure, remove the steering column completely.
9   Remove the left and right HVAC outlets.
10   Remove the radio (see Chapter 12). If the vehicle has upper front speakers, remove them.
11   Remove the heater/air conditioning control module and free its wiring harness from the retainer (see Chapter 3).
12   Remove the panel mounting screw located behind the instrument cluster, and the instrument panel mounting screws located where the glove box was mounted.
13   Remove the screws securing the glove box door latch.
14   Refer to Chapter 12 and remove the passenger airbag.
15   Through the hole left by removing the glove box, remove the one screw holding the instrument panel to the carrier. At each side of the instrument panel, remove the end closure panels and remove the one screw on each side of the instrument panel.
16   Have an assistant help you lift the instrument panel out of the vehicle. Each of you should pull out on the lower corners of the

instrument panel to release the clips securing it.
17   Once the panel is free, release all the wiring harness clips on the back of the instrument panel and remove the panel.
18   Installation is the reverse of removal.

26 Seats - removal and installation

Warning: *The models covered by this manual are equipped with Supplemental Restraint Systems (SRS), more commonly known as airbags. Always disable the airbag system before working in the vicinity of any airbag system component to avoid the possibility of accidental deployment of the airbags, which could cause personal injury (see Chapter 12).*

Front bucket seat/split-bench seat

Refer to illustration 26.1

1   Remove the trim covers from the mounting fasteners, then unscrew the mounting nuts/bolts **(see illustration)**. **Note:** *If*

26.1 The front seat mounting nuts are accessed by removing the plastic covers

27.3 Steering gear crossmember mounting bolts

clips. *Pull up on the seatback to remove it.*
7   Remove the seat assembly as a unit.
Note: *This is a job for two people.*
8   Installation is the reverse of the removal steps.

27   Steering gear crossmember - removal and installation

Refer to illustration 27.3
Note: *This crossmember is removable to make room for steering gear removal.*
1   If the steering gear is to be removed, loosen the wheel lug nuts, raise the front of the vehicle and support it securely on jackstands. Remove the wheels.
2   Remove the splash shield from under the vehicle.
3   Unbolt the steering gear front crossmember from the vehicle and remove it **(see illustration)**.
4   Installation is the reverse of the removal steps. Tighten the steering gear crossmember bolts to the torque listed in this Chapter's Specifications.

equipped with power bucket seats, remove the passenger seat first, since power to the passenger seat would be cut off if the driver's seat is removed first.
2   Position the seat forward as far as it will go and remove the rear mounting bolts. Move the seat rearward as far as it will go and remove the front mounting bolts.
3   Unplug the electrical connector(s), disconnect the harness from the frame, then remove the seat.

Rear folding seat (extended cab)
4   Remove the mounting bolts securing the folding seat to the cab.
5   Installation is the reverse of removal.

Rear bench seat (crew cab)
6   Remove the front and rear seat mounting bolts. **Note:** *On some crew-cab models, the rear seat back is attached to the body with*

Notes

Chapter 12
Chassis electrical system

Contents

1 General information

The electrical system is a 12-volt, negative ground type. Power for the lights and all electrical accessories is supplied by a lead/acid-type battery that is charged by the alternator.

This Chapter covers repair and service procedures for the various electrical components not associated with the engine. Information on the battery, alternator, ignition system and starter motor can be found in Chapter 5.

It should be noted that when portions of the electrical system are serviced, the negative cable should be disconnected from the battery to prevent electrical shorts and/or fires.

2 Electrical troubleshooting - general information

Refer to illustrations 2.5a, 2.5b, 2.6, 2.9 and 2.15

A typical electrical circuit consists of an electrical component, any switches, relays, motors, fuses, fusible links or circuit breakers related to that component and the wiring and connectors that link the component to both the battery and the chassis. To help you pinpoint an electrical circuit problem, wiring diagrams are included at the end of this Chapter.

Before tackling any troublesome electrical circuit, first study the appropriate wiring diagrams to get a complete understanding of what makes up that individual circuit. Trouble spots, for instance, can often be narrowed down by noting if other components related to the circuit are operating properly. If several components or circuits fail at one time, chances are the problem is in a fuse or ground connection, because several circuits are often routed through the same fuse and ground connections.

Electrical problems usually stem from simple causes, such as loose or corroded connections, a blown fuse, a melted fusible link or a failed relay. Visually inspect the condition of all fuses, wires and connections in a problem circuit before troubleshooting the circuit.

If test equipment and instruments are

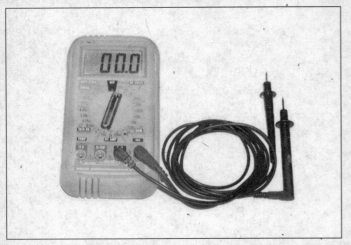

2.5a The most useful tool for electrical troubleshooting is a digital multimeter that can check volts, amps, and test continuity

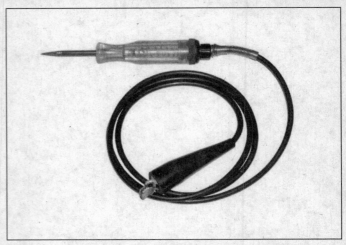

2.5b A test light is a very handy tool for checking voltage

going to be utilized, use the diagrams to plan ahead of time where you will make the necessary connections in order to accurately pinpoint the trouble spot.

The basic tools needed for electrical troubleshooting include a circuit tester or voltmeter (a 12-volt bulb with a set of test leads can also be used), a continuity tester, which includes a bulb, battery and set of test leads, and a jumper wire, preferably with a circuit breaker incorporated, which can be used to bypass electrical components **(see illustrations)**. Before attempting to locate a problem with test instruments, use the wiring diagram(s) to decide where to make the connections.

Voltage checks

Voltage checks should be performed if a circuit is not functioning properly. Connect one lead of a circuit tester to either the negative battery terminal or a known good ground. Connect the other lead to a connector in the

circuit being tested, preferably nearest to the battery or fuse **(see illustration)**. If the bulb of the tester lights, voltage is present, which means that the part of the circuit between the connector and the battery is problem free. Continue checking the rest of the circuit in the same fashion. When you reach a point at which no voltage is present, the problem lies between that point and the last test point with voltage. Most of the time the problem can be traced to a loose connection. **Note:** *Keep in mind that some circuits receive voltage only when the ignition key is in the Accessory or Run position.*

Finding a short

One method of finding shorts in a circuit is to remove the fuse and connect a test light or voltmeter in place of the fuse terminals. There should be no voltage present in the circuit. Move the wiring harness from side-to-side while watching the test light. If the bulb goes on, there is a short to ground

somewhere in that area, probably where the insulation has rubbed through. The same test can be performed on each component in the circuit, even a switch.

Ground check

Perform a ground test to check whether a component is properly grounded. Disconnect the battery and connect one lead of a continuity tester or multimeter (set to the ohms scale), to a known good ground. Connect the other lead to the wire or ground connection being tested. If the resistance is low (less than 5 ohms), the ground is good. If the bulb on a self-powered test light does not go on, the ground is not good.

Continuity check

A continuity check is done to determine if there are any breaks in a circuit - if it is passing electricity properly. With the circuit off (no power in the circuit), a self-powered continuity tester or multimeter can be used to check the

2.6 In use, a basic test light's lead is clipped to a known good ground, then the pointed probe can test connectors, wires or electrical sockets - if the bulb lights, the part being tested has battery voltage

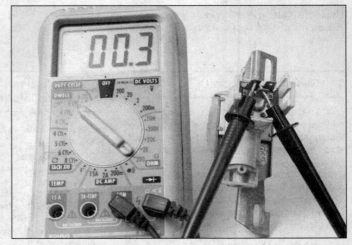

2.9 With a multimeter set to the ohms scale, resistance can be checked across two terminals - when checking for continuity, a low reading indicates continuity, a high reading indicates lack of continuity

circuit. Connect the test leads to both ends of the circuit (or to the power end and a good ground), and if the test light comes on the circuit is passing current properly **(see illustration)**. If the resistance is low (less than 5 ohms), there is continuity; if the reading is 10,000 ohms or higher, there is a break somewhere in the circuit. The same procedure can be used to test a switch, by connecting the continuity tester to the switch terminals. With the switch turned On, the test light should come on (or low resistance should be indicated on a meter).

Finding an open circuit

When diagnosing for possible open circuits, it is often difficult to locate them by sight because the connectors hide oxidation or terminal misalignment. Merely wiggling a connector on a sensor or in the wiring harness may correct the open circuit condition. Remember this when an open circuit is indicated when troubleshooting a circuit. Intermittent problems may also be caused by oxidized or loose connections.

Electrical troubleshooting is simple if you keep in mind that all electrical circuits are basically electricity running from the battery, through the wires, switches, relays, fuses and fusible links to each electrical component (light bulb, motor, etc.) and to ground, from which it is passed back to the battery. Any electrical problem is an interruption in the flow of electricity to and from the battery.

Connectors

Most electrical connections on these vehicles are made with multi-wire plastic connectors. The mating halves of many connectors are secured with locking clips molded into the plastic connector shells. The mating halves of large connectors, such as some of those under the instrument panel, are held together by a bolt through the center of the connector.

To separate a connector with locking clips, use a small screwdriver to pry the clips

2.15 To backprobe a connector, insert a small, sharp probe (such as a straight-pin) into the back of the connector alongside the desired wire until it contacts the metal terminal inside; connect your meter leads to the probes - this allows you to test a functioning circuit

apart carefully, then separate the connector halves. Pull only on the shell, never pull on the wiring harness as you may damage the individual wires and terminals inside the connectors. Look at the connector closely before trying to separate the halves. Often the locking clips are engaged in a way that is not immediately clear. Additionally, many connectors have more than one set of clips.

Each pair of connector terminals has a male half and a female half. When you look at the end view of a connector in a diagram, be sure to understand whether the view shows the harness side or the component side of the connector. Connector halves are mirror images of each other, and a terminal shown on the right side end-view of one half will be on the left side end-view of the other half.

It is often necessary to take circuit voltage measurements with a connector connected. Whenever possible, carefully insert a small straight pin (not your meter probe) into the rear of the connector shell to contact the terminal inside, then clip your meter lead to the pin. This kind of connection is called backprobing **(see illustration)**. When inserting a test probe into a terminal, be careful not to distort

the terminal opening. Doing so can lead to a poor connection and corrosion at that terminal later. Using the small straight pin instead of a meter probe results in less chance of deforming the terminal connector.

---

3 Fuses and fusible links - general information

Fuses

Refer to illustrations 3.1a, 3.1b, 3.1c, 3.3 and 3.4

The electrical circuits of the vehicle are protected by a combination of fuses, circuit breakers and fusible links. The fuse-relay panel is in the engine compartment **(see illustrations)**.

Each of the fuses is designed to protect a specific circuit, and the various circuits are identified on the fuse panel itself.

Several sizes of fuses are employed in the fuse blocks. There are small, medium and large sizes of the same design **(see illustration)**, all with the same blade terminal design. The medium and large fuses can be removed

3.1a The main fuse/relay box is in the engine compartment; disengage the locking tabs and remove the cover . . .

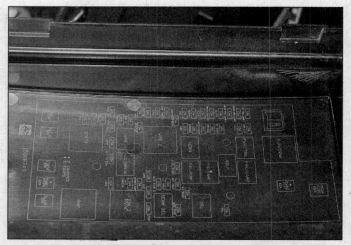

3.1b . . . which has a legend to identify the fuses and relays

with your fingers, but the small fuses require the use of pliers or the small plastic fuse-puller tool found in most fuse boxes.

If an electrical component fails, always check the fuse first **(see illustration)**. The best way to check the fuses is with a test light. Check for power at the exposed terminal tips of each fuse. If power is present at one side of the fuse but not the other, the fuse is blown. A blown fuse can also be identified by visually inspecting it.

Be sure to replace blown fuses with the correct type. Fuses (of the same physical size) of different ratings may be physically interchangeable, but only fuses of the proper rating should be used. Replacing a fuse with one of a higher or lower value than specified is not recommended. Each electrical circuit needs a specific amount of protection. The amperage value of each fuse is molded into the top of the fuse body.

If the replacement fuse immediately fails, don't replace it again until the cause of the problem is isolated and corrected. In most cases, this will be a short circuit in the wiring caused by a broken or deteriorated wire.

Fusible links

Refer to illustration 3.10

Some circuits are protected by fusible links. The links are used in circuits that are not ordinarily fused, such as between the battery and the alternator, or in the circuit to the starter or underhood electrical center.

A fusible link is a short length of heavy wire that is marked "fusible link" on the outer cover.

To replace a fusible link, first disconnect the negative battery cable. **Caution:** *On models equipped with the Theftlock audio system, be sure the lockout feature is turned off before performing any procedure which requires disconnecting the battery (see the front of this manual).*

Although the fusible links appear to be a heavier gauge than the wires they're protecting, the appearance is due to the thick insulation. All fusible links are several wire gauges

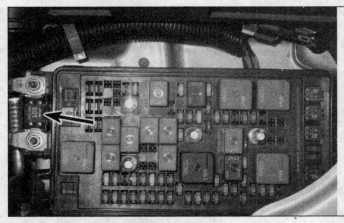

3.1c The primary circuit protection at the fuse/relay box is the 100-amp megafuse

smaller than the wire they're designed to protect. Fusible links can't be repaired, but a new link of the same size wire can be installed. The procedure is as follows:

a) *Cut the damaged fusible link out of the wire just behind the connector.*
b) *Strip the insulation back approximately 1-inch.*
c) *Spread the strands of the exposed wire apart, push them together and twist them in place* **(see illustration)**.
d) *Use rosin core solder and solder the wires together to obtain a good connection.*
e) *Use plenty of electrical tape around the soldered joint. No wires should be exposed.*
f) *Connect the negative battery cable. Test the circuit for proper operation.*

4   Circuit breakers - general information and check

Circuit breakers protect certain circuits, such as the power windows and power seats.

Because the circuit breakers reset automatically, an electrical overload in a circuit-breaker-protected system will cause the cir-

cuit to fail momentarily, then come back on. If the circuit does not come back on, check it immediately.

For a basic check, pull the circuit breaker up out of its socket on the fuse panel, but just far enough to probe with a voltmeter. The breaker should still contact the sockets.

With the voltmeter negative lead on a good chassis ground, touch each end prong of the circuit breaker with the positive meter probe. There should be battery voltage at each end. If there is battery voltage only at one end, the circuit breaker must be replaced.

5   Relays - general information and testing

General information

1   Several electrical accessories in the vehicle, such as the fuel injection system, horns, starter, and fog lamps use relays to transmit the electrical signal to the component. Relays use a low-current circuit (the control circuit) to open and close a high-current circuit (the power circuit). If the relay is defective, that component will not operate properly. Most relays are mounted in the engine compart-

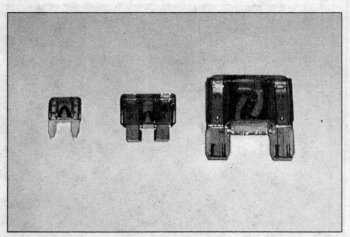

3.3 All three of these fuses are of 30-amp rating, yet are different sizes - make sure you get the right amperage and size when purchasing replacement fuses

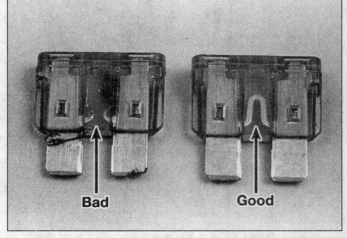

3.4 When a fuse blows, the element between the terminals melts

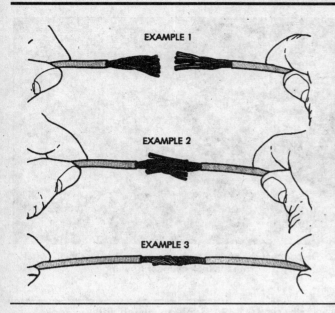

3.10 To repair a fusible link, cut out the damaged section, then join a new section by stripping the wire and twisting it together, as shown here - when securely joined, solder the connections and wrap them with electrical tape

circuit and connect to the relay coil. The other relay terminals are the power circuit. When the relay is energized, the coil creates a magnetic field that closes the larger contacts of the power circuit to provide power to the circuit loads.

5   Terminals 85 and 86 are normally the control circuit. If the relay contains a diode, terminal 86 must be connected to battery positive (B+) voltage and terminal 85 to ground. If the relay contains a resistor, terminals 85 and 86 can be connected in either direction with respect to B+ and ground.

6   Terminal 30 is normally connected to the battery voltage (B+) source for the circuit loads. Terminal 87 is connected to the ground side of the circuit, either directly or through a load. If the relay has several alternate terminals for load or ground connections, they usually are numbered 87A, 87B, 87C, and so on.

7   Use an ohmmeter to check continuity through the relay control coil.

a) *Connect the meter according to the polarity shown in* **illustration 5.2a** *for one check; then reverse the ohmmeter leads and check continuity in the other direction.*

b) *If the relay contains a resistor, resistance should be indicated on the meter, and should be the same value with the ohmmeter in either direction.*

c) *If the relay contains a diode, resistance should be higher with the ohmmeter in the forward polarity direction than with the meter leads reversed.*

d) *If the ohmmeter shows infinite resistance in both directions, replace the relay.*

8   Remove the relay from the vehicle and use the ohmmeter to check for continuity between the relay power circuit terminals. There should be no continuity between terminal 30 and 87 with the relay de-energized.

9   Connect a fused jumper wire to terminal 86 and the positive battery terminal. Connect another jumper wire between terminal 85 and ground. When the connections are made, the relay should click.

10   With the jumper wires connected, check for continuity between the power circuit termi-

ment fuse/relay box **(see illustrations 3.1a and 3.1b)**. If a faulty relay is suspected, it can be removed and tested using the procedure below or by a dealer service department or a repair shop. Defective relays must be replaced as a unit.

Testing

Refer to illustrations 5.2a and 5.2b

2   Most of the relays used in these vehicles are of a type often called ISO relays, which refers to the International Standards Organi-zation. The terminals of ISO relays are numbered to indicate their usual circuit connections and functions. There are two basic layouts of terminals on the relays used in these vehicles **(see illustrations)**.

3   Refer to the wiring diagram for the circuit to determine the proper connections for the relay you're testing. If you can't determine the correct connection from the wiring diagrams, however, you may be able to determine the test connections from the information that follows.

4   Two of the terminals are the relay control

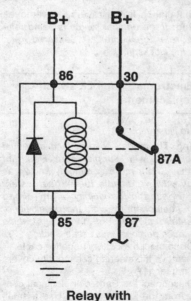

Relay with internal resistor

Relay with internal diode

24053-12-5.2a HAYNES

5.2a Typical ISO relay designs, terminal numbering and circuit connections

5.2b Most relays are marked on the outside to easily identify the control circuit and power circuit - this one is of the four-terminal type

7.5 Remove the three screws to detach the multi-function switch/ airbag coil from the mounting plate (steering wheel must be removed, lower screw indicated here)

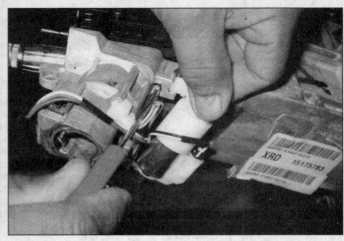

8.3 Disconnect the connector and remove the Park lock switch from the lock cylinder housing

nals. Now, there should be continuity between terminals 30 and 87.

11   If the relay fails any of the above tests, replace it.

6   Turn signal and hazard flashers - general information

The vehicles covered by this manual do not have a traditional, replaceable flasher unit. The function of the flasher is performed by the Body Control Module, which is in communication with the multi-function switch and dash-mounted hazard switch. If the turn signal lights fail to function when the turn signal lever is moved, or when the hazard switch is engaged, check the bulbs and circuits for a problem. If the turn signal indicator on the instrument cluster flashes much more rapidly than normal, the most likely cause is a burned-out turn signal bulb. If these checks do not reveal the problem, have the BCM and multi-function switch diagnosed at a dealer service department or other qualified repair shop.

7   Steering column multi-function switch - replacement

Refer to Illustration 7.5

Warning: *The models covered by this manual are equipped with Supplemental Restraint Systems (SRS), more commonly known as airbags. Always disable the airbag system before working in the vicinity of any airbag system component to avoid the possibility of accidental deployment of the airbags, which could cause personal injury (see Section 27).*

1   The multi-function switch is located on the left side of the steering column. It incorporates into one switch the turn signal, headlight dimmer, windshield wiper/washer, flasher function and cruise control function, if equipped.

2   Place the tilt steering wheel in the center position.

3   Remove the steering wheel (see Chapter 10) and steering column trim covers (see Chapter 11).

4   Trace the multi-function switch wires down to the connectors and disconnect them.

5   Remove the multi-function switch screws, then detach the switch from the steering column **(see illustration)**. **Note:** *The multi-function switch is integral with the airbag clockspring, and is replaced as a unit with its wiring harness. If a new switch is being installed, it will come with a special tab in place to keep the clockspring centered during installation. Do not remove the tab until installation is complete.*

6   Installation is the reverse of removal. **Warning:** *If the original switch is being reinstalled, refer to Chapter 10, Section 15 and center the clockspring.*

8   Electronic Park lock switch - replacement

Refer to illustration 8.3

Warning: *The models covered by this manual are equipped with Supplemental Restraint Systems (SRS), more commonly known as airbags. Always disable the airbag system before working in the vicinity of any airbag system component to avoid the possibility of accidental deployment of the airbags, which could cause personal injury (see Section 27).*

1   Disconnect the battery negative cable.

2   Remove the steering column trim covers (see Chapter 11).

3   Disconnect the Park lock electrical connector from the ignition switch. Use a small screwdriver to depress the tab and release the Park lock switch from the lock cylinder housing **(see illustration)**.

4   Installation is the reverse of the removal steps.

9   Ignition switch and key lock cylinder - replacement

Refer to illustrations 9.3 and 9.7

Warning: *The models covered by this manual are equipped with Supplemental Restraint Systems (SRS), more commonly known as airbags. Always disable the airbag system before working in the vicinity of any airbag system components to avoid the possibility of accidental deployment of the airbags, which could cause personal injury (see Section 27).*

Note: *On these models, the key lock cylinder contains an anti-theft ID chip. Replacing the lock cylinder will result in the vehicle not starting. A dealer service department will have to re-program the Body Control Module (BCM) before the engine will start again.*

1   Disconnect the negative battery cable.

2   Remove the steering column covers and remove the Park lock switch (see Chapter 11 and Section 8).

3   To remove the key lock cylinder, place the key in the lock and rotate clockwise to the Accessory position. Push in the retainer pin and pull the key and lock cylinder from the housing **(see illustration)**.

4   If equipped, slide the theft deterrent control module off the key lock cylinder barrel.

5   To replace the ignition lock/switch housing, remove the multi-function switch/airbag coil from the column (see Section 7), then remove the screws and the multi-function switch/airbag coil mounting plate from the column.

6   Remove the shear bolt from the ignition switch housing. This can be done by drilling a hole in the center of the bolt and using a screw extractor to unscrew the bolt.

7   To remove just the electrical portion of the ignition switch, disconnect the electrical connector, then remove the switch **(see illustration)**.

8   When installing the cylinder, align the retainer with the slot in the housing, then push

9.3 Push the retaining pin in to unseat the lock cylinder, then withdraw the key and cylinder

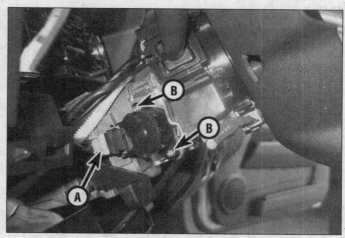

9.7 At the left side of the column, disconnect the electrical connector (A) at the ignition switch, then remove the screws (B) and withdraw the switch

the cylinder in until it snaps into position.
9   When installing the new shear bolt, tighten it until the shear head breaks off. The remainder of installation is the reverse of removal.

10   Instrument panel switches - replacement

Warning: *The models covered by this manual are equipped with Supplemental Restraint Systems (SRS), more commonly known as airbags. Always disable the airbag system before working in the vicinity of any airbag system component to avoid the possibility of accidental deployment of the airbags, which could cause personal injury (see Section 27).*

Headlight switch

Refer to illustration 10.3

1   Disconnect the negative cable from the battery (see Chapter 1).
2   Remove the driver's knee bolster trim

panel (see Chapter 11).
3   Remove the screw at the bottom of the headlight switch, then pull the headlight switch down and out of the instrument panel **(see illustration)**.
4   Disconnect the electrical connectors on the back of the switch.
5   Installation is the reverse of removal.

On/Off switches

Refer to illustration 10.7

6   Depending on the options of the vehicle, there may be one or more switches on the instrument panel, including transfer case shift control and hazard flasher switch.
7   All of the above-mentioned switches are accessible when the instrument cluster bezel or center trim plate is removed (see Chapter 11). The switches are removed from the back of the bezel or trim plate by prying clips with a small screwdriver and pulling the switch out **(see illustration)**.
8   With simple on/off switches, use an ohmmeter or self-powered continuity tes-

ter to check the switch for proper continuity between the terminals. There should be continuity between terminals only when the switch is engaged. If the switch fails the test, replace the switch.

11   Instrument cluster - removal and installation

Refer to illustrations 11.4a and 11.4b
Warning: *The models covered by this manual are equipped with Supplemental Restraint Systems (SRS), more commonly known as airbags. Always disable the airbag system before working in the vicinity of any airbag system component to avoid the possibility of accidental deployment of the airbags, which could cause personal injury (see Section 27).*
1   Disconnect the negative cable from the battery (see Chapter 1).
2   Remove the lower left sound insulator panel and the knee bolster (see Chapter 11).
3   Remove the instrument cluster bezel (see Chapter 11).

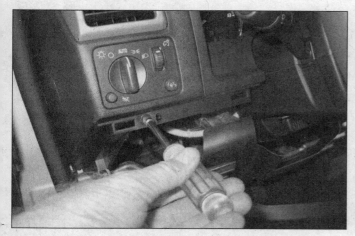

10.3 Remove the headlight switch mounting screw

10.7 Remove On/Off type switches by depressing the clips and pulling the switch out of the panel

**11.4a Instrument cluster upper mounting screws
(left screw shown)**

11.4b Instrument cluster lower mounting screws

4   Remove the screws securing the cluster to the instrument panel **(see illustrations)**.
5   Pull the cluster forward enough to disconnect the electrical connectors at the back, then pull the cluster out, tilting the bottom out first. **Note:** *These models have a Connector Position Assurance (CPA) type of connector. Move the lever away from the wiring end to release the connector.*
6   Installation is the reverse of removal. Push the CPA lever back toward the wiring end of the connector to make a secure connection.

12   Radio and speakers - removal and installation

Warning: *The models covered by this manual are equipped with Supplemental Restraint Systems (SRS), more commonly known as airbags. Always disable the airbag system before working in the vicinity of any airbag system component to avoid the possibility of accidental deployment of the airbags, which could cause personal injury (see Section 27).*

Radio

Refer to illustration 12.3
1   Disconnect the negative battery cable.
2   Remove the center accessory trim plate from the instrument panel (see Chapter 11).
3   Remove the mounting screws, pull the radio out of the instrument panel, disconnect the connectors, then remove it from the vehicle **(see illustration)**.
4   Installation is the reverse of removal.

Speakers

Refer to illustration 12.6
5   Remove the door trim panel (see Chapter 11).
6   Remove the speaker mounting screws **(see illustration)**. Pull the speaker out, disconnect the electrical connector and remove the speaker from the vehicle.
7   Installation is the reverse of removal.

Digital radio receiver

8   Some models have a digital radio receiver, located behind the glove box.
9   To remove the receiver, remove the glove box (see Chapter 11) and the instrument panel right-side end-panel.
10   Reaching through the glove box opening and the end-panel opening, remove the screws securing the radio receiver.
11   Disconnect the two electrical connectors at the radio. One is a CPA (Connector Position Assurance) type, which has a tab that you must push *in* (do not pry it out or up) to release the connector.
12   Installation is the reverse of the removal procedure.

13   Antenna - removal and installation

Refer to illustrations 13.1 and 13.4
1   Use a small open-end wrench to unscrew the antenna mast **(see illustration)**. Be very

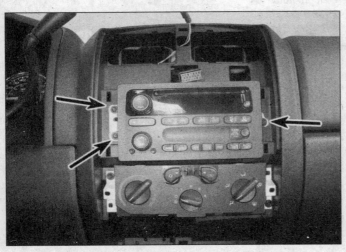

12.3 Remove the mounting screws and pull the radio out

12.6 Remove the speaker mounting screws

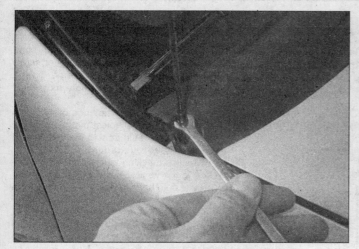

13.1 Use a small wrench to remove the antenna mast

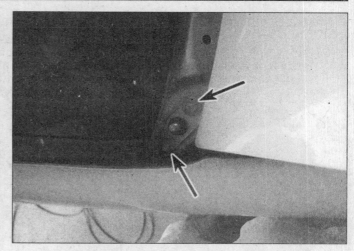

13.4 To remove the antenna base and cable, remove the base mounting bolts

careful - the tool could slip and scratch the body. It's a good idea to surround the base of the antenna with masking tape to prevent scratching. **Note 1:** *An antenna mast removal tool is provided with your vehicle.* **Note 2:** *Models with optional digital radio have a different antenna, mounted to the roof of the cab. Since removal requires the interior headliner to be partially removed for access, it is recommended that this antenna be replaced at a dealership.*

2   If the antenna base/cable assembly must be replaced, remove the glove compartment, the right door sill plate, the right kick panel and detach the lower rear portion of the inner fender liner (see Chapter 11).

3   Disconnect the antenna mast cable from the radio cable where they join in a connector under the far right end of the instrument panel. Attach a "fish" wire to the end of the cable. Working inside the inner fender liner, pass the cable and grommet through the hole in the cowl into the fender opening.

4   Refer to Chapter 11 and remove the cowl cover. Remove the antenna mast base mounting bolts and pull out the base and its cable **(see illustration)**.

5   Attach the new cable to the fish wire and pull the wire back slowly and carefully into the body, routing it as the original cable had been.

6   If the extension cable (between the antenna base cable and the radio) must be replaced, remove the glove compartment and the passenger's airbag module (see Section 27). Release the cable from the clips along the top of the instrument panel and disconnect it from the radio and antenna base cable.

7   Installation is the reverse of the removal procedure.

14   Headlight bulb - replacement

Refer to illustrations 14.2a and 14.2b

Warning: *Halogen bulbs are gas-filled and under pressure and may shatter if the sur-* *face is scratched or the bulb is dropped. Wear eye protection and handle the bulbs carefully, grasping only the base whenever possible. Don't touch the surface of the bulb with your fingers because the oil from your skin could cause it to overheat and fail prematurely. If you do touch the bulb surface, clean it with rubbing alcohol.*

Note: *Low and high beam bulbs can be identified by the color of their sockets; low beam bulbs have gray sockets and high beam bulbs have black sockets.*

1   Open the hood for bulb access from behind the headlight housings.

2   Twist the bulb holder counterclockwise and withdraw the bulb holder and connector from the housing **(see illustrations)**. Unplug the connector from the bulb holder.

3   Handling the new bulb only by the bulb holder portion, reconnect the electrical connector and insert the new bulb/holder into the housing. Twist the holder clockwise to lock it in place.

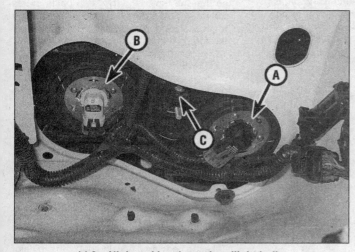

14.2a High and low-beam headlight bulbs

A   High beam headlight   C   Headlight adjuster
B   Low beam headlight

14.2b Turn the bulb holder counterclockwise and remove it from the housing (shown with housing removed for clarity)

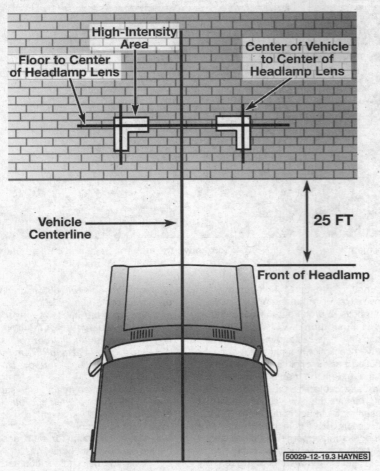

15.2 Headlight adjustment details

4   Installation of the housing is the reverse of the removal procedure.

15 Headlights and fog lights - adjustment

Warning: *The headlights must be aimed correctly. If adjusted incorrectly, they could temporarily blind the driver of an oncoming vehicle and cause an accident or seriously reduce your ability to see the road. The headlights should be checked for proper aim every 12 months and any time a new headlight is installed or front-end bodywork is performed. The following procedure is only an interim step to provide temporary adjustment until the headlights can be adjusted by a properly equipped shop.*

16.1 Headlight housing mounting bolts

Headlights

Refer to illustration 15.2

1   These models are equipped with composite headlights with an adjustment screw controlling up-and-down movement **(see illustration 14.2a)**. Left-and-right movement is not adjustable.
2   There are several methods of adjusting the headlights. The simplest method requires a blank wall 25 feet in front of the vehicle and a level floor **(see illustration)**.
3   Position masking tape on the wall in reference to the vehicle centerline and the centerlines of both headlights.
4   Measure the height of the headlight reference marks (in the centers of the headlight lenses) from the ground. Position a horizontal tape line on the wall at the same height as the headlight reference marks. **Note:** *It may be easier to position the tape on the wall with the vehicle parked only a few inches away.*
5   Adjustment should be made with the vehicle sitting level, the gas tank half-full and no unusually heavy load in the vehicle. There should be a 160-lb person or equivalent on the driver's seat.
6   Turn on the low beams. Turn the adjusting screw **(see illustration 14.2a)** to position the high intensity zone so it is two inches below the horizontal line.
7   Have the headlights adjusted by a dealer service department at the earliest opportunity.

Fog lights

8   Some models have optional fog lights that can be aimed just like headlights. As with the headlights, there are no left-and-right adjustments.
9   Position tape on a wall 25 feet in front of the vehicle **(see illustration 15.2)**. Tape a horizontal line on the wall that represents the height of the fog lamp centers, and another tape line four inches below that line.
10   Use the adjusting screws (torx-type) on the fog lamps to adjust the pattern on the wall so that the top of the fog lamp beam meets the lower line on the wall. On GMC Canyon models, the adjustment bolt is on the side of the fog light housing, loosen the bolt slightly to aim the fog light, then tighten the bolt. On XTREME models, the vertical adjustment screw is at the top of the housing; turn it in or out to adjust the beam.

16 Headlight housing - removal and installation

Refer to illustration 16.1

1   Open the hood. Refer to Chapter 11 and remove the grille.
2   Remove the headlight housing bolts **(see illustration)**.
3   Disconnect the electrical connector(s). Take the headlamp housing out of the radiator support panel.
4   Installation is the reverse of removal. Align the housing locating pins with the holes

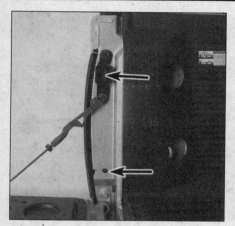

17.7 Remove the taillight assembly mounting screws

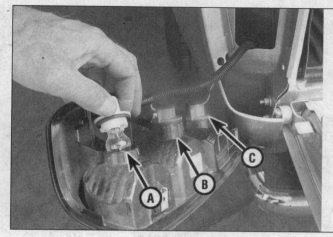

17.8 Twist the bulb holder counterclockwise to release it from the housing

A *Brake light bulb*
B *Taillight/turn signal bulb*
C *Back-up light bulb*

in the panel and push the retaining tabs down to lock the housing in place.

17 Bulb replacement

Warning: *Bulbs can remain hot for up to twenty minutes after they're turned off. Be sure bulbs are off and cool before you touch them.*

Fog lamps

1   Turn the bulb socket counterclockwise and free it from the lamp housing. Remove the bulb from the socket and install a new one.
2   Installation is the reverse of the removal steps.

Turn signal, parking and side marker lights

3   Remove the headlight housing (see Section 16). The park/turn/side marker light bulbs are at the top of the headlight housing.
4   Each bulb is replaced in the same manner. Twist the bulb holder out and pull the bulb straight out of the holder.
5   Installation is the reverse of removal.

Tail/stop/turn/back-up light

Refer to illustrations 17.7 and 17.8

6   On all models, these rear lights are all in one housing.
7   Open the tailgate. Remove the lamp housing screws and take the lamp housing off the body **(see illustration)**.
8   Rotate the socket counterclockwise and pull it out of the housing **(see illustration)**.
9   Pull the bulb straight out of the socket and push a new one in.
10   Installation is the reverse of the removal steps.

High-mounted stop light

11   The center high-mounted stoplight (CHMSL) is located at the top rear of the cab.
12   Remove the mounting screws and detach the stop light from the cab.
13   Each of the four bulbs can be replaced

individually. Rotate each socket counterclockwise and pull it out of the housing.
14   Installation is the reverse of removal.

License plate bulbs

15   From behind and below the rear bumper, remove the screws retaining each of the two license plate light holders. On some models, a single nut retains the license plate light holder.
16   Rotate the bulb holders to remove for bulb replacement.
17   Installation is the reverse of removal.

Instrument cluster lights

18   To gain access to the instrument cluster illumination lights, the instrument cluster will have to be removed (see Section 11). The bulbs can then be removed and replaced from the rear of the cluster, after removing a cover panel. The only bulbs used are for the turn signal indicators, high beam indicator and cruise control indicator. All others are light-emitting diodes (LEDs). If an LED fails, the instrument cluster must be replaced.
19   Installation is the reverse of removal.

Interior lights
Dome light

Refer to illustration 17.20

20   Pull on the sides of the lens for access to the retaining tab at the rear of the lamp. Release the retaining tab with a small screwdriver **(see illustration)**, then lower the lens and pull it rearward to free the front retaining tab.
21   To replace the dome lamp bulb, remove it from the socket.
22   Installation is the reverse of removal.

18 Wiper motor - check and replacement

Wiper motor circuit check

Note: *Refer to the wiring diagrams for wire colors and locations in the following checks. When checking for voltage, probe a grounded*

12-volt test light to each terminal at a connector until it lights; this verifies voltage (power) at the terminal. If the following checks fail to locate the problem, have the system diagnosed by a dealer service department or other properly equipped repair facility. The BCM is capable of storing trouble codes that can be retrieved with the proper equipment.

1   If the wipers work slowly, make sure the battery is in good condition and has a strong charge (see Chapter 5). If the battery is in good condition, remove the wiper motor (see below) and operate the wiper arms by hand. Check for binding in the linkage and pivots. Lubricate or repair the linkage or pivots as necessary. Reinstall the wiper motor. If the wipers still operate slowly, check for loose or corroded connections, especially the ground connection. If all connections look OK, replace the motor.
2   If the wipers fail to operate when activated, check the fuse. If the fuse is OK, connect a jumper wire between the wiper motor's ground terminal and ground, then retest. If the motor works now, repair the ground connection. If the motor still doesn't work, turn the wiper switch to the HI position and check for voltage at the motor. **Note:** *The cowl cover will have to be removed (see Chapter 11) to access the electrical connector.*

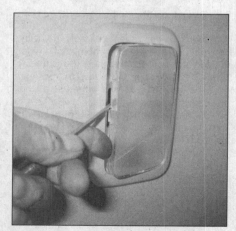

17.20 Use a small screwdriver to release the cover from the dome light

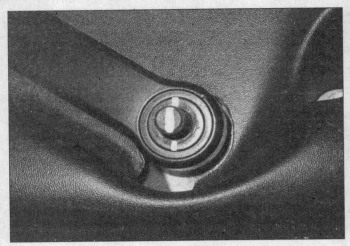

18.7 Remove the nut, mark the wiper arm location and rock the wiper arm to detach it from the shaft - use a small puller if it's stuck

18.9 Remove the wiper linkage mounting bolts, then twist or rock the assembly out from the cowl

3   If there's voltage at the connector, remove the motor and check it off the vehicle with fused jumper wires from the battery. If the motor now works, check for binding linkage (see Step 1 above). If the motor still doesn't work, replace it. If there's no voltage to the motor, check for voltage at the wiper control relays. If there's voltage at the wiper control relays and no voltage at the wiper motor, have the switch tested. If the switch is OK, the wiper control relay is probably bad. See Section 5 for relay testing.

4   If the interval (delay) function is inoperative, check the continuity of all the wiring between the switch and wiper control module.

5   If the wipers stop at the position they're in when the switch is turned off (fail to park), check for voltage at the park feed wire of the wiper motor connector when the wiper switch is OFF but the ignition is ON. If no voltage is present, check for an open circuit between the wiper motor and the fuse panel.

Replacement

Refer to illustrations 18.7 and 18.9

6   Disconnect the negative cable from the battery (see Chapter 1).

7   Remove the wiper arm nuts, mark the positions of the arms to their shafts, then remove the wiper arms **(see illustration)**. **Note:** *If the wiper arm is stuck, try rocking it on the shaft. If that doesn't work, use a small puller such as a battery terminal puller.*

8   Remove the cowl grille (see Chapter 11). Disconnect the electrical connector at the wiper motor.

9   Remove the wiper motor/linkage mounting bolts **(see illustration)**.

10   Remove the assembly and unbolt the motor from the linkage. Some rocking motion may be required to free the wiper drive from the cowl.

11   Installation is the reverse of removal.

19   Horn - replacement

Refer to illustration 19.2

1   Remove the grille (see Chapter 11).

2   Disconnect the electrical connector, remove the mounting bolt and detach the horn **(see illustration)**.

3   Installation is the reverse of removal.

20   Daytime Running Lights (DRL) - general information

The Daytime Running Lights (DRL) system illuminates the low beam headlights at reduced intensity whenever the ignition is On and the headlight switch is in the Auto position. The only exception is with the engine running and the shift lever in Park (automatic transmission models) or with the parking brake on (manual transmission models). Once the parking brake is released or the shift lever is moved, the lights will remain on as long as the ignition switch is on.

21   Cruise control system - description and check

1   The cruise control system maintains vehicle speed with the Powertrain Control Module (PCM), throttle actuator control motor, brake switch, control switches and associated wiring. There is no mechanical connection, such as a vacuum servo or cable. Some features of the system require special testers and diagnostic procedures that are beyond the scope of the home mechanic. Listed below are some general procedures that may be used to locate common problems.

2   Check the fuses (see Section 3).

3   The brake pedal position (BPP) switch (or brake light switch) deactivates the cruise control system. Have an assistant press the brake pedal while you check the brake light operation.

4   If the brake lights do not operate properly, correct the problem and retest the cruise control.

5   Check the wiring between the PCM and throttle actuator motor for opens or shorts and repair as necessary.

19.2 Follow the wiring harness to the horn connector (A), then disconnect it and remove the mounting bolt (B)

6   The cruise control system uses information from the PCM, including the Vehicle Speed Sensor, which is located in the transmission or transfer case. Refer to Chapter 6 for more information on the VSS.

7   Test drive the vehicle to determine if the cruise control is now working. If it isn't, take it to a dealer service department or an automotive electrical specialist for further diagnosis.

22 Power window system - description and check

1   The power window system operates electric motors, mounted in the doors, which lower and raise the windows. The system consists of the control switches, the motors, regulators, glass mechanisms and associated wiring.

2   The power windows can be lowered and raised from the master control switch by the driver or by remote switches located at the individual windows. Each window has a separate motor that is reversible. The position of the control switch determines the polarity and therefore the direction of operation.

3   The circuit is protected by a fuse and a circuit breaker. Each motor is also equipped with an internal circuit breaker; this prevents one stuck window from disabling the whole system.

4   The power window system will only operate when the ignition switch is ON. In addition, many models have a window lockout switch at the master control switch which, when activated, disables the switches at the rear windows and, sometimes, the switch at the passenger's window also. Always check these items before troubleshooting a window problem.

5   These procedures are general in nature, so if you can't find the problem using them, take the vehicle to a dealer service department or other properly equipped repair facility.

6   If the power windows won't operate, always check the fuse and circuit breaker first.

7   If only the rear windows are inoperative, or if the windows only operate from the master control switch, check the rear window lockout switch for continuity in the unlocked position. Replace it if it doesn't have continuity.

8   Check the wiring between the switches and fuse panel for continuity. Repair the wiring, if necessary.

9   If only one window is inoperative from the master control switch, try the other control switch at the window. **Note:** *This doesn't apply to the driver's door window.*

10   If the same window works from one switch, but not the other, check the switch for continuity.

11   If the switch tests OK, check for a short or open in the circuit between the affected switch and the window motor.

12   If one window is inoperative from both switches, remove the switch panel from the affected door. Check for voltage at the switch and at the motor (refer to Chapter 11 for door panel removal) while the switch is operated.

13   If voltage is reaching the motor, disconnect the glass from the regulator (see Chapter 11). Move the window up and down by hand while checking for binding and damage. Also check for binding and damage to the regulator. If the regulator is not damaged and the window moves up and down smoothly, replace the motor. If there's binding or damage, lubricate, repair or replace parts, as necessary.

14   If voltage isn't reaching the motor, check the wiring in the circuit for continuity between the switches and motors. You'll need to consult the wiring diagram at the end of this Chapter. If the circuit is equipped with a relay, check that the relay is grounded properly and receiving voltage.

15   Test the windows after you are done to confirm proper repairs.

23 Power door lock and keyless entry system - description and check

1   The power door lock system operates the door lock actuators mounted in each door. The system consists of the switches, actuators, Body Control Module (BCM) and associated wiring. Diagnosis can usually be limited to simple checks of the wiring connections and actuators for minor faults that can be easily repaired.

2   Power door lock systems are operated by bi-directional solenoids located in the doors. The lock switches have two operating positions: Lock and Unlock. These switches send a signal to the BCM, which in turn sends a signal to the door lock solenoids.

3   If you are unable to locate the trouble using the following general steps, consult your dealer service department.

4   Always check the circuit protection first. Some vehicles use a combination of circuit breakers and fuses. Refer to the wiring diagrams at the end of this Chapter.

5   Check for voltage at the switches. If no voltage is present, check the wiring between the fuse panel and the switches for shorts and opens.

6   If voltage is present, test the switch for continuity. Replace it if there's not continuity in both switch positions. To remove the switch, use a flat-bladed trim tool to pry out the door/window switch assembly (see Chapter 11).

7   If the switch has continuity, check the wiring between the switch and door lock solenoid.

8   If all but one lock solenoids operate, remove the trim panel from the affected door (see Chapter 11) and check for voltage at the solenoid while the lock switch is operated. One of the wires should have voltage in the Lock position; the other should have voltage in the Unlock position.

9   If the inoperative solenoid is receiving voltage, replace the solenoid.

10   If the inoperative solenoid isn't receiving voltage, check for an open or short in the wire between the lock solenoid and the relay. **Note:** *It's common for wires to break in the portion of the harness between the body and door (opening and closing the door fatigues and eventually breaks the wires).*

11   On the models covered by this manual, power door lock system communication goes through the Body Control Module. If the above tests do not pinpoint a problem, take the vehicle to a dealer or qualified shop with the proper scan tool to retrieve trouble codes from the BCM.

Keyless entry system

12   The keyless entry system consists of a remote control transmitter that sends a coded infrared signal to a receiver, which then operates the door lock system.

13   Replace the battery when the transmitter doesn't operate the locks at a distance of ten feet. Normal range should be about 30 feet.

14   Use a small screwdriver to carefully separate the case halves.

15   Replace the three-volt, CR2032 lithium battery.

16   Snap the case halves together.

24 Electric side view mirrors - description

1   The electric rear view mirrors use two motors to move the glass; one for up and down adjustments and one for left-right adjustments.

2   The control switch has a selector portion that sends voltage to the left or right side mirror. With the ignition in the ACC position and the engine OFF, roll down the windows and operate the mirror control switch through all functions (left-right and up-down) for both the left and right side mirrors.

3   Listen carefully for the sound of the electric motors running in the mirrors.

4   If the motors can be heard but the mirror glass doesn't move, there's probably a problem with the drive mechanism inside the mirror. Power mirrors have no user-serviceable parts inside - a defective mirror must be replaced as a unit (see Chapter 11).

5   If the mirrors don't operate and no sound comes from the mirrors, check the fuses (see Section 3).

6   If the fuses are OK, remove the mirror control switch. Have the switch continuity checked by a dealer service department or other qualified shop.

7   Check the ground connections.

8   If the mirror still doesn't work, remove the mirror and check the wires at the mirror for voltage.

9   If there's not voltage in each switch position, check the circuit between the mirror and control switch for opens and shorts.

10   If there's voltage, remove the mirror and test it off the vehicle with jumper wires. Replace the mirror if it fails this test.

25 Power seats - description

1   Power seats allow you to adjust the position of the seat with little effort. These models feature a six-way seat that goes forward and backward, up and down and tilts forward and backward. The seats are powered by three reversible motors, mounted in one housing, that are controlled by switches on the side of the seat. Each switch changes the direction of seat travel by reversing polarity to the drive motor. Some models may also have optional power lumbar support and seat heaters.

2   Diagnosis is usually a simple matter, using the following procedures.

3   Look under the seat for any object which may be preventing the seat from moving.

4   If the seat won't work at all, check the fuses. See Section 3 for circuit breaker testing.

5   With the engine off to reduce the noise level, operate the seat controls in all directions and listen for sound coming from the seat motors.

6   If the motors don't work, check for voltage at the motors while an assistant operates the switch. With the door open, try the seat switch again. If the dome light dims while trying to operate the seat, this indicates something may be jammed in the seat tracks.

7   If the motor is getting voltage but doesn't run, test it off the vehicle with jumper wires. If it still doesn't work, replace it.

8   If the motor isn't getting voltage, remove the switch and check for voltage. If there's no voltage to the switch, check the wiring between the fuse block and the switch. If there's battery voltage at the switch, check the other terminals for voltage while moving the switch around. If the switch is OK, check for a short or open in the wiring between the switch and motor.

9   Test the completed repairs.

26 Data Link Communication system - description

1   The vehicles covered by this manual have a complex electrical system, encompassing many power accessories, and a number of separate electronic modules.

2   The Powertrain Control Module (PCM) is mainly responsible for engine and transaxle control, but also communicates with other modules around the vehicle through a Data Link Communication system, which sends serial port data very quickly between the various modules. Many of the computer functions involved in the operation of body systems are routed through the Body Control Module (BCM), which communicates with the PCM.

3   Among the modules in the Data Link system besides the BCM and PCM are the Sensing Diagnostic Module (airbag system), the Electronic Brake Control Module and the instrument panel cluster. The BCM further communicates with various body subsystems.

4   All of the modules in the vehicle have associated trouble codes. When other troubleshooting procedures fail to pinpoint the problem, check the wiring diagrams at the end of this Chapter to see if the BCM or PCM are involved in the circuit. If so, bring your vehicle to a dealer with the factory diagnostic tools to extract the trouble codes.

27 Airbag system - general information

1   These models are equipped with a Supplemental Restraint System (SRS), more commonly known as airbags, designed to protect the driver and front seat passenger from serious injury in the event of a head-on or frontal collision. Side airbags mounted in the sides of the roof are optional equipment, and are designed to deploy only in a side impact of sufficient force. All models have a sensing/ diagnostic control unit, located under the rear of the center console. **Warning:** *If your vehicle is ever involved in a flood, or the interior carpeting is soaked for any reason, disconnect the battery and do not start the vehicle until the airbag system can be checked by your dealer. If the SRS system is subjected to flooding, the airbags could go off upon starting the vehicle, even without an accident taking place.*

Airbag modules

2   The airbag modules consist of a housing incorporating the cushion (airbag) and inflator unit. The inflator assembly is mounted on the back of the housing over a hole through which gas is expelled, inflating the bag almost instantaneously when an electrical signal is sent from the system. The specially wound wire on the driver's side that carries this signal to the driver's module is called a clockspring. The clockspring is a flat, ribbon-like electrically conductive tape that is wound many times so that it can transmit an electrical signal regardless of steering wheel position. Airbag modules are located in the steering wheel, on the passenger side above the glove box, and on some models, at the upper sides of the roof (side-impact airbags).

Sensing/diagnostic control unit and sensors

3   The sensing/diagnostic control unit contains an on-board microprocessor which monitors the operation of the system, and also contains a crash sensor. It checks this system every time the vehicle is started, causing the AIRBAG light to flash seven times then go off, if the system is operating properly. If there is a fault in the system, the light may not come on at all, or the light will go on and continue, either illuminated steadily or blinking, and the unit will store fault codes indicating the nature of the fault.

4   A pair of impact-activated sensors, called the discriminating sensors, are mounted to the underside of the radiator support. The side airbags are triggered by side impact sensors mounted behind the front door panels, attached to the inner door frame.

Operation

5   For the airbag(s) to deploy, the discriminating sensors and the impact sensor in the sensing/diagnostic control unit must be activated. When this condition occurs, the circuit to the airbag inflator is closed and the airbag inflates. If the battery is destroyed by the impact, or is too low to power the inflator, a back-up power unit inside the SRS system provides power.

Self-diagnosis system

6   A self-diagnosis circuit in the SRS unit displays a light on the instrument panel when the ignition switch is turned to the On position. If the system is operating normally, the light should go out after about seven blinks. If the light doesn't come on, or doesn't go out after a short time, or if it comes on while you're driving the vehicle, or if it blinks at any time, there's a malfunction in the SRS system. Have it inspected and repaired as soon as possible. Do not attempt to troubleshoot or service the SRS system yourself. Even a small mistake could cause the SRS system to malfunction when you need it.

Servicing components near the SRS system

7   Nevertheless, there are times when you need to remove the steering wheel, radio or service other components on or near the dashboard or near other airbag system components. At these times, you'll be working around components and wire harnesses for the SRS system. Do not use electrical test equipment on airbag system wires; it could cause the airbag(s) to deploy. ALWAYS DISABLE THE SRS SYSTEM BEFORE WORKING NEAR THE SRS SYSTEM COMPONENTS OR RELATED WIRING.

Disabling the SRS system

Warning: *Any time you are working in the vicinity of airbag wiring or components, DISABLE THE SRS SYSTEM.*

8   To disable the airbag system, perform the following steps:

a) *Turn the steering wheel to the straight-ahead position and turn the ignition switch to the Lock position, then remove the key.*

b) *Remove the airbag fuse located in the underhood fuse/relay box.*

c) *Wait at least two minutes for the back up power supply to be depleted before beginning work.*

d) *Remove the driver's knee bolster (see Chapter 11) and disconnect the driver's airbag connector at the steering column (see Chapter 10).*

e) Open and drop the glove box door (see Chapter 11) and disconnect the connector to the passenger airbag, which is mounted to the backside of the instrument panel.

f) To disable a side impact airbag, remove the door trim panel on the side to be disabled (see Chapter 11), then disconnect the electrical connector for the side impact sensor.

Enabling the system

9   To enable the airbag system, perform the following steps:

a) Turn the ignition switch to the Lock position and remove the key.

b) Reconnect the passenger and driver's airbag connectors (or the side impact sensor connector), making sure the CPA (Connector Position Assurance) clips are in place so the connectors can't accidentally disengage.

c) Reinsert the airbag fuse.

d) Turn the ignition switch to the On position. Confirm that the airbag warning light glows for 6 to 8 seconds, then goes out, indicating the system is functioning properly.

Removal and installation

Warning: When carrying an airbag module, keep the upholstered (or trim) side of it away from your body, and when you set it down (in an isolated area), have the upholstered (or trim) side facing up.

Driver's side airbag

10   Disable the airbag system (see Step 8). Refer to Chapter 10 for removal and installation of the driver's side airbag.

Passenger side airbag

11   Disable the airbag system (see Step 8).
12   Remove the glove box (see Chapter 11). Remove the access plate from the right end of the dash, then reach through the hole, unbolt the air outlet on the right end of the dash and take it out.
13   Refer to Section 12 and Chapter 3 and remove the radio and the HVAC control unit to access the left side of the passenger airbag.
14   Remove the lower mounting bolts and upper nuts (which face forward and are accessed from underneath the instrument panel, on each side of the airbag module) and gently remove the airbag unit from the dashboard. **Caution:** The airbag assembly is heavier than it looks; use both hands when removing it from the dash.
15   Installation is the reverse of the removal procedure.

Side impact airbags

16   The side impact airbags used on some models are mounted in the sides of the roof interior. Replacement of these airbags requires partial disassembly of the headliner and should be done by a dealer service department or other qualified shop.

28   Wiring diagrams - general information

Since it isn't possible to include all wiring diagrams for every year and model covered by this manual, the following diagrams are those that are typical and most commonly needed.

Prior to troubleshooting any circuits, check the fuse and circuit breakers (if equipped) to make sure they're in good condition. Make sure the battery is properly charged and check the cable connections (see Chapter 1).

When checking a circuit, make sure that all connectors are clean, with no broken or loose terminals. When disconnecting a connector, do not pull on the wires. Pull only on the connector housings themselves.

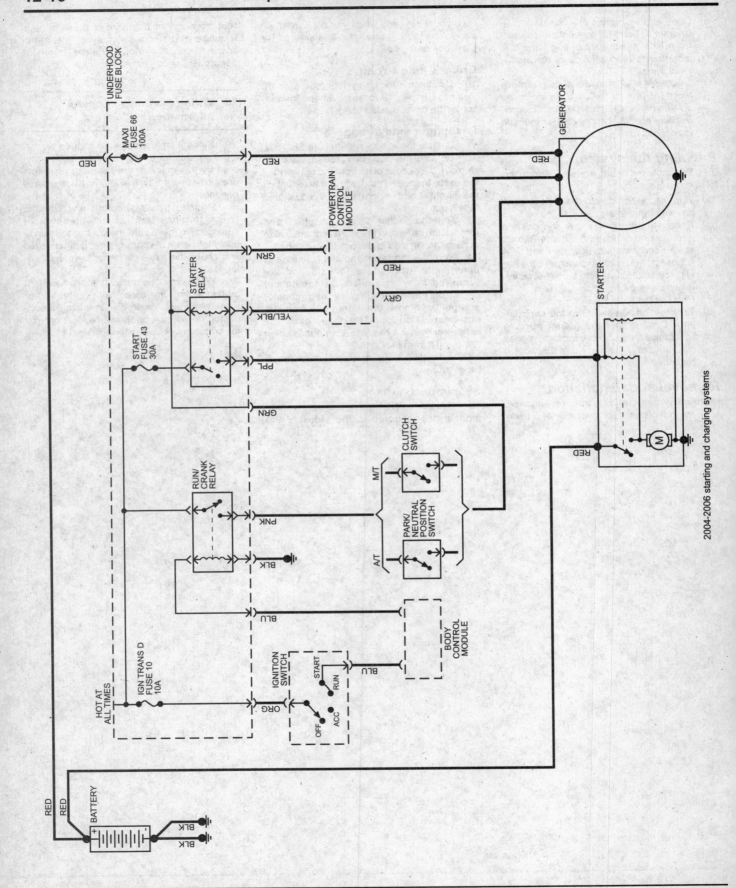

2004-2006 starting and charging systems

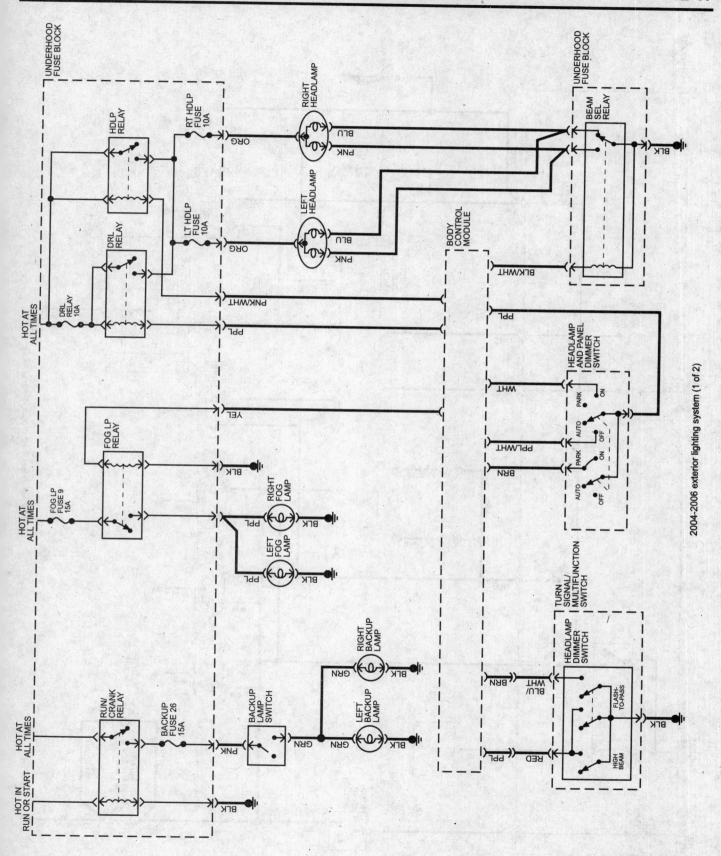

2004-2006 exterior lighting system (1 of 2)

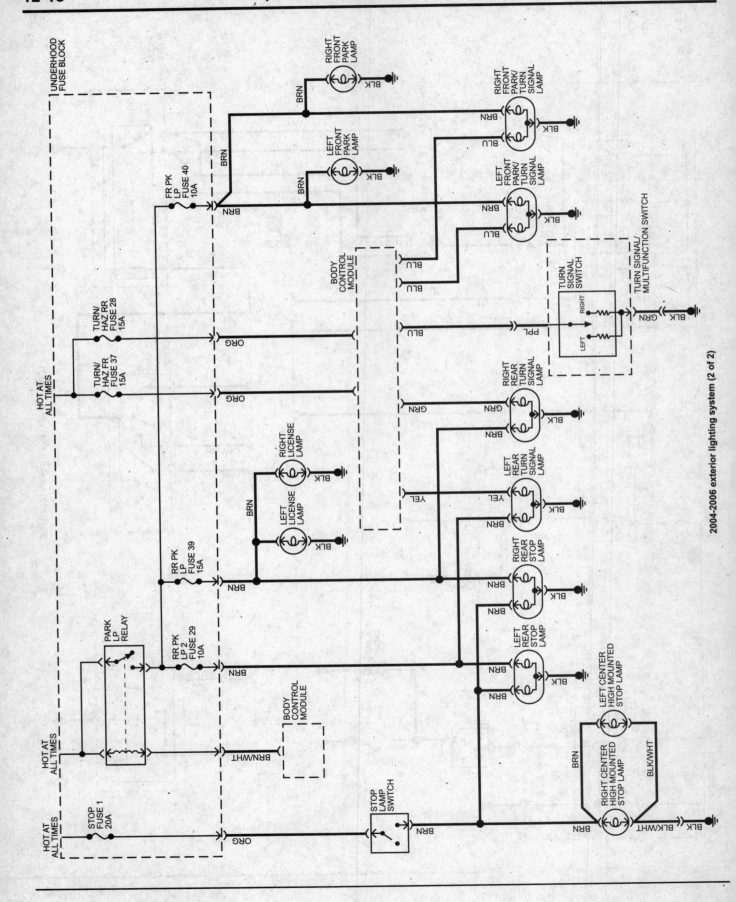

2004-2006 exterior lighting system (2 of 2)

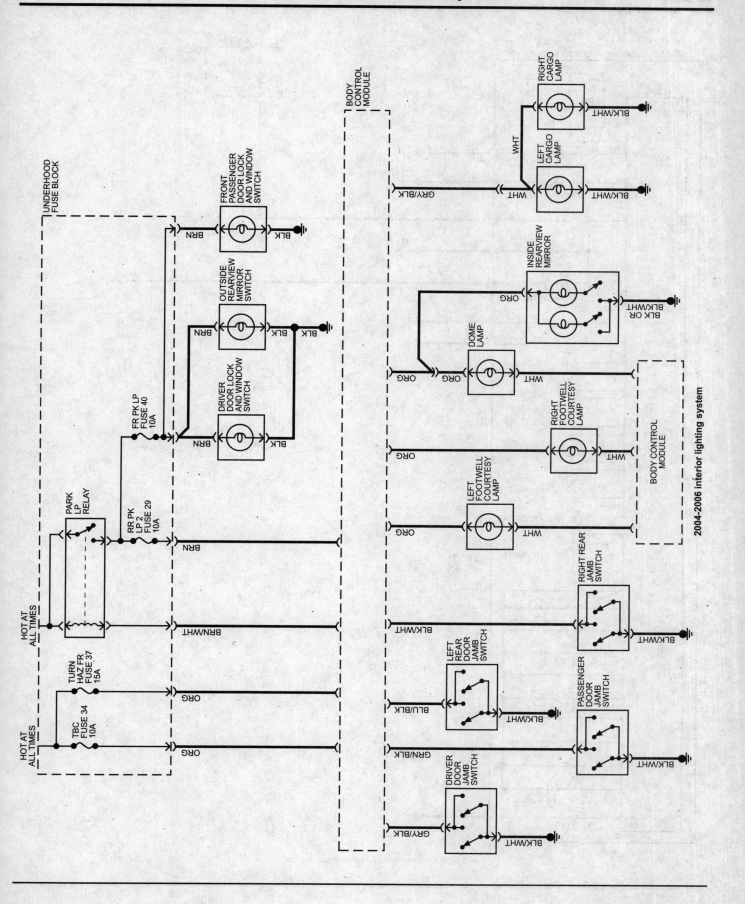

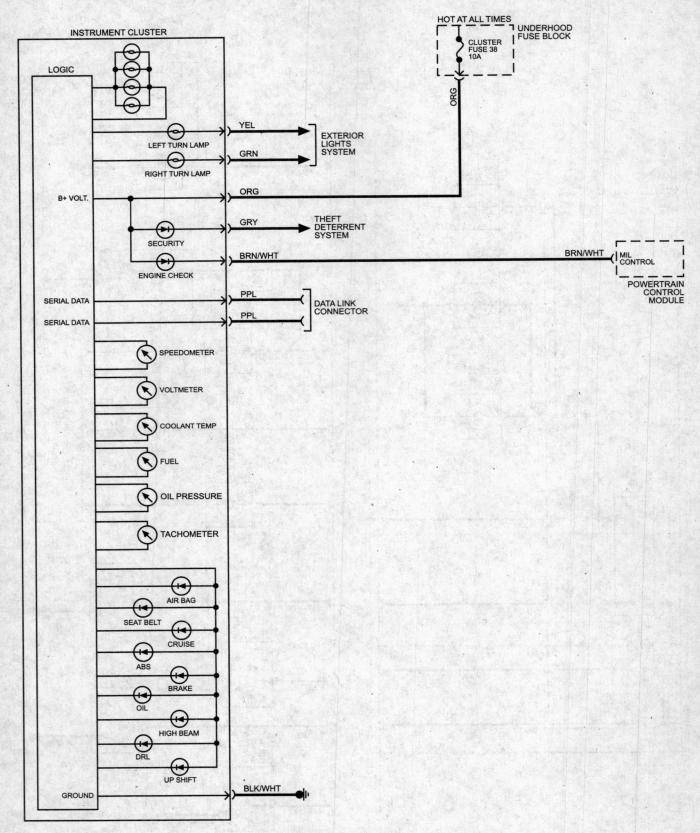

2004-2006 instrument cluster warning system

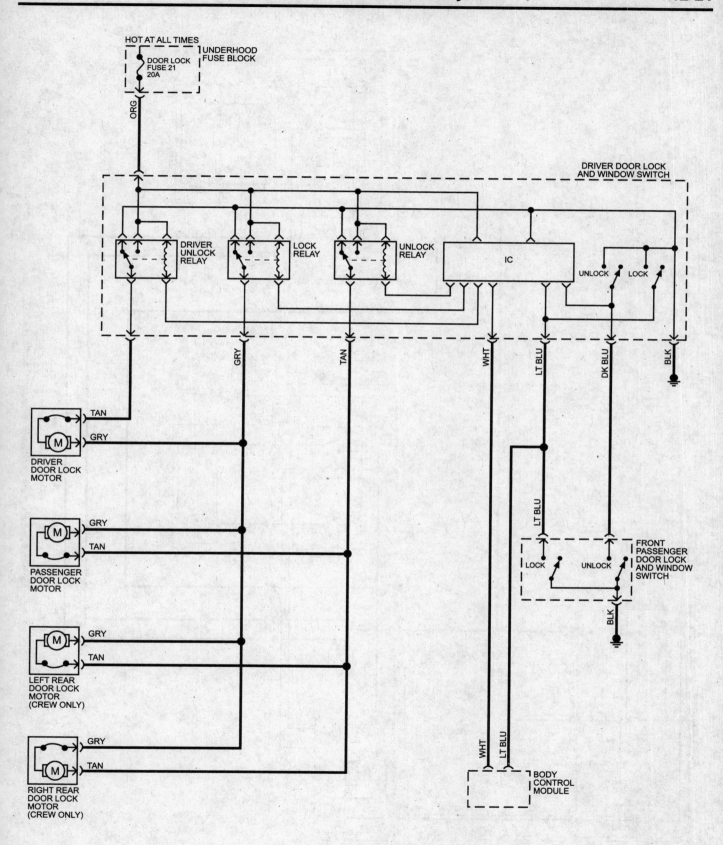

2004-2006 power door lock system

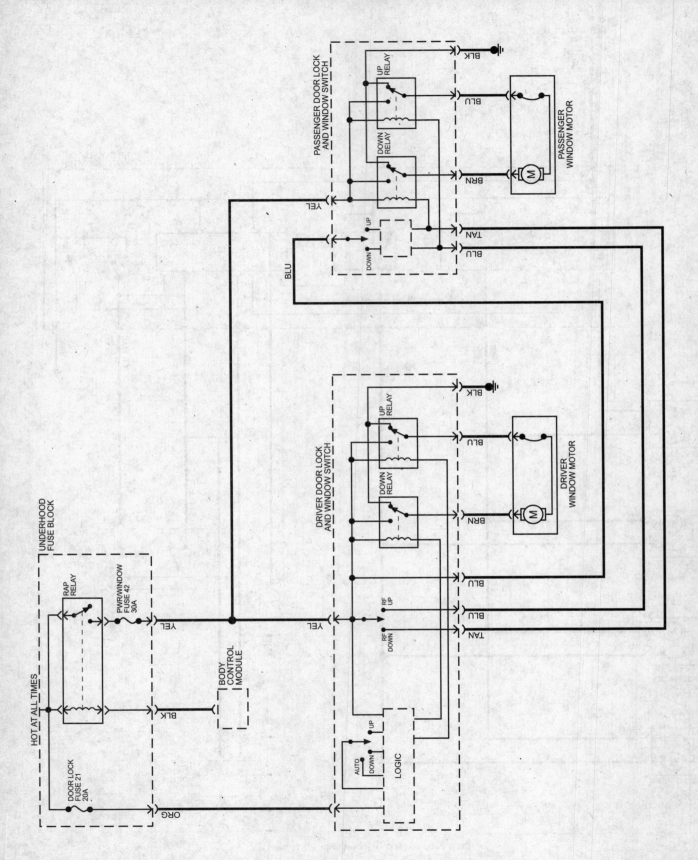

2004-2006 power windows system (Regular and Extended Cab)

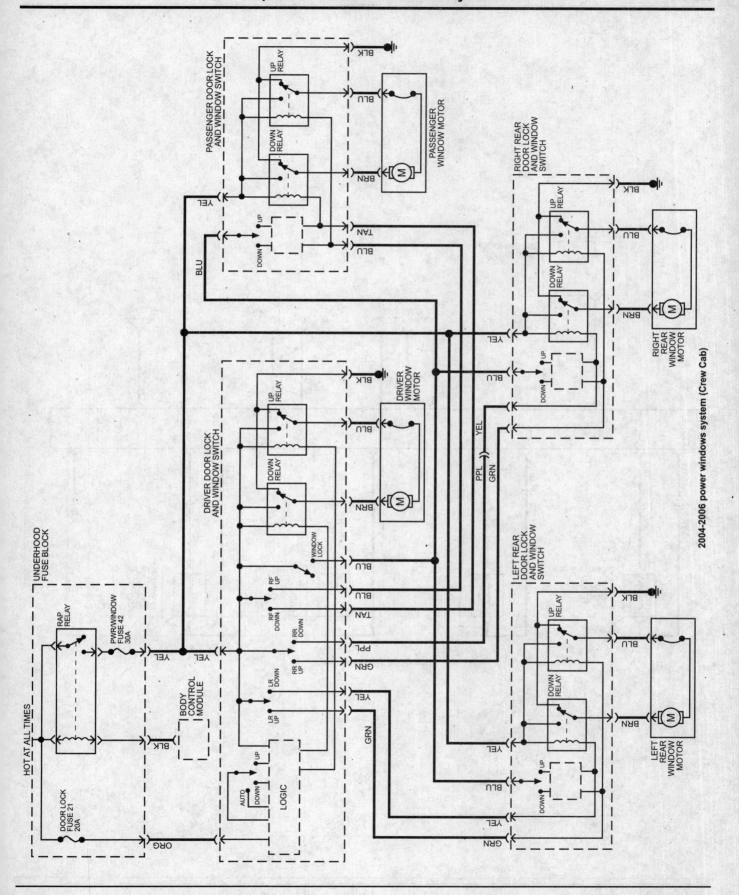

2004-2006 power windows system (Crew Cab)

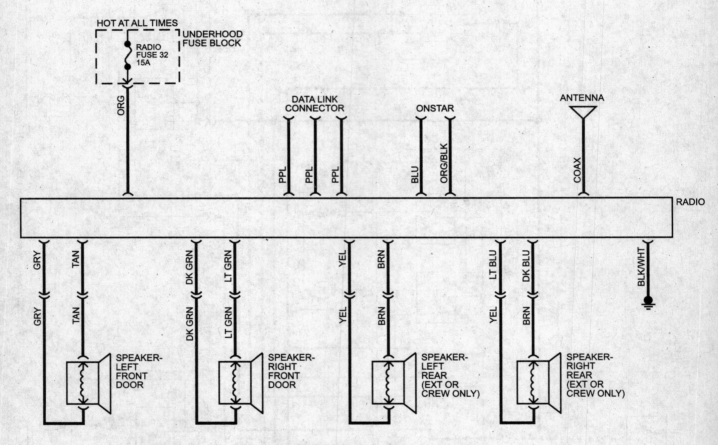

2004-2006 Radio system

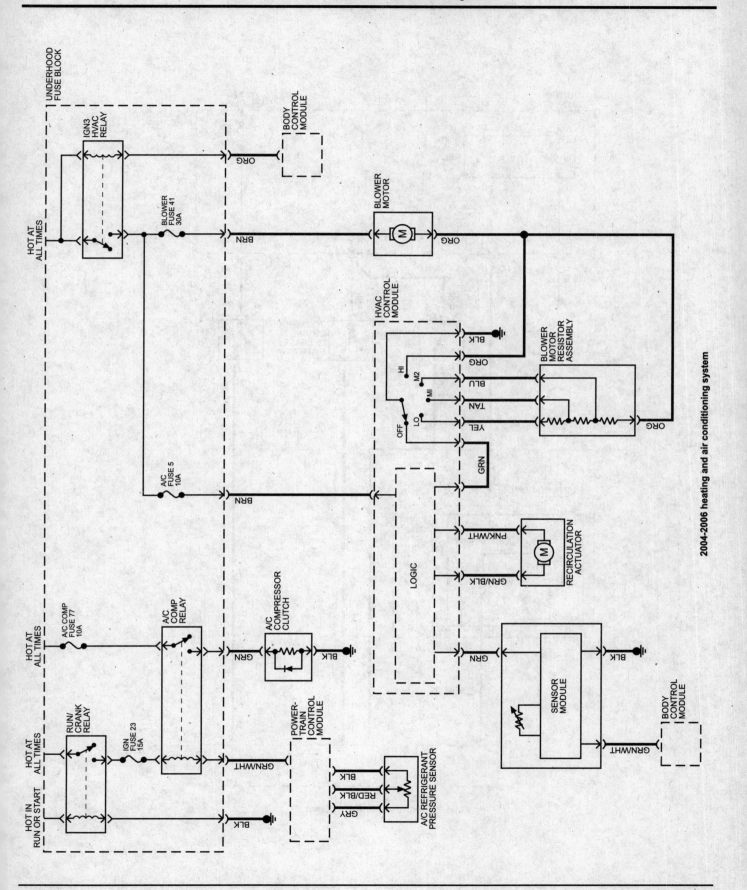

2004-2006 heating and air conditioning system

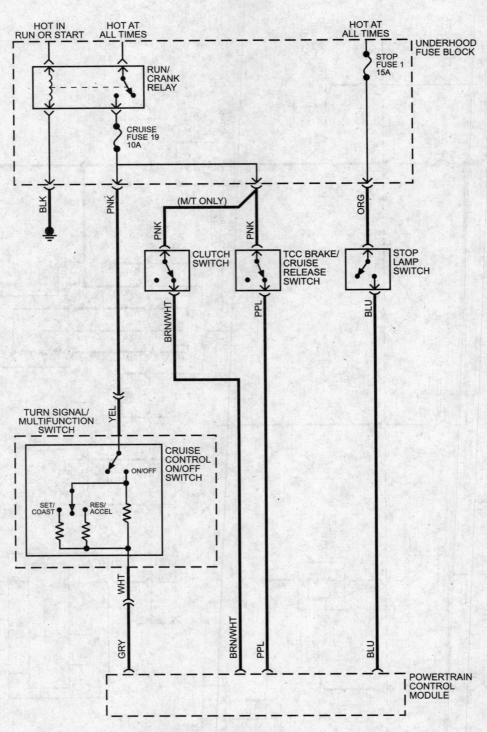

2004-2006 cruise control system

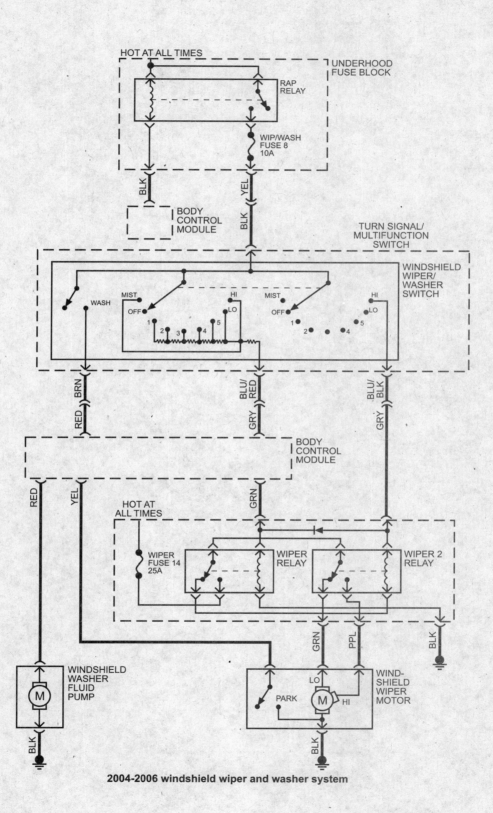

2004-2006 windshield wiper and washer system

Notes

Index

K

Key lock cylinder, ignition, replacement, 12-6
Keyless entry system, general information, 12-13
Knock sensor, replacement, 6-12

L

Lash adjusters, removal and installation, 2A-7
Leaf spring, removal and installation, 10-9
Lubricants and chemicals, 0-17
Lubricants and fluids
  capacities, 1-2
  recommended, 1-1

M

Maintenance
  routine, 1-1 through 1-30
  schedule, 1-3
  techniques, tools and working facilities, 0-8
Manifold Absolute Pressure (MAP) sensor, replacement, 6-9
Manual transmission, 7A-1 through 7A-2
  back-up light switch, replacement, 7A-1
  lubricant
    change, 1-28
    level check, 1-22
    type, 1-1
  overhaul, general information, 7A-2
  removal and installation, 7A-2
  shift lever, removal and installation, 7A-1
Mass Air Flow (MAF) sensor, replacement, 6-9
Master cylinder, removal and installation
  brake, 9-9
  clutch, 8-2
Mirrors, electric side view, general information, 12-13
Mirrors, removal and installation, 11-12
Multi-function switch, replacement, 12-6

O

Oil level tube, removal and installation, 2A-10
Oil pan, removal and installation, 2A-10
Oil pressure check, 2B-3
Oil pump and relief valve, replacement, 2A-9
Oil, engine, level check, 1-7
On-Board Diagnostic (OBD) system and Diagnostic Trouble Codes (DTCs), 6-2
Oxygen sensor, replacement, 6-11

P

Pads, disc brake, replacement, 9-3
Park lock switch, replacement, 12-6
Park/Lock system, description and component replacement, 7B-3
Park/Neutral Position (PNP) switch/back-up light switch, description, replacement and adjustment, 7B-4
Parking brake, adjustment, 9-13
Parts, replacement, buying, 0-8
Pilot bearing, replacement, 8-5
Pinion oil seal, replacement, 8-10

Pistons and connecting rods, removal and installation, 2B-10
Power brake booster, check, removal and installation, 9-12
Power door lock system, general information, 12-13
Power seats, description, 12-14
Power steering
  fluid level check, 1-11
  fluid type, 1-1
  pump, removal and installation, 10-13
  system, bleeding, 10-14
Power window system, general information, 12-13
Powertrain Control Module (PCM), removal and installation, 6-8
Powertrain mounts, check and replacement, 2A-10

R

Radiator
  grille, removal and installation, 11-6
  removal and installation, 3-4
Radio and speakers, removal and installation, 12-8
Rear main oil seal, replacement, 2A-10
Recall information, 0-7
Receiver/drier, air conditioning, removal and installation, 3-9
Recommended lubricants and fluids, 1-1
Regulator, window glass, removal and installation, 11-11
Relays, general information and testing, 12-4
Release cylinder and bearing, clutch, removal and installation, 8-2
Repair operations possible with the engine in the vehicle, 2A-3
Replacement parts, buying, 0-8
Rocker arms and lash adjusters, removal and installation, 2A-7
Rotor, brake, inspection, removal and installation, 9-5
Routine maintenance schedule, 1-3
Routine maintenance, 1-1 through 1-30

S

Safety first!, 0-20
Safety recall information, 0-7
Scheduled maintenance, 1-1 through 1-30
Seat belt check, 1-13
Seats, removal and installation, 11-14
Secondary Air Injection system, 6-14
Shift cable, automatic transmission, removal, installation and adjustment, 7B-2
Shift lever, manual transmission, removal and installation, 7A-1
Shock absorber, removal and installation
  front
    2WD models, 10-4
    4WD models, 10-5
  rear, 10-8
Shoes, drum brake, replacement, 9-6
Slave cylinder, clutch, removal and installation, 8-2
Spare tire, installing, 0-15
Spark plug
  check and replacement, 1-24
  torque, 1-2
  type and gap, 1-2
Speakers, removal and installation, 12-8
Stabilizer bar and bushings, removal and installation
  front, 10-5
  rear, 10-9

APACK

Haynes Automotive Manuals

NOTE: If you do not see a listing for your vehicle, consult your local Haynes dealer for the latest product information.

HAYNES XTREME CUSTOMIZING
11101 Sport Compact Customizing
11102 Sport Compact Performance
11110 In-car Entertainment
11150 Sport Utility Vehicle Customizing
11213 Acura
11255 GM Full-size Pick-ups
11314 Ford Focus
11315 Full-size Ford Pick-ups
11373 Honda Civic

ACURA
12020 Integra '86 thru '89 & Legend '86 thru '90
12021 Integra '90 thru '93 & Legend '91 thru '95

AMC
Jeep CJ - see JEEP (50020)
14020 Concord/Hornet/Gremlin/Spirit '70 thru '83
14025 (Renault) Alliance & Encore '83 thru '87

AUDI
15020 4000 all models '80 thru '87
15025 5000 all models '77 thru '83
15026 5000 all models '84 thru '88

AUSTIN
Healey Sprite - see MG Midget (66015)

BMW
18020 3/5 Series '82 thru '92
18021 3 Series including Z3 models '92 thru '98
18022 3-Series, E46 chassis '99 thru '05, Z4 models '03 thru '05
18025 320i all 4 cyl models '75 thru '83
18050 1500 thru 2002 except Turbo '59 thru '77

BUICK
19010 Buick Century '97 thru '05
Century (front-wheel drive) - see GM (38005)
19020 Buick, Oldsmobile & Pontiac Full-size (Front wheel drive) '85 thru '05
19025 Buick Oldsmobile & Pontiac Full-size (Rear wheel drive) '70 thru '90
19030 Mid-size Regal & Century '74 thru '87
Regal - see GENERAL MOTORS (38010)
Skyhawk - see GM (38030)
Skylark - see GM (38020, 38025)
Somerset - see GENERAL MOTORS (38025)

CADILLAC
21030 Cadillac Rear Wheel Drive '70 thru '93
Cimarron, Eldorado & Seville - see GM (38015, 38030, 38031)

CHEVROLET
10305 Chevrolet Engine Overhaul Manual
24010 Astro & GMC Safari Mini-vans '85 thru '03
24015 Camaro V8 all models '70 thru '81
24016 Camaro all models '82 thru '92, Cavalier - see GM (38015), Celebrity - see GM (38005)
24017 Camaro & Firebird '93 thru '02
24020 Chevelle, Malibu, El Camino '69 thru '87
24024 Chevette & Pontiac T1000 '76 thru '87
Citation - see GENERAL MOTORS (38020)
24027 Colorado & GMC Canyon '04 thru '06
24032 Corsica/Beretta all models '87 thru '96
24040 Corvette all V8 models thru '82
24041 Corvette all models '84 thru '96
24045 Full-size Sedans Caprice, Impala, Biscayne, Bel Air & Wagons '69 thru '90
24046 Impala SS & Caprice and Buick Roadmaster '91 thru '96
Lumina '90 thru '94 - see GM (38010)
24048 Lumina & Monte Carlo '95 thru '05
Lumina APV - see GM (38035)
24050 Luv Pick-up all 2WD & 4WD '72 thru '82
Malibu - see GM (38026)
24055 Monte Carlo all models '70 thru '88
Monte Carlo '95 thru '01 - see LUMINA
24059 Nova all V8 models '69 thru '79
24060 Nova/Geo Prizm '85 thru '92
24064 Pick-ups '67 thru '87 - Chevrolet & GMC, all V8 & in-line 6 cyl, 2WD & 4WD '67 thru '87; Suburbans, Blazers & Jimmys '67 thru '91
24065 Pick-ups '88 thru '98 - Chevrolet & GMC, all full-size models '88 thru '98; C/K Classic '99 & '00; Blazer & Jimmy '92 thru '94; Suburban '92 thru '99; Tahoe & Yukon '95 thru '99
24066 Pick-ups '99 thru '06 - Chevrolet Silverado & GMC Sierra '99 thru '06; Suburban/Tahoe/Yukon/Yukon XL/Avalanche '00 thru '06
24070 S-10 & GMC S-15 Pick-ups '82 thru '93
24071 S-10, Sonoma & Jimmy '94 thru '04
24072 Chevrolet TrailBlazer & TrailBlazer EXT, GMC Envoy & Envoy XL, Oldsmobile Bravada '02 thru '06
24075 Sprint '85 thru '88, Geo Metro '89 thru '01
24080 Vans - Chevrolet & GMC '68 thru '96
24081 Chevrolet Express & GMC Savana Full-size Vans '96 thru '05

CHRYSLER
10310 Chrysler Engine Overhaul Manual
25015 Chrysler Cirrus, Dodge Stratus, Plymouth Breeze, '95 thru '00
25020 Full-size Front-Wheel Drive '88 thru '93
K-Cars - see DODGE Aries (30008)
Laser - see DODGE Daytona (30030)
25025 Chrysler LHS, Concorde & New Yorker, Dodge Intrepid, Eagle Vision, '93 thru '97
25026 Chrysler LHS, Concorde, 300M, Dodge Intrepid '98 thru '03
25027 Chrysler 300, Dodge Charger & Magnum '05 thru '07
25030 Chrysler/Plym. Mid-size '82 thru '95
Rear-wheel Drive - see DODGE (30050)
25035 PT Cruiser all models '01 thru '03
25040 Chrysler Sebring/Dodge Avenger '95 thru '05, Dodge Stratus '01 thru '05

DATSUN
28005 200SX all models '80 thru '83
28007 B-210 all models '73 thru '78
28009 210 all models '79 thru '82
28012 240Z, 260Z & 280Z Coupe '70 thru '78
28014 280ZX Coupe & 2+2 '79 thru '83
300ZX - see NISSAN (72010)
28018 510 & PL521 Pick-up '68 thru '73
28020 510 all models '78 thru '81
28022 620 Series Pick-up all models '73 thru '79
720 Series Pick-up - NISSAN (72030)
28025 810/Maxima all gas models, '77 thru '84

DODGE
400 & 600 - see CHRYSLER (25030)
30008 Aries & Plymouth Reliant '81 thru '89
30010 Caravan & Ply. Voyager '84 thru '95
30011 Caravan & Ply. Voyager '96 thru '02
30012 Challenger/Plymouth Saporro '78 thru '83
30013 Challenger '67-'76 - see DART (30025)
30016 Caravan, Chrysler Voyager, Town & Country '03 thru '06
30016 Colt/Plymouth Champ '78 thru '87
30020 Dakota Pick-ups all models '87 thru '96
30021 Durango '98 & '99, Dakota '97 thru '99
30022 Dodge Durango models '00 thru '03
30023 Dodge Durango '04 thru '06, Dakota '05 and '06
30025 Dart, Challenger/Plymouth Barracuda & Valiant 6 cyl models '67 thru '76
30030 Daytona & Chrysler Laser '84 thru '89
Intrepid - see Chrysler (25025, 25026)
30034 Dodge & Plymouth Neon '95 thru '99
30035 Omni & Plymouth Horizon '78 thru '90
30036 Dodge and Plymouth Neon '00 thru '05
30040 Pick-ups all full-size models '74 thru '93
30041 Pick-ups all full-size models '94 thru '01
30042 Dodge Full-size Pick-ups '02 thru '05
30045 Ram 50/D50 Pick-ups & Raider and Plymouth Arrow Pick-ups '79 thru '93
30050 Dodge/Ply./Chrysler RWD '71 thru '89
30055 Shadow/Plymouth Sundance '87 thru '94
30060 Spirit & Plymouth Acclaim '89 thru '95
30065 Vans - Dodge & Plymouth '71 thru '03

EAGLE
Talon - see MITSUBISHI (68030, 68031)
Vision - see CHRYSLER (25025)

FIAT
34010 124 Sport Coupe & Spider '68 thru '78
34025 X1/9 all models '74 thru '80

FORD
10355 Ford Automatic Transmission Overhaul
10320 Ford Engine Overhaul Manual
36004 Aerostar Mini-vans '86 thru '97
Aspire - see FORD Festiva (36030)
36006 Contour/Mercury Mystique '95 thru '00
36008 Courier Pick-up all models '72 thru '82
36012 Crown Victoria & Mercury Grand Marquis '88 thru '06
36016 Escort/Mercury Lynx '81 thru '90
36020 Escort/Mercury Tracer '91 thru '00
Expedition - see FORD Pick-up (36059)
36022 Ford Escape & Mazda Tribute '01 thru '03
36024 Explorer & Mazda Navajo '91 thru '01
36025 Ford Explorer & Mercury Mountaineer '02 thru '06
36028 Fairmont & Mercury Zephyr '78 thru '83
36030 Festiva & Aspire '88 thru '97
36032 Fiesta all models '77 thru '80
36034 Focus all models '00 thru '05
36036 Ford & Mercury Full-size '75 thru '87
36044 Ford & Mercury Mid-size '75 thru '86
36048 Mustang V8 all models '64-1/2 thru '73
36049 Mustang II 4 cyl, V6 & V8 '74 thru '78
36050 Mustang & Mercury Capri '79 thru '86
36051 Mustang all models '94 thru '04
36052 Mustang '05 thru '07
36054 Pick-ups and Bronco '73 thru '79
36058 Pick-ups and Bronco '80 thru '96
36059 F-150 & Expedition '97 thru '03, F-250 '97 thru '99 & Lincoln Navigator '98 thru '02
36060 Super Duty Pick-ups, Excursion '99 thru '06
36061 F-150 full-size '04 thru '06
36062 Pinto & Mercury Bobcat '75 thru '80
36066 Probe all models '89 thru '92
36070 Ranger/Bronco II gas models '83 thru '92
36071 Ford Ranger '93 thru '05 & Mazda Pick-ups '94 thru '05
36074 Taurus & Mercury Sable '86 thru '95
36075 Taurus & Mercury Sable '96 thru '01
36078 Tempo & Mercury Topaz '84 thru '94
36082 Thunderbird/Mercury Cougar '83 thru '88
36086 Thunderbird/Mercury Cougar '89 thru '97
36090 Vans all V8 Econoline models '69 thru '91
36094 Vans full size '92 thru '05
36097 Windstar Mini-van '95 thru '03

GENERAL MOTORS
10360 GM Automatic Transmission Overhaul
38005 Buick Century, Chevrolet Celebrity, Olds Cutlass Ciera & Pontiac 6000 '82 thru '96
38010 Buick Regal, Chevrolet Lumina, Oldsmobile Cutlass Supreme & Pontiac Grand Prix front wheel drive '88 thru '05
38015 Buick Skyhawk, Cadillac Cimarron, Chevrolet Cavalier, Oldsmobile Firenza Pontiac J-2000 & Sunbird '82 thru '94
38016 Chevrolet Cavalier/Pontiac Sunfire '95 thru '04
38017 Chevrolet Cobalt & Pontiac G5 '05 thru '07
38020 Buick Skylark, Chevrolet Citation, Olds Omega, Pontiac Phoenix '80 thru '85
38025 Buick Skylark & Somerset, Olds Achieva, Calais & Pontiac Grand Am '85 thru '98
38026 Chevrolet Malibu, Olds Alero & Cutlass, Pontiac Grand Am '97 thru '03
38027 Chevrolet Malibu '04 thru '07
38030 Cadillac Eldorado & Oldsmobile Toronado '71 thru '85, Seville '80 thru '85, Buick Riviera '79 thru '85
38031 Cadillac Eldorado & Seville '86 thru '91, DeVille & Buick Riviera '86 thru '93, Fleetwood & Olds Toronado '86 thru '92
38032 DeVille '94 thru '05, Seville '92 thru '04
38035 Chevrolet Lumina APV, Oldsmobile Silhouette & Pontiac Trans Sport '90 thru '96
38036 Chevrolet Venture, Olds Silhouette, Pontiac Trans Sport & Montana '97 thru '05
General Motors Full-size Rear-wheel Drive - see BUICK (19025)

GEO
Metro - see CHEVROLET Sprint (24075)
Prizm - see CHEVROLET (24060) or TOYOTA (92036)
40030 Storm all models '90 thru '93
Tracker - see SUZUKI Samurai (90010)

GMC
Vans & Pick-ups - see CHEVROLET

HONDA
42010 Accord CVCC all models '76 thru '83
42011 Accord all models '84 thru '89
42012 Accord all models '90 thru '93
42013 Accord all models '94 thru '97
42014 Accord all models '98 thru '02
42015 Honda Accord models '03 thru '05
42020 Civic 1200 all models '73 thru '79
42021 Civic 1300 & 1500 CVCC '80 thru '83
42022 Civic 1500 CVCC all models '75 thru '79
42023 Civic all models '84 thru '91
42024 Civic & del Sol '92 thru '95
42025 Civic '96 thru '00, CR-V '97 thru '01, Acura Integra '94 thru '00
Passport - see ISUZU Rodeo (47017)
42026 Civic '01 thru '04, CR-V '02 thru '04
42035 Honda Odyssey all models '99 thru '04
42036 Honda Pilot '03 thru '07, Acura MDX '01 thru '07
42040 Prelude CVCC all models '79 thru '89

HYUNDAI
43010 Elantra all models '96 thru '01
43015 Excel & Accent all models '86 thru '98

ISUZU
Hombre - see CHEVROLET S-10 (24071)
47017 Rodeo '91 thru '02, Amigo '89 thru '02, Honda Passport '95 thru '02
47020 Trooper '84 thru '91, Pick-up '81 thru '93

JAGUAR
49010 XJ6 all 6 cyl models '68 thru '86
49011 XJ6 all models '88 thru '94
49015 XJ12 & XJS all 12 cyl models '72 thru '85

JEEP
50010 Cherokee, Comanche & Wagoneer Limited all models '84 thru '01
50020 CJ all models '49 thru '86
50025 Grand Cherokee all models '93 thru '04
50029 Grand Wagoneer & Pick-up '72 thru '91
50030 Wrangler all models '87 thru '03
50035 Liberty '02 thru '04

KIA
54070 Sephia '94 thru '01, Spectra '00 thru '04

LEXUS
ES 300 - see TOYOTA Camry (92007)

LINCOLN
Navigator - see FORD Pick-up (36059)
59010 Rear Wheel Drive all models '70 thru '05

MAZDA
61010 GLC (rear wheel drive) '77 thru '83
61011 GLC (front wheel drive) '81 thru '85
61015 323 & Protegé '90 thru '00
61016 MX-5 Miata '90 thru '97
61020 MPV all models '89 thru '94
Navajo - see FORD Explorer (36024)
61030 Pick-ups '72 thru '93
Pick-ups '94 on - see Ford (36071)
61035 RX-7 all models '79 thru '85
61036 RX-7 all models '86 thru '91
61040 626 (rear wheel drive) '79 thru '82
61041 626 & MX-6 (front wheel drive) '83 thru '92
61042 626 '93 thru '01, & MX-6/Ford Probe '93 thru '01

MERCEDES-BENZ
63012 123 Series Diesel '76 thru '85
63015 190 Series 4-cyl gas models, '84 thru '88
63020 230, 250 & 280 6 cyl sohc '68 thru '72
63025 280 123 Series gas models '77 thru '81
63030 350 & 450 all models '71 thru '80

MERCURY
64200 Villager & Nissan Quest '93 thru '01
All other titles, see FORD listing.

MG
66010 MGB Roadster & GT Coupe '62 thru '80
66015 MG Midget & Austin Healey Sprite Roadster '58 thru '80

MITSUBISHI
68020 Cordia, Tredia, Galant, Precis & Mirage '83 thru '93
68030 Eclipse, Eagle Talon & Plymouth Laser '90 thru '94
68031 Eclipse '95 thru '01, Eagle Talon '95 thru '98
68035 Mitsubishi Galant '94 thru '03
68040 Pick-up '83 thru '96, Montero '83 thru '93

NISSAN
72010 300ZX all models incl. Turbo '84 thru '89
72015 Altima all models '93 thru '04
72020 Maxima all models '85 thru '92
72021 Maxima all models '93 thru '01
72030 Pick-ups '80 thru '97, Pathfinder '87 thru '95
72031 Frontier Pick-up '98 thru '04, Xterra '00 thru '04, Pathfinder '96 thru '04
72040 Pulsar all models '83 thru '86
72050 Sentra all models '82 thru '94
72051 Sentra & 200SX all models '95 thru '06
72060 Stanza all models '82 thru '90

OLDSMOBILE
73015 Cutlass '74 thru '88
For other OLDSMOBILE titles, see BUICK, CHEVROLET or GM listings.

PLYMOUTH
For PLYMOUTH titles, see DODGE.

PONTIAC
79008 Fiero all models '84 thru '88
79018 Firebird V8 models except Turbo '70 thru '81
79019 Firebird all models '82 thru '92
79040 Mid-size Rear-wheel Drive '70 thru '87
For other PONTIAC titles, see BUICK, CHEVROLET or GM listings.

PORSCHE
80020 911 Coupe & Targa models '65 thru '89
80025 914 all 4 cyl models '69 thru '76
80030 924 all models incl. Turbo '76 thru '82
80035 944 all models incl. Turbo '83 thru '89

RENAULT
Alliance, Encore - see AMC (14020)

SAAB
84010 900 including Turbo '79 thru '88

SATURN
87010 Saturn all models '91 thru '02
87011 Saturn Ion '03 thru '07
87020 Saturn all L-series models '00 thru '04

SUBARU
89002 1100, 1300, 1400 & 1600 '71 thru '79
89003 1600 & 1800 2WD & 4WD '80 thru '94
89100 Legacy '90 thru '99
89101 Legacy & Forester '00 thru '06

SUZUKI
90010 Samurai/Sidekick/Geo Tracker '86 thru '01

TOYOTA
92005 Camry all models '83 thru '91
92006 Camry all models '92 thru '96
92007 Camry/Avalon/Solara/Lexus ES 300 '97 thru '01
92008 Toyota Camry, Avalon and Solara & Lexus ES 300/330 '02 thru '05
92015 Celica Rear Wheel Drive '71 thru '85
92020 Celica Front Wheel Drive '86 thru '99
92025 Celica Supra all models '79 thru '92
92030 Corolla all models '75 thru '79
92032 Corolla rear wheel drive models '80 thru '87
92035 Corolla front wheel drive models '84 thru '92
92036 Corolla & Geo Prizm '93 thru '02
92037 Corolla all models '03 thru '05
92040 Corolla Tercel all models '80 thru '82
92045 Corona all models '74 thru '82
92050 Cressida all models '78 thru '82
92055 Land Cruiser FJ40/43/45/55 '68 thru '82
92056 Land Cruiser FJ60/62/80/FZJ80 '80 thru '96
92065 MR2 all models '85 thru '87
92070 Pick-ups all models '69 thru '78
92075 Pick-up all models '79 thru '95
92076 Tacoma '95 thru '04, 4Runner '96 thru '02, T100 '93 thru '98
92078 Tundra '00 thru '05, Sequoia '01 thru '04
92079 Previa all models '91 thru '95
92081 Prius '01 thru '08
92082 RAV4 all models '96 thru '05
92085 Tercel all models '87 thru '94
92090 Sienna all models '98 thru '02
92095 Highlander & Lexus RX-330 '99 thru '06

TRIUMPH
94007 Spitfire all models '62 thru '81
94010 TR7 all models '75 thru '81

VW
96008 Beetle & Karmann Ghia '54 thru '79
96009 New Beetle '98 thru '05
96016 Rabbit, Jetta, Scirocco, & Pick-up gas models '75 thru '92 & Convertible '80 thru '92
96017 Golf, GTI & Jetta '93 thru '98, Cabrio '95 thru '98
96018 Golf, GTI, Jetta & Cabrio '99 thru '02
96020 Rabbit, Jetta, Pick-up diesel '77 thru '84
96023 Passat '98 thru '01, Audi A4 '96 thru '01
96030 Transporter 1600 all models '68 thru '79
96035 Transporter 1700, 1800, 2000 '72 thru '79
96040 Type 3 1500 & 1600 '63 thru '73
96045 Vanagon air-cooled models '80 thru '83

VOLVO
97010 120, 130 Series & 1800 Sports '61 thru '73
97015 140 Series all models '66 thru '74
97020 240 Series all models '76 thru '93
97040 740 & 760 Series all models '82 thru '88

TECHBOOK MANUALS
10205 Automotive Computer Codes
10206 OBD-II & Electronic Engine Management Systems
10210 Automotive Emissions Control Manual
10215 Fuel Injection Manual, 1978 thru 1985
10220 Fuel Injection Manual, 1986 thru 1999
10225 Holley Carburetor Manual
10230 Rochester Carburetor Manual
10240 Weber/Zenith/Stromberg/SU Carburetor
10305 Chevrolet Engine Overhaul Manual
10310 Chrysler Engine Overhaul Manual
10320 Ford Engine Overhaul Manual
10330 GM and Ford Diesel Engine Repair
10333 Building Engine Power Manual
10340 Small Engine Repair Manual
10345 Suspension, Steering & Driveline
10355 Ford Automatic Transmission Overhaul
10360 GM Automatic Transmission Overhaul
10405 Automotive Body Repair & Painting
10410 Automotive Brake Manual
10415 Automotive Detailing Manual
10420 Automotive Electrical Manual
10425 Automotive Heating & Air Conditioning
10430 Automotive Reference Dictionary
10435 Automotive Tools Manual
10440 Used Car Buying Guide
10445 Welding Manual
10450 ATV Basics
10452 Scooters, Automatic Transmission 50cc to 250cc

SPANISH MANUALS
98903 Reparación de Carrocería & Pintura
98904 Carburadores para los modelos Holley & Rochester
98905 Códigos Automotrices de la Computadora
98910 Frenos Automotriz
98913 Electricidad Automotriz
98915 Inyección de Combustible 1986 al 1999
99040 Chevrolet & GMC Camionetas '67 al '87
99041 Chevrolet & GMC Camionetas '88 al '98
99042 Chevrolet Camionetas Cerradas '68 al '95
99055 Dodge Caravan/Ply. Voyager '84 al '95
99075 Ford Camionetas y Bronco '80 al '94
99077 Ford Camionetas Cerradas '69 al '91
99088 Ford Modelos de Tamaño Mediano '75 al '86
99091 Ford Taurus & Mercury Sable '86 al '95
99095 GM Modelos de Tamaño Grande '70 al '90
99100 GM Modelos de Tamaño Mediano '70 al '88
99106 Jeep Cherokee, Wagoneer & Comanche '84 al '00
99110 Nissan Camionetas '80 al '96, Pathfinder '87 al '95
99118 Nissan Sentra '82 al '94
99125 Toyota Camionetas y 4-Runner '79 al '95

Over 100 Haynes motorcycle manuals also available

10-07

Haynes North America, Inc., 861 Lawrence Drive, Newbury Park, CA 91320 • (805) 498-6703